I0813214

WHAT DID YOU HEAR?

What Did You Hear?

The Music of Bob Dylan

STEVEN RINGS

The University of Chicago Press *Chicago and London*

The University of Chicago Press, Chicago 60637
The University of Chicago Press, Ltd., London

Published 2025
Printed in the United States of America

34 33 32 31 30 29 28 27 26 25   1 2 3 4 5

ISBN-13: 978-0-226-84265-3 (cloth)
ISBN-13: 978-0-226-84331-5 (ebook)
DOI: https://doi.org/10.7208/chicago/9780226843315.001.0001

Library of Congress Cataloging-in-Publication Data

Names: Rings, Steven, author.
Title: What did you hear? : the music of Bob Dylan / Steven Rings.
Description: Chicago : The University of Chicago Press, 2025. | Includes bibliographical references and index.
Identifiers: LCCN 2025008161 | ISBN 9780226842653 (cloth) | ISBN 9780226843315 (ebook)
Subjects: LCSH: Dylan, Bob, 1941– —Criticism and interpretation. | Popular music—United States—Analysis, appreciation. | Popular music—United States—History and criticism. | Folk music—United States—History and criticism.
Classification: LCC ML420.D98 R55 2025 | DDC 782.42164092—dc23/eng/20250226
LC record available at https://lccn.loc.gov/2025008161

∞ This paper meets the requirements of ANSI/NISO Z39.48-1992 (Permanence of Paper).

Authorized Representative for EU General Product Safety Regulation (GPSR) queries: **Easy Access System Europe**—Mustamäe tee 50, 10621 Tallinn, Estonia, gpsr.requests@easproject.com
Any other queries: https://press.uchicago.edu/press/contact.html

FOR JENNIFER

The imperfect is our paradise.
Note that, in this bitterness, delight,
Since the imperfect is so hot in us,
Lies in flawed words and stubborn sounds.

WALLACE STEVENS,
"POEMS OF OUR CLIMATE"

CONTENTS

HOW TO (NOT JUST) READ THIS BOOK

A book about sound faces a challenge of medium: sounds can't be put on the page. For some books on music, that's not a big problem, but for this one, hearing the sounds matters a great deal. It will thus be crucial to your reading experience to get them into your ears. My website, soundingbobdylan.com, includes all of the book's audio and video examples. The site is mobile optimized, so you can use it easily on your phone or tablet as you read. I highly recommend pulling it up before diving into a chapter. To that end, there is a QR code on the page facing each chapter opener, which will take you directly to the relevant examples on the site. I have put the first reference to each audio and video example (as well as each figure) in boldface so that you can easily find your place again on the page after visiting the site. Having easy access to the sounds I discuss while you are reading will make all the difference.

WHAT IF I DON'T READ MUSIC?

This book is still for you! And you're in good company: Bob Dylan doesn't read music either. Nevertheless, some musical terminology and the occasional notated figure are useful in coming to terms with his sounds. I have striven to write so that readers unfamiliar with such musical concepts can still follow the main thrust of the argument. Again, the website will help—listening while following a figure, for example, aids comprehension greatly. Occasionally, I direct traffic around more detailed analyses. But, by and large, you should be able to navigate through the musical discussions and get the overall gist. If there are details that elude you, don't sweat it. The big-picture takeaway is always what matters, and I've worked to make that takeaway clear in each musical discussion.

SOME MUSICAL DEFINITIONS

Having said that, if you wish to understand some of the book's musical content better, I offer simple definitions here for a few terms and symbols that I use relatively frequently. If you find such things tedious or overwhelming, no need to read this just yet! Dive into the book and refer back here if you find yourself curious about a musical detail or concept.

Pitch labels: Sometimes I will refer to a pitch with a number indicating its octave. C4 is middle C. The B immediately to its left on the piano is B3; the D to its right is D4; the C an octave higher is C5; etc. This allows us to make observations like, "Bob Dylan's vocal range early in his career extends from E2 up to A4."

Scale degrees: I often refer to the degrees of the scale using numerals with a circumflex accent above them. If you have ever heard "Do–Re–Mi" ("Do, a deer . . .") from *The Sound of Music*, you already know these scale degrees: $\hat{1}$ = do, $\hat{2}$ = re, $\hat{3}$ = mi, $\hat{4}$ = fa, $\hat{5}$ = sol, $\hat{6}$ = la, $\hat{7}$ = ti, and then back to $\hat{1}$ = do. I sometimes also label this last one $\hat{8}$ if I wish to indicate its positioning at the top of a scale rather than the bottom.

Tonic: The tonic is the first scale degree, or $\hat{1}$. It is musical home base. Most pieces of music end on their tonic note and chord, creating a sense of resolution or, indeed, of homecoming.

Dominant: The dominant is the fifth scale degree, or $\hat{5}$. It is the second most important note in a scale, after the tonic, $\hat{1}$. The dominant often acts as a counterpole to the tonic, a common melodic and harmonic destination—the music's home away from home, if you will.

Chords: Chords are groups of notes that sound together. Think of Dylan accompanying himself on solo acoustic guitar. Those simultaneous handfuls of notes that he strums are chords. I will sometimes refer to chords using Roman numerals, which correspond to the scale degrees discussed above. Roman numeral I represents the chord built on $\hat{1}$; this is also called the tonic chord. Roman numeral V represents the chord built on $\hat{5}$, the dominant chord. It often leads back energetically to the tonic. The IV chord, built on $\hat{4}$, is called the subdominant; it often leads to the dominant. A vast swath of Dylan's music—and much folk and rock music—uses only these three chords: I, IV, and V, that is, tonic, subdominant, and dominant.

Major and minor: The two main "modes" of Western music. Major is generally associated with positive emotional states, minor with negative. To sense the difference, first imagine "Blowin' in the Wind," a textbook major-key song, then contrast it with "All Along the Watchtower," which is minor. The technical difference between major and minor has to do with inflections of certain scale degrees, especially $\hat{3}$, which is lower in minor than in major.

Meter: Meter is a recurring pattern of regularly spaced beats. If you've ever tapped your foot in time to a song you've moved your body to the meter. Meters in Dylan's music come in only a few forms. Some of his songs fall into three-beat patterns (1-2-3, 1-2-3), which musicians often label with the time signature 3/4. Think of "The Times They Are a-Changin'," "The Lonesome Death of Hattie Carroll," or "Time Passes Slowly." Other songs, such as "Like a Rolling Stone," "Tangled Up in Blue," or "Love Sick," fall into four-beat patterns (1-2-3-4, 1-2-3-4), which musicians often notate with the time signature 4/4. Finally, some songs fall into a six-beat meter divided into two groups of three (*1*-2-3-*4*-5-6), usually notated as 6/8. Think "Just Like a Woman," "Every Grain of Sand," or "I've Made Up My Mind to Give Myself to You." Though Dylan largely sticks to these basic meters, his treatment of them in performance is hardly simple—just ask his backing musicians. He often adds and drops beats unexpectedly, transforming the given meter into something new—say, turning a 4/4 bar into a momentary 3/4.

That covers a lot of the technical language in the book. For other terms that I don't define here, there is a wealth of fine information about music theory online these days, including excellent YouTube videos. A quick Google search will turn up an accessible definition for any term I use in the following pages.

Introduction

WORDS-MUSIC B. DYLAN

We begin with a sound. It is not a musical sound per se, but it is rhythmic: the tapping of typewriter hammers against paper. It is a late-summer evening in 1962, and the *tap–tap–tap* emerges from a room above the Gaslight Café in Greenwich Village. Bob Dylan is at the machine, hunting and pecking. Even when writing he is evidently a noisy presence, for his "banging" attracts folksinger Tom Paxton. The typewriter belongs to Paxton's roommate, Hugh Romney, and Dylan is finishing "a long poem" on it; he asks Paxton what he thinks. After commenting on the text's "wild imagery," Paxton asks, "Are you gonna, you know, put music to it?"

> He said, "Well, you think I should?" And I said "*Yeah*. I mean, 'cause otherwise it's just something to go in some literary quarterly or something, but this way, you know, you'll have a song out of it." So the next night . . . he got up [at the Gaslight] and he sang this new song called "It's a Hard Rain's a-Gonna Fall."[1]

The anecdote intrigues. What if "Hard Rain" had never become a song? What if its only "instrumental" sound was that tapping, its only vocal sound—perhaps—some later verbal recitation? If we take Paxton at his word, this was a genuine possibility. There is evidence that the incident indeed happened, at least in some form.[2] A typescript survives. It passed to Romney's in-laws and ultimately to Sotheby's, which estimated its value at £150,000–200,000.[3]

If the story goes down easy, that is in part because it ticks several boxes in the Romantic checklist of (white, male) artistic genius. We see a scruffy loner at work, the model bohemian. He creates in partial confusion, as though drawing inspiration out of the air, as yet unaware of the true nature or value of his artwork. The nonbohemian world will soon enough prize enormously the document he produces, establishing its exchange value as a luxury commodity. And so on. But the anecdote goes down easy for another reason as well. It accords with a familiar hierarchy of critical values: Dylan's words are primary, his music secondary. The story in fact makes this ordering explicit—music becomes a literal afterthought.

The sterling critical reputation of Dylan's lyrics is secure. If nothing else, his 2016 Nobel Prize in Literature has seen to that. His music is another matter. The songs are beloved, but his musical way with them has divided listeners from the first. The asymmetry between words and music in Paxton's anecdote thus passes almost without notice. But we will begin by pausing over it, by making audible that which the anecdote mutes. For this is a book about Dylan's sounds. We cannot fully understand the origin of "Hard Rain," or indeed much else about Dylan, without taking the full measure of those sounds, especially their puzzling mixture of idiosyncrasy and expressive power. In the pages that follow, I will engage Dylan's wayward sounds with the same critical care typically lavished on his words, arguing that his music achieves its effects not despite its many imperfections, but precisely because of them.

Let's tune our ears, then, back to that room above the Gaslight. What do we hear? A clacking typewriter and a conversation. But if we listen closer, might we also hear faint music? To do so, we have to listen past the "music" of the typewriter, and indeed past all of the other sounds vibrating in the room's stuffy, late-summer air. We have to listen instead for fragments of song held in memory, and a new song taking shape—however falteringly—in the mind's ear. For there are reasons to question the story that "Hard Rain" began purely as a poem. Dylan was writing songs at a brisk pace in 1962, but he was not writing many stand-alone poems. He would pen a handful of substantial poems and prose pieces beginning in the *following* year—"Last Thoughts on Woody Guthrie" and "My Life in a Stolen Moment" are the best known—but these differ considerably from "Hard Rain." They are generally not written in stanzas, and most exhibit little to no metrical regularity.[4] Moreover, the circumstances of 1962 called for songs. Dylan was churning them out for his publishers Leeds Music and later M. Witmark and Sons; there was money to be made. He recorded dozens of new songs for the two publishers in 1962, including "Hard Rain."[5] He was also hard at work on his second album, anxious to make a follow-up that would surpass his eponymous debut—which Columbia had released in March—in both sales and creative ambition. While his first album included mostly covers, this one, following his songwriting breakthrough with "Blowin' in the Wind," would include almost all originals. He wrote (and discarded) a great many songs for *The Freewheelin' Bob Dylan*. "A Hard Rain's a-Gonna Fall" would make the cut, anchoring the end of side 1.

Of course, Dylan could have begun "Hard Rain" as a literary exercise and only later figured out how to make it a song. But even here questions press. Each verse begins by invoking the Scots-English border ballad "Lord Randal," a folk-revival staple that Dylan had heard plenty, both in the Village and on recordings.[6] In the best-known folk-revival versions, its first lines are "Oh, where have you been, Lord Randal, my son? / Oh, where have you been my handsome young man?" Could Dylan have written the opening of "Hard Rain" without those lines rattling in his ears? As it happens, Dylan's eventual melody for "Hard Rain" would not resemble any known tune for "Lord Randal"—I will explore the differences in chapter 9—but the ballad was nevertheless an item to be sung, not to be read off the page. Did Dylan really mean *not* to sing his own fantastical rewrite of it? Consider, too, the song's refrain: "And it's a hard, it's a hard, it's a hard . . ." Such folksy repetition makes good sense when sung, but it sits oddly in print. The only portion of the text that does not immediately suggest song is the part that most captivated Paxton—the "wild imagery" in each verse's interior, the blue-eyed son's answers to the parent's questions. Here the text's literary ambitions are at their most pronounced, reaching especially for Ginsberg and Rimbaud.[7] All the same, if one glances from those "flashing images" to the top of the typescript, between the title and the year, one reads "Words-Music B. Dylan."[8]

There is so much compressed in that tiny bit of text. Its hyphenated compound, "Words-Music," is the tersest possible expression for Dylan's alchemical art. I will have much to say about that compound and its world-containing hyphen in the pages to come. For now, we can note that its second word makes clear that Dylan intended to sing "Hard Rain" from the moment he rolled the paper into the machine.[9] But how? He wasn't sure. In a 1964 interview he said, "I wrote the words of it on a piece of paper. But there was just no tune that really fit to it, so I just sort of play chords without a tune."[10] This offhand dismissal of the song's melody is mumblingly true to form, but it's still a stunner. After all, there *is* a tune to "Hard Rain," an especially shapely one, and Dylan sang it with unusual clarity in the 1960s.[11] Moreover, that tune makes the verses' three-stage arc—questions, answers, refrain—sonically vivid, pulling the listener toward the refrain's apocalyptic climax. The music may well have been inchoate while Dylan typed, with melodies mentally tried and discarded. Once he did sit down with his guitar, he may have conceived the tune and chords quickly and with little conscious reflection, perhaps even in one day, as Paxton suggests. The typescript nevertheless makes clear that the volatile words-music compound was in play from an early stage. Moreover, Dylan's groping for sound discloses something about the hyphen between the compound's two terms, suggesting it marks not a space of compositional certainty, but one of experiment, intuition, and risk.

Imagine the risk had failed. Imagine "Hard Rain" had remained text without music, Dylan never finding a melody for it, nor chords, nor rhythm, those wisps of music slipping back into silence. He may not have relegated it to a literary quarterly, as Paxton worried, but it could well have ended up on the back cover of a later album, like "11 Outlined Epitaphs" on the sleeve and insert of 1964's *The Times They Are a-Changin'*. What would be lost? Would Dylan, Nobel laureate in literature, be diminished if "Hard Rain" had remained literature alone?[12] Would we even remember "Hard Rain" had it not become a song? After all, few outside of the most devoted fans know "11 Outlined Epitaphs." If you own the LP, I challenge you to quote a single line of it from memory. (If you can, you know who you are.)[13] By contrast, it is difficult to imagine a world without the *song* "Hard Rain." It has resonated in global auditory culture for over half a century. In so resonating, again and again, what do its sounds *do*? What do they make of the words that initially took shape on that typescript? Why is that hyphenated compound so potent when it begins to vibrate in the air?

These questions open onto deep waters, and it will take us an entire book to dive toward satisfactory answers. But I'll venture some initial observations here. First, think of the compound's hyphen as marking an *encounter* between words and music, one that releases new, emergent affects and meanings, available to neither words nor music alone. This process is especially legible in "Hard Rain." Its words channel a generational anxiety about Cold War brinksmanship, but the music balances that anxiety with sounds that are notably less grim. For "Hard Rain" the song is far from musical doom and gloom. Its mood is as much one of wonder as of foreboding, the result of a singular mix of bleak imagery and buoyant sounds. Its major key, gently cycling triple meter, and ear-catching melody counteract the lyrical darkness, improbably conjuring hope from the wreckage.

To sense how this could have been otherwise, imagine a different, hypothetical encounter: the words of "Hard Rain" set to the guitar part of "Masters of War." The latter is another triple-meter tune on the first side of *The Freewheelin' Bob Dylan*, but it is minor not major, its strumming effortful rather than lilting, its harmony claustrophobically limited to one chord. If "Hard Rain" is awed and expansive, "Masters of War" is vengeful and confined. One could nevertheless set the words of the former to the guitar part of the latter with only a small bit of melodic invention.[14] The emergent effect of *this* encounter would differ drastically from the "Hard Rain" we know. The new compound would double down sonically on the lyric's darkest corners, becoming a sounding emblem of its most nihilistic line: "where black is the color and none is the number." By contrast, the actual "Hard Rain" is luminous, its end-times imagery aglow with prophetic vision.

This description nevertheless risks fixing "Hard Rain" too securely, pinning it to one set of sounds (those of the studio recording) and one set of plausible historical meanings. To do so is to neglect another critical aspect of the "Words-Music" alloy. For, when "Hard Rain" became a song, it became iterable, repeatable. While the 1962 studio recording offers theoretically limitless repetitions of a single sonic copy, each live performance—made by bodies, instruments, and technologies in real time—has its own sonic particularity, its own quirks, blemishes, and triumphs. "Hard Rain" in performance is thus no single, fixed object. It is instead a vivid instance of what Robin Bernstein calls a "scriptive thing," which, "like a play script, broadly structures a performance while simultaneously allowing for resistance and unleashing original, live variations that may not be individually predictable."[15] One can hardly imagine a better description of Dylan's performance practice, with its wildly proliferating variations. As we will discuss below, such variation is to some extent the condition of all musical performance, but when the performer is Bob Dylan, an artist as dedicated to the stage as he is ambivalent about the studio, difference-in-sounding becomes a musical way of life. Variation, flux, flaw: these are constants in a performing career famously short on consistency. Or better, a career in which inconsistency becomes the paradoxical rule, the enduring strategy. We might say, then, that a song like "Hard Rain" is for Dylan the performer an occasion for such difference-in-sounding, for his particular brand of sonic inconsistency.

That inconsistency foregrounds the novelty of each encounter between words and music. Each performance restages the encounter, as Dylan reenters the space of chance and experiment that saw the song's creation. Affects and meanings morph accordingly, as the gentle luminosity of the 1962 studio "Hard Rain" gives way to the raucous roadhouse blues of the 1975 Rolling Thunder version, or to the cool, epic sweep of the 1994 performance with orchestra in Nara, Japan.[16] The little sounds that saw the text's genesis—the tapping of typewriter hammers, the wisps of ballad in memory—give way to a profusion of musical realizations that unfurl across decades, as "Hard Rain" sounds and re-sounds. And this is merely one song, just one red thread in the vast tapestry of Dylan's musical career. Additional threads abound, each tracing the arc of another song through hundreds and even thousands of unique performances.[17]

That cacophonous tapestry is almost entirely archived on recording, an unprecedented sonic corpus that preserves literally thousands of hours of Dylan's voice, his guitar, his harmonica, his piano, his bands. As of this writing, Dylan's official catalog numbers more than eighty albums (the precise number varies depending on how one counts), forty of them original studio albums and the remainder live sets, archival releases, and compilations, many of which include original material unavailable elsewhere.[18] Record sales are now north of 100 million, and individual tracks circulate even more widely through streaming. But as large as this official recorded corpus already is, the archive of unofficial recordings is several orders of magnitude greater. Dylan is the most bootlegged artist in modern popular music, surpassing even the Grateful Dead.[19] Most of his nearly 4,000 concerts have been recorded and are accessible through online trading sites.

Maintaining such a corpus requires labor, money, and technological know-how from an international network of fans. These expenditures signal how highly fans value these sounds, and how much weight they place on their preservation.[20] Such obsessive collecting, cataloging, and organizing instances a phenomenon that Simon Reynolds discusses in his book *Retromania*—it is a belated form of "hyperconsumption" in which fans seek to gain mastery over the recorded past through possession and taxonomy.[21] But Dylan bootlegs are not merely relics to be hoarded. In fan practice they become sounding artifacts, sites of endless aural scrutiny. Aficionados lavish attention on the most granular sonic details in these performances—a hitch in the voice here, a subtle detail of strumming there—comparing and debating the merits of live and studio recordings on sites like expectingrain.com. Nor is this merely a question of collecting recordings. The most dedicated "Bobcats" will spend untold sums to see Dylan perform live night after night; more casual fans will still shell out for tickets when he comes through their town. A night at home with the printed lyrics would be much cheaper.

THE PAGES AND THE TEXT

("Going, Going, Gone," 1974)

And yet, a reader of the Dylan literature would be forgiven for thinking that his sounds are a negligible facet of his art. Academics and critics have spilled rivers of ink on the first term in the "Words-Music" compound, as well as on studies of Dylan's cultural context, his political impact, his status as a media figure, his faith, and so on. The shelves groan under the weight of books on Dylan the poet, Dylan the '60s icon, Dylan the Iron Range enigma, Dylan the rake. But on the musical Dylan—the one that strikes our ears—the literature is surprisingly thin. Actually, it's *astonishingly* thin given the unprecedented corpus of recorded Dylan discussed above, those thousands of hours of meticulously preserved and distributed sounds. This shelf doesn't groan—it has ample room to spare.

Occupying the most space on it is Greil Marcus, who has shown time and again an extraordinary knack for hearing deeply and weaving vibrant prose around his aural objects, mapping the music's historical resonances with breathtaking critical flair. Larry Starr's 2021 book, *Listening to Bob Dylan*, is there too, providing an invaluable foundation for future studies of Dylan's music. Paul Williams's three-volume series *Bob Dylan, Performing Artist* offers a highly personal fan's account of Dylan's studio recordings and live performances. Most recently, Ray Padgett's *Pledging My Time* is an invaluable storehouse of insights into Dylan's music making from his bandmates.[22] That more or less does it for books on Dylan's music.[23] A few other books touch on his music in passing, sometimes brilliantly.[24] Spread over the remaining empty feet of shelf space is a smattering of academic articles, several of which have been invaluable to my thinking.[25] But beyond these writers, the majority of Dylanologists have limited their commentary on the music to the passing adjective. Dylan scholars across the quad have taken notice. One of them, sociologist Lee Marshall, wonders, "Where are the works from musicology, from performance studies, or from drama that could help us develop a critical vocabulary appropriate for [Dylan's music and performances]?" Bemoaning the academic focus on Dylan's art solely as literary text, Marshall calls for studies that explore the ways in which his performances "generate their affects aesthetically, through music, performance, and voice, and not just words."[26]

The lack of a ready critical vocabulary for discussing Dylan's sounds, which Marshall laments, is often apparent in Dylan talk. In a 2009 panel discussion at the Philoctetes Center in New York, eminent Dylan scholars Christopher Ricks and Sean Wilentz bumped into the issue. Some forty-seven minutes in, Wilentz mentioned that "the thing that's sometimes left out [in discussions about Dylan] is sound." The usually loquacious Ricks responded, deflated: "I'm not good on sound."[27] He was selling himself short. Ricks had just spoken eloquently about the importance of the very compound named at the top of the "Hard Rain" typescript, and his book *Dylan's Visions of Sin* contains several passages that illuminate local musical details to dazzling critical effect. But the moment is still telling, as is the fact that it didn't arise until three-quarters of an hour into the discussion. Dylan's sounds are often sidelined in critical discussions; when the subject does arise, his critics can fall curiously mute.

Or perhaps not so curiously. After all, music is difficult to discuss, even for music scholars. Written commentary shares a medium with poetry (or printed lyrics). Both occupy the page and hold relatively still. The critic's words can take up the poet's seamlessly, moving fluidly between quotation and interpretation, or staking out a location somewhere in between, via paraphrase or rewriting. In the hands of a gifted critic, language can handle other language with enviable deftness. But language struggles with music. Words that felt fleet and agile when interpreting poetry can become leaden and awkward when engaging with ephemeral sound. And when the artist is as committed to ephemerality as is Dylan—committed, that is, to the singular moment of performance and all that it affords, as a site of spontaneity, reinvention, and felicitous accident—the task becomes that much harder.

But what of those scholars who make it their business to face such challenges, to think and talk about music? Why haven't more of them answered Marshall's call? There are, I suspect, two broad reasons. First is the suspicion that Dylan's music will not bear the same kind of close attention that his lyrics do. His words are famously ambitious, complex, often difficult—just the sort of thing academics love. But Dylan's music, on first blush, seems simple. The harmonic vocabulary is small. Harlan Howard once quipped that country music is nothing but "three chords and the truth." Dylan has at times gotten by with two fewer than that, in one-chord numbers like "Masters of War," "Ballad of Hollis Brown," "Political World," "High Water (for Charley Patton)," and "Tin Angel." He once sang "I wish I could write you a melody so plain."[28] Music analysts may feel he succeeded all too well—his tunes are compact and often derived from the preexisting stock of vernacular song. As for form, his songs very often fall into humble handed-down forms like the twelve-bar blues and the verse with refrain. Music theorists have developed sophisticated tools to analyze music that is complex precisely where Dylan's seems most artless. No surprise, then, that many have taken those tools elsewhere.

But we should tread carefully here. For the question of simplicity is not always simple. In certain contexts, especially in the academy, attributions of complexity and simplicity bear (often tacit) value judgments, the complex elevated above the simple. Philosopher Theodore Gracyk discusses this in his essay "Valuing and Evaluating Popular Music," arguing:

> We must be wary of the trap of supposing that only complex, challenging music is of real aesthetic value. . . . Simplicity and directness can

> also be of value, and we find artistic achievement when such aesthetic qualities are embodied in appropriate means. The economy and simplicity of Ernest Hemingway's prose does not indicate a corresponding poverty in Hemingway's artistry or cognitive import.[29]

It is hard to disagree with this sentiment, but the qualifiers "simple" and "complex" remain underdefined, their connotative range unspecified. The terms are also subject to imperceptible drift back to their familiar hierarchical ranking, in part *because* of their underdefinition. Furthermore, from the strategic perspective of a musical interpreter or analyst, the assertion that a given bit of music is simple often acts as a claim that it will not reward (or sustain) close attention, stopping analysis before it has even begun. If we indeed stop there, we find ourselves no closer to understanding what gives a song like, say, "Hard Rain" such aesthetic power and political resonance—in a word, such efficacy—for so many listeners. After all, it uses only three chords, has a straightforward diatonic melody, and follows a verse-refrain structure. The same could be said of thousands of other songs. But just how those materials are deployed and arranged—how words, chords, rhythm, and tune align, how Dylan animates them in a given performance—these details make all the difference. The more we focus our attention on the particularity of *this* song, *this* performance, *this* context, the more words like "simple" and "complex" seem a distraction. Indeed, we may eventually find that we can dispense with them altogether, losing little in the bargain.

TALK ABOUT PERFECTION, I AIN'T NEVER SEEN NONE

("Ain't No Man Righteous, No Not One," 1979)

The second likely reason for the academic neglect of Dylan's music is his famously idiosyncratic playing and singing, mentioned at the outset of this introduction. Everyone knows the gibes, and it is not hard to enumerate Dylan's sins against bourgeois "good musicianship." His singing has always been a target, but his guitar, piano, and harmonica playing are equally vulnerable. And not just to academic critique. Serious harmonica players, for example, often bristle at Dylan's ramshackle blowing and drawing, their irritation only increased by the fact that he is one of their instrument's most famous players. For some, Dylan's unkempt sounds are an insurmountable barrier. For others, though, they are extraordinarily compelling, the very source of his appeal and a warrant of authenticity.[30] David Kinney colorfully captures this critical divide, writing about Dylan's most recognizable instrument:

> It starts with the voice. One day we hear its strange, broken glory, and before long everyone else in our lives would rather jam ice picks into their ears than listen to another Bob Dylan song. We know what you're thinking. The man cannot sing, that he yelps, grunts, and caterwauls, that he sounds like a suffering animal or a busted lawn mower, that his throat is a rumbling, grating cement mixer. How can we ever explain this so you understand? Dylan's voice, so reviled and ridiculed by you heathens, is a wonder of the world to us. It's human, real, and above all *expressive*. It embodies rapture, heartbreak, rage, bitterness, disdain, boredom. It can be by turns biting, sarcastic, and deeply funny. It's freighted with weirdly spellbinding magic. It's what pulls us—the faithful—to the foot of the stage, and keeps us there for a lifetime.[31]

The extreme reactions—self-harm with an ice pick versus decades of rapt attention—are a hallmark of Dylan reception. His sounds, vocal and instrumental, surprise and provoke; opinions are rarely moderate. We have a ready critical vocabulary to account for the negative assessments. It is easy to measure Dylan's singing and playing against various institutional standards of professional musicianship and find them wanting. It is much harder to account for those same sounds' allure, their "weirdly spellbinding magic" for listeners on the other side of the critical gulf. That is the challenge facing the music scholar. Rather than dismissing Dylan's "aesthetic of imperfection," as Gracyk calls it, the student of his music must face it head on, asking: What is it about Dylan's imperfect sounds that gives them such potency, for so many?[32]

This book proposes an answer. It does so not by listening past these imperfect sounds or explaining them away. Rather, it takes imperfection seriously, thinking carefully about what it affords. In the following pages I argue that Dylan's idiosyncratic sounds are not incidental to his art, a troublesome husk we can discard once we have extracted his celebrated words. Rather, his art lives and thrives in the noisy encounter between words and music. So much is obvious to any fan, but our critical discourse too often fails to register it. If asked what Dylan's sounds *do*, we can answer briefly: they imperfect. (Accent on the last syllable.) I use this word—and its noun form, imperfection—in a broad, twofold sense that I will develop below. Dylan's music making is founded on a radical openness to this twofold imperfection. That openness is an enabling condition of his extraordinarily prolific musical career—his ceaseless performing and recording activity—and it is at the heart of his music's efficacy. In short, this book argues that imperfection is not a bug but a feature of Dylan's music making.

By its very construction, the word "imperfection" suggests negation or subtraction: *not* or *less than* perfect. For those unmoved (or worse) by Dylan, his errant sounds may well seem subtractive or negative in this way—an absence of polish, virtuosity, decorum, take your pick. But for fans, his ragged practice can seem paradoxically additive or affirmative, a *productive* or *generative* imperfection. The result is a kind of wild superabundance—unruly plenitude rather than lack. Kinney characterizes this as a plenitude of expressive possibility, which provides seemingly direct access to a wide range of human emotion and experience. For many it is also a plenitude of meaning, each errant sound ringing true, disclosing insights from the personal to the political.

To better understand Dylan's generative imperfection, it will be useful to distinguish between two species of imperfection, which I will call "flaw imperfection" and "change imperfection." The first of these encompasses the familiar meanings of the term: imperfection as flaw, blemish, irregularity. In music think of a missed note, a break in the voice, a dropped beat. The word "flaw" needs to be taken with a grain of salt, though. For any attribution of flaw imperfection to a given bit of music is culturally and stylistically contingent. After all, in some traditions—say, in bluegrass and old-time music—dropped beats are the norm, and indeed expected from great players.[33] To play such music *without* dropping certain beats is to miss a central aspect of the style, just as it would be to sing a Carter family song—say, "Wildwood Flower"—with bel canto operatic technique. So, while a classical musician might identify a dropped beat or Sarah Carter's vocal tone as imperfect, cultural insiders in bluegrass or old-time circles would not. Traditional musicians sometimes use the phrase "ragged but right" for such phenomena, as do certain Dylan fans.[34] For example, fan Michael Smith, in his review of a 2001 Dylan concert in Medford, Oregon, states of the night's rendition of "Tombstone Blues," "Bob played back-to-back ragged-but-right guitar and harp solos to finish it off."[35]

But not every ragged sound is right. Dylan's risks are genuine and, to be genuine, as Christopher Ricks stresses, risks must hold the potential for failure.[36] There may be no success like failure, as Dylan puts it in a riddling couplet, but this does not make *every* failure a success.[37] Sometimes a failure is just that. For example, another fan, Mitch Gart, writes of a 1996 show in Springfield, Massachusetts, "I thought a lot of times Bob's voice missed notes he was trying for and sounded really rough. Sometimes it can sound 'ragged but right' and other times just ragged."[38] So, the concept of flaw imperfection retains its force. It captures something that critics and fans have long recognized about Dylan's music making: that it teems with errant sounds, which can fail as well as succeed.

ALL THIS (DIFFERENCE AND) REPETITION

("Queen Jane Approximately," 1965, via Deleuze, 1968)

Our second species of imperfection does not concern fallibility or blemish but change. More precisely, change imperfection is the difference that arises in repetition. All three nouns in that sentence require unpacking. Let's begin with imperfection. Here it has a temporal sense, in which the imperfect is the ongoing, that which is still in process, not (or not yet) in a final state of completion.[39] This usage draws on a grammatical category called the "imperfective aspect." That aspect is at work in the imperfect tense, familiar to students of the Romance languages. This tense indicates an action that was ongoing at a certain time in the past ("I was listening," "she was performing"). The imperfective aspect is also at work in the English present progressive and future continuous tenses ("I am playing," "he will be singing"). In each instance, the imperfective aspect denotes an action that has not reached a state of completion—it is under way. This idea of imperfection is not merely grammatical; it casts a long historical shadow, extending back to medieval scholastic adaptations of Aristotle's physics. For the scholastics, following Aristotle, "perfection" denoted the end state of a process, its completion or full actualization. Any process still under way was considered "imperfect."[40]

Dylan's commitment to change imperfection is obvious to any fan who has marveled at the alteration his songs undergo in live performance. Songs repeat, but their tunes, keys, grooves, and genres change. In some cases words do too ("Tangled Up in Blue" is the best-known example). His songs live in the imperfective aspect of constant flux, always in motion.[41] During the highly confrontational 1965–66 tour, Dylan took to introducing the new, electric version of "I Don't Believe You (She Acts Like We Never Have Met)" with the drowsy sneer, "It used to be like that, now it goes like this." He meant it to provoke the folk purists in attendance, but the line could just as well serve as a compact maxim for his art of change imperfection. The phrase enacts what it describes: repetition with a difference. Its two halves balance each other in sing-song fashion, the parallel structure making us that much more aware of what stays the same and what changes.[42] Note especially the change in verb. Back then, the song merely *was*—note the infinitive "to be"—while now the song *goes*. The shift from static being to active going is suggestive. As it is reanimated onstage, the song is something in process, always on the way, *going*.

All this talk of difference and repetition may put some philosophically savvy readers in mind of Gilles Deleuze. Indeed, this section borrows part of its header from the title of one of his books.[43] I will not dive into the Deleuzian depths here, nor am I qualified to do so.[44] But his title is too apt to resist. For Dylan's art of change imperfection pushes difference and repetition to extremes, at once maximizing them and insisting on their reciprocity. We can answer the question "What does Bob Dylan do?" with a pithy maxim: he repeats and he differs. This unfolds on multiple, nested time scales. Most obviously, in concert he has repeated certain songs hundreds, even thousands of times across the decades, the songs undergoing dramatic change in the process. More globally still, Dylan repeats the music of the past, reanimating old songs and genres, adopting earlier singers' voices, reviving old-timey idioms. But these repetitions also produce difference, for the more strenuously Dylan imitates an earlier singer, the more he tends to sound utterly singular, a paradox we will explore in chapter 2. As we will see there, even at this global scale, Dylan's retrospective art tightly entwines repetition and difference.

At a more local level, repetition is embedded in the songs themselves, in recurring refrains, looped chord progressions, repetitive groove beds, and verse structures that cycle through stanza after stanza. Think, for example, of the cyclical recurrence of the refrain in so many Dylan songs, from "Desolation Row" to "Simple Twist of Fate" to "Murder Most Foul." One of the pleasures of these songs is the diversity Dylan can pull from a repeated refrain. This is partly a question of lyrical meaning, of the different ways his words approach a refrain, illuminating it from ever-new semantic and grammatical angles. But the pleasure also resides in the many different ways he wraps his voice around the refrain. Dylan's most attentive listeners often celebrate this point, its appreciation becoming a sign of true connoisseurship. Michael Gray comically demonstrates, praising Dylan's singing of the chorus in one version of the remarkable 1980 song "Caribbean Wind":

> The different exploratory way that he sings "nearer to the fire" each time around on this recording will divide your friends into those with no patience for such amateur messing about and those who are

> intelligent, warm, generous and possessed of a sense of humour and an enquiring mind.[45]

A commonsense view holds that Dylan varies his performances so much because his songs repeat—and because he repeats his songs night after night, year after year. It would bore him *not* to differ. There is surely some truth to this, but it impoverishes our understanding of difference and repetition, dulling us to their generative potential. It turns repetition into a fault that needs correcting. But why, then, build so much repetition into the songs themselves? And why repeat those songs night after night, across decades? These questions suggest a reframing. Perhaps Dylan doesn't differ because he repeats. Perhaps he repeats so that he can differ. That is, by structuring his performing activity as a vast sequence of nested repetitions, Dylan creates the conditions for the very difference-in-sounding I discussed above, with its unruly plenitudes. In this understanding, change imperfection—difference in repetition—becomes not a lamentable byproduct of Dylan's obsessively iterative career, but a deliberate strategy. He is no Queen Jane, "sick / of all this repetition." Rather, repetition laced with constant change is his musical way of being.

For repetition to realize its full generative potential in difference, the performer must have a particular openness to chance and risk—indeed, to flaw imperfection. Here it will be useful to contrast Dylan's practice with other musical approaches to repetition and difference. For change imperfection is in one sense the condition of all music. As long as there is musical repetition, difference is inescapable.[46] In draping itself across the axis of time, music opens onto difference time and again. Even two soundings of the same recording (on the same system in the same room) differ from one another in that they occur at distinct moments, are embedded in different fields of ambient sound, and accompany a unique set of behaviors, bodily dispositions, moods, and thoughts on the part of the listener. When it comes to live performance, iteration harbors the potential for much greater difference, opening a space for in-the-moment invention by the performer—a new phrasing, a new accent, a new intensity. Flaw imperfection also lurks nearby, affording difference through accident.

But in certain musical traditions, performers cultivate considerable bodily discipline to rein in the proliferating effects of difference in performance. Think of the classical pianist practicing the same phrase hundreds of times to ensure consistency in concert, each iteration hewing as closely as possible to the notated score. In the controlled space of the practice room, the pianist repeats in order to *minimize* difference on the more volatile space of the stage. Of course, gifted classical performers know how to harness the potential of change imperfection in performance, making each phrase breathe and live anew. But such variation rarely involves changes that would contradict the notes in the score, at least not intentionally. Mistakes do happen—those slips of memory and finger—but practice aims to minimize them. The result is fidelity to a work—say, a Beethoven sonata—whose notated form radically delimits the proliferating effects of difference in repetition.

EVERYBODY WANTS YOU TO BE JUST LIKE THEM

("Maggie's Farm," 1965)

Perhaps surprisingly, things were not that different in certain corners of the folk revival in the late '50s and early '60s.[47] Many revivalists practiced incessantly in order to reproduce performances exactly as they sounded on old recordings. The New Lost City Ramblers, for instance, were virtuosos in this regard, matching "authentic" recorded performances of string-band music to the tiniest detail. John Hammond Jr., son of the Columbia executive who signed Dylan in 1961, did the same with Robert Johnson's blues. For such musicians, the old recordings were not unlike the notated scores of classical music, to be learned by rote and reproduced with the greatest possible fidelity. Dylan admired Hammond and was especially impressed—indeed, intimidated—by the technical skill of the Ramblers, especially Mike Seeger.[48] But he was also put off by aspects of this performative purism and quickly saw that it wasn't for him. As he put it in 1984:

> I didn't really play with that much technique. And people really didn't take to me because of that, because I didn't go out of my way to learn as much technique as other people. . . . I mean I know people who spent their whole lives learning John Lee Hooker chords, just hammering on, you know, on the E string, and that was all. . . . Folk people didn't want to hear it if you couldn't play the song exactly the way that . . . Aunt Molly Jackson played it.[49]

Dylan's mild insecurity about his lack of technique is dwarfed by his distaste for the habits of his fellow revivalists, embarked on a lifetime of practice to sound as much as possible like someone else. Here was a species of repetition that Dylan could not abide, one that aimed not at proliferating difference but its opposite.

He began to see an alternative way forward. As he states in *Chronicles, Volume One*:

> If I wanted to stay playing music, . . . I would have to claim a larger part of myself. I would have to overlook a lot of things—a lot of things that might even need attention—but that was all right. They were things that I probably felt totally powerless over, anyway.[50]

In part, Dylan is writing of a turn to songwriting, creating his own music rather than reproducing others'. This is the "larger part of himself" that he would have to "claim." But he is also talking about performing. It is clear from context that the many "things" he would have to "overlook" involve the kinds of musical technique that he saw in Mike Seeger, the bodily discipline that allowed the latter to reproduce earlier musics with such unnerving fidelity, reducing difference, and personal idiosyncrasy, to a negligible ripple. Dylan would move in the opposite direction. As the quote's final sentence suggests, he likely couldn't have done otherwise if he had wanted to.

But Dylan's developing aesthetic was not merely a product of individual temperament, of a performing body allergic to practice and rote repetition. It was also a conscious aesthetic choice, an attempt to carve out a niche within the crowded and competitive Village music scene. As such, it was an example of what French sociologist Pierre Bourdieu calls a *prise de position*, or "position-taking." Bourdieu would describe the Village scene as a cultural "field" structured by various artistic antagonisms and alignments.[51] In order to secure one's place in such a dense relational field, one must take a position, adopt a stance by cultivating *this* artistic practice rather than *that* one. Such choices are never disinterested. They are bound up in a relational network of competing actors, all scrambling to accrue capital, both cultural and monetary.[52]

Why does this matter? Because Dylan is one of postwar mass culture's anointed geniuses. When contemplating such figures, it is all too easy to slip into Romantic habits of thought that elevate them above the fray, treating them as lone, autonomous agents that create out of whole cloth, impervious to the grubby material circumstances of their local social context and historical moment. In such a view, artistic choices arise from a deep reservoir of personal identity or selfhood, not from social entanglements. But Dylan is in fact one of the best witnesses to refute such a view. One can sense the Bourdieuian dynamic throughout *Chronicles, Volume One*, as Dylan makes clear just how profoundly he was shaped by the competitive forces that surrounded him in the Village. Or consider this passage from the liner notes to the 1985 box set *Biograph*:

> [Woody Guthrie] contributed a lot to my style lyrically and dynamically but my musical background had been different, with rock 'n' roll and rhythm and blues playing a big part earlier on. Actually attitude had more to do with it than technical ability and that's what the folk movement lacked. In other words, I played all the folk songs with a rock 'n' roll attitude. This is what made me different and allowed me to cut through all the mess and be heard.[53]

There is much to notice here. First, observe the explicit language of position taking. By leaning on his rock 'n' roll roots, Dylan was able to "cut through all the mess and be heard." Bourdieu couldn't have put it better himself. Second, note that the forces that shaped Dylan's performing aesthetic were not merely negative, things he wanted to avoid. Rather, he sought to channel the spontaneity, energy, and rawness of the music that had thrilled him as a youth.

Third, many of those youthful musical enthusiasms had African American roots. His references to rock 'n' roll and R&B remind us that Little Richard was his first musical hero, whom he raucously imitated at the piano in his earliest performances in Hibbing, Minnesota (discussed in depth in chapter 8). A few paragraphs earlier in the *Biograph* notes, he offers a veritable rollcall of African American musicians as explicit early influences, a few of whom he met and learned from directly in his early Village years: Lonnie Johnson, Tampa Red, Scrapper Blackwell, Jimmy Reed, Sonny Terry, Junior Parker, Victoria Spivey. The notes even include a photo of a twenty-year-old Dylan with Spivey, as though offering documentary evidence of a direct lineage.[54] To be sure, Dylan was also assimilating the sounds of numerous white musicians at this time, Woody Guthrie foremost among them. But he blended these with Black influences, crafting a rough-and-ready style a world removed from that of more commercially polished (and lily-white) folkies like, say, the Kingston Trio. The author of "Blowin' in the Wind" and "Only a Pawn in Their Game" was a champion of the civil rights movement, yes, but he was also a musician in thrall to Black music and expressive culture, seeking to channel its potency in his own music making. Many of his sonic imperfections derive from his emulations of Blackness—a coarse vocal timbre here, a wildly broken blues harmonica note there. Billy Cross, guitarist in his 1978 band, put it bluntly: "Bob is really into black culture. He likes black women. He likes black music. He likes black style. When he asked for musical attitudes, they would always be black."[55] "Love and theft," Dylan himself would later call it, channeling Eric Lott.[56] Such racial appropriation is hardly unique to Dylan, but it remains a vexed aspect of his legacy. We will listen closely for its effects—and their ideological entailments—in the coming chapters.

We should nevertheless be wary of reducing these questions to an overly tidy polemic about white appropriation. One reason is Dylan's Jewish heritage. While I have referred to him above as white, he is a member of an ethnic group that has not historically enjoyed the full privileges of whiteness in the United States.[57] Indeed, white supremacists to this day are keen to police this very border, explicitly excluding Jews from the "white race." Moreover, such racists would not have to look far into Dylan's performing persona to find material ripe for antisemitic stereotype. Think of his stylistic shapeshifting, his ability to adopt others' mannerisms, his comic banter early in his career, with its hints of Borscht Belt shtick. Shapeshifting and mimicry have a long, dark history in antisemitic writing on music, going back to Richard Wagner's diatribes against Jewish composers like Mendelssohn and Meyerbeer.[58] To be sure, Dylan's relationship to his Jewish roots is complex, and it in no way exonerates him from charges of appropriation. He has still benefited handsomely from a culture that rewards non-Black artists for sounding like Black ones. But his Jewishness adds an asterisk to claims of privileged whiteness. More broadly, we do well to remember that Dylan's musical appetite has always been omnivorous. He has assimilated and metabolized *many* musical and cultural traditions: Black, white, rural, urban, Southern, Northern, New World and Old. We will do well to remain critically alert and ethically nimble when it comes to *all* of the ethnic and racial vectors at play in his art.

For now, we can note that, in the mid-'60s, many of Dylan's sonic imperfections fused Black vernacular musical influences with prestigious high-culture aesthetic values. The result was a kind of cultural-capitalist double play. His embrace of imperfection in the volatile moment of performance was of a piece not only with blues, early rock 'n' roll, and R&B, but also with the Beats' aesthetic of creative spontaneity, as embodied in Jack Kerouac's mini-manifesto, "Essentials of Spontaneous Prose."[59] This was a quick route to claiming a certain kind of hipster cred, one with roots both in the academy (Kerouac and Allen Ginsberg had studied at Columbia) and in the nascent counterculture.[60] Even more explicitly highbrow was his alignment with a set of modernist ideals neatly encapsulated in Ezra Pound's dictum to "make it new." Dylan's commitment to bracing novelty in performance, his desire to confront and shock his audience—these are modernist gestures that had a long history before he arrived in New York in January 1961. His scandalous electric performance at Newport in 1965 quickly took on almost mythical status in the annals of folk and rock, becoming a primal scene that would be rehearsed and relitigated for decades to follow. The parallels to the riotous Parisian premiere of Stravinsky's *Rite of Spring* in 1913—another modernist primal scene—are almost too obvious to point out. Dylan himself eventually noted the similarity:

> I was booed at Newport before [the 1979 Christian tour], remember. You can't worry about things like that. Miles Davis has been booed. Hank Williams was booed. Stravinsky was booed. You're nobody if you don't get booed sometime.[61]

Note Dylan's sly intermixing of mass and high culture, Miles Davis and Hank Williams cheek-by-jowl with Stravinsky. This at once inscribes all of these artists into a single pantheon of antagonistic modernists and includes Dylan himself in that tradition. Greil Marcus has stated that Dylan's three electric records in 1965–66 "rank with the most intense outbreaks of twentieth-century modernism," and Timothy Hampton writes extensively about the modernist impulse in Dylan.[62] In the mid-'60s, this impulse fused the scrappy energy of rock 'n' roll with self-consciously poetic language and an aesthetic of high-cultural provocation and difficulty. If booing was the result, all the better—such noises merely confirmed Dylan's modernist bona fides. But this was merely one modernist inflection point in his career. Throughout the decades, his particular brand of modernism has found expression night after night in the moment of performance, in his compulsion not only to confront and challenge his audience but also to "make it new" on stage every night—opening again and again to difference in repetition.

In short, Dylan's rowdy art of twofold imperfection has multiple sources. It developed as a product of temperament *and* cunning calculation, a triangulation between his bodily predispositions, his aesthetic enthusiasms, and sites of cultural prestige both high and low. While this fleshes out our sense of the origins of Dylan's sonic imperfections, it tells us little about how that imperfection works in practice. It is one thing to state, as I do above, that Dylan's "music achieves its effects not despite its many imperfections, but precisely because of them." It is quite another to demonstrate just what those effects *are*. That is the work of the chapters to come.

MUSICKING, SOUNDING, AND THE BOOK AHEAD

This book is organized into three parts: "Voicing," "Playing," and "Sounding 'Hard Rain.'" The gerunds take their inspiration from an influential study by Christopher Small, in which he argues that music is not a noun but a verb. It is something we do, or many somethings—performing, composing, dancing, listening. Small coins a new gerund to encompass them all: musicking.[63] The term is especially apt for Dylan, with his deep commitment to musical process over finished product, imperfective openness over perfective closure. Small's work encourages us to reframe our subject. Not Dylan's music, but Dylan's musicking.

Before giving an overview of the chapters, it is worth pointing out topics that the book does *not* cover. My focus in all that follows is on sounds that Bob Dylan himself makes, whether as a singer or as an instrumentalist. I talk about his backing musicians from time to time, but they do not get their own chapter. This is largely for reasons of space. One could write an entire book on Dylan's guitarists alone, or on his performances with one backing group, say, the Band. This is not that book. Thankfully, Ray Padgett has published a revelatory collection of interviews with Dylan band members, which will be an invaluable resource to all future researchers who want to explore Dylan's interaction with his bandmates in greater depth. It is an extraordinary book and a gift to the Dylan community.[64] I also do not discuss covers of Dylan songs, a thorough study of which could fill an entire library shelf.[65] My focus, again, is on the sounds Dylan makes with his own voice, his own body.

This book is not a comprehensive survey of Dylan's music, were such a thing even possible. There are literally hundreds of Dylan songs I don't mention at all. Conversely, I spend several chapters on just *one* song. As a result, it's almost certain that at least a couple of your favorite Dylan tunes are not mentioned in these pages. My hope, though, is that you will find the book's ideas portable. Once you have read, say, about the styles of vocal delivery I discuss in chapters 4 and 5, or about Dylan's harp playing in chapter 7, you will be able to transport those concepts to any performance you choose. Above all else, I aim for this book to be *ear opening*. If I have succeeded, you can step away from the text with ears transformed and newly sensitized, ready to fill them with your favorite Dylan performances, hearing afresh.

The book's first section, "Voicing," encompasses five chapters that theorize Dylan's voice in all its teeming multiplicity. Chapter 1, "The Fashioned Voice," attends closely to the changeability of that voice over decades. This chapter draws on scholars of voice studies who have thought carefully about the relationship between the sounding voice and the self that emits it, a relationship smudged by Dylan's constant shapeshifting. Chapter 2, "Identity and Plurality," takes up the issue of identity in earnest, addressing the critical commonplace that Dylan's voice is merely a series of "masks," with no persisting core voice. But any fan *also* knows that one can always perceive Dylan within or behind the mask. He is ever recognizable. I argue in the chapter that part of what we recognize when we recognize Dylan's voice is not only his persisting (if aging) body—specifically, its fleshy interior, where the voice originates—but also the sound of that interior under pressure, torqued by other voices, especially voices of strong predecessors. This leads to a paradox of vocal identity: the more strenuously Dylan imitates other singers, the more he sounds unmistakably like himself.

Chapter 3, "The Empathic Voice," turns in a different direction, focusing on Dylan's ability to vocally inhabit characters in his songs, a skill that Greil Marcus calls his "genie."[66] I focus here especially on Dylan's 1961 studio performance of "House of the Rising Sun." Gender and class figure prominently in the chapter. How does the middle-class Jewish kid from the small-town North invest this poor, Southern female character with such searingly believable affect? Dylan, like many great singers before him (Billie Holiday leaps immediately to mind), turns his vocal limitations into expressive resources here, recruiting them to voice the character of the woman "ruined" by the titular house in New Orleans. Nothing mystical, in other words, just tools of the trade. But Dylan pulls it off with such conviction that the dissonances of gender, class, and subject position recede, replaced by something that feels suspiciously like emotional truth. Chapters 4 and 5 conclude the "Voicing" section by theorizing Dylan's fluid traversal of the speech–song continuum throughout his career. Chapter 4 explores the speechward side of the continuum, chapter 5 the songward end. I argue in these chapters that one of the primary ways Dylan imperfects his voice is by shuttling it along this continuum, moving now more toward speech, now more toward song. I provide a typology of stations along the continuum, showing how they correlate with different phases in his career, shifting racial postures, and varied stances toward the word as semantic object of everyday talk (at one extreme) and raw material of musical sound (at the other).

By the end of these chapters, the reader may well have concluded that voice is all in Dylan's music. After all, his voice is the vehicle of his celebrated words, a conveyor of identity and affect, and an object of sonic fascination. His music gathers itself around his voice, the center of its gravitational system. But the next section of the book, "Playing," begins by reminding us that Dylan's choice of instruments has also had seismic implications, capable of throwing entire genres off their axes. Most notable, of course, was his turn to amplified bands in the mid-1960s. The iconic instrument of this turn was the electric guitar, which Dylan wielded on stage at Newport in July 1965 and then in a series of increasingly confrontational shows worldwide over the following ten months. Far from a neutral backing instrument, Dylan's electric guitar was a source of epochal consternation for folk revivalists. For many, it signaled the end of the folk boom, its mere physical and sonic presence seeming to sicken the movement like an airborne pathogen from the despised worlds of rock 'n' roll, the capitalist music industry, and the bourgeoisie that supported it.

The section thus begins here, with an instrument that has been (quite literally) pivotal in Dylan's career. Chapter 6, "Guitar: Sound and Symbol," takes Dylan's infamous 1965 Newport performance as its point of departure. I begin with the irony that the offending noisemaker around Dylan's neck—his Stratocaster—is barely audible in the texture, utterly drowned out by Mike Bloomfield's ferocious leads. Dylan was that night, and has remained, a diffident electric player. His acoustic playing, by contrast, is characterful, driving, and stylistically varied. Moreover, his most overt rock 'n' roll playing has (also ironically) been on the acoustic. The chapter listens intently to the tensions and ironies in this acoustic/electric binary, drawing out their interpretive implications as regards race, genre, gender, and sexuality. Chapter 7, "Harmonica: Breathing Room," listens closely to the one instrument that necessarily stops the flow of Dylan's celebrated words. I argue that his rudimentary rack style makes various histories audible, from a populist history of what Kim Field calls "the people's instrument" to histories of modernist antagonism and high-art difficulty. Chapter 8, "Piano: Seeking and Finding," explores an instrument little associated with Dylan in the popular imagination, but that has been central to his music making for seventy years, beginning with his earliest imitations of Little Richard in Hibbing, Minnesota. He has sought identities as well as songs at the keyboard, his flat-fingered technique coaxing primitive chords and culturally distant musics from this quintessential instrument of the middle-class living room.

Section 3, "Sounding 'Hard Rain,'" concludes by returning to the song with which we began: "A Hard Rain's a-Gonna Fall." I noted above that the song "has resonated in global auditory culture for over half a century," asking: "In so resonating, again and again, what do its sounds *do*?" This section offers one set of answers. Its four chapters listen for the song's musical sources as well as the welter of sounds that Dylan made when performing it on stage over the ensuing six decades. Chapter 9, "What Did You Hear, My Blue-Eyed Son? The

Musical Sources," demonstrates that, despite claims to the contrary from scholars, Dylan's tune is not in fact based on any known tune for the ballad "Lord Randal," though its lyrics partially derive from it. The *musical* sources of "Hard Rain," by contrast, range from a field recording of a Black farmer, collected by John and Alan Lomax; to Woody Guthrie's "1913 Massacre"; to Roy Orbison's "Running Scared." The brief chapter 10, "Six Crooked Highways: Time and Harmony in the Guitar Part," explores Dylan's deceptively simple guitar playing on the studio recording, illuminating its play of "crooked" and "straight" time, so essential to the song's momentum and temporal unfolding. Chapters 11 and 12 then trace a longitudinal history of the song as Dylan performed it night after night across fifty-five years, from 1962 to 2017. What emerges is a sonic portrait of Dylan caught in the act, repeating and differing, draping "Hard Rain" over minutes and years. Dylanesque imperfections crack the song open each time, new meanings spilling out. We cannot hear those meanings—with all they have to teach us about America's roiling history, its social ills, its aspirations—unless we listen.

Think, then, of each of these chapters as a *sounding*, in a dual sense. They are on the one hand exercises in close listening, in attending carefully to Dylan's sounding imperfections. More fancifully, they are also soundings in the nautical sense of depth measures, deep dives into a particular set of sonic behaviors, an inquiry into their social and aesthetic effects, and into their historical, political, and ideological contexts. So, let's dive in. We begin—where else?—with his voice.

PART I
Voicing

Chapter 1 audio examples:
soundingbobdylan.com/ch1

CHAPTER ONE

The Fashioned Voice

Let's start by getting Dylan's voice in our ears. It's October 24, 1963, a bit over a year since we left him typing the words to "Hard Rain." We're no longer in the Village, but in Midtown—at Columbia's Studio A—where Dylan is recording "The Times They Are a-Changin'," the title track for his third album. He is twenty-two. **Audio example 1.1** presents the opening verse. The voice is dusty and weathered, a sonic match for the image that would grace the album's cover: a stoic Dylan in a denim shirt, the black-and-white composition worthy of Dorothea Lange.[1] He at once sounds his age and works to sound older. As so often in these years, Dylan deliberately ages his voice, tensing the laryngeal muscles around the glottis. This prevents the vocal folds from making complete contact, causing them to respond more like the stiffer, less pliable folds of an older singer; some breath escapes between them, preventing clean phonation. The result is the grit so characteristic of early Dylan—"as if sandpaper could sing," in Joyce Carol Oates's memorable phrase.[2] The sound is bright and forward in the mask, creating a timbre many have heard as nasal. But that word can distract us from how sonorous the young Dylan's voice is. He sings here in the upper-middle part of his range—the tune covers only a perfect fifth, from G3 to D4 (that is, the G below middle C to the D immediately above it)—but one senses a deep resonance beneath that register, like a silent bellows powering the resonant vowels.[3] The delivery is at once casual and stately, striding the anthemic tune with folksy nonchalance.

It is one of Dylan's sturdiest melodies.[4] **Figure 1.1** traces its outline in simplified rhythm. Dylan's actual sung rhythm is, as always, alive with subtle detail, but this skeletal representation will serve for now. The figure divides the melody into six phrases, which correspond to the six lines of the verse. Note first the play of ascent and descent: phrases 1 and 3 ascend; phrases 2, 4, and 6 descend; the climactic phrase 5 neither ascends nor descends, holding steadily—and arrestingly—to a single pitch, at the top of the tune's range. Underneath that held pitch, Dylan's guitar progresses through a series of chords whose bass notes descend, as shown in the small black noteheads in phrases 5 and 6. The result is a sounding metaphor for the words, "you better start swimmin' or you'll sink like a stone": the voice holds to the surface, while the guitar sinks beneath.

Tony Bennett is reported to have said of the young Dylan, his label-mate on Columbia, "he may not be able to sing, but he sure can *phrase*."[5] That gift for supple phrasing is especially evident in live performance, where Dylan can be extraordinarily inventive, as we will hear in a moment. But his gift for phrasing is at work here too, in a carefully poised, early studio take. Note first that phrases 1 and 3 are melodically identical, and 2 and 4 are nearly so. The first four phrases thus pair up melodically: 1+2, 3+4. But Dylan's supple, irregular phrasing cuts across this parallelism. He elides the end of phrase 2 with the beginning of phrase 3, dragging the /n/ from "grown" to the beginning of the next line, affixing it to the onset of "and." (The figure shows this with a dashed slur.) The result is an aural enjambment at precisely the moment where a pause or breath would articulate the melodic parallelism of phrases 1+2 and 3+4. Instead, rests separate these paired lines—note the empty bars at the ends of phrases 1 and 3—creating a phrase-level syncopation: instead of 1+2 | 3+4, we hear something more like 1 | 2+3 | 4. Moreover, the pauses themselves manifest a subtle change imperfection. Dylan inserts one bar of extra

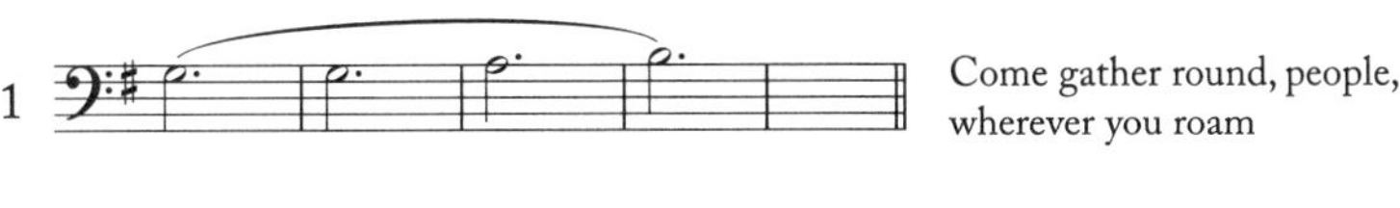

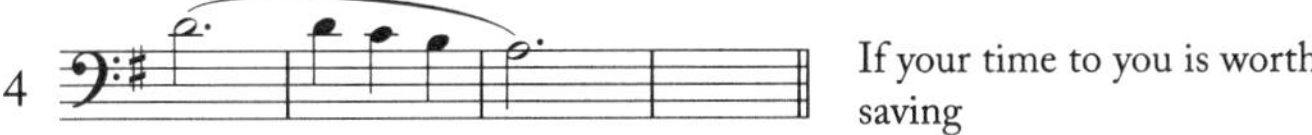

FIGURE 1.1. Skeletal melody of "The Times They Are a-Changin'," as recorded by Dylan on October 24, 1963, in Columbia's Studio A and released on the album of the same name.

strumming after line 1 but expands this to two after line 3. The result is an oddly unpredictable kind of momentum, a sense that the lyric is tumbling falteringly—but inevitably—forward. The effect is apt, given the song's thematics of imminence ("soon," "rapidly") and delay, its push-pull temporality: "The slow one now will later be fast."

That biblical rewrite, with its hints of Ecclesiastes and the Gospels, beautifully captures an aspect of the verse's temporality as it continues to unfold.[6] For, while progress is halting and fitful in phrases 1–3, it gathers momentum in lines 4–6. Note that each of these last three phrases is four bars long, in contrast to the five bars of line 1 and the six of line 3. The regular four-bar phrases in lines 4–6 create a sense of consistent forward motion, of regular and predictable metric progress. Moreover, phrase 4 is left hanging in multiple senses; it points forward, asking for completion. Like phrase 2 it ends on A, the second scale degree ($\hat{2}$), rather than coming fully home with a descent to the first scale degree ($\hat{1}$), the tonic. But unlike phrase 2, phrase 4 ends melodically in its third bar—it is the first phrase to do so—adding a sense of unfinished metric business. The contrast to phrase 2, with its overflowing enjambment, is especially striking. Moreover, the end rhyme in phrase 4 ("saving") dangles, departing for the first time from the /ohm/ohn/ rhyme of the first three phrases. All of this creates a sense of expectation at the end of phrase 4, which is heightened and suspended in the air during the sustained D of phrase 5.[7] Phrase 6 then steps down from this highpoint, resuming the melodic gesture of phrases 2 and 4, but bringing it for the first time to conclusion on G ($\hat{1}$) in the fourth bar. This sense of melodic and metric arrival coincides with a poetic one, as the end rhyme of line 6 reaches back to that of line 4. The dangling rhyme now partnered, all of phrase 4's loose ends are tied up. This kinetic profile—with its gathering momentum and gratifying conclusion—sonically enacts the lyrics' sentiment of hopeful futurity, of a change already under way, the arc of the moral universe seeming to bend toward justice before our very ears.[8]

VOICES COLLECTIVE AND APART

To better sense the particularity of Dylan's voice as it traverses the tune, let's compare it with a contemporaneous performance of the same song. Peter, Paul and Mary were among the first artists to cover "The Times They Are a-Changin'," releasing a live version on their 1964 album *In Concert.* **Audio example 1.2** presents their first verse. In place of Dylan's weathered rasp, we now hear pure-voiced commercial folk singing, with clean tone and careful sustain. The singers begin in unison, breaking out into carefully tuned two-part harmony in phrases 5 and 6; three-part harmony will follow in subsequent verses. The seamless blend of vocal timbres—indeed, their near indistinguishability during the unison passages—is especially striking. Though Mary Travers's alto obtrudes slightly, the overall effect in the unisons is of three individuals singing with one voice. This anonymizes the voices, effacing their timbral differences and the singers' bodily identities. This is no accident. The performance clearly enacts a political ideal, gesturing toward an imaginary collective, a sounding emblem of the civil rights movement and of the resurgent, early-'60s Left more generally. Peter, Paul and Mary's commercial success was due in part to the ways they embodied the ideals of this counterculture to middle-class consumers in a decidedly nonthreatening way—polished, inoffensive, and very white.[9]

If Peter, Paul and Mary's singing style anonymized bodies and voices, Dylan's did quite the opposite. One heard *his* body, in all of its idiosyncrasy, not an anonymized ideal. One could sing along to Peter, Paul and Mary's version of this song, and many did. It was much harder to blend voices with Dylan, as Joan Baez could attest. (I will have more to say about Dylan's harmonizing with women below.) For now, we should note that these two performances sound from different sides of a divide in the early-'60s urban folk revival. As Sumanth Gopinath and Michael Cherlin write:

> When Dylan encountered the Greenwich Village folk revival in full swing in the early 1960s, the scene was divided into two streams: the college-campus and media-friendly "clean" tendency, in which the presumed universality of the folk song was reflected in an apparently neutral voice bespeaking a young, white, middle-class sensibility, and the ethnic particularist perspective, in which musicians attempted to re-create the sound of traditional music rather than abstracting it into some "purer" style.[10]

Peter, Paul and Mary are archetypes of the first camp, while Dylan is the most famous representative of the second, though he had models.[11] As Gopinath and Cherlin note, two Dylan mentors in particular—Ramblin' Jack Elliott, a protégé of Woody Guthrie, and

Dave Van Ronk, the father figure of the Village folk scene—blazed the trail.[12] As Van Ronk himself put it:

> The one limiting factor was the insistence on "authenticity," on reproducing the traditional ethnic styles, all the way down to getting the accents right. It did not matter if you were ethnic à la Furry Lewis, or à la Jimmie Rodgers, or à la Earl Scruggs; that was a matter of personal taste. But it should be authentically ethnic as a matter of principle.[13]

Van Ronk's locution "authentically ethnic"—or as he puts it elsewhere, "neo-ethnic"—is jarring to twenty-first-century ears. It also marks a contradiction: one achieved "authenticity" by imitating someone else.[14] Dylan of course followed exactly this path, famously "finding his voice" by imitating others', most notably Woody Guthrie's, a subject we will explore in chapter 2. Dylan and the rest of Van Ronk's "neo-ethnics" were largely middle-class, urban whites, just like Peter, Paul and Mary. But unlike them, Van Ronk and his fellow travelers self-consciously adopted the vocal techniques of working-class, southern musicians—often rural and often Black. Dave Van Ronk's gruff delivery owed a great deal to Black blues singers, and Dylan himself regularly adopted a bluesy voice in his early recordings and live performances. Just as often, though, he affected vocal mannerisms of the white south, as on "The Times They Are a-Changin'," with its twang, studiously dropped *g*s, and coarsened timbre bespeaking a hard, working-class life. That these were vocal affectations should be obvious to anyone who has ever spent time in northern Minnesota or spoken with someone who hails from there.[15] This carefully imperfected voice constructs a persona: the singer as rural sage.

Though these two performances epitomize the stylistic fissure in the revival, there is one notable similarity between them. For all of their local differences in rhythm—Peter, Paul and Mary sing relatively straight, Dylan syncopates incessantly—the trio largely follows the outline of Dylan's tune as depicted on figure 1.1. They even follow his phrasing as regards the enjambment between phrases 2 and 3 (though they do not vary the length of the rest after lines 1 and 3). The similar phrasing suggests that they learned the song from Dylan's studio recording as released on *The Times They Are a-Changin'* on January 13, 1964, and not from the earlier demo Dylan had recorded for Witmark, the first verse of which is reproduced in **audio example 1.3.**[16] In addition to the piano accompaniment, this version differs from the studio recording in its phrasing. Most notably, Dylan does *not* elide the end of phrase 2 with the beginning of phrase 3. Instead, he pauses carefully between the phrases, as though giving the singer learning the tune from the publisher's demo time to assimilate each line. The result is notably square, lacking the push-pull momentum of the studio version. The comparison makes clear that Dylan *heightens* his stylized vocal imperfections for the album version, carefully fashioning his public vocal persona by blurring the tidy structure he had laid down in the demo.

Such unpredictable singing made him a famously difficult duet partner, especially for female harmonizers. Ask Joan Baez: "if you ever work with him, if he did the song the night before as a waltz, tonight he's gonna do it in 2/4 time just to fuck you up, you know."[17] The gender dynamics in these duets are clear. It is up to the woman to harmonize with Dylan, not the other way around. He bobs and weaves around the melody in his characteristically shambolic style. She then has to find higher pitches that work with the unpredictable sounds emerging from Dylan's throat, gingerly picking out euphonious thirds and sixths against the moving target of his vocal line. This is highly gendered work—the sonic equivalent of dressing up your man to make him presentable. One thinks of Baez leading the rumpled young Dylan onto the stage in their early duo performances, she regal and commanding, he scruffy and hunched. As she herself said, "He would bring out the mother instinct in a woman who thought her mother instinct was *dead*."[18] In short, Dylan the ramshackle singer exercised a prerogative of white masculinity—to reside in a space of disheveled inspiration, while the few female singers to harmonize with him had to draw on their gender training to domesticate his untidy sounds within the code of Western musical convention.[19]

Aside from tensions over musical gender roles, there were various reasons for Dylan's split with Baez after their brief romance. Chief among these was his increasingly awful treatment of her in 1965, painfully documented in D. A. Pennebaker's film *Dont Look Back.*[20] But Baez had additional reasons to take her voice elsewhere. Most notably, she quickly became disenchanted with Dylan's political ambivalence, his wavering commitment to the cause. If we listen closely, we can hear Dylan's political ambivalence in his studio recording of "Times," in the tension between his aspirational lyrics—their explicit calling into being of a movement ("Come gather 'round")—and his highly aestheticized solo performance, with its unpredictable timing and coarse timbre. The lyrics announce a collective, but on Dylan's recording they are delivered by a voice apart—that of the budding auteur, already on his way to the aloof, untouchable paragon of hardened cool.

THE WHEEL'S STILL IN SPIN: 1978–2008

Timothy Hampton writes perceptively of "the distance between the implicitly understood or 'unheard' melody of Dylan's songs . . . and his own dramatic performance of those same songs," wryly observing that "even when singing his own compositions, Dylan seems unable to color inside the lines."[21] If Dylan's vocal coloring strays somewhat outside the melodic lines of the Witmark demo already on the studio recording, it would do so ever more extravagantly on stage over the coming decades, the gap between the "unheard melody" and his vocal performance widening vertiginously. **Audio example 1.4** demonstrates by sampling four live versions of the first verse, beginning in 1978 and then striding forward in ten-year intervals: 1988, 1998, 2008. These performances lift the song out of its 1963 context—civil rights, the nascent counterculture, stylistic squabbles of the folk revivalists—and place it in new ones, from late-'70s malaise to millennial hope. To be sure, the memory of the song's original contexts—or some imagined (and likely romanticized) version of them—presumably accompanied it for many listeners at these concerts, giving the performance an especially strong retrospective charge, like a fragment of '60s culture reanimated in the present. But that reanimation of course unfolded in (and was inflected by) the current context. In 2008, for example, it mapped onto a new generation's sense of changing times, their hope that the arc of the moral universe had just bent a few degrees further: the performance took place on the night of Barack Obama's election.[22]

Most listeners to Dylan that night—and in each earlier rendition in audio example 1.4—surely carried with them not only a fantasy of "the '60s revived" but also an aural memory of Dylan's voice on the 1963 recording. They could then measure the yawning distance between that recording and the sounds emanating from the stage. For the music of Dylan's live performances does not reside only in the sounds that are empirically present in the venue, the noises he and his band are making in real time. His performances also activate a space *between* those sounds and the more familiar versions of the songs, typically the studio recordings. The result is a kind of double-hearing for audience members, as the sounds in the here and now link up with (often very different) sounds held in memory.[23] To some degree, this is a common experience in all live performance—the concert rarely sounds exactly like the record—but Dylan takes it to an extreme. The links between the (recalled) studio recording and the (sounding) live performance bend and buckle as Dylan and his band reshape the song phrase by phrase, words once again encountering music to reforge that hyphenated compound.

One experiences that double-hearing immediately on listening to audio example 1.4, as the memory of the studio version dissonates with the live renditions. The glut of change imperfections, of proliferating difference in repetition, is dizzying. Consider vocal quality.[24] Gone is the dusty deadpan of 1963. In its place we hear the euphoric thrust-and-jab of 1978, the clipped urgency of 1988, the tender resonance of 1998, the guttural rumble of 2008. Dylan's aging voice strikes these familiar words from ever new angles. Take register. He hits the very top of his range in the 1978 performance, on the climactic phrase 5, which touches on A4 ("or you'll sink like *aaay* stone!"). Decades later he inhabits the vocal depths. His register drops notably in 1998 and sinks further in 2008. If in 1963 we heard a young singer trying to sound old, we now hear an actual body aging: thirty-seven years old in 1978, then forty-seven, fifty-six, sixty-seven.[25] And this is not just any body. It is Bob Dylan's, bearer of a voice that has been singing incessantly since well before that 1963 recording, on stage and in the studio. By 2008 that voice is ragged and torn from years of (mis)use. Yet we can also hear how Dylan adapts to the changes in his aging vocal apparatus. Though his upper register is largely gone by the late '90s, he explores the deep recesses of his range with ceaseless ingenuity. What he loses in pitch mobility he makes up for in timbral variety, rhythmic invention, and morphing melodic contour.

In fact, melodic contour varies across *all* of these performances. On this point, it is illuminating to listen to audio example 1.4 while following figure 1.1, which can act as a mnemonic for the melodic up-and-down of the studio recording. Though Dylan stays somewhat close to the tune in the opening lines in 1978 and 1988, the changes elsewhere are stark. Where the melody had once risen, it now falls, or stays put, or traces some entirely new shape. Sometimes he drifts toward speech (for example, near the ends of phrases 3 and 4 in 1988), at other times he launches into an ecstatic or broken upper register (phrase 5 in 1978, phrase 6 in 1998). Changes in rhythm also abound. In 2008 every line arrives in a rhythmic burst, syllables huddled tightly together. In 1998, by contrast, Dylan holds back rhythmically at certain moments, inserting slight but touching pauses ("around you have . . . grown"). Certain words leap out on a given night only to lose their markedness in a different version. Generic signifiers come and go—a country twang here, a bluesy inflection there.

THINKING VOCAL MULTITUDES

What are we to make of this riot of vocal invention? How can we theorize a voice that never stays put, that sounds ever different, that encounters the same words night after night but that weaves around them with such insistent novelty? What does that novelty disclose? About the song? About the singer? About us and our investment in both? What, for example, might listeners in Minnesota on November

4, 2008, have made of the deep rumble delivering those idealistic, defiant words? Did the specific sounds matter less than the simple fact that Dylan was singing the song on the night of Obama's election? Or did his ravaged sounds invest the old tune with new meaning? Answers would of course differ based on whom one asks. Some were no doubt baffled by Dylan's delivery that night, others transfixed.

What can we say with certainty about Dylan's voice, in all of its teeming multiplicity, its wild signifying energy, its sheer *muchness*? Well, at least this. In any era, on any night, Dylan's voice sounds his words and it sounds a persona. That is, his voice conveys both his famous lyrics and (some iteration of) the famous character "Bob Dylan." It is a critical commonplace to view that character as a construction, a collection of influences and put-on identities. "Bob Dylan," in this understanding, is nothing but a series of masks, including vocal ones. In the next chapter I'll put some pressure on that view. For now, it will be useful merely to note the ways in which his voice acts as a vehicle for both words and performed identity in our "Times" examples, at once sounding his lyrics and fashioning an audible self. In 1963 that self emerged from the conflictual forces of the folk revival, the weathered rasp both affiliating with Van Ronk's "neo-ethnics" and laying claim to a kind of timeless, prophetic wisdom. In later eras we hear different fashioned personas, from Vegas entertainer (1978) to inscrutable, ancient bard (2008). All the while, Dylan vocally navigates the song's words anew each night, startling them back into meaning.

WHAT'S IN A VOICE? SOUND, WORD, AND BODY

To think our way further into Dylan's vocal multitudes, we begin with philosopher Brian Kane's insight that voice arises at the intersection of sound, word, and body.[26] We are perhaps most comfortable thinking of voice simply as the sound that comes from our mouths when we speak or sing. But on reflection it's clear that voice often means more than just that. Our voices are also vehicles of words, and thus meaning. Moreover, they also audibly disclose our bodies, and thus our identities—a kind of sonic thumbprint. Kane develops a sophisticated model for thinking through this threefold understanding of voice.[27] I will use his concepts somewhat more casually. **Figure 1.2** provides a useful visual to orient our discussion. Let's explore it a bit before giving it a test drive on our "Times" examples.

When talking about Dylan's voice, we can situate ourselves wherever we like on the figure. We can, for example, occupy each vertex in turn. This is straightforward enough. For example, whenever we puzzle at the sense of Dylan's lyrics, our focus is firmly on the word, at the lower left vertex. Dylan reception has for decades been in thrall to the word, to poring over the most studied body of lyrics in the postwar era. When our attention turns to the peculiarity of his sounding voice, our focus is on sound, at the apex of the figure. And when we wonder about the fleshy configuration that produces that voice, and at the self that it presumably discloses—just who Dylan *is*, another perennial topic—we shift to thinking about the voice as emissary of the body, at lower right.

All of this is relatively obvious and only moderately illuminating. The model reveals more when we consider the terms in pairs, situating ourselves on the lines or *edges* joining the terms.[28] As this is a book on sound, we will be most concerned with the two edges that emanate from that word at the top. These are the two axes I mentioned above: voice as a sounding vehicle of words (the left edge) and the voice as a sounding vehicle of the body, and thus a self (the right). Let's begin

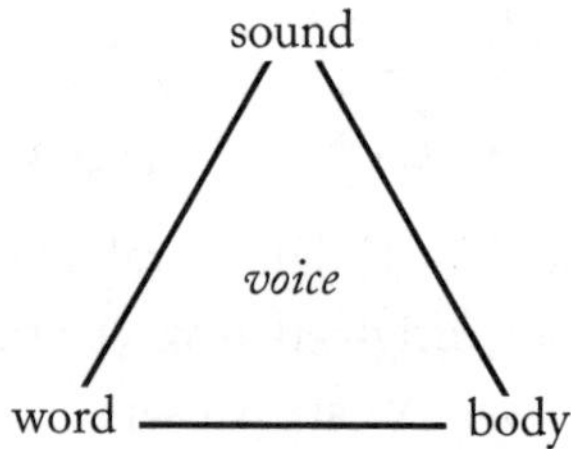

FIGURE 1.2. Voice arising at the intersection of sound, word, and body (after Brian Kane).

on the left, where Dylan's sounding voice—in all of its idiosyncrasy, its breakages and imperfections—bodies forth his lyrics, spinning them first this way and now that, caressing a word at one moment, roughing it up the next. If his voice cracks open when he sings "And though our separation / It pierced me to the heart," we may well believe some deep wound has been disclosed, the raw vocal sound investing the words with the ring of truth, a topic I will return to in chapter 3. Note that it is the *sound* of Dylan's voice that creates this ring of truth. The words alone are one thing, but the delivery supercharges the meaning.

To be sure, we can also delight in this axis—the sound of Dylan's language, its play of rhythm, rhyme, and meaning—on the page:

> Maggie comes fleet foot
> Face full of black soot
> Talkin' that the heat put
> Plants in the bed but
> The phone's tapped anyway
> Maggie says that many say
> They must bust in early May
> Orders from the D. A.[29]

We don't need to hear Dylan sing those lines to revel in the tripping monosyllables, the slant rhymes and eye rhymes, the collision of Chuck Berry's scansion with Beat hipsterisms.[30] We can at the same time delight in how that scansion interacts with the meaning of the words, which themselves come fleet foot, tapping away in our inner ears. To hear "tapped" in that way is to hear a pun, but it's not the only one hereabouts. There is also the pun on plants (growing in flower beds or hidden—as microphones—where one sleeps), as well as the felicitous coincidence of D. A. with the first initials of the filmmaker who would direct the song's iconic video.[31] This reminds us that poetry—even unrecited, in print—resides always at the intersection of sound and word, the two making a volatile alloy.

When Dylan *sings* his lyrics we get all of this and more. Indeed, when hearing his sounding voice we may even wonder about the self that produces it, shifting our attention to the broad category of voice and identity, which lives on the rightward edge of the figure. When we listen from this position, we are less concerned about *what* is said or sung—that is, the linguistic meaning of his lyrics—than we are about the relationship between the resulting noise and the body that makes it. Think here of Dylan's vocal timbre in a given era—gritty or smooth, nasal or throaty, rounded or flat. When we attend to these different textures and timbres as the audible surface of a body, independently of the meaning of the words sung, we find ourselves at the right edge of figure 1.2, poised between sound and body. The central question when we inquire into the body behind a voice is "Who speaks?"[32] When crossed with sound, that question is often inflected toward general categories of identity: race, gender, sexuality, ability, class, age, health, cultural background.[33] Dylan learned early that a change in vocal timbre could signal a change in identity, allowing the middle-class Jewish boy from Hibbing to fade to near inaudibility behind a mutable series of vocal identities: train-hopping hobo, fatalistic bluesman, earnest balladeer, sneering dandy.[34] "Which one is Dylan's *real* voice?" "Who *is* he?" many asked then, and still do. The performance of vexation on this point is one of the chief pleasures of fandom. We retake these questions in chapter 2.

What of the one edge we have not discussed, running along the bottom of figure 1.2, between word and body? As it does not involve sound per se, it will be of less immediate interest to us in this book, but it does illuminate one crucial sense of "voice" in Dylan studies. As Kane puts it, this edge raises questions such as "What does the spoken proposition, apart from its sound, tell us about the body or the source of the speaker? How does the knowledge of the source alter the perceived meaning of the utterance?"[35] Here we might consider Dylan's burdensome nomination as "the voice of a generation." The present model puts that tired cliché in a new light, for it leads us to ask just what sense the word "voice" carries here. How is it distributed among sound, body, and word? Word must surely figure in any answer, for the meanings of Dylan's early lyrics—their calls for social justice, for example—are central to any account of his role as generational spokesman. But it is worth remembering that he first became known to a broader public not through the sound of his voice, but through cover versions, most notably Peter, Paul and Mary's 1963 recording of "Blowin' in the Wind," which was a commercial hit. In that context the "voice of a generation" labeled not a disembodied collection of lyrics, but also a person: the self who wrote them, whoever that was. Fans of the Peter, Paul and Mary performance wanted to know just who had penned this song, to attach a body and an identity to it, to fix an author. "Voice" was in this sense a stand-in for Bob Dylan, lyricist. In the early '60s, then, the voice of a generation arose at the intersection of word and body. But not yet sound. Indeed, such was the early success of Dylan *covers* that Columbia had to do some special pleading for the sound of his words in his own voice: "Nobody sings Dylan like Dylan," the ad copy proclaimed. Soon enough, that voice would be circulating internationally—through radio waves, from record grooves, on stage—opening the door to the wild circulation between sound, body, and word that has constituted Dylan's voice ever since in the popular imagination.

That circulation was fully in evidence in our survey of examples from "The Times They Are a-Changin'." I began by noting the affinity between Dylan's "dusty and weathered" 1963 voice and the image of him on the album cover, situating us on the right edge of figure 1.2 as bodily image and sound reinforced one another. Sound and body were also in evidence in the live versions, as we puzzled at the shifting selves his voice seemed to disclose or considered the ways in which his voice made audible an aging body. On the sound-and-word axis, we observed the ways Dylan's singing enacted his lyrics: for example, in the push-pull temporality of the studio recording, or the touching pauses of 1998. Finally, we found ourselves briefly at the intersection of body and word when we wondered at the ways Dylan's performance may have signified in a given era independent of the sound of his voice, most notably in the 2008 version. As I asked in that discussion, "Did the specific sounds matter less than the simple *fact* that Dylan was singing the song on the night of Obama's election?" In other words, for some that night the idea that they were hearing the fabled "voice of a generation" may have taken precedence over the specific sounds coming from the stage. If so, such listeners sited Dylan's voice at the intersection of word and body, to the relative neglect of sound.

TECHNOLOGY AND TECHNIQUE

Before continuing, we need to add one final piece to this model, which Kane labels with the Greek term *technê*, which encompasses both technology and technique. Here is Kane:

> By *technê*, I do not mean tools or instruments per se, but something broader. *Technê* includes both technologies and techniques alike. Under this heading we must consider the astounding variety of bodily and cultural techniques that subjects apply to themselves as well as the technologies that they employ to shape, define, and alter their experience.[36]

For Kane, *technê* disturbs and rearranges sound, body, and word. This should be clear enough when we consider technology in the familiar sense. When applied to the singing voice it involves microphones, cables, mixing boards, speakers, recording and playback devices, signal processing and other effects. Given the back-to-basics rawness of Dylan's singing, it can be all too easy to forget that we always encounter his voice through such technological mediation.[37] We need only revisit our "Times" examples to sense its thickness, for there is a dramatic difference between the close-miking of the studio in 1963 and PA systems in booming auditoriums and arenas, including the Pavillon de Paris (which seats 10,000) and the University of Minnesota's Northrup Auditorium.[38] In each case we can hear Dylan contend vocally with both technology and resonant space, taking advantage of their affordances and working around their limitations. In Columbia's Studio A, he could afford to sacrifice volume in search of that sandpapery vocal surface; on stage, even with state-of-the-art microphones and amplification, he didn't have this luxury—projection was all. This was especially the case in 1978, in front of an eleven-piece band. The fire of that performance came from the energy Dylan derived from his players and from his need to project above them. Not only the technology of Dylan's vocal miking, but that of the instruments behind him, pushed his voice into a volume and declamatory intensity far removed from the hush of the studio.

Moreover, we hear these performances *now* through an additional layer of technological mediation, as recordings. The voice comes to us via speakers or headphones, receivers, amplifiers, equalizers, compression algorithms, streaming codecs, and so on. Among other things, this severs the sound of the performances from any visual or physical contact with the performers. We hear (some mediated version of) the sounds Dylan and his bandmates made, but we do not see their bodies, which performed these actions decades ago.[39] This technological mediation cannot but shuffle the priorities of sound, word, and body. An audio recording, for example, might encourage us to attend more closely to vocal sound-qua-sound, free as we are from visual information about the singer. Alternatively, we might construct the singer's body imaginatively from the sound we hear, imagining what kind of body would produce that kind of voice. Or, we might use recording technology to help decipher the words. Many early fans attest to transcribing Dylan's lyrics from LPs, picking up and replacing the needle multiple times to do so, a technique unavailable before the historical emergence of sound recording.[40]

All of this is clear enough: technology always intervenes in our encounters with Dylan's voice. It is more radical to assert, as Kane does, that *technê* also encompasses *technique*. In other words, *technê* involves not just technology, in the devices-and-wires sense, but also bodily practices. Both shape the voice, altering, projecting, inflecting, and (at times) disguising it. As for bodily practices, consider the vocal technique discussed at the beginning of this chapter, the young Dylan tensing his laryngeal muscles to prematurely age his voice. This instance of bodily technique blurs our sense of the singer's age, as well as his cultural background. We know that we're hearing the young star of the Village folk scene—who hails from northern Minnesota, we're told—but we hear the voice of a singer who could be older, and who may well be from the white rural South. Dylan's vocal technique thus alters our sense of the body—and hence the identity—that we imaginatively construct in the moment of hearing.

There is no singing without technique, however rudimentary. Indeed, there is no using the voice *at all* without technique. For what is speech but a series of highly complex vocal techniques (pronunciation, inflection, articulation, rhythm, pacing, pitch) in the service of communication? This should ring bells for Dylan fans, who are very familiar with the idea of vocal techniques reconfiguring our sense of who a singer is. After all, what is the search for his "real voice" if not an effort to determine which one is Dylan's voice shorn of the many techniques that he uses to alter it? Yet this search is fruitless. One cannot voice anything without technique.

Through technique, Dylan fashions his voice again and again. That fashioning is amply audible in the "Times" examples from the beginning of the chapter. But, per the previous paragraph, this is the case for all singers, indeed for all *speakers*. Questions thus remain. If technique mediates all voices, why does that mediation feel even *more* conspicuous in Dylan's case? That is, why does the question of vocal technique and its effect on identity seem especially urgent with him? After all, we worry much less about, say, Paul McCartney's identity when we hear him imitate Little Richard (though our vexation here may relocate to questions of race and appropriation). What is it about Dylan's particular techniques of vocal alteration that so trouble the question of identity? Conversely, if Dylan's voice is indeed permanently adorned with an array of vocal masks, how is it that we recognize him so instantly, even—and perhaps especially—when he is strenuously imitating someone else? The following chapter proposes some answers.

Chapter 2 audio examples:
soundingbobdylan.com/ch2

CHAPTER TWO

Identity and Plurality

It's Halloween, 1964. Performing at New York's Philharmonic Hall, Dylan quips, "I have my Bob Dylan mask on. I'm masquerading!"[1] The first sentence gets a big laugh from the crowd, followed by applause. But Dylan himself seems more amused by the second sentence, and the audience soon laughs at *his* laughter. In both cases, the audience's guffaws seem layered, knowing. By now everyone is aware that Dylan is not his family name; a *Newsweek* exposé the previous year had outed him as Robert Zimmerman from Hibbing, Minnesota. Yet few in Philharmonic Hall seem troubled by the previous year's big reveal. To the contrary, the laughter seems in part a moment of self-congratulation, delight at being in on the joke. His flexible relationship to identity was already becoming a source of pleasure and insider connoisseurship, as it would remain for decades to come.

In retrospect, the line seems almost too on the nose, slotting tidily into the familiar tale of "Bob Dylan, shape shifter."[2] And it's notable that *he* utters it. In the years and decades to come he will profess his mutable identity time and again: acting as a character named "Alias" in Sam Peckinpah's 1973 film *Pat Garrett and Billy the Kid*; wearing whiteface and a Nixon mask on 1975's Rolling Thunder Revue;

swapping actor and character identities willy-nilly in 1978's *Renaldo and Clara* (filmed during Rolling Thunder); assigning Ronnie Hawkins the character "Bob Dylan" in that film; naming his next feature film *Masked and Anonymous*; and so on. This, then, is an enduring feature that persists throughout his mercurial transformations: he will constantly remind you that he is masquerading. You don't need to enroll in Bob Dylan 101 to learn that he plays with identity. He'll tell you over and over again.

EYE IS ANOTHER

As he did several months after the Halloween gig, on the back cover of *Highway 61 Revisited*, released in summer 1965. Near the end of his breathless, stream-of-consciousness sleeve notes, he writes:

> I cannot say the word eye anymore. . . . when I speak this word eye, it is as if I am speaking of somebody's eye that I faintly remember. . . . there is no eye—there is only a series of mouths—long live the mouths—[3]

We are now deep in the hipster surreal, far from the folksy stage banter of the Halloween show. But identity is still the watchword, mischievous play still the vibe. Where he once spoke of masks, now he writes of eyes and mouths. The play with the homophone I/eye may at first appear too clever by half, but it is deftly executed, and surprisingly rich on closer examination. For one, it enacts itself. The distinction between I and eye is apparent only to vision, that is, to the eye; when spoken—from a mouth—the distinction disappears. (The excerpt begins with speaking and ends with mouths.) The idea of a bounded, sovereign self—an "I"—dissolves on the page, before our very eyes, precisely when the word "eye" appears. But it doesn't disappear entirely—it keeps bobbing to the surface. Note the careful alternation:

> I . . . eye . . . I . . . eye . . . I . . . eye . . . I . . . eye

The authorial "I" continually reappears, only to profess its own contingency. But this process of hide and seek does not continue indefinitely. "I" submerges for good at "there is no eye," at which point it is replaced with mouths, which also repeat rhythmically:

> I . . . eye . . . I . . . eye . . . I . . . eye . . . I . . . eye . . . mouths . . . mouths

The I/eye homophone disappears into mouths that cannot distinguish the two words. Only the mouths remain.

It is a giddily virtuosic bit of writing. Among other things, it is a Rimbaudian riff, ringing changes on the poet's famous statement "Je est un autre" ("I is someone else" or "I is another").[4] The excerpt is also suspiciously easy to connect to certain strands of poststructuralist thought.[5] As with so much Dylan, it has a kind of plug-and-play applicability for the postmodern scholar, ready for use right out of the box. If one is in thrall to such theories, it is tempting to take Dylan at his word: "See! He says it himself! There is no 'I,' there are only mouths. 'Bob Dylan' is nothing but a series of vocal masks! There is no 'I' lurking behind those masks. Dylan shows us that selfhood is a fiction. He said that too: 'I'm not there, I'm gone.'"[6] The extraordinary variety of Dylan's sounding voices then seems to confirm this thesis. As vocal sound morphs continuously before our ears, our sense of the body behind that voice—the vocal "I," the answer to the question "Who sings?"—shifts and slides, revealing the self to be an ephemeral construction. Our ears verify what Dylan has already confessed: There is no I, there is only a series of mouths.

But in our zeal to take Dylan at his word, and to link those words with the high-prestige discourses of the humanities, we may go too far. For the passage from the *Highway 61* sleeve in fact enacts a *tension* between identity and plurality, between the I and its dissolution. In the *Highway 61* passage, the rhythmic reappearance of the word "I"—repeatedly bobbing to the textual surface—asserts a continued authorial presence, even as it professes its own erasure. There may only be a series of mouths, but we need an authorial "I" to *tell* us that there is only a series of mouths. And telling us, as I've already noted, is something that Dylan does repeatedly. Similarly, Dylan the singer may adopt a variety of sounding voices, idioms, and accents, but we marvel at them precisely because they emerge from a single body, whose fleshy persistence we hear in each new vocal guise. We hear a voice that constantly changes—adopting now this idiom, now that; imitating singers of diverse ethnicities, classes, and musical traditions; exploring the new resources of his aging apparatus—but the very fact that we can speak of a changing voice attests to an identity amid this plurality. We don't, in other words, hear a string of utterly unrelated voices, as though sung by many different singers. Rather, we hear many voices emerging from one singing body, a unique configuration of lungs, glottis, larynx, tongue, lips.

Italian philosopher Adriana Cavarero presents a theory of vocal identity that rests precisely on this fleshy, bodily configuration—the voice as the sonic marker of a unique body. The voice makes certain of the body's visually hidden, inner recesses accessible to sense, that is, to hearing:

> The play between vocal emission and acoustic perception necessarily involves the internal organs. It implicates a correspondence with the fleshy cavity that alludes to the deep body, the most bodily part of the body. The impalpability of sonorous vibrations, which is as colorless as the air, comes out of a wet mouth and arises from the red of the flesh.[7]

Neil Verma pithily glosses this passage: "To speak is to turn oneself 'inside out.'"[8] The particularities and peculiarities of Dylan's vocal apparatus, emanating from his "deep body," sound in and through each new vocal mask. His vocal plurality strikes us precisely because of the thrumming tension it establishes with his unmistakable vocal identity, his idiosyncratic deployment of a persisting vocal instrument.

Here, then, is one answer to a question with which the previous chapter ended. Dylan's voice troubles questions of identity because his conspicuous technique at once maximizes our sense of plurality *and* identity. Cavarero's idea of the deep body provides one way to understand this paradox. For Dylan's is a voice that seems almost to externalize its inner workings, to disclose with unusual vividness the idiosyncrasy of the body producing it and the labor involved in that production. This is especially evident in Dylan's vocal imperfections, those moments of strain, breakage, and coarse tone that seem to make audible a pocked and pitted interior surface. Imperfection thus becomes one marker of bodily identity, of the flawed particularity of Dylan's deep body, situating us on the right edge of figure 1.2. Crucially, we sense Dylan's vocal identity even, and perhaps especially, when he is working hard to sound like someone else. His labors of vocal imitation disclose his bodily uniqueness with particular vividness. Dylan's voice becomes paradoxically *more* singular, not less, in its effortful acts of imitation.

EARLY VOICES

To hear this, let's turn to some examples from the young Dylan. In Martin Scorsese's *No Direction Home*, harmonica player Tony Glover says that Dylan in 1959–60 "was like a sponge in a way. . . . [He would] pick up people's mannerisms, accents." Scorsese sets this quote amid a comparison of the Clancy Brothers and Tommy Makem singing "Johnny I Hardly Knew Ye" and Dylan singing the same in September 1960.[9] The nineteen-year-old's Irish brogue is impressive, especially the tightly snapped syllables on "beguiled" and "m'child."[10] Still, we can hear the coarse vocal surface that he would deploy three years later on his studio recording of "The Times They Are a-Changin'"—and, for that matter, on all of his early records for Columbia. In other words, there is difference in this repetition. Dylan's unmistakable vocal apparatus seems even *more* conspicuous through this act of vocal imitation, the very effort of which discloses the fleshy resistance of his deep body, with its characteristic dry grit.

Scorsese provides other side-by-side comparisons hereabouts, including ones with Odetta ("Muleskinner Blues," 22:36–23:02 in the film) and the Memphis Jug Band ("K. C. Moan," 24:40–24:56). In each of these comparisons, images of Dylan appear when he is singing, underwriting the link between the voice we hear and the body producing it, shuttling us along the right edge of figure 1.2. In "K. C. Moan" the visual link is hardly necessary, as one recognizes Dylan's familiar nasal rasp immediately, though one may be struck by the youthfulness of that voice here, the sonic equivalent of baby fat. The performance of "Muleskinner Blues" is another story. Here the voice is rounded, the throat relaxed, the vowels plummy and full. This sound is far enough from the gritty Dylan norm that Scorsese places text on the screen confirming that it is in fact the "voice of Bob Dylan." This recording comes from the so-called St. Paul Tape or Karen Wallace Tape, recorded in May 1960, excerpts of which we'll hear in a moment. Dylan's voice on this tape has puzzled many commentators, with some even questioning its authenticity.[11] Scorsese's documentary laid that debate to rest, as have reports from those who knew Dylan in Dinkytown in 1960.[12] Spider John Koerner, for example, has commented on his "pretty voice," while Karen Wallace's sister Terri states:

> He had . . . the most beautiful voice. . . . I really thought he had a good singing voice. Which I might add was something of a disappointment after he became well known, and I heard the voice that made him famous. . . . It was so different from the voice that I had first heard coming out of him.[13]

Moreover, Dylan *returned* to this voice nearly a decade later, for 1969's *Nashville Skyline*, the same year's Isle of Wight concert, and selected tracks on 1970's *Self Portrait*.[14] This has led some to the opposite extreme: rather than an inauthentic recording, might the 1960 Wallace Tape in fact document Dylan's "real voice," to which he reverted when in retreat from fame (and "Woodstock Nation") in the late '60s?[15] In short, even this exceptional voice has been heard as both a put-on vocal mask and as disclosing a true vocal self.

But the vocal "I" that seems, for some, to bob to the surface here submerges on closer examination. For, an earlier 1958 recording—made in Hibbing with his friend John Bucklen—challenges the idea that this is somehow Dylan's "real" voice. On **audio example 2.1** we hear Dylan and Bucklen singing an original called "Hey, Little Richard," seemingly composed on the spot. When Dylan sings his lead breaks, one clearly recognizes that familiar rasp; the rounded, plummy voice is nowhere in evidence.[16] More generally, after our discussion of *technê* in chapter 1, I hope the reader is by now sufficiently skeptical about the idea that Dylan's (or anyone's) "real voice" comes in just one form—and perhaps skeptical of the idea of a "real voice" altogether. Such skepticism is not the same as skepticism about a persisting, embodied self that fashions those voices. One can be skeptical about "real voices" and yet stop short of the theoretical extravagance that there is no such thing as an enduring self. That self endures, and we can hear it in the persistence of a fleshy deep body, which anchors our sense of vocal identity. But the self must *deploy* that deep body, fashioning voices through labor and technique. And that effortful fashioning, as discussed above, braids identity and plurality, disclosing a persisting fleshy self through the very act of trying to sound like someone else. Already in the late '50s and 1960 the youth from Hibbing—about to adopt a new name—was making that point emphatically.

GUTHRIE VIA ELVIS

One fact about the Wallace Tape is especially interesting for our purposes: it contains the first known recordings of Dylan singing Woody Guthrie songs. He was on the cusp of his Guthrie obsession, though it wasn't until he devoured the latter's semifictional autobiography *Bound for Glory* in September 1960 that the mania would take hold in earnest.[17] The Wallace Tape thus offers a fascinating document of the young Dylan trying out Guthrie's songs but with vestiges of his prefolk musical enthusiasms still audible. Consider "This Land Is Your Land," excerpted in **audio example 2.2**. The recording is frustratingly fragmented, consisting of snippets played by Karen Wallace directly from her reel-to-reel, interrupted by fast-forwarding; at the time of this writing, the full performance of the song does not circulate. Even so, what we hear is startling. For Dylan sounds much closer to Elvis Presley than to his emerging hero from Oklahoma. Note especially the jaunty pause he inserts in his guitar part at the end of each verse. The sharp downstroke chop that opens a space for the voice is a classic rockabilly gesture, familiar from Sun Records–era Elvis and Carl Perkins.[18]

His singing is reminiscent of theirs too, the vocal line shot through with syncopations and blue notes. **Figure 2.1** demonstrates.

The upper staff, labeled (a), transcribes the second (incomplete) verse in Dylan's recording (included in audio ex. 2.2), above a rendering of the tune as typically sung, shown in staff (b). Numerals above the staves label the phrases 1 through 4. Dylan nowhere sings the square-cut rhythm familiar to all children who learn the song in school: short–short–short–*long–long* ("this land is *your land*"). Figure 2.1(b) notates this as three quarter-notes followed by two halves.[19] The various configurations of ties and eighth-notes in Dylan's part above attest both to the pervasiveness of his rockabilly syncopations and to their variety. We can also detect a nascent hallmark of the singer who would later change the tune of "The Times They Are a-Changin'"—and, for that matter, the tune of nearly every song he would sing on stage—so radically. For even at this young age, Dylan treats melodic contour with great freedom. Note especially the melodic variant in phrase 2, which neither proceeds in the same direction as the familiar tune (it descends while the tune as usually sung ascends) nor even

FIGURE 2.1. "This Land Is Your Land," excerpt: (a) as sung by Bob Dylan in May 1960; (b) as typically sung.

ends on the same note. Instead, he begins with syncopated Gs before sliding down through a blue third—at the word "my," drawlingly delayed—to the tonic D.[20] Dylan then leans hard on the same blue note at the beginning of phrase 3, when he sings "From Cali-." In phrase 4 one can almost hear Presley or Perkins in the sprung syncopations ("To the New York") before the tape maddeningly cuts off. There even are hints of an Elvis technique that Richard Middleton calls "boogification": vocal pulsations that infuse a boogie-woogie rhythm into sustained syllables. Elvis's 1956 recording of "Heartbreak Hotel" is saturated with the technique, as Middleton shows.[21] Such boogification is evident in Dylan's upbeats to each verse, in the break created by the guitar chop. Here, strangely, he twice seems to forget the words, but each time—and especially the second, presented in **audio example 2.3**—he slyly boogifies Guthrie's upbeat figure. Elvis and Guthrie tussle in that break, and the former wins, crowding out the latter's words.

To be sure, Presley and Perkins are not the only voices one hears in this performance. There are traces of more traditional country singers too—for example, the two Hanks (Williams and Snow) that had captivated the Hibbing youth glued to his radio—and the country and blues inflections mix in ways that do not always echo rockabilly, sometimes sounding more like the "Singing Brakeman" Jimmie Rodgers.[22] When Dylan returned to this voice at the end of the decade, the country connection would become stronger . . . but so would that to Elvis. Consider his 1970 recording of "Blue Moon," one of the least loved tracks on that little-loved record, *Self Portrait*. **Audio example 2.4** compares the first verse with that in Elvis's 1954 recording for Sun Records. Note first that Dylan matches Elvis's key and pitch level exactly: both versions are in C major, and both vocal performances begin on the G below middle C. Dylan is famous for changing keys on a whim, in the studio and on stage; the fact that he matches Elvis exactly here, pitch for pitch, suggests that he listened to the latter's 1954 recording in the studio right before producer Bob Johnston called the take and the engineer hit the record button.[23] Elvis's voice having just entered Dylan's ears, we now hear it emerging from his body. It both shapes and is shaped by Dylan's singular vocal apparatus.

Which of course doesn't mean that we "hear Elvis" when we hear the *Self Portrait* recording. We hear Dylan's voice encountering Elvis's. And the result sounds difference as loudly as it does similarity. For one, Dylan does not adopt Elvis's breathy delivery, which creates a sense of proximity and intimacy—indeed, for many, sexiness.[24] Instead, he hams it up with a deliberately dopey croon, adding an ornament on "moon" and a cheeky scoop into "aloooone." His tone is fuller and more sonorous than Elvis's, the mood arch rather than seductive.

THE SWERVING VOICE

As with the 1960 recording of "This Land Is Your Land," it is difficult to know whether we are hearing a send-up, a sincere homage, or some curious combination of these in the 1970 "Blue Moon." The ambivalence calls to mind Harold Bloom's well-worn theory of the "anxiety of influence," in which artists (Bloom is interested mostly in poets) create by misreading their "strong" precursors.[25] It is a highly Freudian—and lamentably masculine—theory, with influence often figured in Oedipal terms, the artist seeking to vanquish the oppressive father through a violent act of rewriting.[26] As Richard Taruskin, a skeptic, puts it, in Bloom's theory "success as a poet is achieved through parricide."[27] That may feel like too strong a word for Dylan's lighthearted "Blue Moon," but the theory's applicability remains clear enough. How better to grapple with Elvis's looming influence than through an affectionate tribute laced with mockery?

Dylan is a quintessentially belated artist, the past always close behind. Precursor voices haunt all of his singing, and no precursor was stronger for Dylan in the early '60s than Woody Guthrie. Which may be why he sounded so little like him when he arrived in New York in January 1961, in part to visit the ailing dustbowl balladeer at Greystone Park Hospital in New Jersey. His Guthrie fever was at its peak, his performing repertory dominated by Guthrie tunes. Yet Tom Paxton, who first heard Dylan in 1961, states it plainly: "They were accusing him of being a Woody Guthrie clone, which was nonsense. He didn't sound like Woody Guthrie."[28] What Paxton could not have known is that Dylan also didn't sound like *himself*—or at least like he had sounded in Karen Wallace's apartment the previous May. The gulf between his 1961 voice and that on the Wallace Tape is every bit as startling as is the gulf between either of those voices and Guthrie's. The differences are not subtle. To hear them, consider **audio example 2.5**, an excerpt from Dylan's performance of "This Land Is Your Land" at Carnegie Chapter Hall on November 4, 1961, and **audio example 2.6**, the same verse as Guthrie recorded it for Moses Asch in the 1940s.[29]

The Carnegie Chapter Hall show was Dylan's first high-profile headlining gig in New York, in a prestigious midtown location.[30] Attendance was sparse, but many of the folk-revival intelligentsia had made the trip up from the Village. At a couple points in his between-song banter, Dylan speaks about Guthrie. He is clearly nervous; his comic timing, usually so sharp in these years, is slightly off. (A seemingly overrehearsed shtick about getting lost on the trip up to the hall falls largely flat.) When discussing his relationship with Guthrie, Dylan veers between cocky and diffident. He at once asserts his connection to Guthrie, explicitly invoking a lineage, and at the same time downplays it. "I haven't done too many Woody Guthrie songs since a long time ago." If this play of claim and disclaimer were not evidence enough of his tussle with Guthrie's legacy, the performance of "This Land Is Your Land" makes it palpable.

One first notices the contrast in vocal timbre. As always, Guthrie's sound in audio example 2.6 is mildly nasal but bouncy and resonant, with clean tone and a relaxed Oklahoma twang. He sings comfortably in the middle of his range and doesn't push. Dylan, by contrast, pushes a great deal on Carnegie's recital stage, tightening into the sandpapery, prematurely aged tone that we heard in the 1963 "Times" recording. As already noted there, the young Dylan's strategically aged voice sounds vaguely rural, southern, poor, and white—all things that Guthrie in fact *was*—but the result sounds very little like Guthrie. Dylan's voice instead seems to index a kind of archetype, that of a wise southern bard, the voice even *more* worn by hard travelin' than Guthrie's was.[31]

The differences in timing and phrasing are also striking. Guthrie's rhythm is simple and direct, befitting his plainspoken persona. He adheres largely to the square-cut short–short–short–*long*–*long* rhythm discussed above, with only minor variations. This persists until the refrain, "This land was made for you and me," which differs rhythmically. As on the Wallace Tape, Dylan never once sings this rhythm onstage at Carnegie Hall. But now his phrasing completely eschews rockabilly syncopation. Instead, it floats relatively free of the meter, the syllables clustering together somewhat in the manner of **figure 2.2(a)**.

The figure aligns his loosely triplet-based rhythm above the square-cut rhythm from Guthrie's performance and countless singalongs at (b). Dylan's rhythmic clustering is evident in the narrower span of the syllables, and the loose triplets indicate his freedom from the quarter-note beat, which his guitar projects. Arrows mark one result of this metric freedom: "your" lands squarely on a downbeat in Guthrie's version, but with Dylan it arrives early, before the beat.[32] Nor is there any longer a distinction between short and long syllables: all are short in Dylan's version. The result is not so much hurried as metrically loose, free, and spacious. The tempo is slow, providing ample space around the sung lines, which the guitar fills with simple strumming. The overall effect is monumentalized and reverent, a mood established by Dylan's long guitar-and-harmonica introduction—he plays for nearly a minute

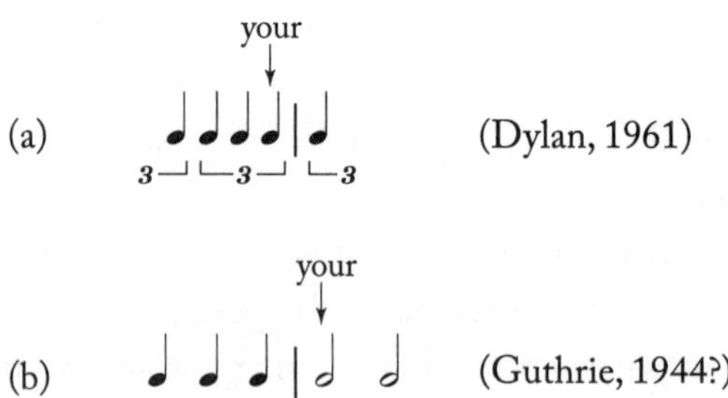

FIGURE 2.2. Sung rhythm in "This Land Is Your Land": (a) as performed by Dylan at Carnegie Chapter Hall, New York City, November 4, 1961; (b) as sung by Woody Guthrie for Moses Asch's Folkways Label, 1944(?).

before he begins singing. The performance as a whole conjures a sense of wide-open spaces. We are, in short, a world away—geographically, culturally, stylistically—from the homey informality of the Wallace Tape, with its irreverent humor and blue notes. And we are remote in a different direction from Guthrie matter-of-factly singing into Moe Asch's machine. In Carnegie Chapter Hall Dylan delivers, above all, a connoisseur's performance, sacralized and weighted with history.

In the introduction, I stated that Dylan's engagement with predecessor voices is a global instance of his art of change imperfection, of difference in repetition. We can hear this vividly in all of the audio examples in this chapter, as Dylan's voice at once engages and swerves from Guthrie's and Elvis's. I borrow the word "swerve" once again from Bloom, who uses it in discussion of one of his six "revisionary ratios," which he labels with the related Latin word *clinamen*. That word comes from the Epicurean philosophy of Lucretius,

> where it means a "swerve" of the atoms so as to make change possible in the universe. A poet swerves away from his precursor, by so reading his precursor's poem as to execute a *clinamen* in relation to it. This appears as a corrective movement in his own poem, which implies that the precursor poem went accurately up to a certain point, but then should have swerved, precisely in the direction that the new poem moves.[33]

The Lucretian swerve is an agent of change in the universe, at the atomic level. Put in our present terms, the swerve yields difference in repetition, imperfecting the regular fall of atoms into the bewildering diversity of repeating, differing life. Bloom adopts this Lucretian image as a metaphor for the poetic act, as poets follow the course of their precursors, only to swerve from it at a precise moment, charting a new path. As we have heard throughout this chapter, Dylan similarly engages and swerves from the voices of his predecessors in diverse ways, producing global difference in repetition, change imperfection writ large.

Such swerves need not be intentional and may not even be conscious. And when it comes to the sounding body in the voice, they may not even be entirely volitional. For, however much Dylan may have *wanted* to sound like Guthrie, it may simply be that his body had other ideas—his particular vocal apparatus simply would not produce Guthrie's timbre, his Okie twang. Ditto for Elvis's breathy intimacy. What we hear instead is a kind of triangulation, Dylan's voice equidistant from these precursor voices (Elvis's, Guthrie's), but shaped by the encounter with them. His idiosyncratic voice emerges from this pull of forces, imitation and desire to "see who he could be" held in check by fleshy resistance, the unique affordances and limitations of his own body.[34]

We could go on in this fashion, listening to Dylan's many other vocal forebears and teasing apart the ways he does and does not sound like them, but the point should by now be clear. Dylan never sounds entirely like his vocal models. For all of his evident gifts at imitation and mimicry, his voice remains stubbornly singular. And that singularity is paradoxically heightened through imitation. This is the paradox of Dylan's vocal identity: as his voice engages others', the particularity of his own vocal instrument emerges with ever more clarity. Another way to put this is that Dylan's vocal swerves are not toward or away from some "real voice." Rather, when we recognize Dylan's voice, part of what we recognize is *the sound of the swerve itself.* That is, we hear a persisting vocal apparatus torqued by predecessor voices. Swerving in response, it issues from his mouth sounding like no one else. Whether this is due to a bodily inability to pull off the imitation fully; to a Bloomian brew of anxiety, desire, and Oedipal aggression; or (quite possibly) to some mixture of the two, ultimately may not matter. What does matter is the sounding result. And that is the sound of a torqued voice, swerving under pressure. More than any particular vocal guise, Dylan's voice is the sound of this swerve—a singular voice amplified, not diminished, by its tussle with others'.

Chapter 3 audio examples:
soundingbobdylan.com/ch3

CHAPTER THREE

The Empathic Voice

DYLAN'S GENIE

On November 20, 1961, sixteen days after the Carnegie Chapter Hall concert, Dylan recorded a batch of songs for his debut album; among them was "House of the Rising Sun." The song had become a folk-revival standard by the time Dylan had arrived in the Village ten months earlier, with recorded versions by Hally Wood, Lead Belly, Libby Holman, Woody Guthrie, Joan Baez, Josh White, Carolyn Hester, and others in circulation.[1] But it was Dave Van Ronk's arrangement that provided Dylan's model. Van Ronk drew on his knowledge of jazz harmony to outfit the song with a new descending bass line, which Dylan promptly adopted, recording it before the older musician had a chance to do the same, to the latter's great frustration.[2] It shouldn't surprise us, then, to hear bits of Van Ronk in Dylan's vocal performance. Nor, based on the discussion in the previous chapter, should it surprise that his voice departs from Van Ronk's in striking ways. We'll hear some details below.

But Van Ronk's is not the only voice that we should listen for in this performance. There is also the voice of the lyric persona, the "I" of the song.[3] In this number, tellingly, that persona is female, the woman ruined by the titular house in New Orleans.[4] Her gender is never in doubt, yet neither is it audible in Dylan's voice. What *is* audible are the song's emotional stakes, the cornered fear and rage accumulated over a life lived hard against the abyss. The effect is so potent as to conjure the lyric subject before our very ears, even though the voice we hear is clearly not hers. How does this empathic conjuring work?

That it *does* work is an article of faith among critics, many of whom have praised Dylan's ability to inhabit a song, to project its protagonist's voice as though it were his own. "House of the Rising Sun" shows that this effect can hold even when Dylan's voice discloses a body notably different from the protagonist's. In contemplating this puzzling act of impersonation—I choose the word carefully—our attention shifts from Dylan's engagement with precursor singers, our focus in chapter 2, to his projection of characters in the songs themselves. Ian Bell makes the distinction explicit when writing of another track on the first album, Blind Lemon Jefferson's "See that My Grave Is Kept Clean." He states that Dylan "isn't Blind Lemon Jefferson, or even close, but he is wholly present within the cold universe of the song. He inhabits the thing like an actor consumed by a role."[5] Glenn Hughes writes similarly of Dylan's

> uncanny ability to experience an imaginative empathy with the figures in both inherited songs and those of his own invention—to "inhabit" these personae and communicate feelingly their passions and perspectives, whether they were fictional characters of legend, historical persons told of in ballads, archetypal hoboes or outlaws or orphans or disillusioned lovers or persons of the present whose stories Dylan had read about in the newspapers.[6]

Hughes's list of personae opens toward a new kind of vocal plurality, one made up of characters real and fictitious in the songs themselves.[7] We can think of this as an act of impersonation, in a rather literal sense: stepping into a person. Hughes uses the term "empathic mimicry" for the phenomenon, citing Greil Marcus, who writes:

> Empathy has always been the genie of [Dylan's] work, of the tones of his voice, his sense of rhythm, his feel for how to fill up a line or leave

> it half empty, his sense of when to ride a melody and when to bury it, so that it might dissolve all of a listener's defenses—and this is what allowed Dylan, in 1962 at the Gaslight Café in Greenwich Village, at home in that secret community of tradition and mystery, to become not only the pining lover in the old ballad "Handsome Molly," but also Handsome Molly herself.[8]

Marcus's example is characteristically extravagant. Molly's voice sounds nowhere in Dylan's 1962 version of the ballad that bears her name, which is sung entirely from the perspective of her "pining lover." Nevertheless, this critical flourish suggests that Dylan's empathy can extend to characters other than the lyric "I" of a song, not only Molly, but also Hattie Carroll, Ramona, or Reilly's daughter.[9] That the young Dylan could convey compassion—and, at times, outrage—for these second- and third-person female characters is remarkable enough, a testament to his powers of vocal empathy even at this early stage. But his performance of songs in the female first person—like "House of the Rising Sun"[10]—make Marcus's point even more emphatically.

A skeptic might nevertheless argue that no amount of theorizing or analytical close reading can support such critical articles of faith. They are entirely subjective, the argument might go: one either hears Dylan projecting vocal empathy for these characters—along with Marcus, Bell, Hughes, and similarly minded listeners—or one doesn't. Scholarly chin-stroking won't change anyone's mind. And yet, as Marcus states, Dylan produces these effects through vocal details: "the tones of his voice, his sense of rhythm, his feel for how to fill up a line or leave it half empty, his sense of when to ride a melody and when to bury it." Hughes similarly attributes Dylan's gift for "empathic mimicry" to "precision in timing, control of emotional tone, and inventive and surprising phrasing."[11] Such details are, at least in principle, illuminable by music analysis.

Moreover, the argument that such convictions are "entirely subjective" ignores the *inter*subjectivity of meaning creation and the many ways such meanings are socially and historically conditioned. When we hear Dylan, say, adopting the perspective of a Black persona—as in the slave hymn "No More Auction Block" or the spoken-word piece "Black Cross (Hezekiah Jones)"[12]—we respond not in a vacuum ("entirely subjectively") but from within a particular social, historical, and ideological context, which (in this case) deeply informs our ideas on race, appropriation, authenticity, class, and so on. These networks of value and meaning formed an especially dense weave during the folk revival.[13] And within that context, gifted performers could enroll listeners in a compelling fiction: that their voice and that of the song's lyric persona were one.

Joan Baez enrolled a young Bob Dylan in that very fiction before he even arrived in Greenwich Village. While still in Minnesota, he was an avid listener to her first record and had seen her on television. He was especially struck by her ability to inhabit and project a character:

> Not everyone can sing these songs convincingly. The singer has to make you believe what you are hearing and Joan did that. I believed that Joan's mother would kill somebody that she loved. I believed that. I believed that she'd come from that kind of family. You have to believe. Folk music, if nothing else, makes a believer out of you.[14]

The almost obsessive repetition of "believe" is striking, the incantatory effect not unlike Baez's own singing. Note, too, its transformation by the end of the excerpt from something you do to something you become—a "believer." On hearing Baez Dylan became a believer. He believed, for example, that she was the protagonist in "Silver Dagger," the song he alludes to in the quote, whose mother sleeps beside her, dagger in hand, ready to stab her daughter's paramour.

VOICING GENDER

"Silver Dagger" is the opening track on Baez's debut album. On the following song, "East Virginia," the lyric subject is male. It is a haunting performance, Baez's keening vibrato resounding in the space above her understated fingerpicking, the harmony wavering between minor and major. The emotional impact is such that one can be swept into belief—wholly taken in by the fiction, in the way Dylan describes—and yet remain only dimly aware of the gender mismatch. Later on the record, the gender mismatch is more pronounced on the song "Rake and Rambling Boy," if only because it is made explicit the first line: "Well, I'm a rake, and a ramblin' boy." The fact that Baez can sing that line with such carefree insouciance is telling; it makes clear just how common such gender shifting was in the folk revival, no big deal.[15] At least, no big deal for a woman. While females in the revival often sang songs from a male perspective, the reverse was less common. Though the revivalists shared a general commitment to progressive causes, their scene was by no means immune to patriarchal asymmetries.[16] This is to say nothing of the patriarchal cultures from which the revivalists' repertory was drawn—say, the music of white Appalachia or the Jim Crow prison farm—most of them an ideological world away from the progressive enclaves of the Village and Harvard Yard. The male lyrical perspective was the default in those repertories, the unmarked term.

Songs from a female perspective, though hardly unheard of, were less common. If female revivalists wanted to sing as broad a repertory as their male colleagues, they would need to perform songs from a male subject position. A survey of albums by a range of female revivalists, from Peggy Seeger to Barbara Dane, Odetta to Judy Collins, bears this out—songs sung from a male perspective pop up everywhere. By contrast, female lyric personae are rare on releases by male revivalists. For example, of the seventy-eight songs on Dave Van Ronk's first six albums, only two are in the female first-person: the comic "You've Been a Good Old Wagon" (on 1962's *Folksinger*), and "House of the Rising Sun" itself (on *Just Dave Van Ronk*, from 1964). By contrast, nine out of twenty tracks on a single record (!) by Odetta—*Odetta Sings Ballads and Blues* (1956)—are sung from a male perspective.

A female singer could reclaim her subject position by changing the gender of the lyric subject. For example, many female singers, including Seeger, Baez, Dane, and Collins performed a version of the Stanley Brothers' "Man of Constant Sorrow"—which Dylan would cover on his first album—with the title's first word changed to "Girl" or "Maid." Such a change at once thematizes gender, in its departure from a well-known original, and resolves the gender dissonance between singer and lyric subject. For a somewhat more complex later example, consider Nina Simone's version of "Just Like a Woman."[17] In her 1971 studio performance of the song, she switches pronouns for the last chorus, replacing "she" with "I," thus identifying vocally with the woman of the title.[18] This subtly subverts the song's vexed gender politics, as Simone's resigned melancholy invests the woman in question with psychological depth, a three-dimensional inner life arguably denied her in Dylan's barbed original. In Simone's voice the final line is no longer a misogynistic jab but a moment of genuine pathos ("But I break just like a little girl").

AND ME, OH . . . GOD, I'M A-ONE

How to account, then, for the pathos in Dylan's "Rising Sun"? For here the future author of "Just Like a Woman"—which, alas, would not be his last song to admit of a misogynistic reading—disappears so thoroughly and empathically into a female lyric subject as to leave hardly a trace.[19] One way into this question is (once again) to resist being drawn into a quixotic search for the "true" Dylan—What were his *real* feelings about women? in 1961? in 1966?—and to recognize that "House of the Rising Sun" achieves its effect through details of performance. We can listen closely to those details while remaining agnostic about their connection to Dylan's deeper beliefs about gender. To do so is to recognize that these vocal techniques are just that—techniques, learnable tricks of the trade. To be sure, as Dylan himself says of Baez in the quote above, a gifted performer can make one believe precisely the opposite—that what one is hearing is not mere artifice, much less (gasp!) show business, but an authentic expression of some deep emotional truth about the lyric persona, mysteriously channeled through the singer's voice, perhaps in the manner of a gifted method actor.[20] The idea that such effects might be the result of studied artifice dissonates with the ideology of the folk revival, with its professed commitment to unvarnished "authenticity" and its rejection of mainstream polish. But the revivalists relied no less than mainstream singers on tried-and-true techniques for hooking listeners, drawing them in, and creating an affective bond.

Dylan sensed such a bond from Baez and knew he could achieve a similar effect. But he would have to use different means, as his voice was so far from hers: "She had the fire and I felt I had the same kind of fire. I could do the songs she did. . . . I could make them drop into place like she did, but in a different way."[21] Dylan would need to look elsewhere for specific vocal techniques, for means of achieving Baez's empathic identification with character. He found them in Dave Van Ronk, himself no slouch at vocal empathy. A comparison between Van Ronk's and Dylan's versions of "House of the Rising Sun" is instructive.

Audio example 3.1 provides the first verse as Van Ronk sang it in a live concert at Yale University in 1961; **audio example 3.2** is the first verse as Dylan recorded it in Studio A on November 22 of that year.[22] There are various vocal similarities, which we will explore in a moment. But we should also note some striking contrasts. They perform the song in different keys, Van Ronk in F♯ minor, Dylan in A minor.[23] This places their voices in different registers—Dylan's lower to start—a fact that will have considerable implications for where the performances can go from here. Van Ronk projects an extremely loose sense of meter, the chords and vocal pitches changing at irregular temporal intervals, the steady up-down strumming (with the flesh of his fingers or thumb) providing only a very thin, surface layer of metric regularity.

We can see this in **figure 3.1(a)**, a transcription of Van Ronk's first verse. The transcription is complex; you need not fret over the details. The main thing to notice is the extreme fluidity—indeed, unpredictability—of Van Ronk's timing via constantly shifting time signatures: 9/8, 13/8, 8/8, 7/8, and so on. The length of each bar is dictated by the irregular durations of the chords in his guitar playing.[24] Dylan, who at other times can be every bit as metrically free as Van Ronk is here, by contrast projects a fixed meter throughout, a loping compound duple that **figure 3.1(b)** notates in 6/8.[25] If Van Ronk's rhythm unsettles with its unpredictability, Dylan's entrains us, pulling us forward with even strides.

Van Ronk's vocal performance is shot through with abrupt contrasts in dynamics, register, timbre, and articulation, every word minutely textured. The result is highly perforated; it is a performance of hushes, pauses, outbursts, catchings of breath. Note, for example, the rests in bar 2 of figure 3.1(a), marked with asterisks, which set off the word "house." Van Ronk sings the words surrounding these pauses with an unusually straight tone, free of vibrato, which makes the florid, bluesy melisma on "New" that much more striking. (A melisma is a vocal gesture in which multiple notes are sung to one syllable of the lyric.) Note, too, the vertiginous leap down of an octave near the beginning of phrase 3 ("It's been the [octave drop] ruin of many a poor girl"). This is matched by a similarly extreme dynamic contrast: high and loud at the start of the phrase, low and soft for "ruin."

As in so much of his singing, Van Ronk makes extensive use of what linguists call "creaky voice" or "vocal fry," a species of noisy phonation in which the vocal folds are only loosely compressed, so that they go slack and one hears individual pulsations rather than a clean fundamental pitch. (To produce the effect, say "Ah" in your lowest speaking register, then descend several steps lower.) Creaky voice acts as a kind of unstable default in all three of Van Ronk's recorded performances of the song, a ravaged vocal edge to which he returns again and again to stage vocal failure.[26] He knew well that one way to draw an audience in—to enlist their affective involvement—is to sing quietly. His default creaky voice achieves this, the voice barely there, seemingly always on the verge of withdrawing back into the body. This performance of fragility is central to his rendition, especially when it is set off by the opposite extreme: brief moments of rage, usually in the higher octave, the volume increasing dramatically, only to fall away again with an immediate and precipitous drop in pitch and dynamics, back to the creaky failure zone. It is a performance of quicksilver contrasts, conjuring a lyric subject in extremis, barely coherent.

(a) Van Ronk (Live at Yale University, 1961)

(b) Dylan (*Bob Dylan*, 1961)

FIGURE 3.1. "House of the Rising Sun," verse 1, as sung by (a) Dave Van Ronk and (b) Bob Dylan, both in 1961.

Dylan's version differs dramatically. For while he also deploys a range of vocal timbres and articulations at the phrase level, these are held in check by a focus on the architecture of the song as a whole, its long-range dynamic and emotional trajectory. His is a performance rich in signifying moments, but it is not *only* a performance of moments, as Van Ronk's can at times seem. While the latter's version exhibits often-violent vocal contrasts at the micro level of each line, Dylan's is structured around just one, now at the macro level: a great emotional and musical hinge at the halfway point of the song, between the fourth and fifth verses.[27] The performance progresses from the quiet, contained tension of the opening four verses to the vehement plateau of the last four. As we will hear, the shift occurs at a crucial nodal point in the lyrics, animating an aspect of the protagonist's psychology largely missed by Van Ronk, to devastating effect. It is, above all, a remarkably *disciplined* performance, a word we do not often associate with Dylan, especially as a singer. But we should, for the control of pacing and emotional tone that he displays here is the norm in his singing, not the exception.

To focus our ears on these local and global dynamics, let us first return to the opening verse (audio ex. 3.2). We can hear aspects of Van Ronk's influence immediately, most notably in the dips into creaky voice ("There iii*is* a house . . . *down* in New Orleans") and the use of subtly contrasting vocal timbres from phrase to phrase. But these contrasts are less extreme, less tightly concentrated than Van Ronk's. Dylan's opening verse is instead marked by restraint along multiple axes—volume, articulation, vocal effect. While Van Ronk displays basically all of the vocal techniques he will use in the song in his first few lines, Dylan holds much in reserve. This allows the local details to speak with particular eloquence. Consider the subtle shift from the nasal, creaky, and underpowered first line to the throaty, blues-inflected holler of the second ("They call the Rising Sun"). The first line reports the existence of the house; the second names it. But the slight shift in delivery establishes a tension between them. If the first line seems wary and inward, the second turns outward. It is, fittingly, a call. And Dylan gives the word "call" extra emphasis with a bluesy ornament, a minor third. The change in delivery draws attention to those doing the calling—the "they" of the lyric—and sets up a contrast between that public, collective voice (judging, threatening) and the private world of the lyric persona, disgraced and isolated.

Dylan's melody traces a melodic arch across the verse, peaking in the call of line 2 and bottoming out in the abject self-recognition of line 4. **Figure 3.2** fleshes out the idea, showing the rough contour of each phrase, as well as the contrasting timbres of Dylan's performance (via different notehead types).[28] This notation greatly simplifies a vocal line rich in ornaments—slides, turns, bends—but doing so brings out the overall profile of the verse. Note the descent from the melodic apex on "call"—decked out with its ornament in little notes—to the nadir on "God," which Dylan delivers in a breathy, almost toneless voice, the low E2 pitch merely hinted at. This aspirated delivery is also evident in other words hereabouts, for example, "many a p(h)oor girl" and "I'm a-(wh)one." We hear a voice almost disappearing, phonation giving way to mere air, halfway to silence.

Dylan heightens the effect through the exquisite timing in his delivery of the final line. On the page, one would likely parse it "And me / oh God / I'm a-one," and many singers phrase it exactly this way (among them Dave Van Ronk and Eric Burdon of the Animals). But Dylan's phrasing cuts across this parsing. He first slurs "me" directly into "oh," fusing them into a twisting diphthong, a self already distorted. He then inserts a pause before "God." Only an instant in musical time, this pause is like a chasm that yawns wide at the very

FIGURE 3.2. General contour and timbre of Dylan's first verse in "House of the Rising Sun."

moment of shamed self-recognition. "God" then arrives in an aspirated shudder.

The big emotional hinge of Dylan's performance re-engages these themes of private shame and public reckoning. Beginning with the fifth verse, he shifts the melody up one octave, where he remains for the rest of the song. He is able to make this shift because of the key he has chosen (A minor), which allows him to begin in a lower register than Van Ronk. The latter starts quite high in his range and thus has nowhere to go but down. Dylan, by contrast, leaves himself room to ascend, as the protagonist's agita mounts. **Figure 3.3** illustrates, comparing the register of the first and fifth verses. As the figure shows, the fifth verse begins precisely at the apex of the first, on the minor-third ornament of "call." **Audio example 3.3** juxtaposes this ornamented "call" from verse 1 with the beginning of verse 5, so that the reader can hear the connection shown by the dashed arrow in figure 3.3.

The registral shift in verse 5 also corresponds to a shift in grammatical mood. In the first four verses the lyric "I" had narrated her past—the house, her ruin, her poor mother, her gambling sweetheart. With verse 5, narration ends, replaced by the imperative voice: "Oh, tell my baby sister / Not to do what I have done." The imperative has an implied second person: "*you* go tell my baby sister." The way Dylan sings the line, it is hard to shake the feeling that we listeners are the target, his voice a sonic finger pointed directly at us. The effect is similar to one that Christopher Ricks discusses in the 1964 song "The Lonesome Death of Hattie Carroll." Ricks likens the line that begins that song's

FIGURE 3.3. Contour and registral outline in Dylan's first and fifth verses in "House of the Rising Sun."

refrain—"You, who philosophize disgrace"—to a tank turret pivoting to take direct aim at the listener.[29] The turret effect in "House of the Rising Sun" differs in that it is a product of Dylan's vocal performance, not his lyric writing, but it is no less unnerving for that.

Nor does the unnerving effect ebb. Dylan maintains this new vocal plateau for the remainder of the song, his intensity never flagging. Each verse climaxes more than two octaves above the aspirated E2 of "God" in verse 1, topping out in a knot of tension centered on the pitches E4 and G4. **Figure 3.4** transcribes this moment in verse 5; you can hear it in **audio example 3.4**. Note the sustained E4s, Dylan boring into the pitch for several beats before leaping up to the accented yelp of the climactic G4 (on "what" and "have").[30] Tension builds across the sustained pitches, then snaps with the leaps upward. After the second such leap, Dylan lands back on E4 with the word "done." But his vocal timbre now edges into a gravelly snarl, smearing from E4 down a step to D4 (indicated by a wavy line in the figure). Dylan sings the corresponding line in each of the remaining verses similarly, each time landing hard on the snarling E4-to-D4 descent. We are not only at the other end of the pitch spectrum from the aspirated E2 of "God," we are at the other end of the affective spectrum. If "God" was the song's abject interior—its nadir—this is its apex, a peak of externalized anger in which pitches are not aspirated but bored into with such intensity that they smear and blur, like vision distorted by rage.

Unlike Van Ronk, who ends with verse 7, Dylan appends a repeat of the first verse to round off the song. This at first might seem overly formal, even prim. But Dylan avoids any hint of superfluity with his delivery, which adds something new to words we've already heard.

FIGURE 3.4. Vocal climax in Dylan's fifth verse in "House of the Rising Sun."

Audio example 3.5 presents the final two lines of the verse. He traverses the first of these, "It's been the ruin of *many poor girls*," with a wobbly stagger, the italicized words sung in a voice that Cherlin and Gopinath call the "drunken fool," all whoops and exaggerated diphthongs.[31] But the lyric persona here sounds less drunk than contemptuous, taking aim in turret fashion at upstanding middle-class listeners who would shake their heads in self-satisfied pity at such "ruined" women. The line is grotesquely comic, the sonic equivalent of a clown with fists balled in his eyes, mocking the crocodile tears of his audience: "boo *hoo*!" The line that follows—"And me, oh . . . God I'm a-one"—was the abject crux of the first verse, but now any hint of abjection is gone. Dylan snarls his way in with the opening "*And* me" before once again perforating the phrase between "oh" and "God." This time, though, "God" arrives not in an aspirated shudder, but with a desperate lunge. There is still some wobble in the voice, but the overall tone is one of fuck-you confidence, of defiantly claiming an identity in the face of bourgeois reproach. Instead of balled fists, a middle finger.

IMPERFECT TRUTHS

On the subject of Bob Dylan, Sam Cooke is said to have told his guitarist Bobby Womack, "from now on it's not going to be about how pretty the voice is. It's going to be about believing that the voice is telling the truth."[32] Many years later, *New Yorker* editor David Remnick said something similar: "Dylan has something better than a 'good voice.' He has a true voice. He has a voice that brings out what truth there is in a song—particularly his own."[33] Many fans agree. Consider this 2016 Quora post from user Radosław Gorny:

> It all depends who we call "a singer." If you mean a person that makes sounds, then yes—Bob Dylan sucks. His vocal abilities are extremely limited. On the other hand, if by "a singer" you mean a person who sells emotions by voice, then Bob Dylan is a master of his profession. The keyword is TRUTH. When he sings, I feel like he is being honest with me and I truly believe in his beautiful lyrics.[34]

Here, then, is another article of faith among Dylan devotees: his voice discloses the truth. This is a close cousin to the article of faith discussed near the beginning of this chapter, that Dylan is a master of vocal empathy. For what is such empathy if not an impersonation that has the ring of truth?

Note that the quotes from Cooke, Remnick, and Gorny all contrast the truthful aspects of Dylan's singing with conventions of "good singing" or "pretty voices." It is not hard to connect such thinking to this book's main thesis. For the supposed truthfulness of Dylan's voice, in each of these quotes, is closely related to its imperfection. One senses these three each saying, in their own way, that prettiness and conventional technique can act as a veneer that *blocks* truthful communication in song. Dylan's voice, raw and untutored, has no such veneer. As a result, it strikes sympathetic ears with an emotional intensity and seeming honesty in inverse proportion to its lack of technical polish. The result is belief—truth taken in through the ears.

Such, at least, is the critical conviction. With "House of the Rising Sun," it may well make us uneasy, especially in our current era, when truths are so often viewed relativistically, as inseparable from one's embodied subject position. On such a view, is it not in fact preposterous to say that Dylan discloses a truth in this performance? After all, what could *he* possibly know about the lived experience of women who have experienced what the song's protagonist has? When I taught this material to a group of graduate students in 2022, they were indeed discomfited along these lines. One of them likened the image of Van Ronk and Dylan arguing over who would record this version of the song to two white guys pulling on the suffering lyric persona, each one holding an arm. Some preferred Joan Baez's version of the song, in which the protagonist bears her burden with upright dignity and not a hint of inward shame.

To this discomfort we can add another: the jarring dissonance between what we know about Bob Dylan's own relationship to the truth in real life and his supposed truth-disclosing abilities in song. For it's no news that Dylan is one of mass culture's great fibbers. He changed his name, lied about his origins when he arrived in New York, and has ever since played a cat-and-mouse game with fans and critics about who he "really is." As Ian Bell puts it, speaking of Dylan's early years in the Village, right around the time he recorded "House of the Rising Sun": "he lies outrageously, lies when there is no need, habitually, even compulsively."[35] How could this incorrigible fabulist possibly have a hotline to truth in performance?

Perhaps we can work our way toward an answer if we shift the emphasis from truth to belief. Cooke and Gorny both explicitly mention belief in their quotes. Cooke says that after Dylan "it's going to be about believing that the voice is telling the truth." Gorny puts it even more plainly: "When he sings, I feel like he is being honest with me and I truly believe in his beautiful lyrics." Remnick does not mention belief, but it is arguably implicit. Another way to say that Dylan has a "true voice" is to say "when hearing his voice, I believe what he sings." Recall that Dylan himself uses the word believe (or a variant of it) no fewer than six times in the quote about Joan Baez near the beginning of this chapter, which ends with a credo of sorts: "You have to believe. Folk music, if nothing else, makes a believer out of you."

You have to believe, that is, in a fiction. Joan Baez is not a "rake and a ramblin' boy." Bob Dylan is not a woman ruined by sexual exploitation and violence. But in the moment of aesthetic encounter, the coordinates and conditions of belief shift. We regularly speak of a "suspension of disbelief" when discussing theater, opera, or film. Is song that different? As the examples of gender-shifted songs above make clear, we are very used to suspending disbelief when hearing a singer deliver a story they never could have lived. Indeed, the suspension is so reflexive we may not even realize we are doing it. It is entirely possible to listen to Dylan's "House of the Rising Sun," and even be moved by it, and remain oblivious to the gender mismatch. When pointed out, it is glaringly obvious, but before that it can reside below the threshold of awareness, so accustomed are we to such aesthetic licenses.

Our disbelief suspended—or not even raised to consciousness—we may well feel ourselves compelled toward a kind of "as if" belief. This is not necessarily to say that we believe in the fiction of the character per se. We are never really in doubt that we are hearing Bob Dylan or Joan Baez sing, not the actual characters they impersonate. But their singing may carry a ring of truth. Or—to borrow another felicitous musical metaphor—their sounds may strike a chord in us. What resonates is a plausible *emotional* truth. To experience this ring of truth, this struck chord, is to experience a flash of recognition: I recognize that emotion. It seems plausible to this character and this situation. Maybe even: it moves me. And in moving me, it rings true.

But we don't all believe the same things, especially in the "as if" space of the aesthetic. One person's true voice can be another's emotional counterfeit. Nor are these merely differences of taste. Gender, generation, race, class, ability—all inflect our aesthetic judgments. Moreover, as I have argued above, we do not have to delve deep into Dylan's own psyche to query such beliefs. This is not a matter of probing the artist's personal psychology, or of judging sincerity. We can, again, remain agnostic on those points while still cocking an ear for the techniques he uses to make believers out of so many of his listeners, even if one personally remains unmoved (like my graduate students).

To bring this point home, we will turn to a different song to close this chapter. In this song, Dylan is not impersonating anyone. He is ostensibly singing about his own experience—fittingly, about his belief. Though this is not an example of empathy per se, it can teach us much about Dylan's art of impersonation, illuminating the relationship between imperfect technique and the ring of truth.

THEY ASK ME HOW I FEEL / AND IF MY LOVE IS REAL

Dylan recorded "I Believe in You" in 1979 for his first Christian album, *Slow Train Coming*. The song is in E major, and his voice peaks at several points on the same E4 that he had bored into during the climactic plateau of "House of the Rising Sun" eighteen years earlier. But in "I Believe in You" the pitch has a very different character—it is precarious. And that precarity seems to be precisely the point. The lyrics speak of certainty, of a belief maintained steadfastly in the face of worldly incomprehension and contempt, but Dylan's voice tells a different story. As he struggles over and over to ascend to E4, we hear a belief that is far from secure. It trembles. When he succeeds in holding the pitch, it is effortful; when he fails, his voice splatters wildly. The lyrics proclaim an unshakable faith, but the voice says otherwise.

Crucially, E4 is not at the top of Dylan's range in 1979; he can sing it cleanly, as he can sing several pitches above it. In audio example 1.4(a)—the live version of "The Times They Are a-Changin'" from July 1978 in Paris, a mere ten months before the *Slow Train* sessions—we heard him hit an A4 squarely and securely, a full perfect fourth above E4. In live versions of "I Believe in You" from the fall of 1979, he regularly hits a G4, a minor third above E4. And yet in these same live performances of the song he often causes his voice to break on or near E4, just as it does in the studio recording. In other words, these vocal failures aren't accidents. They're deliberate.

Moreover, he stages them carefully. He ascends to E4 once in each verse, first on "How I know I'll make it through," then, in verse 2, on "Cause I don't be like they'd like me to." **Audio example 3.6** presents both lines as he sings them on the studio recording. He hits the pitch relatively squarely in each verse, though it has a certain nasal tremulousness. One senses its instability, its potential to break apart. But it doesn't—yet. Once the chorus arrives, the singer's confidence seems to grow, E4 resounding over and over (**audio ex. 3.7**): "Even through the tears and the laughter," "Even though we be apart," "Even on the morning after." E4 is now full, impassioned. In the lead-up to the chorus's climax, the chords change more rapidly and Dylan offers two quick lines ("When the dawn is nearin'—ah! / When the night is disappearin'—ah!") that have the effect of a pitcher winding up. He is clearly aiming at the strike zone of E4. But he misses. At the chorus's climax, the ball drifts wildly just before crossing the plate, like a vocal instance of the yips. At the last word of "This feelin' still here in my *heart*," he effortfully attains D♯4, right on E4's threshold. But his voice begins to wobble and lose control, eventually breaking luridly on the E4 that follows on "Don't!" This word is simultaneously the last note of the chorus's buildup and the first word of the next verse. It is pivotal in the song—a crux—both musically and lyrically. And Dylan breaks it open every time. **Audio example 3.8** presents this process as it sounds in verse 1, beginning with the wind-up.

The second chorus follows the progression of the first chorus exactly: impassioned confidence, pitcher's wind-up, effortful wobble, yips-like loss of control right before E4. Tellingly, live versions of the song from late 1979 include the same failures, at the same spots. **Audio example 3.9** presents snippets from two concerts during his fourteen-show residency at the Fox Warfield Theater in San Francisco in November. The example begins with the complete first chorus from November 6, which includes plenty of solid E4s. It also includes two G4s, at these underlined spots: "I believe in you / Even though we be apart // I believe in you / Even on the morning after." Dylan's voice here surpasses E4 with confidence. But E4 itself remains precarious, his voice often peeling off it with a ragged upward break. He leans into this effect at the climactic crux moment, exaggerating the break on the D♯4 right before "Don't!" This is followed on audio example 3.9 by three more instances of the very same break, beginning with the second chorus on November 6, then both choruses on November 16. By this later concert, many in the audience have dialed in the new, gospel Dylan. They cheer after each splattered climax.

It's an interpretively complex moment every time. Dylan's voice belies the lyrics, sounding doubt and strain where the words proclaim certainty. Whatever the words say, his voice tells us that his faith isn't easy. He has to struggle to maintain it. Given the intensity of his vocal performances of the song—in the studio and on stage—it is very tempting to hear the voice as true, in Cooke's, Remnick's, and Gorny's senses. We hear what seems to be evidence of the singer's own effortful belief. But the repeated staging of the same failure, his clear *choice* to fail in the same way over and over, on a note that he can otherwise sing just fine—these raise a doubt. For they make clear that these moments of intensely imperfected singing, just like those in "House of the Rising Sun," are products of technique and calculation.

Rather than the yips, which are involuntary, perhaps these are instead knuckleball pitches, *intentionally* wobbly and unpredictable, meant to throw the batter off.

Or, in this case, the interpreter. For we are left wondering once again at the spacing between the "I" of the lyric persona and the "I" of the singer. With "House of the Rising Sun," that spacing was obvious once we attended to it: male singer and female protagonist. With "I Believe in You," though, it's much less clear. For here Dylan is singing *his* story, not another's. And yet his performative calculation, his choice to fail vocally again and again at the same moment, cause us to doubt our own belief. Is he really, here in 1979, a Christian with shaky but determined faith? Or is he having us on? Again? All of this casts the song's opening lines in a new light: "They ask me how I feel / And if my love is real."

If the voice that breaks again and again in "I Believe in You" rings true, we have strategic imperfection to thank. Dylan's breakages on the word sound a very human frailty, a struggle to hold on to belief in the face of doubt. In a dizzying moment of interpretive doubling, we the listeners may experience something similar, a compulsion to believe in a "true voice" undercut by a nagging doubt that it may all be for show. The spacing between lyric persona and singer may be smaller in this song than in "House of the Rising Sun," but it is a spacing all the same. The gulf is just as deep, for we can never know the precise relationship between what we hear and what is in the singer's heart. Dylan makes us acutely aware of that spacing, singing of "this feeling still deep in my heeeeeaaaart" right before the first break. Faced with such a spacing, we have options. Some will choose to remain on this side of the gulf, arms skeptically folded. But Dylan's most faithful listeners regularly choose otherwise. They become believers, just as he did when hearing Joan Baez. Belief carries them across the spacing, with sounding imperfection as the bridge. In the face of doubt, the ears believe.

Chapter 4 audio examples:
soundingbobdylan.com/ch4

CHAPTER FOUR

Words-Music (1)

Speechward

In the introduction I waxed poetic about the "world-containing hyphen" in Dylan's words-music compound. This chapter and the following one are a meditation on that hyphen. Our question is simple but far-reaching: how do words and music meet in Dylan's voice? To answer it, we will listen closely to how he traverses the continuum between speech and song at various points in his career. In the present chapter we will explore the speechward end of the continuum, while in the next we will progress toward song proper. Given the scope of both the question and the career, we will have much to consider and will require a good number of musical figures. But if you don't read music, never fear! The main purpose of the figures is to show the contour of Dylan's singing—its play of rising and falling. You can trace that up-and-down motion visually on the page even if you don't follow the finer points of the notation. Doing so while listening to the excerpt in question will help even more.

CHAPTER FOUR

VOICING THE FRINGE

Dylan's lyrics are the raw material that he must navigate each night, the material stuff against which his voice rubs in each performance. Arrangements change, keys shift, and melodic lines alter, but the lyrics persist.[1] His words are thus always there, and not only as sounding material. They retain their potential to flicker back into meaning with the right vocal nudge. I will argue here that one way Dylan provides that nudge is by manipulating "the fringe of contact between music and language," to borrow a felicitous line from Roland Barthes.[2] When we attend to that fringe, we shift our location on figure 1.2, the triangle depicting voice at the intersection of sound, word, and body. The preceding chapters focused largely on questions of identity, situating us on the right edge of the figure, as we puzzled at the relationship between the sound of Dylan's voice and the body that emits it. In chapter 3 we also wondered about the spacing between that sounding body and the protagonist in a given song. In this chapter and the next, by contrast, we shuttle to the left edge, contemplating the fringe of contact between sound and word. With Dylan, as we will see, that fringe never stays put for long. Indeed, its *mobility* is one of the hallmarks of his singing, reanimating long-familiar lyrics and startling old words back to life.

How does this work? Let's begin with the observation—hardly new—that Dylan's voice moves fluidly on a continuum from speech to song.[3] Dylan is one of the iconic speak-singers in postwar mass culture. I will have more to say about speech in song in a moment. But let's begin with **figure 4.1**, which offers a rudimentary image for the continuum.

Think of the arrow as modeling the motion of Dylan's voice between the two poles. We can conceive of that motion at various times

speech ◄- -► song

FIGURE 4.1. Speech and song on a continuum.

scales, from momentary shifts in delivery within a given performance to large-scale changes in vocal style across his career. At this latter, macro level, various locations along the spectrum act as centers of gravity in a given era. For example, in his late turn toward the Great American Songbook—in three albums released from 2015 to 2017—Dylan hews to the composed melody with great care, treating it with even more fidelity than seasoned practitioners in the style (for example, his principal influence on these recordings, Frank Sinatra). In these years he resides very near the "song" pole. By contrast, in the amplified burst of 1965–66, his voice often settles somewhere in the middle, neither speech nor song, but roving mercurially in between, dragging the fringe of contact to ever-new locations. In his earliest, acoustic years he straddles this middle zone, either singing clear melodies (at the far right of the figure) or delivering talking blues (at the far left). And so on.

Figure 4.1 is nevertheless a bit too smooth. It doesn't give a good sense of the tug-of-war between speech and song that one sometimes senses in Dylan's delivery, nor does it capture their interaction and co-presence at various intermediate stages. **Figure 4.2** thus offers a refinement, adapting a bit of music notation: hairpins typically used to indicate crescendos and decrescendos (volume is greatest when the hairpin is at its widest). At the left edge of the figure speech predominates, while song is at its weakest. As we move rightward, song increases in strength while speech inflections attenuate, until we reach the right edge, with sung delivery predominant. Each stratum is dynamic and is oriented toward its pole, the point toward which its metaphorical crescendo aims. At any point on the spectrum, one can imagine Dylan's voice subtly tugged in both directions, leftward by the pull of speech, rightward toward the etched contours of melody. The alignment of the hairpins also suggests that neither speech nor song is ever completely absent. Even at the extremes, the attenuated hairpins do not disappear entirely. This is attractive, as there is arguably always a residue of speech in Dylan's vocal delivery, even when he is at his most melodically well behaved. Emphasized fricatives,

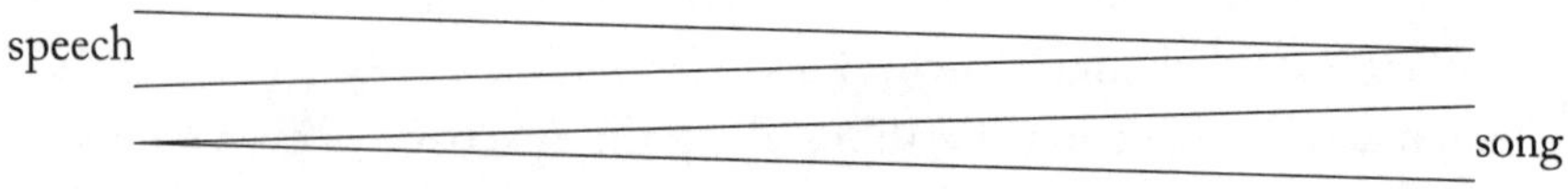

speech

song

FIGURE 4.2. The speech–song continuum as aligned dynamic hairpins.

palatals, and plosives, bent and inflected vowels that suggest a persisting fidelity to the word as an object of everyday talk—these never leave Dylan's voice. In the 1961 review that made Dylan famous Robert Shelton states memorably that "all the 'husk' and 'bark' are left on his notes."[4] That husk and bark consists, in part, of the residues of speech, so often trained out of voices in traditions that value purity of sung tone. In short, all of the articulative labor of speech remains perceptible even when Dylan is at his most singerly, on the rightmost edge of the figure. Similarly, at the leftmost extreme, there is an incipient musicality even in Dylan's everyday talk.[5] Think of his delivery in interviews, from any era—the playful rhythm and impeccable timing, the varied articulations (from slurred to staccato), the dynamic range, the arched melodic contours. The aligned hairpins capture these dynamics nicely. Speech and song taper, but they never fade to complete inaudibility.

Figure 4.3 offers a further refinement, identifying five nodal points at which Dylan often resides along the speech–song continuum. (I will refer back to this figure often in what follows, so you may want to bookmark or dogear its page.) These nodal points are neither hard-and-fast nor exhaustive. They shade into each other and intermix in ways much more fluid than the discrete points of the arrowheads suggest. Nevertheless, they provide a useful starting point for thinking about Dylan's diverse modes of vocal delivery across the continuum. The figure numbers them 1–5, gives them descriptive names, and provides an example of a studio recording to get the given vocal style in the reader's ears. The odd-numbered nodes have straightforward titles and are familiar from various vocalists and

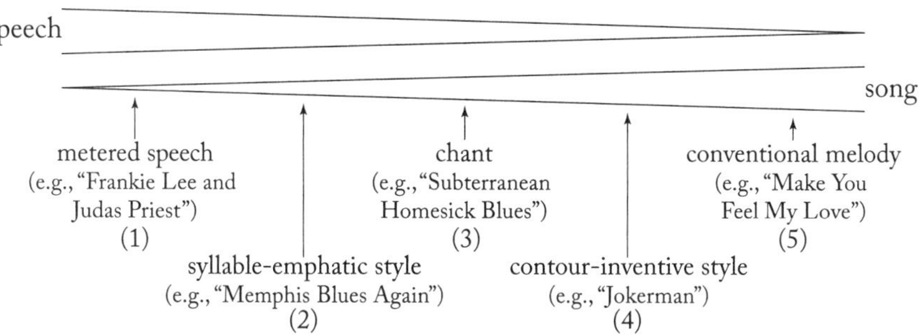

FIGURE 4.3. The speech–song continuum with five nodal points.

genres. The even-numbered nodes are more elaborately named. They are intermediate stages between the odd-numbered nodes, more or less sui generis to Dylan.

As with figures 4.1 and 4.2 before, one can imagine Dylan's delivery ranging across this spectrum at various timescales, from the micro scale of local shifts in delivery within a given line, to the macro scale of his entire career. We can now be more precise about the latter. In the early, acoustic years, his voice divides its time between nodes 1 and 5, metered speech and conventional melody. In the early part of the electric period, on *Bringing It All Back Home* and *Highway 61 Revisited*, chant (3) is a central point of reference, Chuck Berry crossed with the Beats. The syllable-emphatic style (2) comes into its own first on 1966's *Blonde on Blonde* and then becomes a special effect available in all subsequent eras. On the so-called Never-Ending Tour, Dylan regularly resides at node 4, inventing new melodies nightly. In his Sinatra era, he hews carefully to node 5, which then remains a prominent station in the *Rough and Rowdy Ways* era.

Across this chapter and the next, we will survey each node, listening closely to examples as we move left to right across figure 4.3. At the end of each chapter, we will revisit the question of imperfection and meaning at the vocal fringe.

NODE 1: METERED SPEECH

Spoken delivery in song foregrounds the word *as* word. It asserts language's autonomy from the musical code—chords, rhythms, melodies, timbres, the whole fabric of musical syntax. The spoken word is not subsumed by melody but retains its stubborn particularity as an object of everyday talk. As I have discussed elsewhere, speaking in song can heighten the material presence of spoken language.[6] In our everyday social interactions, when we are attending to our interlocutor's meaning, we typically discard the sound of their voice as soon as we have gleaned their meaning. As Mladen Dolar eloquently puts it, in such everyday talk the voice "goes up in smoke in the meaning being produced."[7] Or, to switch metaphors, the everyday speaking voice is transparent to meaning; we "hear through it" to the meaning being conveyed. Think of this in terms of our three categories from chapter 1: word, sound, and body. In everyday speech, word—meaning—is ascendant. We think little about the specific sound of our interlocutor's voice once we have gleaned her meaning, nor do we puzzle over the body that emitted that voice. We instead extract the sense of the words, leaving sound and bodily source behind.

But speech *in song* is another matter. Heard against the background of the musical code, the speaking voice can seem to regain its materiality, set off like a figure in front of the musical ground. Its relative independence from that ground—its refusal to settle into the music's pitch system, for example—brings out its texture and intonation, its dips and rises, its articulative micro-details, encouraging us to attend to them with renewed focus. Speech in song does not bring us in contact with the word as a transparent vehicle of meaning. It brings to our ears a word that is stubbornly opaque and material, its sound newly audible.

By allowing residues of speech to persist in all of his vocalizing, to various degrees, Dylan influenced a whole raft of later vocalists: Patti Smith, Leonard Cohen, Lou Reed, Rickie Lee Jones, Jonathan Richman. It is no accident that these are all vocalists with literary ambition.[8] But Dylan's speaking in song is not only indebted to the literary high style. While it does have roots in the elite practice of Beat recitation—think of Allen Ginsberg reading "Howl"—it also draws on more modest vernacular traditions such as Woody Guthrie's talking blues and Hank Williams's spoken homilies (delivered as Luke the Drifter). As these two examples suggest, these vernacular traditions range from the comic to the devotional. As an example of the latter, consider the 1967 song "Sign on the Cross."[9] Dylan sings the first half of the song over gospel organ from Garth Hudson and gently pealing 6/8 arpeggios from guitarist Robbie Robertson. But he then begins to speak in the style of a radio preacher, with an arch huckster's cadence and a smile in his voice.[10] **Audio example 4.1** provides an excerpt including the end of the earlier, sung section and the beginning of the spoken one. Greil Marcus hears much in the contrast:

> Hudson's organ and the piety in Dylan's [singing] voice have made a church, but the uncertainty of God's existence produces [in the spoken section] only mockery and nervousness, ridicule and isolation, speech the first singer is sure no one will hear, God least of all.[11]

This stylistic downshift into vulgar, mocking speech is realized in part through a shift into an *unmetered* vocal delivery. That is, Dylan's speech here makes no concessions to the regularities of musical meter. He speaks instead in the fluid, flexible rhythms of the pitchman.

But much of Dylan's speaking in song is loosely hitched to the musical meter. This is why I have labeled node 1 in figure 4.3 "metered speech" and placed it slightly to the right of the "speech" pole. This slight rightward shift indicates that this is minimally musicalized speech, in that it involves musical rhythm and meter. "The Ballad of Frankie Lee and Judas Priest," from 1967's *John Wesley Harding* illustrates. **Audio example 4.2** presents the first line, which is transcribed in **figure 4.4**. Dylan's spoken delivery is clearly coordinated with the song's meter. The phrases cluster around each metric downbeat, and

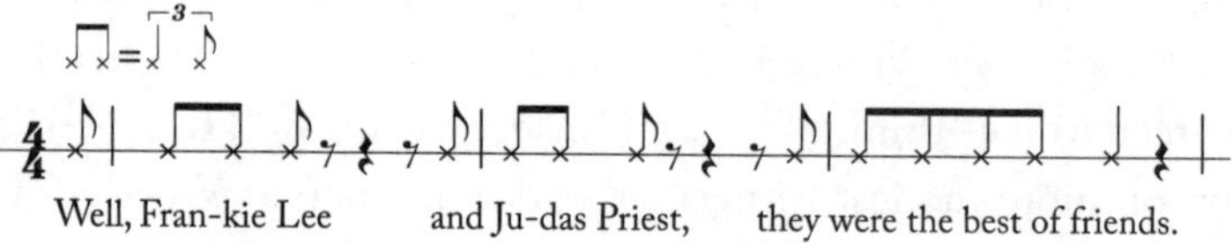

FIGURE 4.4. Metered speech in "The Ballad of Frankie Lee and Judas Priest" from *John Wesley Harding* (1967), first line.

the rhythm within each phrase aligns with the song's relaxed, swung groove. We can hear the first hint of the fringe of contact between music and language here, as Dylan's speech rhythms are bent and pulled into alignment with the music's meter. In this particular song the effect is in keeping with Dylan's lyric. The music pulls the story forward toward the unsettling climax, and the voice does not resist its rhythmic momentum. It is matter of fact, moving along with the meter like a train passenger commenting on the scenes passing by through the window, his affect flat.

In other speaking songs, Dylan's alignment with the meter is looser, hovering somewhere between free and metered speech. Much of the comic charm in his early talking blues comes from his subtle shifting in and out of phase with the musical meter, a technique he heard in Woody Guthrie and heightened in his own practice. There is a tussle between musical and linguistic priorities here, but the tussle is worn lightly and manipulated for laughs. Consider the fourth verse of "Talking World War III Blues" from 1963 **(audio ex. 4.3)**:

Well, I got up and I walked around
2 *Up and down the lonesome town*
I stood a-wondering which way to go
4 I lit a cigarette on a parking meter
And walked on down the road [pause]
6 It was a normal day

Dylan delivers the first two lines, which I've italicized, in explicit alignment with the meter, the plodding rhythm offering a sonic analogue for the monotonous business of trudging around the city.[12] But with lines 3–6 he shifts back into a metrically free delivery, his tone returning to one of impish bewilderment. As he stands wondering and lights his cigarette, he takes a beat. The beat removed, he slips out of the dreary routines of city life, with its regular (read: metric) grids of blocks, streets, sidewalks, traffic signs, and a whole dense web of laws indicating how one should traverse them. Inching leftward on figure 4.3, Dylan's Guthrie-meets-Chaplin vocal persona shakes off grid-like confinement with a shrug. In the pause after line 5—idiomatic in the talking blues, a setup for the droll punchline of line 6—one can almost see Chaplin's tramp walking away, cane swinging.[13]

Though talking blues quickly left his repertory, Dylan continued to explore node 1 and its environs in later years, though mostly as a local effect, a brief dip into speech inflection within an otherwise sung number. We heard an instance of this in the 1988 live version of "The Times They Are a-Changin'" in audio example 1.4(b): as I put it there, his voice drifts toward speech at the ends of lines 3 and 4. Occasionally, though, he still speaks a song throughout, as in "Long and Wasted Years," from 2012's *Tempest*. Here he recruits his aging voice for a delivery that is equal parts sly and rueful. **Audio example 4.4** provides an excerpt. There is also a hint here of figure 4.3's node 2, in lines like "The sun can burn your BRAINS right out." The punched word protrudes from the general flow of speech, suddenly higher in pitch and volume: sonic all-caps. It is one of Dylan's most idiosyncratic—and imitable—vocal mannerisms.

NODE 2: SYLLABLE-EMPHATIC STYLE

On episode 102 of his radio show *The Theme Time Radio Hour*, broadcast in 2020, Dylan discusses a performance of Kurt Weill and Bertolt Brecht's "Alabama Song" as sung by Weill's wife Lotte Lenya:

> Lotte utilizes a singing technique called *Sprechstimme*, which the Oxford English Dictionary defines as a style of dramatic vocalization intermediate between speech and song. You know, half speaking, half singing. I've been known to use that, myself.[14]

Dylan was more correct than he may have realized. For, some of his vocal delivery bears more than a passing resemblance to *Sprechstimme*, which literally means "speech song." But *Sprechstimme* is not just any old mixture of speech and song. It is a very particular technique, best known from the expressionist music of atonal composer Arnold Schoenberg, whose 1912 work *Pierrot lunaire* famously uses *Sprechstimme* throughout (he employed it in other compositions too).[15] In Schoenberg's introduction to *Pierrot*'s score, he describes the technique, stating that the singer must be

> precisely aware of the difference between a *sung tone* and a *spoken tone*: the sung tone maintains the pitch unaltered; the spoken tone does indicate it, but immediately abandons it again by falling or rising. . . . The goal is certainly not at all realistic, natural speech. On the contrary, the difference between ordinary speech and speech that collaborates in a musical form must be made plain. But it should not call singing to mind, either.[16]

The crucial detail here is the difference between pitch in singing and pitch in *Sprechstimme*. In the former, the singer holds a pitch relatively steady, whereas in the latter the singer merely brushes that pitch before sliding away. The result is a highly mannered vocal style, a series of parabolic arcs as the singer ascends to a given pitch only to depart immediately upon touching it. The effect, when done well, is neither speech nor song, as Schoenberg notes, but an idiosyncratic amalgam.

Now consider Dylan's delivery on the 1966 studio recording of "Stuck Inside of Mobile with the Memphis Blues Again" (**audio ex. 4.5**):

Well SHAKEspeare HE'S in the alley
With his pointed SHOES and his BELLS
Speaking to some FRENCH girl
Who SAYS she knows me WELL
And I would SEND a MESsage
To find out if she's TALKed
But the POST office has been STOlen
And the MAILbox is LOCKed
OH, MAma, can this REALly BE the END,
To be STUCK inSIDE of MObile
WITH the MEMphis BLUES aGAIN?

Or consider "Million Dollar Bash," recorded the following summer in Woodstock (**audio ex. 4.6**):

Well, I LOOKed at my WATCH
I LOOKed at my WRIST
I punched myself in the FACE with my FIST
I took my poTAtoes DOWN to be MASHed
And I made it on over to that MILLION DOLLAR BASH!

In both songs, Dylan's voice swoops up on the all-caps syllables, only to fall away again just as quickly—a parabolic lunge. These lunges are reminiscent of Schoenberg's *Sprechstimme* both in their contour and in their loose tethering to the music's underlying pitch structure.[17] I mean by this that Dylan only occasionally swoops up to a note that fits the local scale or harmonic context. The rest of the time his parabolic arcs are largely oblivious to the music's tidy pitch systems.

But we shouldn't push the comparison to *Sprechstimme* too hard. Delightful as it is to hear Dylan himself make the comparison in the *Theme Time Radio Hour* quote, there is no obvious lineage from

Schoenberg to him, nor should we rush to create one, in a search for high-cultural prestige. Moreover, the affect is not the same in Dylan's delivery and in *Sprechstimme*. The latter is grotesque and dysphoric, expressionist angularity in the service of emotional extremes. Dylan's affect in these songs, by contrast, ranges from laconic to amused, from the ironized paranoia of "Memphis Blues Again" to the comic, stoner surreal of "Million Dollar Bash." So let's give Dylan's delivery a new name: the syllable-emphatic style.[18]

To be sure, Dylan emphasizes syllables in various ways in all of his singing. But at this node the contrast between emphasized and non-emphasized syllables is elevated to a first principle. It is the primary logic of a vocal style whose anarchic rising and falling is all about punching *this* syllable and not that one. As for which syllables are emphasized, note that, in the above two examples, the all-caps words would all receive an accent in normal speech. Dylan doesn't generally punch unstressed syllables. For example, in "Memphis Blues Again" he does not emphasize, say, the second syllable of "alley" in line 1, or "and" in line 2. One need only imagine him doing so—it's not hard—to sense how remote the effect would be from his actual syllable-emphatic delivery. Instead, his voice seizes on syllables we would typically accent, but exaggerates the contrast to the point of mannerism. We hear the contours of everyday speech, but in a funhouse mirror.

We can assemble a gallery of further examples from *Blonde on Blonde*, all of them following the same principle (**audio ex. 4.7**):

Well early in the morning
'Til LATE at NIGHT
I got a POIson HEADache
But I FEEL all RIGHT

"Pledging My Time"

Inside the museums
Infinity GOES up on TRIAL
Voices echo this is what
Salvation must be LIKE after aWHILE

"Visions of Johanna"

But I did it because he LIED
Because he took you for a RIDE
Because TIME was on his SIDE
And because I . . .

"I Want You"

It is Dylan's most imitated style. When mimics put on a Dylan voice, it is usually this one. This speaks to how singular it is, how distinctive to him and no one else. The style is particularly emblematic for the popular image of "Bob Dylan, poet," taking as it does one of the central techniques of spoken-word delivery—syllabic emphasis—and amplifying it.[19] In the resulting friction between word and melody, word wins. That is, in this style, the priorities of speech accent run roughshod over the priorities of melodic accent. In melody proper the music creates its own patterns of accent and emphasis through contour, duration, volume, metric placement, and so on. When the melody is sung, these melodic priorities occasionally come into conflict with the accents of spoken language. A famous example is the first line of "Somewhere" from *West Side Story*. Stephen Sondheim's lyric is "There's a place for us." In normal speech we would usually accent the word "place," though in particular contexts we might emphasize "us" or even "There's." But the one word we would likely *never* accent, in any context, is "a." And yet Leonard Bernstein's melody leaps up right at this word, giving it musical pride of place, in tension with its lowly station in the prosody of the line as spoken. As so often in these cases, music wins. That is, the integrity of the melody trumps the integrity of prosodic emphasis.[20]

But now imagine performing that first line of "Somewhere" in Dylan's syllable-emphatic style. Use your best "Memphis Blues Again" voice: "There's a PLACE for us!" Now "place" comes roaring back, reclaiming its role as the phrase's center of gravity, melodic contour be damned. The lowly "a" is all but lost in the rush. This is what I mean by speech priorities running roughshod over musical ones. In the syllable-emphatic style, the word as an object of everyday speech insists on *its* accentual priorities, a fitting reversal for a poet-musician.

Language bends the music surrounding it into the exaggerated contours of speech. This, then, is the next station in the mobile fringe of contact between music and language mapped out by figure 4.3. It is rightward of node 1 because pitch is now a central musical parameter in a vocal style that is all about exaggerated ups and downs—even if the pitches in question are often unmoored from the musical background.

Despite the centrality of this mode of delivery in the popular imagination of Dylan's voice, it is merely one of his vocal styles among many. Moreover, it is historically particular. First arising around 1966, it features heavily on *Blonde on Blonde*, the spring 1966 leg of his world tour, and *The Basement Tapes*, but is largely absent from the vocally restrained *John Wesley Harding*, before vanishing completely with the country crooning of 1969's *Nashville Skyline*, the Isle of Wight concert, and 1970's *Self Portrait*. It nevertheless remained a special effect throughout the remainder of Dylan's career—as in that line from 2012's "Long and Wasted Years"—though it arguably never regained the prominence it had on *Blonde on Blonde*.

To measure the distance between Dylan's classic 1966 syllable-emphatic delivery and the remotest nodal point on figure 4.3—node 5, where we find melody proper—let's consider two performances of "I Don't Believe You (She Acts Like We Never Have Met)": the 1964 studio recording and the live performance in Manchester's Free Trade Hall on May 17, 1966.[21] **Figure 4.5** is a transcription of the vocal melody as he sings it on the 1964 studio recording; **audio example 4.8** provides the first verse. Capital letters along the left edge of the figure label the melody's phrases. The A phrase is repeated, resulting in a conventional AABA′ form. Brackets above the first line indicate a repeating figure, which music analysts would call a motive; I have labeled it *x*. The motive, which involves only three pitches (E, F♯, and A), is hectoring and repetitive, apt for a lyric of such sustained pique. In the B phrase, as the singer recalls the previous night's erotic encounter, his excitement increasing, the melody ascends. It begins at a new highpoint, D4, before rising a step further for the E4 climax on the second syllable of "forget," marked with a dagger (†). Phrase

FIGURE 4.5. Melody for "I Don't Believe You (She Acts Like We Never Have Met)," as sung on *Another Side of Bob Dylan* (1964).

A′ then fuses aspects of both A and B: it begins on the D4 of phrase B, but integrates it into a variant of motive *x*, which I have labeled "*x* var" on the figure, as the singer descends back into hectoring repetition, incredulous. Tetchy affect aside, the melody is compact and orderly, its pitches never once leaving the D-major pentatonic scale.[22]

On stage in Manchester two years later, that pentatonic scale is long gone. This is one of the most storied concerts from Dylan's combative 1966 tour, at which a fan infamously shouts "Judas!" at the singer.[23] This tour is also, perhaps not coincidentally, the highwater mark of Dylan's syllable-emphatic style on stage. During the electric sets especially, he seems to relish the anarchic energy of the vocal style, its wild disregard for musical propriety, and its confrontational energy. **Audio example 4.9** presents verse 1; **figure 4.6** is a loose transcription. It is all but impossible to notate Dylan's singing in this style precisely; the difficulty is itself telling, indicative of his swooping freedom with pitch when singing syllable-emphatically. So all noteheads in the figure should be taken with a grain of salt. More important than precise pitch is how the noteheads look: ×-shaped ones indicate relatively unstressed syllables, while regular noteheads indicate syllable-emphatic ones. The figure also includes only the punched words in the lyric, both to avoid clutter and to capture visually the aural effect of the style, especially in the noisy context of Dylan's backing band. Many attendees complained about the sound at these concerts—not just the sheer volume, which many found assaultive, but also the poor acoustics, which C. P. Lee, who was there, has called "appalling."[24] One can imagine an audience member in Manchester, pinned to the back of her seat by the volume, catching only these emphasized syllables.[25]

The original tune is all but obliterated. The only hint of it comes at the climactic second syllable of "forget," again marked with a dagger.[26] Here Dylan for a moment slips into a singing voice, sustaining the pitch over a three-note melisma before again drooping back into syllable-emphatic terrain. But the hectoring *x* motive—the song's melodic thumbprint, so omnipresent in the original—is entirely absent. At least, absent from Dylan's voice. If you listen closely, you can

FIGURE 4.6. Emphasized syllables in "I Don't Believe You (She Acts Like We Never Have Met)," as sung in Manchester, May 17, 1966.

still hear it, relocated to Robbie Robertson's guitar.[27] Robertson plays the motive not only in the song's intro but behind Dylan's singing as well. It thus serves both as an aural reminder of how the song used to go, almost mocking in its insistence, and a direct point of comparison against which we can measure how far Dylan's voice has drifted since 1964. In this connection, recall that this is the number Dylan prefaced with his sleepy taunt, "It used to be like that, but now it goes like this," as discussed in the introduction. And Dylan shows that he can still hector just fine without singing the motive. But now the target of that hectoring seems less the "she" of the lyric and much more the audience arrayed in front of him, as he hurls each punched syllable their way. Indeed, later in the same concert, right after the infamous "Judas!" shout, Dylan repeated the name of the song in his retort, at once weary and contemptuously ablaze: "I don't *believe* you. You're a liar!" And then, just before launching into "Like a Rolling Stone," he added a line almost as famous as the fan's shout: "Play it fucking loud!"

Here it is tempting to bring back the Schoenberg comparison, for this is Dylan as confrontational modernist. But, in a fitting inversion, instead of shocking the bourgeoisie he is shocking an imagined proletariat—the UK folk revivalists who attended these gigs:

> The people who booed, slow hand-clapped, heckled, whistled, and walked out belonged to a fraternity, an almost semi-mystical coalition of like-minded purists who referred to themselves as "Folk Fans."[28]

These ascetic Leftists, headed by figures like Ewan MacColl and Bert Lloyd, had many complaints against Dylan: he was a folk impostor, his songs were "tenth-rate drivel," he didn't know his history (or his Marx).[29] But such complaints were drowned out in Manchester, as at every other stop on the tour, Dylan braying down the hecklers in a voice worlds removed from the ballad-singing tradition—syllable-emphatic style as cudgel.

NODE 3: CHANT

While Dylan was touring England the previous spring, British radio listeners were hearing a different voice. "Subterranean Homesick Blues" was a hit. It would in fact break into the UK top 10, peaking at number 9 on May 26, 1965, remaining there for two weeks. The track was both a thrill and a shock. For here was Dylan not only backed by electric instruments but singing in a way no one had yet heard from him, the lyrics unfolding—line after witty line—on one insistent pitch. But listeners had only to think back to earlier rock 'n' roll to hear its antecedents in Chuck Berry.

Figure 4.7 transcribes three phrases from Berry's 1956 song "Too Much Monkey Business," the template for "Subterranean Homesick Blues," as Dylan himself has acknowledged.[30] **Audio example 4.10** presents the three phrases. The line at 4.7(a) is the closest prototype for Dylan's delivery as regards rhythm, prosody, and pitch. Berry delivers the phrase entirely on one pitch, A♭3, the blue third in the key of F.[31] For this and subsequent examples, I will refer to this repeated pitch as the "reciting tone."[32] In 4.7(b), Berry begins on that blue third—bent a bit sharp, hence the arrow—before descending to a reciting tone of F3. In 4.7(c), A♭3 is once again the reciting tone, though in this example Berry breaks away from it at line's end, in comic exasperation.[33]

Compare the three phrases from the studio recording of "Subterranean Homesick Blues" shown in **figure 4.8** and hearable in **audio example 4.11**. Like Berry, Dylan delivers each line almost entirely on one note, C4, which is again the blue third (the key is now A, in contrast to Berry's key of F). Dylan does drop away from C4 on a couple occasions, down to a barely brushed A3, indicated by ×-shaped noteheads. But these brief detours hardly shake the stability of the reciting tone, which reverberates throughout every phrase of the verse. This was not a one-off. Dylan employed reciting-tone chants extensively in 1965. They anchor "Maggie's Farm," "On the Road Again," "Bob Dylan's 115th Dream," "It's Alright, Ma (I'm Only Bleeding)," "Like a Rolling Stone," and "Tombstone Blues." A subvariant of chant that toggles

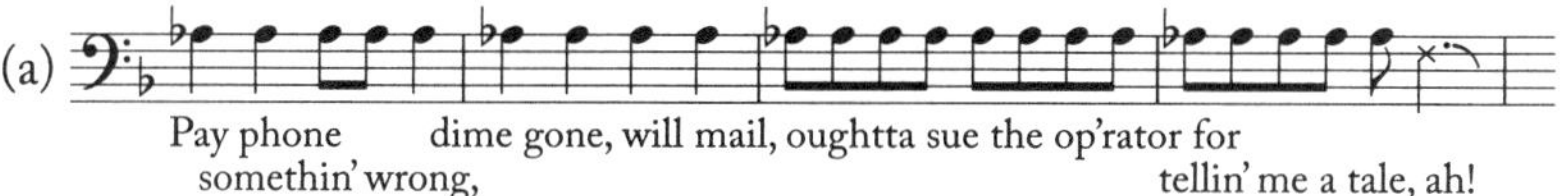

(b)
Blonde haired, tryna get me hooked marry, get a home, write a book, ah!
good lookin' want me to settle down,

FIGURE 4.7. Three phrases from Chuck Berry's "Too Much Monkey Business" (1956).

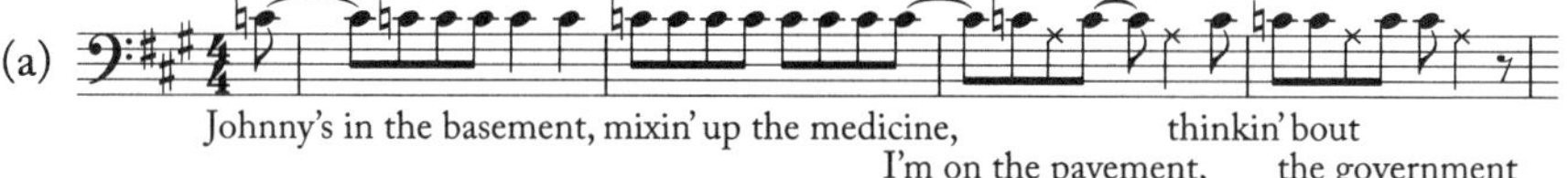

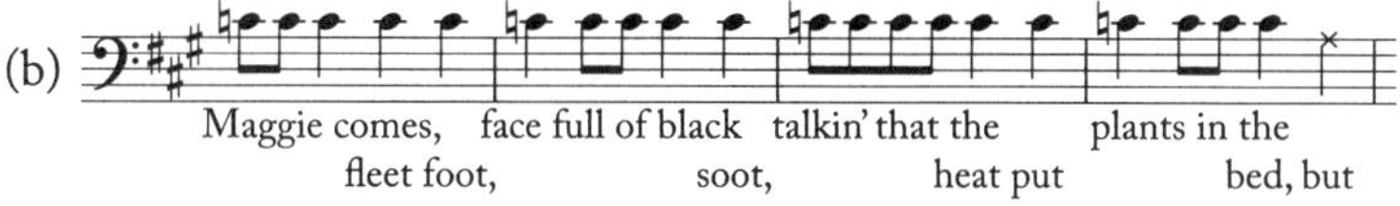

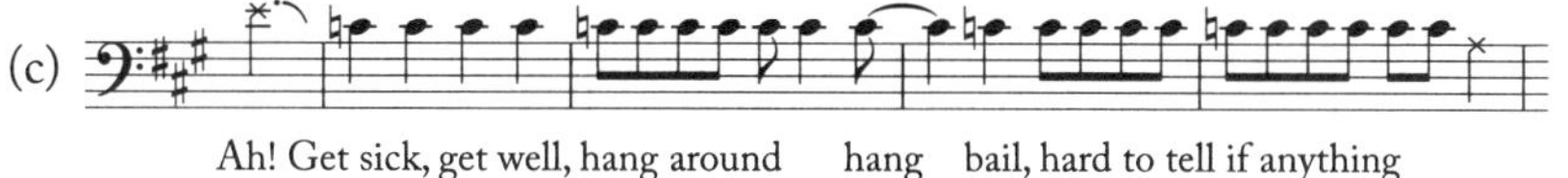

FIGURE 4.8. Three phrases from Dylan's "Subterranean Homesick Blues" (1965).

between two reciting tones, which I will discuss below, provides the foundation for yet more songs: "Outlaw Blues," "Gates of Eden," "From a Buick 6," "Ballad of a Thin Man," and "Highway 61 Revisited."

What made chant so appealing to Dylan in the first blush of his electric phase? Clearly, its rock-'n'-roll lineage back to Chuck

Berry had more than a little to do with it. Dylan was channeling his youthful musical enthusiasms. But crucially, he was doing so at a moment when his lyrics were also becoming ever more fantastical, as Woody Guthrie gave way to Rimbaud and Ginsberg in his pantheon of models. With chant he could deliver his new, ambitious words in a streamlined musical idiom that maximized both verbal clarity and sheer words per second. Even better, the style wedded Beat prestige with rock-'n'-roll propulsion. The result, at times, could sound like a surrealistic patter song, overstuffed lines tumbling out in a syncopated wave, at once invigorating and legible. Every word in "Subterranean Homesick Blues"—and in "Like a Rolling Stone," for that matter, or any of the songs listed above—sounds out clear as a bell, its accentual contours projected through precise rhythm, with no melodic up and down for competition. Crucially, like the later syllable-emphatic style, the sounding result also punched a hole in the noisy wall of Dylan's bands, his nasal reciting tones—usually in the resonant middle of his register—boring through the racket like an auger.

Chant is located rightward of the syllable-emphatic style on figure 4.3 because now Dylan's sung pitch is plugged into the scalar context of the song. Moreover, he holds the reciting tone more or less steady, rather than swooping up and down as in the syllable-emphatic style. To be sure, chant is less mobile in pitch space than the syllable-emphatic style, but it is more securely woven into the musical background. And some chant variants are more mobile than the one-note chant of "Subterranean Homesick Blues." One important variant I call the "chant/escape." The archetypal examples are "It's Alright, Ma (I'm Only Bleeding)" and "Like a Rolling Stone." In both songs Dylan chants several lines on the reciting tone before leaping up to a higher pitch, which I call the "escape tone."[34] Crucially, in both songs the escape tone corresponds to a change in end vowel in the lyrics. **Figure 4.9** illustrates; **audio example 4.12** presents the relevant excerpts. The pattern holds throughout the songs' verses: Dylan sings lines with repeated end rhymes on the reciting tone, leaping up to the escape tone at the change in end vowel that follows.[35] In the first line

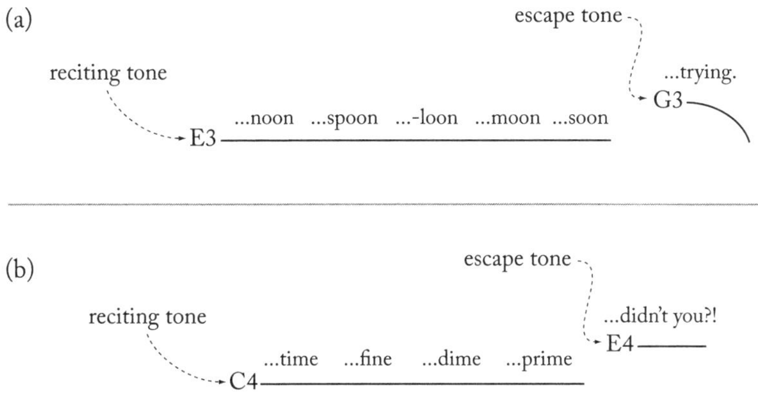

FIGURE 4.9. Chant/escape delivery and vowel alignment in the 1965 studio recordings of (a) "It's Alright, Ma (I'm Only Bleeding)" and (b) "Like a Rolling Stone."

of "Rolling Stone," the leap up to the escape tone also nicely matches the interrogative of the lyric, rising like a question.

Dylan would continue to use the chant/escape at various points later in his career.[36] Consider the opening lines of "Simple Twist of Fate," as recorded in 1974 for *Blood on the Tracks* (**audio ex. 4.13**):

> They sat together in the *park*
> As the ev'ning sky grew *dark*
> She looked at him and he felt a *spark*
> Tingle to his bones

For the first three lines, Dylan chants the words in roman type on a G♯3 before leaping up to B3 for the line-ending, italicized words, which all rhyme. He then departs from this pattern when the end rhyme changes in line 4 ("Tingle to his bones"), the melody now descending. A more extreme example from around this time is the 1974 live version of "Most Likely You Go Your Way (and I'll Go Mine)," as released on *Before the Flood*. Dylan begins each line in the vicinity of G3 before leaping up an octave to deliver the line-ending word with a gravelly shout on G4, **Audio example 4.14** presents the opening.

Such line-ending leaps resurfaced in Dylan's singing in an insistently mannered way in the early 2000s. Fans called it "upsinging."[37] It consisted of a variable opening in lower register—often chant-based, but sometimes more mobile—which then gave way to a single sung pitch near the top of Dylan's register, which I call the "upsung target." The style peaked in 2002 but lingered in various forms for years; one could provide examples by the hundreds. **Audio example 4.15** is one especially vivid instance, from a 2002 performance of "Mr. Tambourine Man" in Aspen, Colorado. As **figure 4.10** shows, in this chorus Dylan begins each line with a chant on C3 before leaping up an octave to C4 for the upsung target. This tic perplexed Dylan fans, especially when he seemed to fall into a rut with it, upsinging for long stretches at a given concert. What was this about? His ravaged voice clearly had much to do with it, especially his challenges in producing a strong fundamental pitch. The technique was arguably a way to mitigate this, to pull a single clean pitch from the tatters of his aging larynx. Upsung phrases at this time almost always began in his then-default low growl, before a leaping up to an almost bell-like target pitch, with focused fundamental and little timbral noise. In other words, the technique seems to have been aimed—quite literally—at producing this one clear pitch at line endings, when clear pitches were otherwise so hard to come by. The resulting target pitches spotlight line-ending syllables, which stand out like an illuminated letter in a medieval manuscript.

Before leaving chant, let's return to 1965 for one final variant, which I dub the "minor-third toggle." It is just what it sounds like: a chanted vocal line that toggles between two pitches a minor-third apart. The easiest way to understand this technique is as an extension of the chant/escape, but the escape tone is now no longer limited to line's end—it can also pop up at stressed words mid-line. "Ballad of a Thin Man" is a classic example. Dylan's vocal line in the verses on the studio recording consists almost entirely of just two notes a

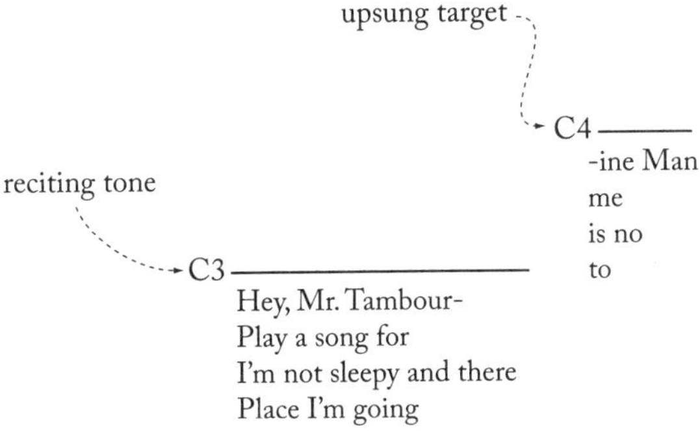

FIGURE 4.10. Upsinging on "Mr. Tambourine Man," Aspen, Colorado, September 1, 2002.

minor-third apart, B and D. Here is the first verse; words chanted on B are in roman type, words and syllables on D are italicized (**audio ex. 4.16**):

> You walk into the *roo*m,
> With your pencil in your *hand,*
> You see somebody *nak*ed and you
> Say "*Who* is *that* man?"
> You try so *hard*,
> But you don't under*stand*
> Just what you will say when *you get* home.

The refrain that follows ("Because something is happening here") departs from these two pitches, but the B/D toggle returns for each verse. It also saturates the bridge ("You have many contacts"), though here D and B switch roles: the higher pitch becomes a new, upper reciting tone. The intensification is apt, as here the lyrics reach a new plateau of contempt.

The minor third is an especially prominent interval in everyday speech, particularly in what Jeremy Day O'Connell calls "stylized interjections":

> The stylized interjection is a brief, attention-getting, but endearing (and, occasionally, mock-endearing) exclamation. It encompasses short- and long-distance calls (*yoo-hoo*; *dinner*), infant-directed formulas (*peek-a-boo*) and certain adult-directed derivatives (*bye-bye*), playground taunts (*nya-nya*), ad hoc group chants (*air-ball*), and various other playful exchanges (*uh-oh*).[38]

Imagine or say any of the italicized interjections, and you will hear a descending minor third. What is notable is that such minor-third interjections hover between speech and song in *everyday vocalizing*. That is, they are moments when everyday speech drifts toward song, when pitch contour takes on proto-musical importance. It should not surprise us, then, to find Dylan's voice also gravitating toward minor thirds when poised between speech and song, in the vicinity of node 3 on figure 4.3. But for Dylan, these minor thirds are rarely endearing, or even "mock-endearing." Rather, in his practice they often become stylized "hipster sneers," as Pete Dale and Adam Fairhall have argued.[39] They are closer to the schoolyard taunt, or the jeer of the hostile basketball crowd, now translated into a voice of untouchable, contemptuous cool.

The reader has likely noticed that the minor-third toggle in some ways resembles the syllable-emphatic style. Both involve a play of up and down that rides on the stress contours of everyday speech. The principal difference is that in the minor-third toggle, both pitches are defined, snugly attached to the music's underlying scale. In "Ballad of a Thin Man," for example, Dylan consistently sings scale degrees $\hat{1}$ and $\hat{3}$, the tonic and its minor third. Moreover, he generally holds and sustains these pitches. In the syllable-emphatic style, by contrast, Dylan's voice swoops and slides freely in pitch space, with little regard for scale degrees, tonics, and the like. Nevertheless, it is plausible—indeed, likely—that the syllable-emphatic style grew out of the earlier toggling chant, as a mannered intensification of it. **Figure 4.11** sketches one account of this development.

Consider these slightly whimsical line drawings in sequence. Beneath each of them, I have included a representative lyric from a song we've already studied: (a) "Subterranean Homesick Blues,"

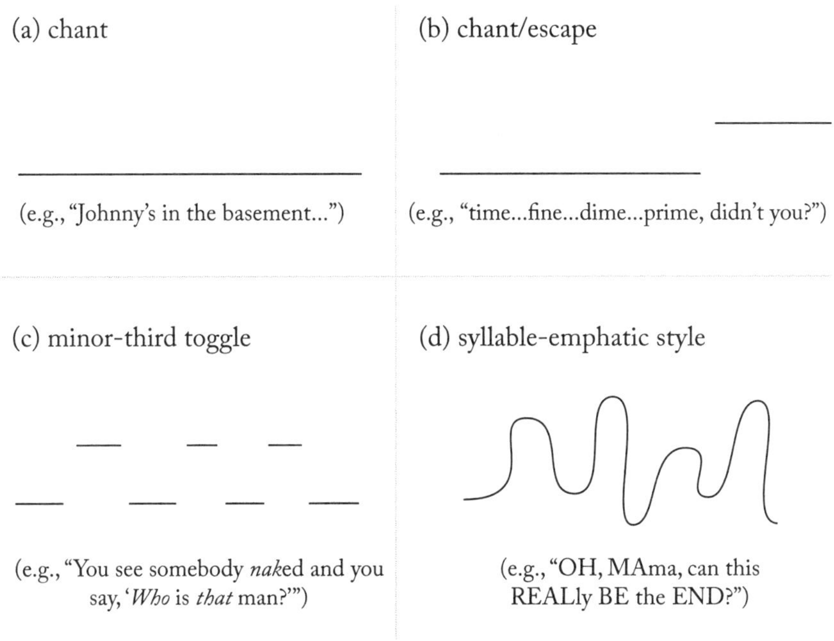

(a) chant

(e.g., "Johnny's in the basement...")

(b) chant/escape

(e.g., "time...fine...dime...prime, didn't you?")

(c) minor-third toggle

(e.g., "You see somebody *nak*ed and you say, '*Who* is *that* man?'")

(d) syllable-emphatic style

(e.g., "OH, MAma, can this REALly BE the END?")

FIGURE 4.11. Pitch contour from chant to the syllable-emphatic style.

(b) "Like a Rolling Stone," (c) "Ballad of a Thin Man", and (d) "Stuck Inside of Mobile with the Memphis Blues Again." We begin, at (a), in the flatlands of chant, with pitch held absolutely steady. The lyrics animate this pitch with syncopation and rhythmic verve, but do not depart significantly from it. With (b), the escape tone at line's end offers the first substantive departure from the reciting tone. A change in linguistic stuff—in this case, end rhyme—bumps the otherwise flat surface of the chant out of true. Such bumps multiply at (c), as various stressed words leave their mark in departures from the reciting tone. Finally, with (d), this syllable-emphatic speech energy becomes wild enough that it dents and bends musical pitch entirely out of shape. Sustained pitch is gone. Nothing remains flat.

* * *

Let's take stock. In this chapter, we have surveyed the speechward end of Dylan's vocal continuum, up through chant, where the balance begins—but just begins!—to tilt more songward. What big-picture conclusions can we draw thus far? First, Dylan's speechward delivery is remarkably diverse, ranging from droll talking blues to the mannered extravagance of the syllable-emphatic style. "Dylan can't sing," goes the familiar jab. But this chapter tells a different story. It tells of a Dylan who deploys his voice in an astonishing variety of ways, even when he's closer to speech than song. His speechward inflections are in fact a richly expressive resource. That they imperfect familiar musical values—conventional melody, sustained pitch, clean tone—is only as it should be for a songwriter whose commitment to the word looms so large. It should not surprise us that Dylan the poet often delivers his lyrics in a manner that emphasizes their wordiness. Moreover, as I wrote above, speech in song makes that wordiness even more palpable. If the sound of the voice recedes in everyday talk, gone as soon as we glean the speaker's meaning, speech in song returns the word to us in all its sonorous materiality. Heard against the musical background, spoken words regain their sonic texture, their heft, their peculiarity. As such, Dylan's speechward delivery turns up the volume on his poetry. His celebrated words are not in one ear and out the other when he speak-sings them. Rather, they lodge in our aural imaginations, resonating.

I wrote above that the mobility of the fringe between music and language in Dylan's voice "startles his words back to life." That is, as he nudges the fringe this way and that on the continuum, his words "flicker back to meaning." We heard that in "Talking World War III Blues," with his gentle shifts between metered and unmetered speech suggesting an entire physical world and the Chaplinesque tramp that inhabits it. We heard the process even more dramatically in the

1966 live version of "I Don't Believe You," whose lunging syllable-emphatic delivery utterly denatures the tidy tune of the studio album. This big nudge makes the words no longer an expression of a spurned lover's pique, but invests them with a new venom, weapons in Dylan's frontal assault on the censorious, slow-clapping folkies. We will hear more such examples of words startled into meaning in the next chapter, as melody comes to the fore, bending language ever more to *its* priorities.

Chapter 5 audio examples:
soundingbobdylan.com/ch5

CHAPTER FIVE

Words-Music (2)

Songward

In the previous chapter we explored the speechward side of Dylan's vocal continuum. We now begin to drift toward song, starting at node 4 on figure 4.3, where Dylan's voice edges improvisationally toward melody but stops just shy. To tune our ears to this style, we begin with a famous 1983 song.

NODE 4: CONTOUR-INVENTIVE STYLE

Question: What is the melody in the verse of "Jokerman"? Listen to the first verse, and you will give one answer. Listen to the second, another. Ditto for all later verses. **Figure 5.1** illustrates with verses one and two, which you can hear in **audio example 5.1**. The figure divides each verse into two parallel phrases, further parsing each of them into three subphrases, labeled A, B, and C.[1] Even those who don't read music should be able to follow the general contour of the melody, its play of rising and falling.[2] There are a couple ways to traverse the figure visually. The most obvious is to follow along while listening to audio example 5.1. Or, if you know the track well—as I suspect many readers do—you can simply recall it in your mind's ear while following the figure. As you listen to the song or play it back in memory, note the variety of melodic patterns. No two vocal gestures on the figure are exactly the same.

FIGURE 5.1. Inventive contour in the first two verses of "Jokerman," as sung on *Infidels* (1983).

Another way to read the figure is to compare the subphrases. This brings out the contrasts even more. For example, consider the four A subphrases. Each has its own contour. The first of them, in the first phrase of verse 1, is an old friend: the chant/escape. Dylan chants the opening words on B♭3 (which is $\hat{1}$ in the local key of B♭ major), before leaping up to D4 ($\hat{3}$) for the line-ending "bread."[3] The chanted portion is a lovely aural pun: Dylan's voice "stands" on the tonic pitch, just as he sings "standing on the water." As memorable as this opening chant/escape is, Dylan never again sings it on the studio recording. Every subsequent A subphrase differs. The next one ("Distant ships sailing into the mist") is the closest, but it begins with something new—a striking descent from two high pitches, F4 and D4, which I've marked with asterisks in the figure. These two pitches will become quite important as the recorded performance proceeds. At the outset of verse 2 ("So swiftly the sun sets in the sky"), we have something new again: a three-note descending scale, repeated. The final A subphrase in the figure, in verse 2, phrase 2 ("Fools rush in where angels fear to tread"), also consists of two descending figures. But now they are more widely spaced, Dylan's voice skipping rather than stepping. The second descending gesture ("angels fear to tread"), projects a motive I have labeled *y*. This resounds into the B subphrase, where Dylan sings it twice more, in pointed rhythm ("both of their futures so full of dread"). This differs from the three preceding B subphrases, which all involved some variant of quick melodic toggling between pitches a step apart. In phrase 2 of verse 2, by contrast, the *y* motive, headed by the striking F4 and D4, takes over.

Note that those two pitches proliferate over the course of the figure, all but saturating its final phrase, in the lower-right quadrant (look at the accumulating asterisks). A vocal impulse that Dylan first hits on with "Distant ships" thus comes to imbue much of the music that follows. This reaches its apotheosis in phrase 2 of verse 5, as **figure 5.2** and **audio example 5.2** show. Here the F4-then-D4 gesture saturates the A and B subphrases—a minor-third toggle with a vengeance. Dylan's vocal insistence on the toggle fits hand in glove with the lyrics, both in mood—urgent, alarmed—and in prosody, as the iterated strong-weak feet in the list of weapons make their mark on the pitch contour. Subphrase C then begins once more with the F4-then-D4 gesture, before cadencing on the B♭3 tonic ($\hat{1}$).[4]

In short, figures 5.1 and 5.2 show a vocal line whose pitch contour constantly morphs. This is most pronounced in the verses of the song, but the prechorus and chorus show their own variations. Every melismatic "Oh!" before the last "Jokerman!" of the chorus differs from the others, in ways subtle and not so subtle. The main body of the chorus ("Jokerman dance to the nightingale tune / Bird fly high by the light of the moon") is more fixed, but even here Dylan can't help but mess with the contour eventually. **Figure 5.3** and **audio example 5.3** illustrate. Figure 5.3(a) sketches the repeated melodic figure that Dylan usually sings for these two lines: a descent from F4 to B♭3, with an ornamental, stepwise toggle on the way down. But in verse 5, shown in 5.3(b), he completely abstracts this contour for the second line ("Bird fly high . . ."). Now he simply leaps directly from F4 to B♭3, iterating the gesture three times, in even note values. Michael Gray speaks admiringly of Dylan "moronising" his delivery in one of the versions of "Caribbean Wind."[5] Though Gray states that this is the only Dylan recording with such a voice, the "Bird fly high" line from the fifth verse of "Jokerman" is arguably another example, with its delectably "moronic" sing-song, a contrast to the florid, ecstatic melismas that always follow the line. As if to compensate for this

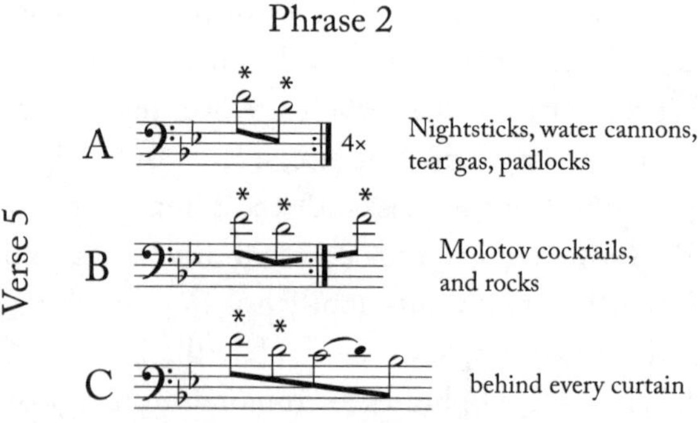

FIGURE 5.2. Further variants in the fifth verse of "Jokerman," as sung on *Infidels*.

transgression against the joyous chorus, the next time it rolls around, shown in figure 5.3(c), the florid contours of the "Oh!" melisma find their way into "Bird fly high" line itself. It is the euphoric climax of the performance, its final vocal achievement.

It should be clear by now why I call this the "contour-inventive style." Dylan's vocal contours across the song change constantly. In answer to the question that began this section, there *is* no fixed melody to the verse of "Jokerman." Dylan invents new melodic lines in each verse, pitch contours emerging flexibly from the stress patterns of his words but falling now into vocal lines more melodically elaborate than chant or its variants. These melodic lines *move*, but in ever-novel ways. Such protean melodic invention is apt in "Jokerman," whose chorus celebrates instinctive melody in the form of the "nightingale tune."

But the technique is far from unique to this song. It has especially flourished on stage. Beginning with his return to touring in 1974, as Dylan sought to reanimate a '60s catalog that at times felt burdensome and distant, he departed more and more from his songs' original melodies. By the time of the Never-Ending Tour, begun in 1988, the contour-inventive style had come into its own. In this era,

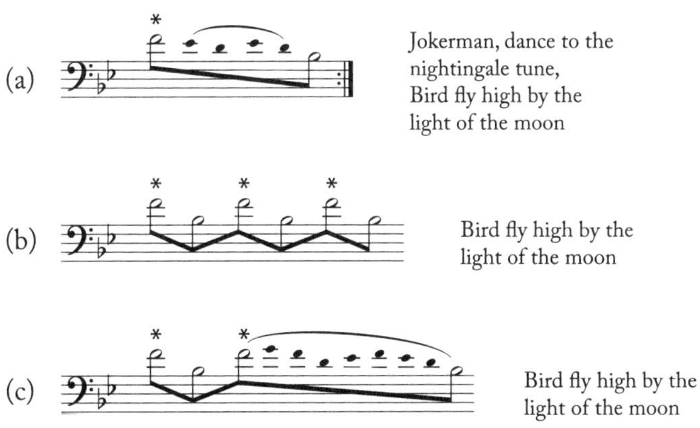

FIGURE 5.3. "Jokerman" chorus (a) as usually sung, plus variants in (b) the fifth and (c) the sixth choruses of the 1983 studio version.

he almost never sings the song's original melody, instead shuttling between newly invented melodic fragments and nodes 1–3 of figure 4.3. As one example, let's return to the 2002 performance of "Mr. Tambourine Man" at Aspen, a portion of which we encountered in audio example 4.15 and figure 4.10. That excerpt was all upsinging, but he does not upsing the entire song. At various points he conjures new melodic phrases, like a magician pulling a rabbit out of a hat. **Audio example 5.4** includes the first and third choruses, which bookend the upsung second chorus of audio example 4.15. As **figure 5.4** shows, both choruses begin with chant on C4 (middle C) for the opening "Hey, Mr. Tambourine Man," but they then diverge for two new melodic variants. In chorus 1, Dylan descends, leaning on the perfect fifth G3–C3 (at "song for me"). In chorus 3, he remains in the upper register, producing a scale that descends from E4 to A3. In each case he sings the variant in question for both iterations of the chorus, allowing us to hear each one twice.

Once Dylan has settled on a new melodic invention, he will often repeat it in just this way. As such, the contour-inventive style often consists of a series of vocal "riffs." A riff is a short musical gesture that is typically repeated.[6] Usually the term refers to an accompanimental figure, not a sung one. Think, for example, of the repeated blues riff in the guitar and bass that underpins the 2012 song "Early Roman Kings," already well known from tunes like Muddy Waters's "Mannish Boy" and Bo Diddley's "I'm a Man." This is a classic instrumental riff—a repetitive groove bed for the voice. But in

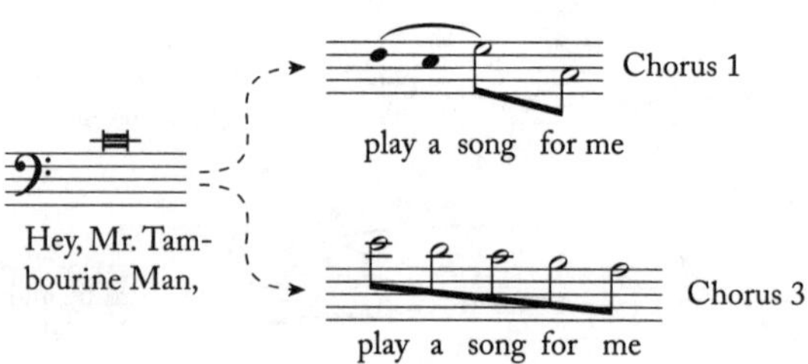

FIGURE 5.4. Contour variants in the first and third choruses of "Mr. Tambourine Man," as sung in Aspen, Colorado, September 1, 2002.

Dylan's contour-inventive singing, his *voice* also occasionally projects riffs, settling on a melodic figure and repeating it several times before moving on to the next melodic idea. Consider **audio example 5.5**, which presents two excerpts from a Halloween 1999 performance of "It's Alright, Ma" in Chicago. **Figure 5.5(a)** shows the modified chant/escape that he inhabits for much of the song. It is modified in that Dylan moves between two reciting tones, one of them a striking blue seventh (F♮). At times his line shades into a minor-third toggle, with bluesy alternation between G and B♭. His singing of the figure is drawling and wry, shot through with seen-it-all-before cynicism. All of which makes the change in tone and musical material in verse 7 that much more striking. At "Advertising signs, they con you," he leaves the chant/escape behind and switches to the descending four-note blues tetrachord shown in **figure 5.5(b)**, which he sings no fewer than eight times.[7] Dylan's voice comes alive here, his pointed repetitions projecting the iterative banality of mass consumer culture and the advertising that drives it. This is a vocal riff if ever there was one, and it gets the audience's attention; they respond with the loudest cheer in the song.

An altogether more peculiar example of vocal riffing occurs in a 2011 "Desolation Row" from Bethel Woods Center for the Arts in New York. **Audio example 5.6** excerpts verse 5, which contains two vocal riffs.[8] The first, transcribed in **figure 5.6(a)**, is a resonant descent into the vocal depths, which Dylan sings in ostentatiously even rhythm. He follows this with the new riff of **figure 5.6(b)**, a stuttering motive on G3 and A3, which he sings a whopping twenty-two times. Such obstinate repetition is a common technique in Dylan's

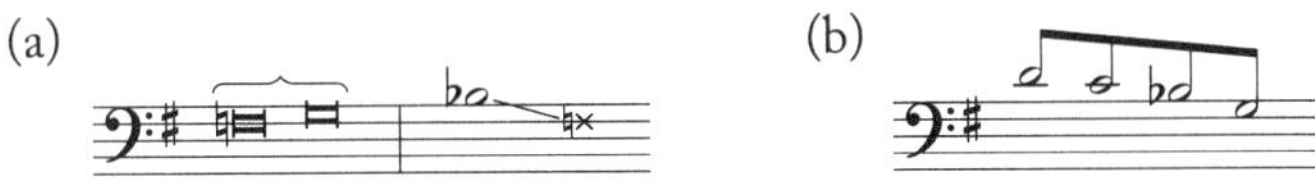

FIGURE 5.5. Contour invention in "It's Alright, Ma," Chicago, October 31, 1999: (a) modified chant/escape used in many lines (bracketed pitches are reciting tones); (b) descending blues tetrachord in verse 7 ("Advertising signs, they con you").

live singing and playing, especially later in his career. Musicians in fact use the word "ostinato," Italian for obstinate, for just such moments. These vocal ostinati unfailingly get the crowd's attention, as in the moment from "It's Alright, Ma" in Chicago twelve years earlier. Here as there, the crowd in Bethel responds to the ostinato with a rousing cheer.

It is worth pausing over a distinction between these two examples. Both musical gestures in figure 5.5, from the 1999 "It's Alright, Ma," strongly evoke the blues, which inevitably bring with them a whole host of cultural associations regarding race, systemic oppression, resilience, the liberatory potential of Black sound, its cooptation by white singers, and much else.[9] By contrast, the two riffs from the 2011 "Desolation Row" in figure 5.6 are more generically puzzling. If anything, 5.6(a) seems incongruously operatic, the kind of thing sung by a comic bass; if you know Mozart's *Don Giovanni*, you can probably imagine it coming out of Leporello's mouth. That's weird enough, but 5.6(b) is quite literally sui generis. I know of nothing like this stuttering figure in popular song, especially repeated at this length. Here a distinction drawn by Richard Middleton between "overcoding" and "undercoding" in popular music is useful.[10] Overcoded music is saturated with conventional musical configurations ("codes") that call to mind a certain genre, say the blues. Undercoded music is short on such familiar musical stuff—it is raw musical material, hard to fit into a genre or style. That much of Dylan's singing is generically overcoded should come as no surprise, given how much American vernacular music he has metabolized. Folk, country, blues, rock 'n' roll,

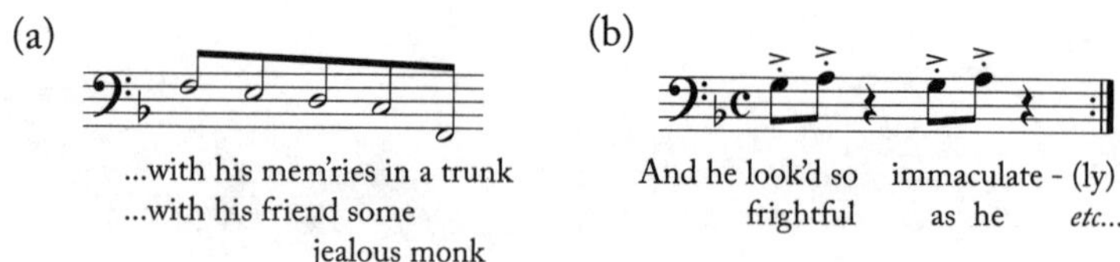

FIGURE 5.6. Two riffs in verse 5 of "Desolation Row," Bethel, New York, August 12, 2011.

Tin Pan Alley, parlor song—all jostle for prominence in his singing and playing over the years. But at times, as in the 2011 "Desolation Row," his late-career contour-inventive singing seems to leave generic codes behind altogether. We struggle to make sense of these undercoded gestures and puzzle at their meaning.

And yet the crowd cheers. Why? What moves fans in these moments of ornery, undercoded repetition? It would be foolish to answer for all in attendance. Crowd dynamics are complex things, and we should not interpret a cheer as a sign of unanimity. For every transported witness there was surely at least one other who was quietly befuddled. The befuddlement is pretty easy to understand. But what about the transport? Any answer must be provisional, but I suspect it might have something to do with the prominence such moments give to Dylan's sounding voice, over and against the meaning of the words. Thinking of our three terms from chapter 1, sound and body are ascendant, while semantic meaning is attenuated. This squares pretty well with how I, at least, experience such moments. I find it hard, for example, to focus on Dylan's lyrics in the fifth verse of the 2011 "Desolation Row," so distracted am I by his puzzling melodic inventions. I can't quite dial in the surreal wit of the lyric. There is humor and invention in his singing, to be sure, but I find it hard to line it up with lyrical meaning. As writer and astute Dylan fan Adam Selzer puts it, in this era it often "seemed as though he wasn't really thinking about the words he was singing so much as he was thinking about the noise they made."[11]

And yet there's that cheer. What to make of it? Maybe this surge of excitement arises from the way Dylan's singing in such moment foregrounds his sounding body, inventing on the spot before listeners' very ears. The fringe of contact between voice and language is especially palpable in these moments. As the meaning of the words retreats, Dylan's sounding body—in all of its idiosyncrasy—becomes more present. The result is a sense of co-presence. As one fan wrote in a review of a 2023 show in Chicago, "it is breathtaking thinking you are in the same room, same space, twenty feet away from Bob Dylan."[12] In that mindset, when Dylan begins to experiment vocally, his puzzling new melodies taking center stage, fans may well sense a heightening of that presence: "I'm in the same space as Bob Dylan, and he's doing something surprising. He's here with me, inventing." His voice, in all its novelty, confirms his attentive co-presence. If lyrical meaning recedes momentarily, it is perhaps a small price to pay.

NODE 5: CONVENTIONAL MELODY

Contour-inventive vocal lines approach the condition of melody without quite stepping across the threshold. We'll consider that threshold—between melody and its absence—more below. But first, let's turn to one of Dylan's best-behaved tunes. **Figure 5.7** presents an analytical sketch of the melody for "Make You Feel My Love," from 1997's *Time Out of Mind.* The song is in a thirty-two-bar AABA form, the norm for a great many Tin Pan Alley standards. This foreshadows a surprising turn that Dylan's musicking would take in the new millennium, when he would record three albums dedicated exclusively to tunes from the Great American Songbook.[13] "Make You Feel My Love" is an early essay in the style. As the labels on the left edge of the figure indicate, the music for A is in the first line, B in the second. **Audio example 5.7** includes the first instance of each in the song. I will sometimes refer to B as the bridge, following Tin Pan Alley practice. I have labeled each subphrase with lowercase letters for ease of reference. Note that subphrase (e) occurs twice in the bridge; to reduce clutter, I have not renotated it.

The A phrase is a model of melodic etiquette. Subphrases (a), (b), and (c) are motivically related: an initial turning figure followed by a leap down. These are followed by the cadential subphrase (d), which contrasts motivically. But it also completes a process begun with subphrase (a). As the upstemmed, open noteheads show, the phrase also embeds a long-range melody.[14] The notes before each downward leap trace out a descending scale: A♭ (in)—G♭ (on)—F (warm)—E♭ (feel)—D♭ (my love). And this is not just any descending scale. It ends on the tonic scale degree, the musical home base, $\hat{1}$.[15] It thus brings melodic closure to the line at the very moment

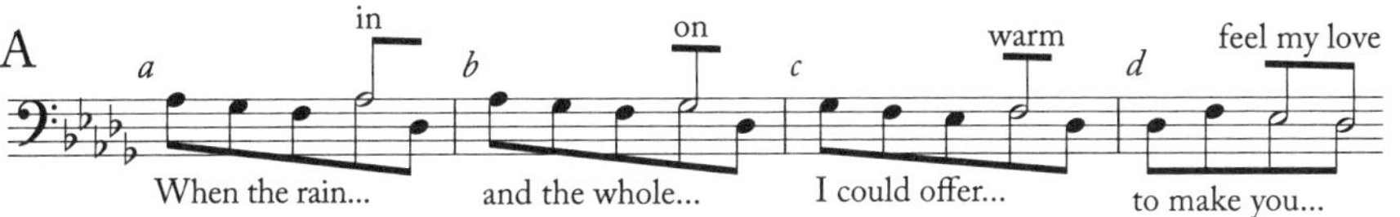

FIGURE 5.7. Melodic analysis of "Make You Feel My Love," from *Time Out of Mind* (1997).

that we hear the refrain. The chords also return to the tonic here, supporting the melody with harmonic closure. The bridge (B) is more wide ranging, spanning an octave rather than a fifth. But the two cadential subphrases—(f) and (g)—offer another stepwise connection, the F of "wrong" descending a step to the E♭ at the second syllable of "belong." The latter is *not* the tonic, but $\hat{2}$, which creates a sense of incompletion. Music theorists would call this a half cadence. The bridge's unfinished business is then finished when the following A phrase concludes, rounding out the AABA structure. The lyrics promise secure emotional attachment and the music delivers: there is never any doubt that the melody will end well. The vicissitudes of life—rain in your face, people on your case—are gently cushioned in the warm embrace of an assured melodic descent.

No wonder many Dylan fans don't like the song. Not only are the sentiments conventional, the musical means are too. But outside high-church Dylan fandom, the song has many devotees, Adele first among them. Indeed, it is the second most-covered songs of his entire catalog, topped only by "Blowin' in the Wind."[16] And can that be any accident? Here is a tune that a polished singer can navigate with ease and flair. One can't say the same of speaking song such as "Long and Wasted Years."[17] Dylan at his most melodically well mannered is Dylan at his most coverable.

But what does it mean to call this tune "melodically well mannered"? Indeed, what does it mean to identify something as a "conventional melody" at all? Why aren't Dylan's vocal improvisations in the contour-inventive style also melodies? What about the various subtypes of chant? It all depends on how one defines melody. And defining it is no easy task, as generations of music theorists have found.[18] This is not the place to get deep into those weeds, nor do we need to. Instead, I propose a quick-and-dirty heuristic definition of "conventional melody" for present purposes: A conventional melody is a vocal line that makes good sense when played by an instrument. This may at first seem far too simplistic, but bear with me. It is a surprisingly useful formulation. Try it out yourself. Imagine a Dylan song you know well. Now ask if the vocal line would make sense played by a melodic instrument. If it does, Dylan is singing a conventional melody. If not, he is somewhere leftward of node 5 on figure 4.3.

Let's do a few together, starting with the example nearest to hand: "Make You Feel My Love." Imagine the vocal line played by a cello.[19] It passes the test with flying colors. The melody is shapely and clear. It has a structural integrity independent of the words. The long-range linear descent, upstemmed in the first line of figure 5.7, gives an overall direction, while the motivic repetitions create coherence through varied repetition. The tune may well still strike some readers as maudlin, but one cannot argue with its shapeliness. Now consider "Memphis Blues Again." Can you imagine, say, a saxophone playing Dylan's syllable-emphatic vocal part? The result would be bizarre at best, even comical. The sax player would struggle right out of the gate in picking specific notes to correspond to Dylan's swooping speech-song. And even if the player could find those notes, the result could not but recall Dylan's sung part. The only way to make sense of it would be to hear Dylan's voice in one's head simultaneously. For anyone who had never heard the original, the result would be nonsense. This is an extreme case, though. What about a song whose vocal part has clearer pitches, say the studio version of "Tangled Up in Blue" that opens *Blood on the Tracks*? The verse is a modified chant, toggling between two pitches: C♯4 and B3. This would be trivially easy for our saxophonist to play.

But would it be a melody? Without the words, the pitch material is paltry. The tune, such as it is, goes nowhere. Not, that is, until the line breaks out at "I was standin' on the side of the road / Rain fallin' on my shoes." Now both voice and harmony begin to move—aptly, given the lyric's turn here to Kerouac-style *On the Road* imagery.[20] This part would sit well on a saxophone or a fiddle. But those same players would have a hard time selling *whole* the vocal line as a legit melody.

One sign of a legit melody is the occasional mismatch between melodic and prosodic emphasis, discussed above in connection with the example from Sondheim and Bernstein's "Somewhere." Such mismatches do indeed pop up in Dylan's conventionally melodic numbers. Indeed, there's one right at the outset of "Make You Feel My Love." The melodic contour leaps up right at the word "in" on the first line, rendering it "When the rain is blowing *in* your face." Most speakers, in most contexts, would likely emphasize "rain" and "face" instead. But the motivic shape that the melody will repeat throughout the phrase insists on giving "in" contour emphasis here. Melody wins. Or consider "With God on Our Side," whose tune is based on "The Patriot Game" by Dominic Behan.[21] Dylan traverses the tune's rangy contours with bounding confidence, most of his words fitting well with the melody's accent patterns. But there is friction at a couple points, for example at the beginning of verse 5: "Oh the Spanish *Aayy*-merican War had its day." Again, a melodic apex falls infelicitously, throwing stress onto the first syllable of "American."[22] Here, once more, is a tussle between music and language. But now melody is in the driver's seat, imperfecting language's everyday stress patterns.

Dylan's borrowing of Behan's tune here recalls a 2003 interview, in which he disavows his melodic gifts:

> "Well, you have to understand that I'm not a melodist," he says. "My songs are either based on old Protestant hymns or Carter Family songs or variations of the blues form."
>
> "What happens is, I'll take a song I know and simply start playing it in my head. That's the way I meditate. . . . At a certain point some of the words will change and I'll start writing a song."[23]

There is much to notice here, but for now I am most interested his claim that he is "not a melodist." It is clear what he means in context, that he often borrows melodies rather than composing them from scratch. But even here, he sells his melodic gifts short. As I mentioned in chapter 1, note 4, though Dylan based the tune for "The Times They Are a-Changin'" on the traditional hymn "Deliverance Will Come," he made telling changes to it, which fit both the sound and sense of his words. The same is true of "With God on Our Side," which departs from Behan's tune in various ways. Other melodically ambitious songs, from "The Lonesome Death of Hattie Carroll" (1964) to "Mother of Muses" (2020), have no known melodic antecedents.

Whatever he says about himself as a melodist, Dylan is also well aware that many of his tunes, borrowed or not, stand on their own, as melodies:

> For sure my lyrics had struck nerves that had never been struck before, but if my songs were just about the words, then what was Duane Eddy, the great rock-and-roll guitarist, doing recording an album full of instrumental melodies of my songs? Musicians have always known that my songs were about more than just words, but most people are not musicians.[24]

The album in question, 1965's *Duane Eddy Does Bob Dylan*, includes eight early Dylan songs, among them "Don't Think Twice," "It Ain't Me, Babe," and "Mr. Tambourine Man," along with a few non-Dylan tracks. The album's a hoot, but it's also instructive. Eddy plays the melodies in the lower register, making ample use of the tremolo bar, in his twangy proto-surf style. The songs are immediately recognizable by their melodies, which cohere beautifully without the songs' lyrics, even when Eddy's tremolo technique is at its most exaggerated.

Dylan himself would follow Eddy's example for his 1978 tour, beginning each concert with an instrumental version of one of his songs. At the tour's outset, in Japan and Australia, it was "Hard Rain," the subject of the final section of this book. Halfway through the European leg it became "My Back Pages." For both songs, guitarist

Steven Soles first plays the tune on a capo-ed acoustic, before saxophonist Steve Douglas takes over. The band begins the song before Dylan comes out on stage. One can always tell when he emerges by a cheer on the tape, as though the musicians melodically conjure him. "My Back Pages" is especially inspired for this purpose, as it is a tune that at once stands on its own and that aptly gestures toward the "Back Pages"—that is, early songs—that will dominate the setlist to come. It is a wonderfully ambivalent gesture, given that the song's lyrics repudiate his earliest, "finger-pointing" material ("I was so much older then / I'm younger than that now"). The fabled voice of a generation is not yet singing, but the melody already signifies, heavy with irony.

The most melodic periods of Dylan's singing bookend his career. His early catalog is rife with ear-catching melodies, some adapted from existing tunes, others wholly invented. A half century later, in the mid-2010s, conventional melody once again moved front and center, as a result of his turn toward the Great American Songbook, via Sinatra. On the albums dedicated to this repertory—*Shadows in the Night* (2015), *Fallen Angels* (2016), and *Triplicate* (2017)—Dylan hews to the composed melody with great care, choosing each melodic foothold with caution. He is generally *less* adventurous in his phrasing in this music than is the supple, conversational Sinatra, to say nothing of the breathtakingly agile Ella Fitzgerald, or the devil-may-care Sarah Vaughan. Dylan does not have these singers' technique. As a result, he gingerly steps through the notated melody like a climber carefully choosing footholds, never venturing from the route.

As a result of this exercise in melodic discipline, Dylan's singing of his own material changed in the years following the Sinatra albums. This was evident in concert and even more so on *Shadow Kingdom*, first released as a black-and-white performance film in 2021 and then on album in 2023.[25] The film and album are subtitled *The Early Songs of Bob Dylan*, which puzzled some commentators, as the earliest track ("It's All Over Now, Baby Blue") dates from 1965, four prolific years into Dylan's career, and the latest comes twenty-four years later (1989's "What Was It You Wanted"). Whatever the meaning of "early," the recording gave fans a chance once again to measure the distance between today's Dylan and yesterday's.

What they heard was more melody. **Figure 5.8** and **audio example 5.8** present three examples. "Most Likely You Go Your Way (and I'll Go Mine)" was a classic syllable-emphatic song on *Blonde on Blonde*. On *Shadow Kingdom*, as shown at (a), Dylan outfits the vocal part with a three-note melodic riff, doubled by the accordion. This acts as

(a)

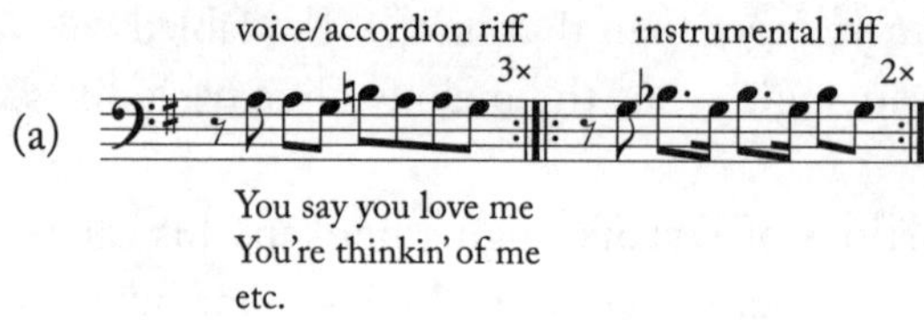

(b)

a The sweet, pretty things...
b The city fathers...
a The reincarnation...
c But the town...

(c)

FIGURE 5.8. Three of the new melodies on *Shadow Kingdom* (2021): (a) "Most Likely You Go Your Way (and I'll Go Mine)"; (b) "Tombstone Blues"; (c) "Queen Jane Approximately."

a partner to the instrumental riff that abuts the sung phrases, already familiar from the original version. The vocal riff is admittedly not much of a melody, but the accordion doubling at least satisfies our definition. And Dylan's care in settling on its three pitches—G3, A3, and B3—is in marked contrast to the syllable-emphatic swooping of the 1966 recording.

More melodically expansive is the reworking of "Tombstone Blues," shown at **figure 5.8(b)**. On *Highway 61 Revisited*, this was an archetypal chant-based number, Dylan's voice drilling away at one pitch. Now, as shown in the figure, he ranges across an entire octave, from B♭2 to B♭3. In between those pitches, Dylan traverses a bluesy minor-pentatonic collection. In subsequent verses, he shuffles and varies the melodic modules, resulting in a vocal line that at times has hints of the contour-inventive style, all in free-time declamation. We get a genuine, closed melody with "Queen Jane Approximately." This was originally another chant-dominated song on *Highway 61 Revisited*. No longer. As shown at **5.8(c)**, the Dylan of 2021 sings shapely arcs for each phrase, picking his phrase-ending pitches especially carefully. These pitches, shown in open notcheads, link up with ending pitches in neighboring phrases to create an overall melodic progression from F♯3 down to D3, which arrives with the second iteration of "Won't you, come see me, Queen Jane?" Dylan subtly varies the melody in each subsequent verse, but the overall shape remains, as does the tone of tender empathy, a far cry from the exultant, bounding original.

The newly melodic Dylan caresses words differently. Listen, for example, to the way he sings "tired" in the first verse: it droops down a fifth from A3 to D3, his weathered voice conveying a lifetime of weariness. It is, on the one hand, a moment of genuine compassion for the song's second-person addressee, Queen Jane.[26] But there's additional pathos in the line. "You're tired of yourself and all of your creations," sings the eighty-year-old musician, ruefully. Could anyone blame him if he was?

THE IMPERFECT FRINGE REVISITED

Such an interpretation of the line runs counter to an idea I floated in the introduction. There, I suggested that Dylan's countless, nested repetitions across his career—for example, performing the same song night after night, year after year, decade after decade—were strategic. Such repetitions are occasions for change imperfection, for proliferating difference: the same song but with a new groove, a new genre, a new melody. In this understanding, Dylan doesn't change songs because he is bored—tired of himself and all of his creations—but because repetition with a difference is his musical way of being. Of course, both could be true in some measure, and it would stand to reason that by 2021 the strategy of change imperfection might be wearing thin. Nearly fifty-six years after he recorded "Queen Jane Approximately" the call to "make it new" could well feel less like a modernist rallying cry and more like a mission-critical strategy for artistic survival.

If so, Dylan could hardly do better than to continue worrying the fringe of contact between music and language. For that fringe is a renewable resource for producing both species of generative imperfection discussed in the introduction: flaw imperfection and change imperfection. As for flaw imperfection, throughout the last two chapters we have encountered examples in in which the residues of speech disrupt the smooth functioning of melody, or—conversely—in which music bends language to fit its contours. Dylan himself has spoken about this tussle between words and music. In a 1964 *New Yorker* interview with Nat Hentoff, he stated:

> It's hard being free in a song—getting it all in. Songs are so confining. Woody Guthrie told me once that songs don't have to rhyme—they don't have to do anything like that. But it's not true. A song has to have some kind of form to fit into the music. You can bend the words and the meter, but it still has to fit somehow. I've been getting freer in the songs I write, but I still feel confined.[27]

Dylan speaks of the words-music relationship here as one of confinement, of mutual limitation—especially of music limiting words.

He goes on to state that he is turning his attention more toward poetry and prose than songwriting. But with his book *Tarantula*, written across the next two years, he would learn the limitations of his particular approach to the word without the friction of music to hold it in check.[28] Put in the present chapter's terms, the pressures or frictions to be found at the fringe of contact between music and language—the two pushing on and bending each other—produce Dylan's best work.

As I wrote in chapter 4, the wavering site of contact between words and music is a place where old words can "flicker back into meaning." We have just heard one such moment, in the caressed "tired" of the 2021 "Queen Jane." Dylan's newly melodic delivery invests that word with a pathos absent from the studio recording. Or consider the version of "It's All Right, Ma" from Halloween 1999, with the repeated blues tetrachord sounding the numbing iterations of late capitalism. Again, old words signify afresh as Dylan shifts the thrumming contact point between words and music. But this is not only a matter of difference in repetition as Dylan repeats a song across days and years. Shifts on figure 4.3 can startle words to life even *within* a single performance of a song. Consider one of Dylan's most virtuosic midcareer vocal performances: "Brownsville Girl," from 1986. He spends much of the song in the vicinity of node 1 and leftward on figure 4.3, delivering the lyrics' shaggy-dog story (co-written with Sam Shepard) in a bemused speaking voice. But at various points he dashes rightward—songward. Indeed, across the performance he will inhabit nearly every station on figure 4.3.

The chorus contains the most conventionally melodic delivery, from both Dylan and his background singers. As for the verses, **audio example 5.9** provides a representative excerpt. Heightened speech is the default, but at moments he moves from this into contour-inventive terrain, for example, at "As the dying gunfighter lay in the sun and gasped for his last breath." One almost doesn't notice the shift to improvised song here, so smooth is Dylan's transition. But it invests the line with emotional intensity, signaling a shift in register from the humorous befuddlement of the narration up until now. The stakes are higher than we thought. The following line—"Turn him LOOSE, let him GO!"—is pure syllable-emphatic style. It strikes the ear that much more forcefully for following the musically pitched, contour-inventive line that preceded it. The entire performance is saturated with such quicksilver nudges of the word-music fringe, which infuse the lyrics with life, wit, and mystery.

The folksinger Will Oldham, a.k.a. Bonnie "Prince" Billy, sensed this too, stating that "the song is concrete, cathartic and epic, humorous and charming. It rolls across unmapped territories and hints at a way of realizing musical ideas that has yet to be pursued since by anyone, anywhere, including by Bob Dylan."[29] This new "way of realizing musical ideas" also makes it one of the hardest Dylan songs to cover, as Billy knows—he is one of the few to have done it.[30] If the melodic Dylan is the most easily coverable, the mobile Dylan, shuttling constantly between speech and song, is at the other extreme. For what is one to do? Imitate him inflection for inflection? Sing throughout? Nudge the fringe in new ways? Billy opts largely for option two, singing over an arrangement that matches Dylan's closely.[31] It is a brave, even moving performance, but if one knows the original recording well, it is hard not to hear it behind Billy's singing. The perspicuous physicality of Dylan's voice sticks tenaciously to these words. Perhaps that is because the performance is such a potent reminder of the stubborn particularity of his voice, and of the encounter that it stages and restages between word and music, mutually imperfecting one another to the last.

PART II
Playing

Chapter 6 audio and video examples:
soundingbobdylan.com/ch6

CHAPTER SIX

Guitar

Sound and Symbol

GUITARS SEEN AND HEARD (NEWPORT '65, PART 1)

Let's start with some famous footage. **Video example 6.1** shows the beginning of Dylan's electric performance at the Newport Folk Festival on July 25, 1965, as shot by Murray Lerner for his film *Festival!* We see Dylan in a leather jacket and button-down shirt, strumming his Stratocaster in the spotlight as "Maggie's Farm" begins. Mike Bloomfield, in the shadows to Dylan's right (our left), plays distorted blues licks on his Telecaster, bending the strings furiously. Lerner's camera focuses almost exclusively on Dylan, the other players largely lost in the dark or outside of the frame. This directs our focus—the camera chooses what we can see—but one imagines it replicates the focus of most attendees relatively faithfully. All eyes were on Dylan, in the bright spotlight.

But is that where all of the *ears* were? When it came to the two Fender guitars being played, very likely not. As reproduced in Lerner's film and on circulating recordings, Dylan's strumming is only the faintest shimmer in the texture, entirely overwhelmed by

Bloomfield's fatter, distorted sound, especially during the latter's solo breaks. To be sure, the sound that night was famously bad; by most accounts this was at least one cause of the booing.[1] So we should be careful not to take the circulating recordings as faithful representations of how the music struck every listener's ears that day. All the same, the overpowering volume of Bloomfield's guitar is borne out by several firsthand reports. Eric Von Schmidt, for example, said that "Bloomfield was out to kill. He had his guitar turned up as loud as he could possibly turn it up, and he was playing as many notes as he could possibly play."[2] This, coupled with the circulating audio, strongly suggests that fans saw Dylan's guitar, but heard Bloomfield's.

Here, then, is one of the great ironies of Dylan's electric turn. The electric guitar, that famous noisemaker, makes very little noise in Dylan's hands. The Stratocaster around his neck at Newport was more symbol than sound. But it was a *potent* symbol. For many fans in attendance, the stakes were clear. The acoustic guitar equaled folk music and all that it entailed: resistance to mainstream culture, commitment to the civil rights movement and other Left causes, a connection to deep tradition, and—often—a kind of coffeehouse-intellectual connoisseurship. The electric guitar, by contrast, equaled rock 'n' roll, and all that *it* entailed: capitulation to the market, teen culture, frivolous partying, sex, and the technologies of our fallen world. This is why the apocryphal anecdote about Pete Seeger wishing to cut the cord with an axe rings so true, and likely why it has stuck so tenaciously to the story all these decades later. The axe is a good, honest, working-class tool of premodern origin. What better implement to sever the tie to the thrumming electric grid, and with it all the ills of the modern world?[3]

But Seeger *didn't* cut the cord, leaving one guitar on stage—Bloomfield's, not Dylan's—making a great noise. That noise reordered the physical and social space of the festival. For the sheer volume of Bloomfield's guitar forced a change in the dynamic between performer and listener, violating certain cherished ideals of the folk revival. As Steve Waksman notes, within the revival,

> acoustic instruments were valued for the intimacy they promoted as people gathered around to hear the musician. An acoustic guitar was just loud enough to make music, but not so loud as to drown out the voice of the singer, or of any in the audience who wanted to sing along. An electric guitar, by contrast, made too much noise, and in so doing converted an audience comprised of individuals into a mass whose attention was overwhelmed by the sound of it all.[4]

The folk revivalists were fundamentally committed to a participatory model of music making.[5] Think not only of the many Newport attendees playing together in fields or at various locations around town (Lerner's documentary includes some choice footage), but also of Seeger's ceaseless efforts, at Newport and beyond, to lower the boundary between performer and audience by insisting that the audience sing along. Participatory performance not only offered a nonhierarchical model of collective musicking, it also enacted the ideal of the collective *as such*, a dream of the New Left. By contrast, the electric instruments Dylan assembled onstage at Newport that Sunday night made such participatory musicking impossible by their sheer volume. In the face of such volume, the audience became a mere spectating mass. The wall of poorly amplified sound—of which Dylan's Stratocaster was only a negligible part—sundered performer from audience. The politics of refusal, the rejection of deeply held folk-revival values, could not have been more legible. In that context, the first line out of Dylan's mouth that night ("I ain't gonna work on Maggie's farm no more") seems almost redundant.

This chapter explores the tension between sound and symbol in Dylan's guitar playing. I argue that the familiar electric-vs.-acoustic tale of Dylan lore oversimplifies a much more complex story, one in which the guitar signifies *both* as a symbol and as a noisemaker, often in contradictory ways. This is true of Dylan's playing on both acoustic and electric, as we will hear in a moment. First, though, it will be useful to pause over some crucial terms.

GENRES, GUITARS, AND RACE

I've mentioned quite a few genres in this book so far: folk, rock, country, blues, rock 'n' roll, and so on. I mention a few more below. Each time, I do so hoping that you'll know what I mean by the terms. This is often how genre labels work, as a kind of shorthand, not only for certain kinds of musical sounds, but for the social groups that produce and consume those sounds. But one can never be sure if the reader has the same understanding of a genre as the author. Thus, as we survey Dylan's various guitar styles, each of which comes trailing a raced and classed genre history, I will do my best to specify my understanding of the characteristics and histories of the genres we encounter.

Genre is complex. I outline here a capacious understanding of the concept, drawing on several prominent scholars, including David Brackett, Charles Kronengold, Jennifer C. Lena, and Eric Drott.[6] Though there are crucial distinctions between these authors' approaches, all agree that musical genre involves far more than musical details. Genres are mutable social phenomena that are as much about configurations of people as they are about configurations of sounds. They involve local communities of practice as well as institutions large and small. Their affiliations with specific raced populations are strongly reinforced by the music industry, radio formats, record labels, and marketing practices. All of this combines to make genre histories inseparable from the histories of the people who predominantly make and consume the music. The Chicago urban blues, for example, is a music of the urban Black working class, the sound of musicians who relocated to Chicago during the Great Migration. They brought with them the musical traditions of the southern, rural blues but modified them—through amplification and a host of smaller performance details—to suit noisy urban performance spaces like bars and clubs. Then labels like Chess Records recorded and marketed the resulting sounds to Black consumers, who heard them either direct from vinyl or over the airwaves.

And yet genres are not racially or demographically exclusive. White folks could also consume urban blues, and even perform it, as

Mike Bloomfield and harmonica player Paul Butterfield did. Bloomfield hailed from the wealthy northern Chicago suburb of Glencoe, while Butterfield grew up in Hyde Park on the South Side (where I live and work, incidentally). Both developed an early fascination with urban blues, from recordings as well as from regular visits to clubs. They were soon playing the music themselves with virtuosic gusto, occasionally even sitting in with such luminaries as Howlin' Wolf, Muddy Waters, Little Walter, and Otis Rush. But if genres are not racially exclusive, neither do they float free of race and class, as neutral spaces in which anyone can participate equally. That white musicians like Bloomfield and Butterfield could tune into R&B radio or enter South Side blues clubs does not negate the fact that the urban blues was still predominantly a Black genre, developed by Black musicians for largely Black audiences.

Genres are socially enacted, negotiated and renegotiated, policed and contested. We need look no further than our opening vignette about Newport for an instance of genre policing and contestation. For genre is arguably *the* central term in the Dylan-goes-electric controversy, which is often told as the story of one genre (folk) infiltrated by another (rock). But, as the above comments suggest, this is not merely a question of musical sound, or even of instruments, plugged-in electrics vs. old-timey acoustics. It is a story of people, ideologies, institutions, and physical spaces. The Newport Folk Festival was an enclave of ostensibly like-minded people—mostly white, middle-class, and highly educated—who defined themselves and their musicking in opposition to the mainstream world that surrounded them. When Dylan played with his amplified band in their midst, the result wasn't merely a musical dissonance. It was a breaching of the charmed circle, an intrusion of generic behaviors that didn't fit with the festival's prevailing ethos. In the hullaballoo that followed, genre was never far from the surface. Some polemicists wondered "whither folk music?" while others welcomed the rock barbarians at the gates.[7] Yet others—especially journalists and disc jockeys—wondered what to call the kind of music Dylan playing. Was it electrified folk? Rock with more ambitious lyrics? Something entirely new under the sun? The label many eventually settled on—"folk-rock"—never pleased Dylan.[8] For now, it is enough to register the term as a symptom of generic confusion, a residue of the whole Newport kerfuffle, as participants in various genre cultures struggled to come to terms with music that seemed to fit tidily into none of them.

In this connection, it is worth returning to the sounds Dylan was making at Newport, noting how they contributed to this generic confusion. Bloomfield was filling the sonic space with the sounds for which electric guitars were known—bluesy leads and ostinato riffs. But Dylan was quietly strumming an open-position D-major chord like a folkie. Any musician could see that. Members of the Hawks—soon to become Dylan's backing band—certainly did when they eventually heard him. "He's a *strummer*," Richard Manuel jeered.[9] Robbie Robertson similarly complained that "there was a lot of strumming going on in this music, and for us, anyone who strummed just seemed to take the funkiness out of it."[10] Robertson was at first openly dubious about the folk tradition behind Dylan's strumming: "The whole folkie thing was still very questionable to us—it wasn't the train we came in on."[11]

Why was Dylan's strumming so objectionable to Robertson and his fellow Hawks? Beyond the sonic qualities of simplicity and squareness, their remarks point toward race. Robertson's train—"the train we came in on"—was fueled in large part by Black traditions, notably urban blues and R&B. His worries about "funkiness," and Dylan's lack thereof, gesture not so subtly in that racialized direction. Is it a step too far to say that Robertson heard Dylan's electric playing as painfully *white*? It was, after all, completely free of the bending so characteristic of Black blues guitar playing, bearing far more resemblance to Buddy Holly's cheerful strumming on, say, "Peggy Sue."[12] Dylan's backing band at Newport, by contrast, came directly out of the Chicago urban blues tradition. The two African American players onstage, drummer Sam Lay and bassist Jerome Arnold, had played in Howlin' Wolf's band. They were now members of the Paul Butterfield Blues Band, as was Mike Bloomfield.[13] During "Maggie's Farm" these players set up a hard-driving, very fast groove that would presumably have pleased Robertson. But Dylan's strumming struck a generic bum note. It was the one stylistic dissonance in the otherwise unified urban blues sound, an incongruous major-key jangle in the middle of the chugging texture.

In short, though the Dylan-goes-electric controversy is often drawn in stark generic terms—acoustic equals folk, electric equals rock—Dylan's playing smudges that distinction. The electric and acoustic may signify tidily as *symbols*, but when it comes to the sounds Dylan makes on them, the generic picture, and all that it entails about raced traditions, is far more complex.

ROCK-FOLK

And it had been for years, as attentive listeners at Newport knew. For Dylan often performed his acoustic folk material in the early '60s with the rhythmic energy and drive of rock 'n' roll. Many observed this at the time, and Dylan has made the point more than once.[14] Here, then, is another irony, the flipside of our first one: Dylan's most overt rock 'n' roll playing has invariably been on the *acoustic* guitar. One example can stand for many. "Highway 51," from Dylan's eponymous first album, is based on Tommy McClennan's "New Highway No. 51," but the two performances could hardly differ more.[15] McClennan's is a mid-tempo blues shuffle, complete with subtle lead breaks, while Dylan's has a barreling rockabilly groove, the tempo much faster, the shuffle gone. As though wishing to make the rockabilly affiliation unmistakable, Dylan explicitly cites the Everly Brothers' 1958 hit "Wake Up, Little Susie" in the song's main guitar riff.[16] **Audio example 6.1** presents the guitar part, which **figure 6.1** transcribes. Annotations above the staff mark the location of a syncopated figure that acts as a kind of tattoo in the Everlys' song. Walter Everett defines a tattoo as "a short, one-phrase unit that may reappear as if to bring the song back into focus."[17] I'll discuss the chords in the tattoo—and the labels ♭III–IV–♭III—below.

For now, note that Dylan plays the tattoo on the guitar's three lowest strings, giving them a hefty sonority.[18] The effect is much

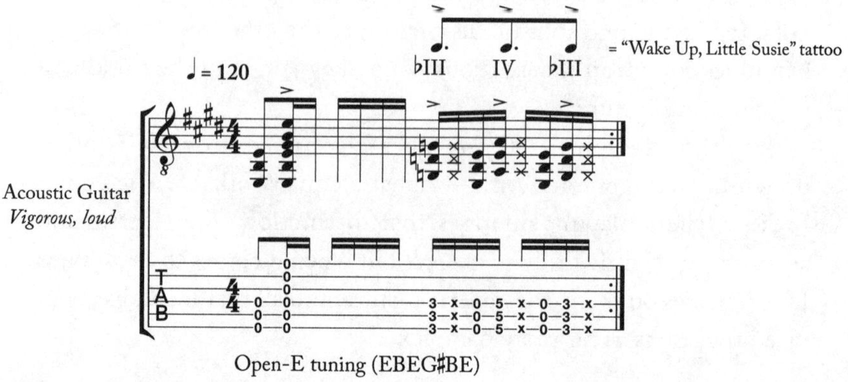

FIGURE 6.1. Dylan's main guitar part for "Highway 51," with the Everlys' tattoo highlighted. Recorded November 22, 1961, for his debut album.

closer to rock 'n' roll than anything he would play on his Strat at Newport three and a half years later. His acoustic guitar sound here has far more weight and body than his thin, jangling electric. This in part has to do with the physics of the instrument: a steel-string acoustic has heavier strings than an electric does, offering considerable resistance and allowing the player to dig in emphatically with the right-hand pick. Dylan's acoustic thus responds much more energetically to raw strumming than does his electric, with its lighter-gauge strings, which wobble and bounce under this kind of pressure.

But rock 'n' roll (or rockabilly) is not the only generic coordinate to consider here. Consider for a moment of all of the other musics that meet in this guitar riff. There is, for one, the blues. "Highway 51" is, after all, a blues—both in its AAB lyric structure and its twelve-bar form—and the guitar figure's blue ♭III chord explicitly indexes that tradition. Here the roman numeral III indicates that it is a chord built on the third scale degree ($\hat{3}$); the flat (♭) indicates that the $\hat{3}$ chordal root has been lowered a semitone, from G♯ to G♮, in a manner typical of the blues scale. This lowered $\hat{3}$ rubs bluesily against the major sonority of the open-E tuning.[19] That tuning also calls up rural blues guitar styles, in which such open tunings are often used to facilitate slide work. Dylan doesn't use a slide here—as he does on "In My Time of Dyin'," earlier on the same side of his first record—but his barre chords work in largely the same way, stopping multiple strings at the same fret.

The ♭III–IV–♭III tattoo not only cites the Everlys' song but affiliates with various actual blues examples, most from the urban, electric tradition. The tattoo is a cousin of the "stop-time" (I)–IV–♭III–I riffs in urban-blues classics like Bo Diddley's "I'm a Man" and Muddy Waters's "Mannish Boy," both recorded in 1955.[20] If we hear forward incrementally from Dylan's 1961 recording of "Highway 51" we encounter examples that echo the ♭III–IV–♭III riff more precisely, including the 1962 hit "Green Onions" by Booker T. and the MGs (house band of Memphis's Stax label), and Sonny Boy Williamson II's "Help Me" from the following year (itself based on "Green Onions"). These two examples did not yet exist when Dylan recorded his first album in 1961, but they were certainly in the air (and on the airwaves) when he created the guitar part to "It's Alright, Ma (I'm Only Bleeding)" in 1964, a song also based around the ♭III–IV–♭III tattoo. Dylan surely had "Highway 51" and "Wake Up, Little Susie" in his ears and fingers when he made the "It's Alright, Ma" guitar part but, given his voracious listening habits, "Green Onions" and "Help Me" may not have been far from his ears and fingers. These intertexts make explicit the ♭III–IV–♭III tattoo's affiliations with African American traditions, via Memphis soul and Chicago blues.[21] Nevertheless, "It's Alright Ma" and "Highway 51" also draw on white traditions. Most notably, the vigorous strumming—in *straight* eighths and sixteenths, that is, even rhythm—points away from the blues shuffle toward the more square-cut rhythms of old-time music and country. These musics—labeled by the prewar record-industry term "hillbilly"—were, after all, the source of the suffix in "rockabilly."

Think, then, of the ♭III–IV–♭III tattoo making a kind of round trip. It begins in African American blues, especially the urban blues of Muddy Waters, Bo Diddley, and others. The "blue" ♭III chord is the most explicit sounding marker of this origin. The Everlys then export the figure to a very different musical context, drawing on various white musics to create a driving rhythmic bed for a lyric explicitly bound up with white teen culture. The bluesy tint of the ♭III–IV–♭III tattoo adds a hint of danger to the mildly risqué lyric. The teen lovers' transgression of middle-class, suburban mores finds sonic expression in the music's importation of the sounds of Blackness, of racialized otherness.[22] The return trip then occurs when Dylan brings the tattoo *back* into an explicit blues context for "Highway 51." Gone is the clean harmonizing of Don and Phil Everly and in their place is Dylan's strident, bluesy tenor. Gone, too, is the teen drama, and in its place is a song about a rural highway and its amorous, illicit traffic. Dylan, we might say, repatriates the ♭III–IV–♭III tattoo, restoring it to a deep blues context. The performance is of such intensity that it seems an attempt to outshout the Everlys' clean-cut whiteness, a constructed blues "authenticity" now taking its place.

But Dylan was of course no Black musician. He accrued authenticity the same way countless white rock 'n' roll musicians had, by adopting Black performance styles. It's a story as old as rock 'n' roll, told by Margo Jefferson, Jack Hamilton, Maureen Mahon, and countless others.[23] We can hear that story in miniature in the round trip that is Dylan's "Highway 51," a performance that barrels ahead with the energy of rock 'n' roll—and late-'50s teen culture more generally—but yokes this to a blues that proclaims its authentic bona fides, to the white artist's profit.

Further examples of rock 'n' roll propulsion in Dylan's early acoustic playing are all over the first album. "You're No Good," "Fixin' to Die," "Pretty Peggy-O," "Gospel Plow," "Freight Train Blues," "See that My Grave Is Kept Clean"—all move with a momentum much closer (again) to Buddy Holly than to any of Dylan's folk and blues sources. Perhaps the most extreme is "Gospel Plow," which has him strumming at a blistering clip of 270 beats per minute. One senses that he is pushing the acoustic as hard as he can, his right hand all force and velocity, transforming the wooden box into a conduit for rock energy. In four short years, he would have a whole band to harness that energy for him, and his vigorous right hand would find itself out of work.

In the ensuing decades Dylan of course continued to play acoustic guitar, his spirited strumming especially evident in live acoustic sets. But it wasn't until the early '90s that his right hand would find full-time employment again in the studio, on two records of traditional songs, *Good as I Been to You* (1992) and *World Gone Wrong* (1993). Dylan performs alone on both, just voice and acoustic guitar. These records are usually credited with reviving Dylan's muse, renewed by contact with this rich store of old songs. There is also a liveliness in the performances that I attribute to the return of the acoustic guitar as sole bearer of the music's rhythmic momentum and affective scene-setting. It's a dramatic shift from his overproduced '80s albums. In the absence of slick machines, celebrity cameos (Slash, Stevie Ray Vaughan), and drenching reverb, his humble acoustic must once again do all the work. And in the process, all of the raw spontaneity, telling imperfection, and signifying richness of his playing return. On some songs, like "Frankie and Albert," "Little Maggie," and "Step It Up and Go," we hear once again his boyhood enthusiasms for rock 'n' roll. But there are many other styles on offer too, including a deceptively simple strumming style on songs like "Jim Jones," "World Gone Wrong," and "Two Soldiers," which had mesmerized listeners three decades earlier.

BARDIC STRUMMING

One of them was Daniel Mark Epstein. Consider his account of Dylan's playing of the intro to "The Times They Are a-Changin'" at a concert in Washington, DC, on December 14, 1963:

> We heard the guitar first, a powerful sound that was percussive, modal, and clarion. He was strumming a full G chord with a flat pick in moderate tempo, 3/4 time. What made it distinctive and commanding was the force of the first stroke of the measure, and that the guitarist had added a high D on the second string to make a perfect fourth with the G next to it. That was the trick, the special magic that transformed the chord from a simple major triad to a mystical, ancient strain, Celtic perhaps, medieval or Native American, a mood transcending time.[24]

No bootleg of the DC gig circulates. But one need not hear a bootleg to experience the effect Epstein describes, for his evocative language also aptly describes Dylan's guitar playing on the studio recording of the song, made seven weeks prior.[25] **Audio example 6.2** presents the beginning of the track, in which the chord is especially audible.

Epstein describes two aspects of Dylan's playing: his strumming (right hand) and his chord voicing (left). Let's start with the right hand. Epstein draws attention to Dylan's emphasis on the downbeat of each measure, calling it "distinctive and commanding." It is an astute observation. For even Dylan's simplest strumming pulses with a subtle rhythmic life, a sense of propulsion often achieved through emphasis on the first beat of each bar. That emphasis is like a strong pull on an oar, gently propelling a skiff across the water. The gliding rhythm that results sends the ear through the bar to the next downbeat, the next pull of the oar. All of this has the effect of entraining the listener, establishing a regular sense of impulse and expectation, which the listener's body can incorporate in subtle ways (foot tapping, gentle swaying). This makes the listener *part* of the music's irresistible temporal flow, which in "Times" is yoked to the song's thematics of futurity and imminent change, discussed in chapter 1.

Poet and critic Robert Graves puts it plainly but wonderfully when he states that traditional ballads have "music of a repetitive kind that excites and sustains."[26] The wording is apt for Dylan's simplest strumming, which is indeed repetitive, but also excites and sustains. It is clear from Graves's discussion where the listener's attention should be when hearing a ballad—on the story. The music excites and sustains our interest in *that*, working in the background to keep our concentration on the words nimble and alert. Given the persistence of Dylan's simplest strumming in songs that are, or are modeled on, old ballads, I refer to this style as "bardic strumming." I choose the word "bardic" both for its archaism as well as for its links to storytelling. For, when listening to a bard, our attention is on the words. The music excites and sustains that attention but it does not *occupy* it.

In "The Times They Are a-Changin'" we hear downstrokes on each beat, with only the occasional partial upstroke, as Dylan's pick lightly brushes a couple strings on its return trip, like the carriage return on a typewriter. By contrast, syncopated rock 'n' roll strumming, as in "Highway 51," makes much of upstrokes. For example, the middle chord of the ♭III–IV–♭III tattoo is a sharply accented upstroke, the two downstrokes on either side of it muffled by the left hand. In "The Times They Are a-Changin'," though, downstrokes are all. It is the simplest of folk rhythms, achieving a kind of affective neutrality, a blankness.

Epstein also comments on Dylan's left-hand chord voicing of the G chord that resonates throughout so much of "Times," a voicing that heightens the sense of musical antiquity. **Figure 6.2** compares the chord in question with more typical voicings. Dylan's chord, shown at 6.2(a), contains no third. He fingers a D on the third fret of the second string, creating a chordal fifth instead of the third that would be present had he instead played the open second string. The resulting chord contains only Gs and Ds, an archaic-sounding open fifth. Medieval music teems with such open-fifth sonorities. Figures 6.2(b) and (c) show two more traditional, less archaic, fingerings of the chord, the first containing one third, the second two (the thirds are shown with black noteheads). Those thirds flesh out the chord, "humanizing" it. The third is like the beating heart of a chord, communicating emotion, whether positive (major) or negative (minor). When the third is removed altogether the effect is impersonal, premodern, mysterious. This wording resonates with the proliferation of generic referents in Epstein's language as he attempts to characterize the chord's sound: it is mystical, ancient, maybe Celtic, maybe medieval, maybe—most incongruously—Native American. The unusual voicing was, for him, not an undercoded moment of sonic novelty, but a moment of abundant meaning, the hollow sonority summoning a numinous musical past. It is the sound of the folk revival at its most antiquarian.

Variants of bardic strumming abound in Dylan's early work, including some of his most famous songs: "Blowin' in the Wind," "A Hard Rain's a-Gonna Fall," "The Lonesome Death of Hattie Carroll," "Chimes of Freedom," "Gates of Eden." Not all of these involve archaic voicings as in "The Times They Are a-Changin'," but they do

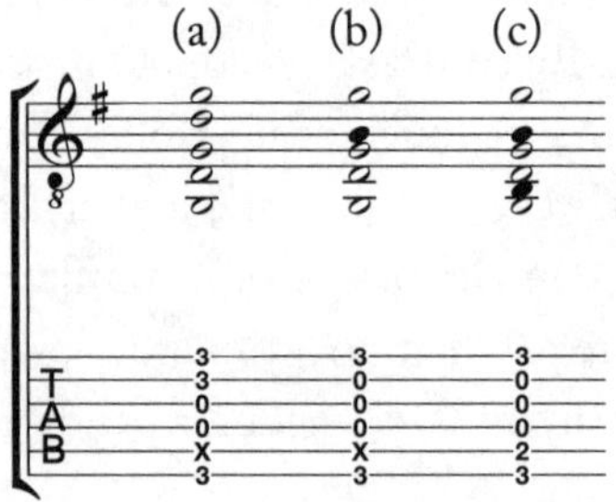

FIGURE 6.2. (a) Dylan's G chord (without third) in "The Times They Are a-Changin'"; (b), (c) two more-conventional voicings, with thirds in solid noteheads.

all have the simple, oar-pull strumming. There is, though, one notable free-meter variant, in which the archaism and neutral affect remain, but the metric entrainment disappears.[27] In this style Dylan strums rapidly but variably, in free tempo, chord changes occurring at irregular intervals, based on the speed of his vocal delivery. Notable examples are the studio versions of "With God on Our Side" and "Restless Farewell," both on *The Times They Are a-Changin'*. The archaism now has a specific cultural source in Irish balladry, as both songs are based on specific Irish precedents. In place of hypnotic metric entrainment, we hear a genuinely bardic time, in which vocal declamation determines the sparse, variable accompanimental rhythm, rather than the reverse. This style sounds, if anything, even older than rhythmically regular bardic strumming, gesturing beyond Dylan's Irish sources to a yet deeper past of accompanied epic narration—think of Homeric recitation accompanied by the lyre. This simple strumming style casts a long historical shadow.

FINGERPICKING I: THE LONGING SELF

If Dylan's bardic strumming tends toward the impersonal, the ancient, and the affectively blank, the sound of his fingerpicking—fleshy fingertips directly on strings—often evokes something entirely different, a present tense of intimacy, vulnerability, and fallible interiority.

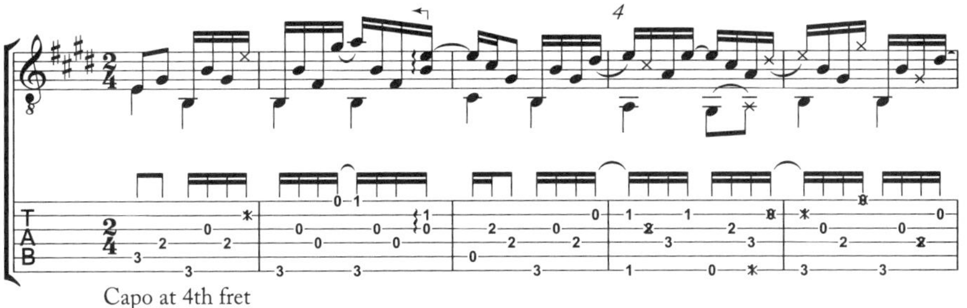

FIGURE 6.3. Dylan's guitar intro to the studio version of "Don't Think Twice, It's All Right," recorded November 14, 1962.

Consider the most famous bit of Dylan fingerpicking on record: the opening of "Don't Think Twice, It's All Right."[28] **Audio example 6.3** presents the fingerpicked opening of the song; **figure 6.3** provides a transcription. Dylan is playing with a capo at the fourth fret, using C-major chord shapes, resulting in a sounding key of E major. The fingerpicking pattern is a traditional one, sometimes called "Travis picking," after Merle Travis, in which the right-hand thumb alternates back and forth between bass notes as the fingers add syncopated interjections and melodic fragments on the higher-pitched strings above. Dylan's Travis picking is jaunty and buoyant, but it is also audibly imperfect, peppered with muffled notes and buzzes. I have used ×-shaped noteheads to indicate these flubbed notes in the transcription. There are many. They especially pile up in measures 4 and 5, but there is one already at the end of bar 1. In the next measure, Dylan stumbles on the final note, playing it slightly early (note the leftward arrow) and accidentally brushing two strings instead of one. Most professional players would likely scrap the entire take at this point, starting over. But Dylan doesn't, to the track's great benefit. For the result is deeply affecting. Such flubbed notes make us acutely aware of the fallible human fingers that make them. A perfect technique, by contrast, can often seem to make the body disappear; it becomes inaudible through discipline. Dylan's imperfect performing body, by contrast, retains its opacity and presence. The fleshy pads of his fingers are ever audible as the strings buzz and thump beneath them.

Literary theorist Roland Barthes, whom I mentioned in chapter 4, speaks to this issue, discussing not the guitar but the piano:

> As for piano music, I know at once which part of the body is playing—if it is the arm, too often, alas, muscled like a dancer's calves, the clutch of the finger-tips (despite the sweeping flourishes of the wrists), or if on the contrary it is the only erotic part of a pianist's body, the pad of the fingers whose "grain" is so rarely heard.[29]

Barthes's concept of grain is complex; I won't digress on it here.[30] Suffice it to say that grain makes the sound of the performer's body a site of erotic attachment for the listener. If the pad of the finger is indeed one locus of grain in instrumental technique, then Dylan's fingerstyle playing is grainy par excellence. It is guitar playing of audible tactility. In "Don't Think Twice," the bodily intimacy and vulnerability of his fingerstyle playing counterbalances the lyrics' moments of defensiveness and blame. The result is exquisitely poised. That poise has sometimes been lost in concert versions where Dylan replaces the fingerpicking with aggressive strumming, as on the 1974 tour. Daniel Mark Epstein, on hearing the song at Madison Square Garden that year, states that Dylan was "strumming furiously instead of finger-picking, the subtlety of which would have been drowned in that din. Oppressive anger, I thought, steamrolled the nuances of tone."[31] On record, by contrast, those nuances are palpable—and moving—in the tender fallibility of Dylan's fingertips.

Despite this effect of intimate disclosure, it is important to recognize that such fingerpicking is not some personal invention, as though Dylan stumbled upon it magically when translating emotion into song. Rather, this playing style has a history, its generic codes traceable back to particular social origins. In "Don't Think Twice," those codes are largely from the country tradition, not only Merle Travis but Chet Atkins, Darby and Tarlton, and Don Gibson.[32] In the fingerpicked song on the other side of *Freewheelin'*, "Girl from the North Country," the generic codes have a different geographical and historic origin: not the North Country of the lyric, but the British Isles. The song contains a striking chord that Dylan learned from British guitarist Martin Carthy during Dylan's first trip to the UK in December 1962.[33] The chord in question comes from Carthy's arrangement of "Scarborough Fair," the fingerpicked vamp of which can be heard in **audio example 6.4**; a transcription is shown in **figure 6.4(a)**.[34] The vamp consists of one unusual fretboard configuration, which Carthy fingerpicks throughout, in gently curling arpeggios. As the tablature shows, this voicing involves stopping the fourth string

(a)

(b)

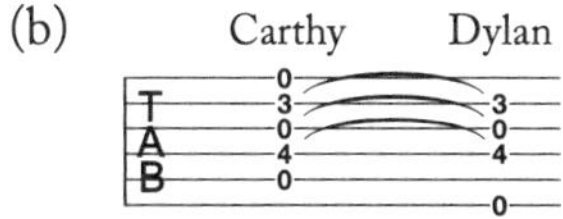

FIGURE 6.4. (a) Martin Carthy's "Scarborough Fair" vamp; (b) Dylan's adaptation of the first chord for the opening of "Girl for the North Country."

on the fourth fret and the second string on the third fret; the remaining strings are all open.

The sounding result is enigmatic, chilly, and static, suggestive of an antique past. The antique flavor comes in part from the music's modality, specifically the Dorian mode projected by the note on the fourth fret of the fourth string. The Dorian mode is like the minor scale, but with $\hat{6}$ raised, giving a wistful, major-key tint to the upper portion of the scale. The right side of figure 6.4(a) shows the sonority that accumulates from Carthy's fingerpicking, which rings throughout much of the song. This configuration of pitches frustrates any traditional harmonic analysis.[35] Rather than acting in a functionally purposeful way, it simply resonates in place, sounding the gentle melancholy of the rain-soaked British pastoral.

Figure 6.4(b) shows how Dylan adopted and ever so slightly modified Carthy's voicing. As the curved lines (i.e., ties) show, the stopped pitches on strings 4 and 2 are the same, as is the open string in between, but the other two open strings are different. While Carthy plays an open fifth and first string, Dylan plays an open sixth string. The result is a somewhat different chord, with more functional potential. And indeed, as **figure 6.5(a)** shows, Dylan deploys the chord very differently than does Carthy. **Audio example 6.5** presents the first verse of the song, so that we can hear the chord in context, as it initiates a purposeful, directed progression, over and over. I discuss some of the technical reasons for the chord progression's momentum in the next two paragraphs. Nonmusicians may wish to skip or skim them. The main thing to notice is how Dylan animates the opening chord, which he borrows from Carthy. In Carthy's "Scarborough Fair," it is a static sonority, resounding in place and going nowhere. In Dylan's song, by contrast, it *moves*, longingly pulling to the next two chords in the progression.[36]

Figure 6.5(a) labels the three chords in this progression as *x*, *y*, and *z*. Chord *x* is the mysterious sonority borrowed from Carthy. **Figure 6.5(b)** isolates the three chords and analyzes their progression; I'll discuss the brackets below. First note the annotations below the staff. The P–D–T stands for predominant–dominant–tonic, the standard functional

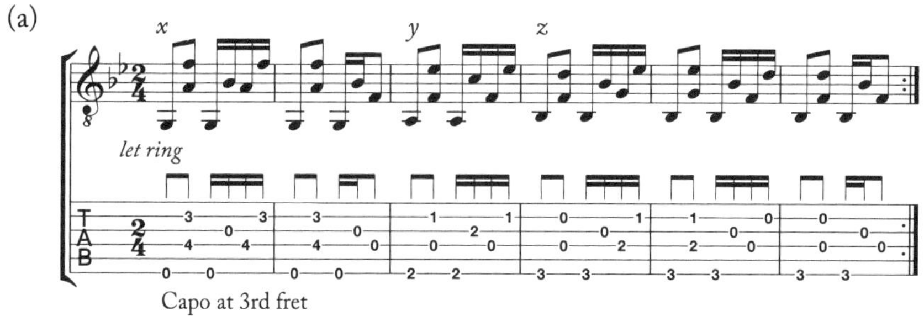

FIGURE 6.5. (a) Dylan's guitar part to "Girl from the North Country"; (b) an analysis of same.

progression of Western tonal music. Unlike Carthy's static modality, Dylan's chord *x* has a clear syntactic role within this functional progression, pointing to the dominant, which in turn points to the tonic. This sense of directedness is heightened by the contrary motion between the outer voices, as chord *x* proceeds to *y* proceeds to *z*. This creates a funneling effect, directing our ears toward the goal chord, *z*. Rather than a site of static, cultural melancholy—as in Carthy's arrangement of "Scarborough Fair"—the chord is a locus of personal nostalgia, of rueful longing. The *x*–*y*–*z* progression encodes that longing, giving it a musical teleology. Chord *x* yearns for chord *z*, over and over, just as the song's protagonist continually sends his thoughts northward, in worry and muted regret. It is telling that *x* yearns for *z* via an intermediary—chord *y*—just as the protagonist channels his nostalgia through his second-person interlocutor (the "you" of the lyric).

The progression is also driven by dissonance. The brackets mark the dissonances in chords *x* and *y*. The most striking dissonance is the minor second in chord *x*—the two pitches right next to each other. It is this dissonance that gives the chord its wistful pang. But there are two *further* dissonances in the same chord as well, both involving its bass pitch. This "charges" that bass note, so to speak, making it unstable and urging it to move forward. When it does move, to chord *y*, it participates in yet another dissonance with the highest voice. But the overall amount of dissonance has decreased, from three dissonant intervals to just one. When chord *y* resolves to chord *z*, that final dissonant interval dissolves into the stable, wholly consonant tonic triad. The *x–y–z* progression thus proceeds from greatest dissonance to least, from three dissonances (*x*), to one (*y*), to none (*z*), as the music settles into tonic resolution. Recall the music-theoretical metaphor of the tonic as a kind of "home." The metaphor is especially apt here, as the lyric persona of the song yearns for his frozen childhood home and the long-haired girl he left there. Dissonance—yearning in sound—drives his thoughts there again and again, as the *x–y–z* progression cycles continually.

Before leaving this song, we should note one crucial way in which Dylan transplants Carthy's chord to American soil: the picking. While Carthy uses a wispy curling pattern in 3/4, Dylan adopts a variant of the same Travis-picking pattern he uses in "Don't Think Twice." As a result, "Girl from the North Country" steps with a distinctly American gait, its mild syncopations infusing Carthy's chilly chord with the rhythmic life of the New World. The result was so effective that Dylan would use the same guitar part for "Boots of Spanish Leather," a song explicitly about encounter between the Old World and the New, now with a thread of amorous longing stretched between them.

FINGERPICKING II: BLUES SUBJECTIVITIES

But fingerpicking is not only a technique for conveying white subjectivity, heartbroken or otherwise. There is a venerable Black tradition of fingerstyle blues playing, extending back to Charley Patton, Blind Lemon Jefferson, Lonnie Johnson, Blind Willie McTell, Peg

Leg Howell, Big Bill Broonzy, Robert Johnson, and countless others. Especially notable is the Piedmont blues style, known for its distinctive fingerpicking patterns, with bass alternations played by the thumb. Piedmont players generally hailed from Georgia, Virginia, and the Carolinas, but some Delta players also picked up elements of the style. The best-known living exemplar of the latter when Dylan was coming up in the folk revival was Mississippi John Hurt, whose rolling, genial playing gives his version of "Frankie and Albert" such

FIGURE 6.6. Dylan's guitar part for "Buckets of Rain," as recorded on September 19, 1974, and released on *Blood on the Tracks*.

warmth and compassion.[37] When Dylan recorded that song for 1992's *Good as I Been to You*, he did not play fingerstyle, instead flat-picking in a driving rock-'n'-roll rhythm. But earlier in his career he finger-picked his way through several blues in a style not far from Hurt's.[38] *Blood on the Tracks* includes two notable examples.[39]

The closest to Hurt is "Buckets of Rain." **Figure 6.6** shows Dylan's main guitar part for the song, which can be heard in **audio example 6.6**. The transcription tidies things up a lot—the performance abounds in stray sounds, just the kind of grainy, imperfect details I discussed above. This is especially evident in the bracketed lick in mm. 4–5 of the transcription, which Dylan rarely plays cleanly. It is a moment of adventure each time it rolls around, some notes sounding clearly, others lost in the rush, muffled or buzzing.

Hurt's influence is evident in the gently droning oscillation between two Es in the bass, played by Dylan's thumb. One can also hear Hurt in the song's sunny major key, which is notably free of blue notes. Free, that is, until a striking journey into the upper register, which one can hear in **audio example 6.7**, and see transcribed in **figure 6.7**. Here, Dylan shifts his sliding sixths up to the tenth fret, producing a blue $\hat{7}$ (D♮). Dylan does this three times on the recording, at 1:05–1:11, 2:11–2:17, and 3:01–3:07. Each time, he snaps the string on the D♮, pulling it away from the instrument and allowing it to slap back into the frets on the fingerboard. The jarring accent reminds us both of his fingers and of the guitar, in all its physicality. Though the song generally preserves the gentle lull of Hurt's blues, it is also peppered with snaps like this, which puncture the sense of humming calm. Though the introduction has few of these pinched notes, they accumulate as the performance goes on. Figure 6.6 indicates some of the most commonly snapped notes with accents. The song may well be "Zen in a bucket," as Eyolf Østrem delightfully puts it,[40] but it is a Zen state perforated by these brittle accents, metal wires startling us back to the world.

"Meet Me in the Morning" includes similar snapped notes, but these are more consistently bluesy. **Figure 6.8** shows the main riff that Dylan plays throughout the song, hearable in **audio example 6.8**. The

FIGURE 6.7. An upper-register variant in "Buckets of Rain."

FIGURE 6.8. Dylan's main guitar figure for "Meet Me in the Morning," as recorded on September 16, 1974, and released on *Blood on the Tracks*.

accent in the figure shows the pitch that Dylan snaps: the bluest of blue notes, a lowered $\hat{3}$, bent slightly upward. Note that Dylan often plays this against a major $\hat{3}$, G♯, shown in parentheses, which makes the clash with the blue, bent G♮ that much more stinging. Dylan adds to the sting by once again yanking the string with his plucking finger to produce the metallic ricochet between string and fret. This moment—the snapped blue note followed by the open string—distills blues sonority and ethos to its essence. It sounds like a shooting pain, arising quickly, and then just as quickly reabsorbed into the swung groove.

If such snaps bear little resemblance to Hurt's hypnotic playing, they do recall a passage from *Chronicles, Volume One*, in which Dylan speaks of another blues fingerstylist, Robert Johnson, saying that the "stabbing sounds from [his] guitar could almost break a window."[41] The snapped notes here are about as close to "stabbing sounds" as one can get when playing with the right-hand fingers. We can hear, and see, Dylan emulate Johnson's playing yet more explicitly in **video example 6.2**, a clip from *Renaldo and Clara*, shot in the year following the *Blood on the Tracks* sessions. This is the fourth scene in the film, beginning about ten minutes in, and it's the first scene in which we encounter Dylan in the character of Renaldo. He is playing guitar in a repair shop, a woman (played by Helena Kallianiotes) hanging on his shoulder and watching closely.[42] Dylan is idly playing a blues in A, using chord shapes popularized as idioms by Robert Johnson. **Figure 6.9** shows the most notable of these. The first, in 6.9(a), is a series of planing diminished triads on the top three strings, which Johnson regularly used for introductions when playing blues in A. Second, in 6.9(b), is a particular fingering of the A chord favored by Johnson, which guitarists call a "long A," as the pinky stretches upward to play the fifth fret of the first string, thus lengthening the hand (and the chord's registral span). This is followed by melodic stepping down from that high A to the blue $\hat{7}$, G♮, another Johnson idiom. Finally, 6.9(c) shows the most characteristically Johnsonian shape Dylan

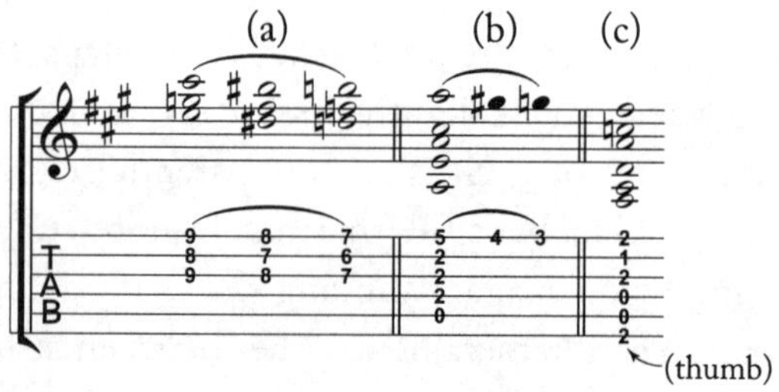

FIGURE 6.9. Robert Johnson–style chord shapes in scene 4 of *Renaldo and Clara*: (a) planing diminished triads; (b) long-A chord with melodic descent; (c) D7 chord in first inversion.

plays: a first-inversion D7 chord, with the left-hand thumb playing on the second fret of the sixth string. Much more common in an A-based twelve-bar blues would be a root-position D7, with D in the bass.

None of these chord shapes is *unique* to Johnson's playing, but their combination is highly suggestive of his style and would have been especially so by the mid '70s, as his posthumous fame had grown. Johnson loomed especially large for Dylan. Just two years before this scene was shot, he had published his first collection of lyrics, *Writings and Drawings by Bob Dylan*, giving Johnson pride of place alongside no less than Woody Guthrie in the book's dedication.[43]

Crucially, though, Dylan's playing in the film clip is languid, without Johnson's taut rhythmic pulse. He is noodling, improvising with Johnson shapes. His plucking motions are exaggerated, almost sensual, as he extends his fingers slowly to caress a new chord, long fingernails gently brushing the strings. The sensuality is obviously intentional, for the erotic charge between Dylan and Kallianiotes is palpable. Indeed, the scene ends with them kissing, oblivious to the mechanic also in the shop. The intimacy of fingers on strings is suggestive, drawing the lover into the player's charmed erotic circle. But that fingerpicked intimacy also has a clear racialized vector. The white player, Dylan, channels the sexual potency of Black sound. Dylan had done something similar on stage at Newport a decade earlier—appropriating Black idioms to create a sense of allure and risk—though with an electric guitar in his hands.

BLACK SOUND, WHITE SPOTLIGHT (NEWPORT '65, PART 2)

To get that evening's music back in our ears, let's begin with **figure 6.10**, which transcribes Dylan's and Bloomfield's guitar parts in "Maggie's Farm." The top system (staff and tab) notates Dylan's part, an open-position D-major chord in drop-D tuning. His strumming is spirited and very fast, immediately recalling his rock 'n' roll style acoustic playing, as in "Highway 51," "Gospel Plow," and many others. But the sounding result is so much different. All the heft, power, and sheer kinetic energy of the acoustic playing is gone. Without the heavy steel strings of an acoustic to resist Dylan's rapid up and down strokes, the strumming falls flat, the skinny electric strings jangling feebly.

The electric guitar speaks more persuasively when the player relies on pickups and amp to provide oomph, focusing less on right-hand vigor and more on clarity and accuracy. Single-note lines work especially well, as Mike Bloomfield knew. The lower system in **figure 6.10** notates the repeated riff that he plays throughout much of the song.[44] His sound is full-bodied and loud, thickened by distortion. It's also thickened by his left-hand position on the fingerboard. Bloomfield plays high on the neck, far from Dylan's open strings. Because of the way fretboards work, guitarists have some flexibility as to where they locate pitches. The same pitch can be found in multiple locations, different combinations of string and fret. He begins the riff on the tenth fret of the sixth—that is, the thickest—string, near its point of greatest flexibility. He could have played it in a lower position (beginning, say, on the fifth fret of the fifth string, or, much less likely, the open fourth string) but neither would have had the chunky resonance of this fingering, nor its options for muting, articulating, and punching.

By placing the riff here on the neck, Bloomfield also situates himself well for the higher-register solo breaks that he will insert between Dylan's sung lines. Bloomfield's riff grounds the music within R&B and blues idioms, making up for the generic dissonance of Dylan's thin, jangling guitar. Dylan's voice also makes up for it, engaging in call-and-response gestures with Bloomfield's lead breaks. This harks back to one of the most potent sources of musical interaction in postwar American popular music: the Black church. Dylan's voice sounds almost as one with Bloomfield's guitar as they trade lines, both of them bright, hectoring, and coarse, Dylan's nasality matching the trebly sneer of Bloomfield's bridge pickup.[45]

Moreover, as **figure 6.11(a)** shows, Dylan's voice and Bloomfield's guitar occupy the same register. Dylan's vocal line is a modified chant/escape that uses three notes: C, D, and F. Bloomfield plays these three notes as well, adding two more, G and A. Note that Dylan's melodic line ends on the same note with which Bloomfield begins his first solo

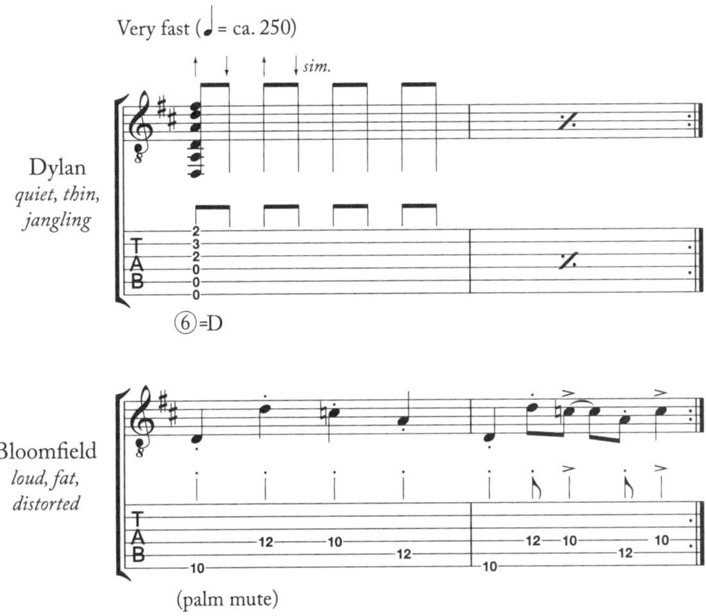

FIGURE 6.10. Dylan's and Bloomfield's guitar parts for "Maggie's Farm," Newport Folk Festival, July 25, 1965.

break (D). The effect is like a baton handoff in a relay race, Dylan's last note identical to Bloomfield's first. **Figure 6.11(b)** shows the pitch overlap between Dylan's vocal and Bloomfield's guitar.[46] Note that they share the two blue notes in the key of D, C♮ (♭$\hat{7}$) and F♮ (♭$\hat{3}$). The F♮ rubs against Dylan's underlying D-major chord (which contains an F♯), amplifying the performance's generic dissonance with an actual, bluesy sonic clash. Throughout the song, Dylan's voice and Bloomfield's guitar chase each other in just this fashion, two white bodies trading gestures and licks from Black musical tradition, harnessing their expressive force and transgressive threat, and funneling them into the one fully visible body on stage—the white dandy in the spotlight.

As this suggests, the electric guitar at this point in its history was bound up in a complex racial dynamic, whose fraught energies Dylan's performance harnessed. Steve Waksman writes that the electric guitar

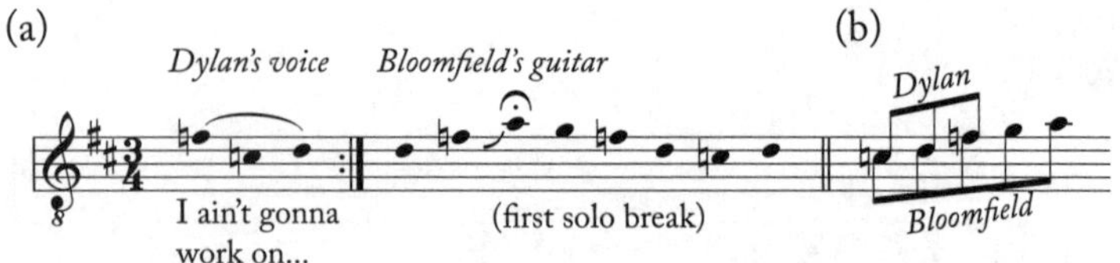

FIGURE 6.11. Dylan's vocal line and Bloomfield's first lead break on "Maggie's Farm," Newport Folk Festival, July 25, 1965.

> came to embody a certain set of countercultural desires that hinged upon the transference of racial and sexual identity between African-American and white men. African-American bluesmen became the ideal type of electric guitarist after whom legions of young white guitarists (like Mike Bloomfield) sought to pattern themselves; and the resulting "rebellion" reproduced patterns of racism and sexism even as it aimed to produce an effective model of resistance rooted in musical practice.[47]

Waksman's language captures the contradictions of the moment. The folk revivalists—pretty much to a person, from the players on down—were deeply committed to racial justice and the civil rights movement.[48] And Black musicians, especially rural blues artists, were central to Newport from the beginning. But Bloomfield expressed discomfort at how Black musicians were presented at the festival, especially as regards amplified blues:

> Lightnin' Hopkins had made electric records for twelve years, but he didn't bring his electric band from Texas. No sir, he came out at Newport like they had just taken him out of the fields, like the tar baby.[49]

To be clear, Hopkins did in fact play his electric guitar at Newport in 1965—Bloomfield introduced him—but he played without his band (drummer Sam Lay sat in on a few numbers). And two electric bands *did* play before Dylan: the Chambers Brothers, an African American foursome from Mississippi, and the Paul Butterfield Blues Band, a racially integrated ensemble from Chicago that included Mike Bloomfield. While both groups reportedly received enthusiastic receptions, the Butterfield Blues Band's performance on Friday afternoon was the site of a legendary confrontation between Albert Grossman (Dylan's manager, as well as Butterfield's) and folksong collector Alan Lomax.[50] The dust-up resulted in the two of them literally rolling in the dirt next to the stage. While the dispute is sometimes portrayed as centering on Lomax's objection to electric blues altogether, Elijah Wald makes clear that Lomax's agitation had more to do with the fact that Butterfield's band included two middle-class white kids.[51] Their performance was part of a carefully curated history of the blues that Lomax was presenting that afternoon, featuring a wide range of Black blues performers; a band that included non-Black players troubled the narrative.

By the time Dylan took the stage on Sunday night, then, the fraught question of Black sounds and white bodies had already shaken up the festival. Dylan's performance capitalized on this energy. Here it is especially fascinating that Bloomfield resides in the shadows at Newport. The sounds of Black blues blare forth from his guitar—overpowering every other instrument on stage—but their source is visually obscured. The transference of racial and sexual identity that Waksman discusses thus receives a special inflection in this performance, as it is distributed across two guitarists: one audible but largely invisible, the other largely inaudible but visible. Even if Dylan is not making especially bluesy sounds on his instrument, Bloomfield's wailing bends fill that gap, providing a sonic correlate for the offending instrument around Dylan's neck.[52] Dylan's almost inaudible playing creates a sonic opening that Bloomfield's playing fills, mapping the sounds of Black blues onto Dylan's body.

It would be hard to imagine a more vivid instance of the guitar's status as both sound and symbol, reified by the two instruments on stage. In the decades since the concert, Dylan's Strat has become one of the most symbolically freighted electric guitars in rock history, selling at Christie's in 2013 for $965,000. The Associated Press notes that this was "the highest price ever paid for a guitar at auction."[53] One can hardly imagine the new owner making any music on it. In the auction photos it looks pristine, barely played. Which, in a sense, it was.

Chapter 7 audio and video examples:
soundingbobdylan.com/ch7

CHAPTER SEVEN

Harmonica

Breathing Room

CRASH IN THE CZECH REPUBLIC

On stage at the Kongresový sál in Prague, Dylan's evening of harmonica playing begins inauspiciously. It is March 11, 1995, the first concert of the year. Near the end of set-opener "Crash on the Levee (Down in the Flood)," he produces a discordant blast from his harp—he's picked up the wrong instrument.[1] **Audio example 7.1** excerpts the moment. The band is playing in G, but Dylan has just blown into a D harmonica. To be sure, harpists often play an instrument whose key differs from that of the song as a whole, a technique known as cross-harp, common in blues playing. But only certain keys will do the trick. Had Dylan chosen a C harmonica, he would have been in good shape to fire off some bluesy licks. But D moves in the wrong direction, making the notes available to him *less* bluesy, not more.[2] For this raucous twenty-bar blues, it is an especially grievous slip, just the sort of moment that makes serious harmonica players shake their heads.

But the Prague audience is unfazed. On this night, as so often, it seems that *any* sound Dylan produces on the instrument raises a rowdy cheer. The discordant blast, the first harmonica sound of the night—and of the 1995 touring season—sure does. Nor has this harp clam diminished the show's reputation among bootleg connoisseurs, many of whom view the concert as an exhilarating return to form after a couple spotty years. Dylan had canceled the previous night's gig due to a bout of flu. Taking the stage the next evening, he decided to forgo the guitar for all but two songs, presumably so as not to weigh down his convalescing body. He instead spent most of the night with a handheld mic in one hand and a harmonica in the other, alternately singing and blowing his way through the set. Devotees praise the show's harp playing as much as they do its vocals.

What is it about Dylan's ramshackle harp that inspires such a rapturous response from his fans, even as serious players sniff at his amateurism? Stated thus, the question may well be unanswerable or, just as troublesome, answerable in as many unique ways as there are unique Dylan listeners. We will gain more traction if we approach the question indirectly, asking, What does Dylan's harmonica playing disclose? Or simpler still, What can we hear in it?[3] I will argue in this chapter that there is no single answer to this question, but a welter of them, which I will corral into four categories: history, identity, emotion, and eloquence. I suspect that all four of these categories—to varying degrees—are at play each time Dylan's harmonica rouses his fans to shout back.

Also at play is a structural feature of the harmonica so obvious that it might escape notice, but so crucial that it underwrites everything that follows: the harmonica is the only instrument that necessarily stops the flow of Dylan's words. He can sing while playing the guitar or piano, but not while playing the harmonica, which occupies the same channel as the voice, riding on the same breath. It's true that he pauses his singing at other points—say, for a solo from his lead guitarist—but it is only the harmonica that *forces* such a substitution, noisily blocking the language channel. The harmonica, in short, conveys to our ears a Bob Dylan momentarily deprived of words.

This substitutional logic has encouraged some to think of Dylan's harmonica as a kind of surrogate voice.[4] While that idea is attractive, I am more interested here in the *relief* Dylan's harp provides from the voice, and especially from linguistic meaning. As it perforates the flow of his language, it clears space for nonlinguistic sounding breath. True, the resulting sounds emerge always alongside his words. The harp solo is often a place to reflect on what Dylan has just sung, or to anticipate a verse to come. But it is also a place in which meaning can drift, where the listener is momentarily freed of the burden of the semantic, of decoding dense lyrics. Dylan's harmonica is thus an instrument of the breath in an additional, less obvious sense: it creates breathing room. It opens a clearing within the thicket of his language. In this breathing room, without the shiny objects of Dylan's words to distract us, we can hear much. Let's listen first for the past.

HISTORY

The harmonica is a relative newcomer on the instrumental scene, though it has ancient roots. These extend back several millennia, to the earliest free-reed aerophones in the Far East, most notably the Chinese *sheng*.[5] But it wasn't until the eighteenth century that *shengs* began to circulate in Europe—along the routes of global exchange and colonial encounter—eventually leading to the invention of the harmonica in the 1820s. It was a humble piece of technology, an instrument of plucky entrepreneurs and clever tinkerers. One of these, a Bohemian named Richter, devised a system using two metal reed plates, one for blowing, the other for drawing (i.e., inhaling). These plates were attached to a wooden "comb" consisting of ten holes, corresponding to two reeds each, one blow and one draw.[6] The harmonica thus became one of the few wind instruments that could produce sound on the inhale as well as the exhale. Richter's ingenious arrangement caught on, and the harmonica was soon swept into the surging Industrial Revolution, ripe for capitalist mass production. It became ubiquitous in Europe and (especially) America, largely through the efforts of a particularly enterprising manufacturer named Matthias Hohner. Hohner's success in global marketing was such that the harmonica has, for nearly its entire existence, been all but synonymous with his name. Many harpists—including Dylan—still play Hohner harmonicas exclusively.

The ubiquity that Hohner fostered has led Kim Field to call the harmonica "the people's instrument," asserting that it is "arguably the most popular instrument in history," second only to the human voice in its "universality."[7] Michael Licht is only slightly more circumspect, stating that it is "probably the most played instrument in the history of the United States."[8] These are bold claims, but borne out by the data. Licht cites a 1967 study that put the number of American players at a staggering forty million. How did the instrument find its way into so many mouths? From the first it was compact, inexpensive, and unpretentious—accessible to all, both economically and technically. Not only could working-class people afford them, anyone could produce a good sound on the instrument right out of the box. Blow into a few adjacent holes on a standard diatonic harmonica and you produce a pleasing chord, a major tonic triad. Draw and you produce another one, a dominant seventh.[9] This latter chord is a bit more dissonant and seems to call for a return of the first, which you can produce by blowing out again. Draw breath long enough and you, too, will need that first chord to return—your body will demand it. Thus, the natural oscillation of breath that we require to survive—exhalation and inhalation, blow and draw—produces a similarly foundational oscillation in tonal harmony when we channel that breath through a harmonica. It's an ingenious mapping of bodily survival mechanics onto instrumental design.[10]

The harmonica is in this sense a great social leveler. Everyone breathes. This is partly why it has long been a popular child's gift, a common stocking stuffer or birthday-party souvenir, frequently "a child's first, and often only, musical instrument."[11] Anyone, from toddler to adult, can produce on it the most important harmonic pairing in tonal music—tonic and dominant—with no training at all, simply by doing what they do every minute of their lives. Consider for a moment the collective cacophony of all of that blowing and drawing across the twentieth century, millions of Americans—young and old, Black and white, rural and urban—delightedly translating respiration into a musical first principle. That cacophony is the soundtrack for one history of the harmonica. Call it a "populist" history. It isn't the kind of history we're most used to telling. Such histories are usually centered on great players—for example, the honor roll of blues, country, jazz, and classical virtuosos that populate Kim Field's book on the instrument.[12] To be sure, several of those famous players had their influence on Dylan, as we will hear in a moment. But the populist history provides a useful corrective to such "great men" narratives, an apt alternative for this humble and ubiquitous instrument.[13] Such a history is orders of magnitude greater in scale than the great-men tale, whether one measures magnitude in number of players or in sheer volume.

Is it too much to suggest that this populist history is audible in Dylan's harp playing? After all, there is a homely accessibility in Dylan's approach to the instrument. A child picking up a harmonica can, on first try, produce certain sounds not far from Dylan's own. To be sure, some of Dylan's sounds—his wailing bends, for example—are well out of reach for the beginner. But others will be quite familiar to any novice. Consider that most elemental musical particle, a single note. Producing a single tone on the harmonica is one of the first challenges new players face, as one must direct air through only one hole (it is much easier to blow into several). There are two methods for playing single notes. One is the pucker technique, which is just what it sounds like: a pursing of the lips so that their opening is the size of one hole. The other is tongue blocking, in which the player's mouth covers multiple holes but the tongue blocks some of them. Dylan uses the pucker method, as do most beginning players, but he rarely does it cleanly. There is very often a blur, a shadow around each melodic note, as air escapes through neighboring holes. This sound is familiar to any student who has tried to master puckering. At first it feels all but impossible not to blow inadvertently into adjacent holes. Dylan's blurred melodic lines thus conjure the sound of an amateur first navigating the instrument.

Now consider the techniques he employs when playing the harp on his famous neck rack. Dylan was not the first to use such a rack—Gwen Foster, Jesse Fuller, Jimmy Reed, and indeed Woody Guthrie were the best-known antecedents—but it was Dylan who made the rack iconic.[14] When using such a rack, the player foregoes a certain amount of control that the hands can provide when cupping the instrument. The hands can create various wah-wah and vibrato effects, as well as position the instrument, allowing the player to select notes by moving the harp while keeping the head relatively stationary. With a rack, by contrast, the sole point of contact is between lips and instrument, the sole means of selecting holes a side-to-side motion of the head. Dylan turns this limitation into a hallmark of his rack style, in which he distills harmonica technique down to its most basic elements. As Jonathan De Souza notes, the harmonica "offers two basic ways of moving—side to side and in and out. It has two 'dimensions.'"[15] We might think of these as right-angled axes with respect to the player's head, head and lips moving side to side, breath moving forward and back. In Dylan's rack technique, we hear these two dimensions especially vividly, as his playing often shuttles between side-to-side sweeping and rhythmic chugging in place (alternating blow and draw). Again, these two techniques are familiar to the novice, who often begins by experimenting in just this way, sweeping side-to-side one moment, chugging in place the next.

Among more advanced players, however, the sweeping technique is uncommon, making it stand out that much more in Dylan's playing. He sweeps in diverse ways throughout his career, at times subtly, at others less so. Unsubtle examples abound in the acoustic sets of the 1966 tour. Consider **audio example 7.2**, from "Desolation Row," as performed in Manchester on May 17.[16] Here Dylan's solo reduces to pure sweeping—swinging wildly from one end of the harp to the other, in time with the swaying pulse of his guitar. The result is a kind of antivirtuosity, a musical de-skilling—harp playing as raw gesture. There is something confrontational and abrasive in these moments of wild sweeping, and indeed in Dylan's harp playing throughout the 1966 acoustic sets. The solos are often long and loud; indeed, their length and loudness seem precisely the point.

Though there are moments of tenderness, much of the playing is coarse, aggressive, and chaotic. The sweeping technique in particular is wildly splattered, the sonic equivalent of Jackson Pollock waving a paint-filled brush. The comparison reminds us that Dylan in 1966 was leaning hard into a familiar modernist pose—the artist as loner-antagonist—whose historical roots date back at least to his hero Rimbaud's proclamation that "one should be absolutely modern."[17] Abstract expressionists like Pollock were merely the most recent American iteration of the type. Mid-'60s Dylan slipped into the role with ease, finding in his studied amateurism the perfect tool to shock the bourgeoisie.

We've jumped tracks from one history—the populist history of the ubiquitous pocket instrument—to a new one, that of modernist confrontation. It is a vertiginous shift, but crucial to understanding the multivalence of Dylan's harp. His harmonica playing at once traffics in a kind of populist antivirtuosity and at the same time harnesses it for the high-prestige cultural work of artistic "difficulty." There is a bifocal quality to his playing, which can be both familiar and alienating, accessible and bracing, shuttling between low culture and high. His lack of technical polish serves both ends. But there is more to say about the low-cultural side of this equation. For, the same harp that can produce de-skilled, modernist splatter can in the next breath suggest a range of humble vernacular traditions whose historical and geographical origins are a world away from the elite enclaves of modernist high culture.

Consider the chugging technique. This vigorous alternation of blow and draw, typically involving several holes, is most familiar as a crucial component of the "train style" of harp playing.[18] This style was part of the common stock of Black and white players in the rural South harnessing one of the instrument's basic affordances—its front–back, in–out dimension—to evoke the most advanced, and most awe-inspiring, mode of transportation in the early twentieth century. The train was an Industrial Revolution wonder. It thrilled avant-gardists like the Italian Futurists as much as it did the American rural poor. For the latter, as countless songs attested, the train became the vehicle that leads one out into the wide world, helping its riders achieve escape velocity from lives of grinding drudgery into a space of freedom, risk, and the unknown. Harmonica players could evoke this entire romance through a few skillful blow-and-draw chugs, the tiny instrument conjuring the headlong rush of industrial modernity and its attendant dislocations.[19]

For a classic instance of the technique, consider Sonny Terry's playing on Woody Guthrie's aptly named "Railroad Blues," excerpted in **audio example 7.3**. Terry's playing is dominated by a chugging *long*–short–short rhythm (♩♫), which forms the foundation for countless syncopated variations. It is not hard to hear a resemblance to Dylan's early harp playing in up-tempo numbers. **Audio example 7.4** collects four of these, all from his first album: "You're No Good," "Pretty Peggy-O," "Gospel Plow," and "Freight Train Blues." Note that only the last of these is a train song per se—the style is not limited to such songs. Conversely, in some explicit train songs we hear no chugging at all. "It Takes a Lot to Laugh (It Takes a Train to Cry)," from 1965's *Highway 61 Revisited*, is a notable instance. **Audio example 7.5** presents a bit of the solo. Instead of chugging we hear mostly long, sustained pitches. This is of course also mimetic: we now hear a train whistle. This effect is also part of the train style, in which players would punctuate their chugging with whistle-like sustained pitches, adding bends to imitate Doppler shifting.

As his career progressed and his playing developed, Dylan made increasing use of sustained, bent pitches or chords in his harp playing, especially live. Are all of these reminiscent of the train style? Surely not. Many simply point to the blues, as I will discuss below. And yet the resonance is there as a potential interpretive affordance. Larry Starr, for example, hears train whistles in Dylan's solos on the studio version of "Don't Think Twice, It's All Right":

> The analogy is appropriate to this song of departure, even though the singer is departing (initially, at least) on foot, because of the extensive history that train imagery has in folk ballads and blues—as a symbol of movement and freedom.[20]

Another song that ostensibly has nothing to do with trains but a great deal to do with movement and freedom is "Mr. Tambourine Man." Though the song is about artistic inspiration, a secondary theme concerns stasis and movement, and especially the transition between them, which Dylan relates to the transition from sleeping to waking. Consider the following lines; underlines indicate stasis, italics motion:

I'm not sleepy and there is no place I'm going to

In the jingle-jangle morning *I'll come following you*

My weariness amazes me, I'm branded on my feet

Take me on a trip upon your magic *swirling* ship

My toes too numb to step

Wait only for my boot heels to be wandering
I'm ready to go anywhere, I'm ready for to fade
Into *my own parade*
Cast your *dancing spell* my way, I promise to *go under it*

Though you might hear *laughing, spinning, swinging* madly across the sun
It's not aimed at anyone
It's just *escaping on the run*

And if you hear vague traces of *skipping* reels of rhyme

It's just a shadow you're seeing that he's *chasing*

Far past the frozen leaves
The haunted, frightened trees

Yes, *to dance beneath the diamond sky*
With one hand waving free

The metaphorical network is clear enough. Stasis/sleep is akin to creative blockage, while motion/waking is the dawning of artistic inspiration through newly tingling senses. This leads—eventually—to ecstatic, dancing production.[21]

Crucially, it is *sound* that will catalyze this transition, specifically, the "jingle jangle" of the tambourine. But an actual tambourine sounds nowhere in Dylan's studio version.[22] Instead the closest analogue is his harmonica, whose contented chugging evokes rhythmic taps on the tambourine's head. **Audio example 7.6** provides several instances of a figure that dominates Dylan's two solos. It's a rhythmic gesture more than anything else, a kind of time keeping—harmonica as percussion instrument. **Figure 7.1** transcribes the figure's rhythm, using a plus sign (+) to indicate blow and a dash (–) for draw (in accord with conventional harmonica notation).

Note the regular alternation of + and – through most of the gesture, the in-and-out technique in action. The bracket shows a moment of increased animation, a brief burst of blow-and-draw sixteenth notes. We might hear this as a quickening of the rhythmic tattoo on the tambourine head, or maybe a shake, activating its cymbals. This injection of energy and motion is just the sort of enlivening sonic impulse that the lyrics celebrate, the sound that will jolt the artist into creative action.

The bracketed figure also hints at the train style, its rapid alternation of blow and draw reminiscent of chugging. To be sure, this is a subtle hint only, a train more dreamed or remembered than physically present. But the hint is strengthened by one moment of sustained, train-whistle bending in the first of two solos. **Audio example 7.7** excerpts the moment. Dylan holds the pitch for five full seconds, bending throughout a vigorous draw on hole 4.[23] This produces the

FIGURE 7.1. A recurring rhythmic gesture in Dylan's "Mr. Tambourine Man" solos.

second degree of the scale (in this case, the note G). That second degree has an unsettled, yearning quality—it yearns, specifically, for the first scale degree and a return of tonic harmony. When the tonic does return, Dylan's harp celebrates by revisiting the rhythmic pattern in figure 7.1, with its hints of chugging locomotion.

The chugging is far less subtle in Dylan's live performances of the song in the spring of 1966. In these concerts "Mr. Tambourine Man" ended the first, acoustic set. The song always had a blissed-out, dreamlike quality—a product of its surrealistic lyrics, easy rhythmic step, and chiming major chords—but in 1966 it became more dreamlike still, extended as it was by two long harmonica solos. **Audio example 7.8** provides three excerpts from the solo as he played it in Manchester on May 17. As he invariably does on this tour, he quickly settles in with a version of the rhythmic tattoo from figure 7.1. But in 1966 Dylan repeats and varies it more vigorously than on the studio version, playing variations on it up and down his instrument. Train-like chugging soon becomes incessant, wall to wall. But this remains a surreal distortion of the train topic, most notably because Dylan achieves it by chugging *and* sweeping simultaneously, combining the instrument's two axes of motion—in and out, side to side—into one continuously swirling action path. The only breaks come from long, bending, train-whistle draws on hole 4, which sometimes surpass ten seconds. The 1966 live "Tambourine Man" solos present the train style blurry and smeared, less a literal image than an impressionistic emblem of ecstatic, hypnotic motion. The result is a state of suspended animation—breathing room at its vastest—in which Dylan's chugging and bending create their own version of escape velocity, now aimed at a kind of spiritual transcendence. The song is far removed from Woody Guthrie, but one can hear in its distant train echoes a psychedelic fantasy on the gospel lyric that gave Guthrie's book its name: "This train is bound for glory, this train."

The sustained, bent pitches in these 1966 performances strengthen the train metaphor. But a bent harmonica note can conjure more than one history. Let us return for a moment to "It Takes a Lot to Laugh (It Takes a Train to Cry)." On the one hand, the lyric prods us to hear

Dylan's bent pitches as train whistles. But the song is also a blues—indeed, the most overt slow blues on *Highway 61*.[24] If we tune our ears to *this* tradition, we hear not doppler-shifted whistles but a whole history of Afro-diasporic musicians bending notes, producing pitches that fall "in the cracks" between adjacent keys on the piano. The two histories sound atop one another in "It Takes a Lot to Laugh." But if the train whistle evokes an optimistic image of modernity's liberatory potential, the bent blues pitch signifies something quite different: a history of unfreedom; of musical traditions under the pressure of the Middle Passage; and of white fascination with, and appropriation of, the bent sounds that resulted.

That Dylan participated in this history of fascination and appropriation we know. Bent pitches and blue notes saturate his guitar playing and singing, as we have already heard. As for the harmonica, Dylan deeply admired blues players like Little Walter, Sonny Boy Williamson II, Sonny Terry, and Junior Wells. We can hear this on the very first recording session he participated in after arriving in New York, backing Harry Belafonte on the harp for the latter's rendition of "The Midnight Special" (another train song, as it turns out). **Audio example 7.9** provides the beginning of one of the takes. Here Dylan plays handheld, demonstrating a surprising command of some basic urban-blues harp techniques, including wah-wah effects, bends, and fluttering tonguing. Such techniques became rarer once he settled into the familiar guitar-and-harmonica-rack configuration, but still there are moments of handheld playing, both in the studio and on stage to this day. One example is "Outlaw Blues" from *Bringing It All Back Home*, excerpted in **audio example 7.10**. Though Dylan plays electric guitar—with heavy, clangorous downstrokes—he doesn't use his harmonica rack; he chose to overdub the harp part instead.[25] We hear Dylan bend, wah, and chug his way behind his own voice, much as Little Walter would back Muddy Waters (though Dylan does so much less virtuosically). This is a rare occasion when the harmonica does *not* interrupt Dylan's voice, thanks to some basic studio trickery.

Dylan's harp in "Outlaw Blues" is nevertheless most audible when the voice isn't present, lending a sense of the call-and-response so familiar from Black blues and gospel traditions. In a track he recorded the next year, this antiphonal call-and-response is even more vivid. "Pledging My Time," from *Blonde on Blonde* contains some of Dylan's most strident harp playing. He again plays handheld, adding interjections after each sung line, call and response emerging from the same mouth. **Audio example 7.11** provides two excerpts. The harp tone becomes progressively more distorted as the track progresses, approaching and then surpassing the amplified harp sound pioneered by Little Walter and familiar from various Chicago blues players. Dylan likely used a "bullet" mic, which helps produce such a sound. Alternatively, producer Bob Johnston may have added the distortion in the control room.[26] All of these sonic signifiers point unmistakably to the harp traditions cultivated by the blues virtuosos of the South Side. And yet Dylan's actual playing bears little resemblance to theirs. The Chicago harmonicists "played with more emphasis on a big multi-layered sound with a wide variety of tonal variations and greater technical agility."[27] Dylan's playing, by contrast, is loose and wild, almost proto-punk in its DIY crudeness. There is a good deal of sweeping in his interjections, like the Pollock splatter of the 1966 gigs to come, but here with greater distortion. The mixture of modernist gestures and blues timbre is singularly bracing, a sonic analogue to the lyrics' "poison headache."

Thus far we have surveyed a populist history of the "people's instrument," a history of modernist antagonism, and two historical styles—the train style and the blues—which bring with them a range of social entailments involving race, technology, class, and mobility. To these I add one more history before closing this section: Dylan's harmonica playing as itself a historical phenomenon. A few months after the recording of "Pledging My Time," Dylan retreated from public life as the result of a motorcycle accident. His sudden absence from the world stage in 1966 was initially met with panic and speculation. Was he dead? Disfigured? Permanently retired? Soon enough, albums began to emerge, but Dylan played only a few isolated shows over the next eight years. And the albums received mixed reviews; 1970's *Self Portrait* was especially reviled. The historical '60s Dylan thus grew in stature, as a phenomenon past, perhaps for good. The vacuum created by his lack of touring created space for his historical myth to expand unchecked. Thus, when he returned to live performance in earnest in 1974, on an arena tour with the Band, his sounds generated a very particular response. For it is *here* that the lusty cheers for Dylan's harmonica playing truly begin. The first harp sound of the night was invariably met with a whoop from the audience. Live recordings from the '60s rarely feature such harmonica cheering. What did Dylan's harp mean in 1974, which it had not meant in 1966 or earlier?

I argue that Dylan's harmonica playing had itself become a part of history. As Greil Marcus puts it:

> The sound of his hammered acoustic guitar and pealing harmonica became a kind of free-floating trademark, like the peace symbol, signifying determination and honesty in a world of corruption and lies.[28]

By 1974 that free-floating trademark was *itself* historical, a sonic emblem of an idealistic moment now receding in the rearview mirror, as the "me decade" lurched uneasily forward. To judge by the cheers, Dylan's harp, arguably more than his guitar, became that sonic peace symbol. Those cheering the harmonica in 1974 were, in part, cheering the very idea of Bob-Dylan-playing-the-harmonica. This is what they'd paid for. To this day, Dylan's harp likely first triggers *this* history for most concert attendees—I'm hearing *Bob Dylan playing the harmonica!*[29] The italicized phrase brings with it a whole imagined history, a romance of Bob Dylan as (say it with me) the voice of a generation. From 1974 forward that history solidified into a kind of gospel: this man changed the world once, by singing and blowing.

IDENTITY

The previous section funneled from the sound of millions of amateur harmonicists to the sound of one player, Bob Dylan as world-historical individual. Note the tension between Dylan's harp playing as, on the one hand, a product of multiple intersecting histories and, on the other, as *itself* a singular historical phenomenon. The shape of the argument should already be familiar from chapter 2, in which we explored questions of identity and plurality as regards Dylan's voice. He fashioned that voice through strenuous imitation, yet the result is immediately recognizable as distinctly *his* voice—indeed, one of the most immediately recognizable voices in popular culture. Just so with his harmonica playing. In it we hear a jumbled mass of histories and influences, yet we also hear *Dylan*, one of the most idiosyncratic and influential players the instrument has known.

What do we hear when we "hear Bob Dylan" in his harp playing? In part, we hear a body—lips, mouth, lungs as bellows. So much could be said about any harpist, perhaps, but I propose that Dylan's imperfect technique on the harmonica discloses his body with particular vividness. I made similar arguments about his voice in chapter 2 and his guitar playing in chapter 6. As I stated there, a highly trained technique can, in part, "train out" individual idiosyncrasy, in favor of more broadly accepted standards of vocal or instrumental polish and virtuosity. Imperfect technique, by contrast, reveals the sounding body in all its particularity. When it comes to the harmonica, we hear *this* mouth, *this* bellows, *this* quirky approach to navigating their interface with the Hohner. Dylan's untutored sweeping technique is a prime example of such a bodily quirk, a sonic thumbprint as unmistakable as his flubbed fingerpicking.

His ramshackle technique also discloses a socially and historically determined body, a type. It is the unkempt sound of the scruffy bohemian who, as we noted in the introduction, is most often white and male. Unkempt playing is the privilege of the white male genius, for whom—in rock ideology—it becomes a warrant of authenticity and principled resistance to the high-gloss falsity of mainstream culture. Dylan's harp is in this sense of a piece with his voice and guitar, all of them combining into the sonic image of a countercultural male body, as disdainful of instrumental polish as it is of bourgeois good manners. If this, too, is a historical type, Dylan nevertheless gives it a singular instantiation in his harp playing, lips meeting the instrument with the casual abandon of one who simply cannot be bothered.

The result was so effective that Dylan's harp playing became a reliable style to imitate, especially for white male players interested in cultivating their own authentic bona fides—think Neil Young and Bruce Springsteen. But even when we hear those players adopting, say, Dylan's rack style, it is, crucially, *Dylan's* rack style, now itself a historical reference point.

In an article on Dylan's body, Ann Powers makes a passing reference to the harp, but it is rich with implications that take us in a different direction. She states that, before he strapped on an electric guitar, rock's archetypal phallic instrument, "Dylan employed the harmonica as his detachable penis—a vehicle for accessing explosive libidinal energy."[30] It is an obviously provocative line, and it provoked many when she delivered it at a keynote address for the World of Bob Dylan Symposium in Tulsa in 2019. That reaction in fact confirmed her argument that many fans and scholars are more comfortable thinking of Dylan as a mind rather than as a body. The idea also provokes because we are not used to thinking of the harmonica as "sexy." Though plenty of virtuosic blues players offer vivid counterexamples, in the context of folk and rock the harp is more typically understood as a humble instrument of rough-hewn, unpretentious honesty: a denim work-shirt in sound. But if we take Powers's provocation seriously, we can hear his pealing harp as releasing libidinal energy, expelled on the breath. This goes some way to accounting for the rowdy cheers. Perhaps fans are not only cheering the historical idea of Bob-Dylan-playing-the-harp, but also reacting to the physical co-presence of his body sounding its erotic energies.

Does it also sound his biography? That is, can we hear in it not only the influences of previous historical styles and big-name players, but also sounds particular to the life experience of the young Robert Zimmerman? Scottish poet Lachlan Mackinnon proposes just such a hearing in his 2003 poem "Bob Dylan's Minnesota Harmonica Sound."[31] Not all poems have an argument, but this one does. It begins with images of the Iron Range: the mine-ravaged earth, metal in the ground and metal vehicles to dig it out, a gray autumn landscape, the blowing wind. It is with this last that the harmonica comes into earshot: "the wind that seemed to be always blowing, / blowing and sucking."

The sly nod to "Blowin' in the Wind" is clear enough, but it is the enjambed extension to "blowing and sucking"—which occurs across a stanza break—that gives the poem its thematic core and its explicit connection to Dylan's harmonica playing. There is a crude, even blunt music in Mackinnon's use of the word "suck" rather than the more genteel "draw." But that crudeness and bluntness are apt poetic echoes of Dylan's coarse harp, as is the words' unpredictable repetition throughout the poem, like a malleable musical motive:

> [. . .]
>
> The freight-train whistles blew and sucked. Their wail
> hung in the steady and insistent gusts
> like a come-hither fading with the dusk.
>
> [. . .]
>
> Small wonder, then, if home became a spotlight,
> as, blowing and sucking, you count the changes,
> wearing a hood like a cowl to shut
> out the sound of the everlasting wind
>
> that blows from childhood, blows to suck you back.

Here, then, is the argument. Dylan's harp blowing and drawing is not just a musical technique. It also resonates with childhood experiences of being buffeted by the wind, of the train's whistle, of bodily exertion when trudging in the snow, breathing hard, heading home.[32] Mackinnon ultimately makes it a higher-level metaphor for memory, perhaps even for Dylan's attempts to escape his Hibbing roots: "the everlasting wind / that blows from childhood, blows to suck you back." Mackinnon reminds us that Dylan grew up in a windy, metallic place, panting in a hood against the cold, the dull landscape regularly punctured by roaring, whistling trains. No wonder he plays the way he does.

Dylan himself points to another sound from his childhood when discussing his harp playing, though it is such a throwaway comment you'd be forgiven for missing it. Speaking to Cameron Crowe for the booklet notes to *Biograph*, he lists players who inspired him, before making a surprising turn:

> The harmonica part, well, I'd always liked Wayne Raney and Jimmy Reed, Sonny Terry . . . 'Lil Junior Parker . . . but I couldn't get it in the rack like that or adjust the equipment to an amplified slow pace so I took to blowing out . . . actually Woody had done it. . . . I had to do it that way to be heard on the street, you know above the noise . . . like an accordion.

Like an accordion? It seems almost like a slip, truth escaping between the cracks. One of course expects Dylan to mention influential blues and folk players, both white (Raney, Guthrie) and Black (Reed, Terry, Parker). They all come from traditions that Dylan worshipped, all of them worlds removed from Hibbing. But the accordion? That was a northern Minnesota staple, the polka instrument par excellence. While the young Robert Zimmerman gravitated to remote musics of rebellion and risk—rock 'n' roll, urban blues, honky tonk, folk—he clearly heard the music surrounding him too, whether he liked it or not. Add to this the fact that the accordion is also, like the harmonica, a free-reed aerophone, and this becomes a forehead-slapper. How did I not hear *that* before? Once one calls to mind the chugging accordion in a polka band it is almost impossible to shake the similarity to Dylan's own harp playing. To be sure, his harmonica also indexes other styles, but it is hardly divorced from the sounds of Dylan's youth, however much he may have wanted to distance himself from them. When we hear "Bob Dylan" in the sound of his harmonica, perhaps we are hearing farther back than we knew, to the Hibbing noises that surrounded a young Robert Zimmerman, blowing to suck him back.

EMOTION

Let us return to Prague, March 11, 1995. As the set swings into its final stretch, Dylan and his band play a hushed, taut "It's All Over Now, Baby Blue." The entire song is haunted by a repeated rhythmic figure that John Jackson plays with palm-muted downstrokes on his acoustic guitar: short–short–short–short–*long*–*long* (♫♫♩ ♩). The overall effect is wary, uneasy—music in a defensive crouch. "Baby Blue" offers one side of a relationship-ending lover's quarrel, but there is no shouting in this version. The tone is instead mistrustful, wounded, vulnerable. Dylan's voice veers from tremulous to quietly focused, often locking into Jackson's palm-muted rhythm, as though hiding behind it.

But the song breaks open emotionally in its two harmonica solos, one after verse 3, the other after verse 4. In the first of these, Dylan remains silent for the music corresponding to the first part of the verse ("You must leave now"), waiting until the second portion ("Yonder stands your orphan") to begin. We will discuss such expressive silences—negative spaces, breathing room *within* the breathing room—in the next section. For now, we can note that, when he does play, his entire solo centers on just two pitches, D and C. Both of these are played on hole 4 of a C harp, D with a draw, C with a blow. **Audio example 7.12** presents the solo. The effect is somewhere between a moan and a wail. Dylan's lips don't need to move to get from D to C, he just needs to switch from draw to blow. But he *does* move his lips, making a quick sweep—a right-then-left whipping motion—as he leaves D for C. These whipping transitions sound like a catch in the voice, a gulp—or even better, a sob.

In a series of blog posts celebrating Dylan's harmonica playing, Mike Johnson (a.k.a. kiwipoet) singles out this very performance for praise. He focuses especially on the second solo, which you can hear in **audio example 7.13**:

> Listen to how Dylan lifts his voice in the last verse, how the harmonica takes over from where the voice leaves off, lays bare the real heartbreak and gives unrestrained voice to grief. Dylan can't cry onstage, but his harmonica can, and boy it sure does, and how painful it is at the end

> as he repeats the same notes over and over, like one of those protracted goodbyes everybody hates but sometimes you just can't escape. Just one more goodbye . . . one more . . . all the way to emotional exhaustion.[33]

Note the arresting claim that Dylan cries through his harmonica—or more precisely, that his harmonica provides an outlet for a kind of emotional expression not otherwise permitted onstage. Then there is the observation about repetition at the end of the solo. Here Dylan fixates on a four-note figure, which he plays no fewer than nineteen times, plus a few interspersed variants. Starting at about the eighth iteration, audience members cheer. This is another moment obstinate repetition, reminiscent of the repeated vocal ostinati discussed in chapter 5. In his harp playing, such ostinati almost always get a reaction from the audience, once they realize what is happening—that Dylan is burrowing into one figure, mining it for all it's worth. For Johnson, Dylan's fixation on this figure is mimetic of an anguished leave-taking, repeated goodbyes all the way to exhaustion.

In an influential midcentury study, music scholar Leonard Meyer proposed that music generates emotion by subverting expectations.[34] I have always found the argument somewhat overstated—music that does just what we expect it to can also arouse emotion—but it seems apt for Dylan's harp playing. As regards his solos on the instrument, the expectation is presumably for a certain degree of novelty and change across a solo—new phrases and ideas following one another. When Dylan instead obsessively fixates on one phrase, repeating it over and over, it subverts audience expectations, removes them from the normal flow of the performance, causes them to notice that something unusual is happening.

This can even happen with a single, elongated note. Consider this comment from the reddit channel r/bobdylan: "Anyone else get kinda choked up at the end of Girl from the North Country? Freewheelin' version, not Nashville Skyline. There's so much emotion in that long harmonica note. I love it so much." The first response: "I'm with you, man. It's very emotional."[35] **Audio example 7.14** presents the moment. The note in question subverts expectations, à la Meyer. It lasts for twenty-two beats, an eternity in a song whose sung lines typically occupy six or seven beats. No other harp note earlier in the song comes close to it in length; the longest are about four beats. Moreover, the extended harp pitch slows time in the guitar too. Though Dylan maintains the underlying pulse, the rate of change among the chords, which music theorists call the "harmonic rhythm," slows considerably. Dylan extends the first chord—that mysterious sonority he learned from Martin Carthy—under the held note from four beats to fourteen, the second chord from two beats to eight. The sustained harmonica pitch and the slowed harmonic rhythm open up a new temporality in the song, drawing out its rueful melancholy into another reluctant leave-taking.

As for the 1995 live version of "Baby Blue," its obsessive repetitions are interpretively legible along various lines, including Johnson's hearing of an agonizing goodbye. There are other interpretations, as well, including emotional flooding, which can freeze our thinking, narrowing our perspective on the world into a binary of threat and nonthreat. Or it can sound like a refusal to let go of something past. Indeed, this hearing seems especially apt to me, as the notes Dylan plays hold always to the same pitches, even when they conflict—sometimes jarringly—with the harmonies played beneath by guitar and bass. The song is ready to move on, but the harp isn't. There is then also the simple fact of intensity. Dylan does not merely repeat this figure nonchalantly; the repetitions have a sharp-edged urgency. They also teeter on the edge of incoherence, with blurred notes, air escaping through adjacent holes, countless micro-variations from iteration to iteration, threatening to pull the motive apart and turn it into something else.

Larry Starr has argued that Dylan's harmonica can access emotion that a singing voice cannot. Writing of the studio version of "Girl from the North Country," the very recording referenced in the reddit discussion, he states: "The delicate melodic curves Dylan plays on the harmonica serve as a voice for what is not (or cannot) be stated (or sung) in words. It might be said that the instrument intones the singer's silent prayer." He says something similar about "Chimes of

Freedom": "It is the previously taciturn harmonica that can now bring this intensely poetic, verbally dense song to its climax, expressing deep feelings that lie beyond the scope of even Dylan's words."[36] Or consider Paul Williams's comments on a 1981 performance of "Forever Young":

> Spirit is definitely present: you can hear it in his voice, and in the things the lead guitar player does, but mostly it's in the two harmonica solos, an extended one in the middle of the song, full of Dylan's feelings about all sorts of unnameables, and a brief brilliant one that ends the performance.[37]

Note especially the reference to "unnameables." We tread close to cliché in these comments—the old saw about music expressing what words cannot—but the idea is richer than that when it comes to Dylan. For his lyrics set up a web of emotional potentials that the harmonica can then exploit. Or express, in the literal sense—press out.

Williams proposes a direct link between the emotion of Dylan's harp playing and audience responses to it. Speaking of the performance of "Song to Woody" at the Gaslight in late September 1961, he states:

> Dylan plays a few notes of harmonica at the start of the Gaslight version of "Song to Woody," then puts the instrument away aside until the very end, and those three seconds of mouth harp at the end tie the whole song together . . . and offer an early taste of a certain sound Dylan creates with the harmonica, the same sound that pierces the heart of everyone who hears *Bringing It All Back Home* or "Just Like a Woman," the sound that has caused audiences through the years to clap and cheer whenever Dylan starts playing his harmonica on stage.[38]

In addition to drawing a link between fans' cheers and the way Dylan's harp can "pierce the heart" of his listeners, this quote provides a useful pivot to our final section. For it is worth underlining how *little* harp there is in this performance: a few seconds at the beginning and a few seconds at the end. You can hear both moments on **audio**

example 7.15. And yet Williams rightly notes that these brief harp figures achieve much, both setting the tone of the performance and creating a frame around the song, even wrapping it with an affective bow to close. Indeed, Dylan's harp playing can at times be at its most affecting when it is most minimal—a sparing eloquence.

ELOQUENCE

The *Oxford English Dictionary* defines eloquence as "the action, practice, or art of expressing thought with fluency, force, and appropriateness, so as to appeal to the reason or move the feelings." The *American Heritage Dictionary*, for its part, defines it as "persuasive, moving, or graceful discourse." Both definitions lean explicitly or implicitly on language—discourse—as the proper vehicle of eloquence. Given the word's etymology, this isn't surprising. Its second portion derives from the Latin *loqui*, which refers to speech (think "loquacious"). This raises a question. If we say that Dylan's harp playing is eloquent, are we saying that his harp speaks? This moves in contrary motion with the argument thus far, in which I have stressed the ways in which the harmonica opens space for specifically nonlinguistic modes of expression, interrupting the language channel. But perhaps the divide between language and the harp isn't as crisp as this dichotomy suggests. Perhaps, in moments, Dylan's harp approaches the condition of speech.

I am not proposing that Dylan adopts a speechlike rhythm in moments of harmonica eloquence, though he may. Instead, I am more interested in Dylan's use of space in certain solos, such that the harmonica notes he *does* play gain a quasi-semantic heft. Consider the celebrated pair of solos on "Every Grain of Sand," from 1981's *Shot of Love*. Both are exemplary instances of Dylan's minimalist eloquence. The first solo, which comes after the second verse, is a still point at the center of the song, Dylan carefully draping the simplest of melodies over three pitches: E♭, F, and G. **Audio example 7.16** presents the beginning of the solo. The phrases are brief, separated by pregnant rests. His playing is aptly tentative, even fragile, echoing the vulnerability of the lyrics. The solo follows the most Blakean couplet of this, Dylan's most Blakean song: "Then onward in my journey, I come to understand / That every hair is numbered, like every grain of sand." As those words linger in memory, it is not hard to hear the harmonica tune as a sounding emblem for the simplicity and wonder of Blake's mysticism. When the harmonica returns as an outro it follows another Blakean couplet, though this one is laced with Shakespeare: "I am hanging in the balance of the reality of man / Like every sparrow falling, like every grain of sand."[39] As one can hear in **audio example 7.17**, the harp tune is now slightly more complex, extending upward in register and finding a new lyrical breadth in the process. But the spare eloquence remains, each phrase speaking into the silence that follows it.

Dylan's eloquent spareness need not always involve silence. Sometimes it is simply a question of reduction—of the "persuasive, moving, or graceful" use of very few notes. Consider the traditional song "Moonshiner," which Dylan recorded in the studio on August 12, 1963, during the sessions for *The Times They Are a-Changin'*. It did not appear on that album, and was not released until 1991, when it became one of the most praised tracks on the first *Bootleg Series* release.[40] This is another performance of long, held pitches. **Figure 7.2** presents a transcription of the opening harp part above guitar annotations. You can hear the passage in **audio example 7.18**. As the plus sign (+) followed by a line at the top of the figure indicates, Dylan blows out for this entire phrase, merely adjusting his lips on the rack-mounted harp to change pitches. As a result, the only notes available to him on his E harp are those of the E-major triad: E, G♯, and B. His guitar nevertheless plays a set of chords that move in and out of agreement with these pitches. The song in fact hovers between a melancholy C♯ minor and an E major that offers a brief respite, like a momentary shaft of sun through the trees in the hollow where the singer has set up his still.

The first event in the song is a heart-catching shift between these two keys, marked with an arrow in the figure. We have just heard seven uneasy beats of a single sustained pitch in the harmonica—a G♯, made by blowing through hole 5 on the E harp—which hangs above a gently fingerpicked C♯-minor guitar chord. The shift in guitar

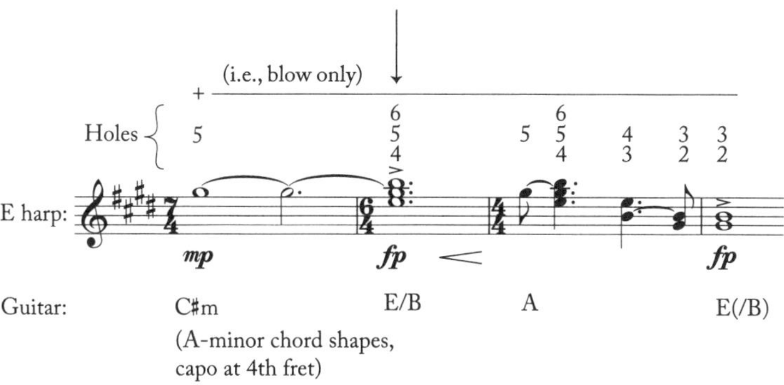

FIGURE 7.2. Harmonica and guitar at the opening of Dylan's 1963 version of "Moonshiner."

and harmonica after seven beats is surprising. Usually, such chord changes happen after regular multiples of three or four beats, marking out a familiar meter like 3/4 or 4/4. The metric surprise throws the moment into sharp relief. Dylan catches us off guard. He does this through the smallest motions, relocating one finger on the guitar and merely opening his mouth wider to cover holes 4, 5, and 6, while also using his tongue to add slight accent.[41] But the economy of motion belies the sounding result, which is affectively arresting. It is a shift in lighting and mood, the music opening up from the quiet claustrophobia of C♯ minor to a sunlit clearing of E major, the fragile single note on the harmonica expanding to a resonant chord.

But it is not entirely untroubled. The sense of repose is undercut by the guitar voicing. Dylan plays a B bass note under the E chord, giving it an unsettled feeling. Such chords are not points of rest, but typically on the way somewhere else. That somewhere else here is the A chord that arrives in the next bar. This chord dissonates with the harmonica notes above, which remain fixed to the pitches of the E-major triad.[42] Harmonica and guitar then come into harmonic realignment in the last bar of the figure, before the voice starts. We have found rest, it seems, in E major. But then Dylan begins to sing, and we are back in C♯ minor, the major-key light extinguished.

This opening is, on the whole, a masterclass in Dylan's eloquent economy of means, wringing maximum aesthetic oomph out of a minimum of notes. The effect differs dramatically from the wall-to-wall chugging and sweeping of the 1966 "Mr. Tambourine Man" solos. But later years would hear him approach that song with more and more eloquent restraint, as the 1995 Prague show demonstrates. After a couple desultory puffs on the instrument at the song's outset, Dylan plays two deeply affecting solos, one after the second verse and one at song's end. The first solo, hearable in **audio example 7.19**, is a simple paraphrase of the chorus's vocal melody.[43] **Figure 7.3(a)** shows its first phrase. Dylan's harp here paraphrases the chorus's opening line, "Hey, Mr. Tambourine Man, play a song for me."[44] He does not match the vocal melody exactly, but it is a close approximation, clearly tracing the skeleton of its octave descent, from the high C of "Hey!" marked with a dagger (†), down to the lower C of "me," marked with an asterisk.[45]

Note that Dylan does not begin immediately with the high C (†). Instead, he leads up to it with two quick sixteenth notes (G and A), creating what musicians call a pickup or anacrusis. Usually this would be a small detail, but in this performance it isn't. For, in his second solo, Dylan abstracts this anacrusis from the melodic paraphrase, making it the focal point of his entire solo. **Figure 7.3(b)** shows two

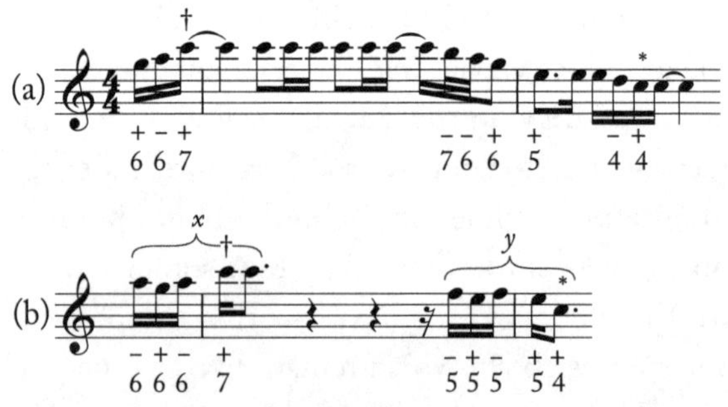

FIGURE 7.3. Two harmonica breaks from "Mr. Tambourine Man," as performed by Dylan in Prague on March 10, 1995: (a) the first phrase of the first solo; (b) principal motives of the second solo.

motives that dominate the second solo, labeling them *x* and *y*. **Audio example 7.20** provides the entire solo. Note first how *x*-then-*y* follows the outlines of the melodic line in 6.3(a), tracing the same path from high C (†) to low C (*). But in between there is not a continuous melody as in the mid-song paraphrase. Instead, there is silence. The process is one of abstraction by deletion.

Indeed, in the second solo silence is as important as sound. Dylan begins the solo with a long silence, resting for a full four bars before playing. Later in the solo he inserts another two-bar rest. One might at first wonder if these pauses were for technical reasons—say, to pick up the proper harp, or to adjust his grip on the microphone. But the fan-shot video of the concert shows otherwise: these were deliberate choices. **Video example 7.1** shows the start of the solo. He stands at the ready, mic in one hand, harp in the other, waiting for his moment. When that moment does arrive, it is with the abstracted anacrusis motives, *x* and *y*, which alternate at regular intervals, their flow perforated by silence. Dylan twice extends his phrases to play cadences that correspond to the end of the vocal lines. But more often than not, the solo is one of charged silences setting off motives *x* and *y*, which become more eloquent with each iteration.

Dylan plays less in this concluding solo, but motives *x* and *y* say more. In their eloquence they gain the quasi-semantic heft I discussed above, approaching the condition of musical words. What do they say? Perhaps they murmur something quiet about trains or tambourines. Note that the two motives share the same blow-draw pattern, as indicated in figure 7.3(b): – + – + +. The first four of these notes trace the sixteenth-note in-out figure that we explored in connection with figure 7.1, where we discussed both their similarity to the train style and their resemblance to gentle taps on a tambourine head. Here, though, any sense of chugging or tambourine playing is muted. The gesture is sublimated into a reduced, eloquent lyricism. Note too that the two motives also involve minimal motion side-to-side. Motive *x* moves one hole right (up in pitch, from hole 6 to 7), while *y* moves one hole left (down in pitch, from hole 5 to 4). This, too, is a distillation of the sweeping-plus-chugging of the 1966 "Tambourine

Man" solos. Gone is the modernist splatter of wild sweeps. In its place are incremental steps right, then left, cautiously exploring before slipping back into the song's dreaming silence. Indeed, the tenuousness of the solo is not unlike the tenuousness of early-morning consciousness, as ideas fitfully stir across our awareness before slipping away again.

But maybe this is too much interpretive specificity. As stated at the chapter's outset, Dylan's harp provides a space necessarily free of his language, a breathing room in which semantic meaning can drift. As it does, much else becomes audible: histories (of the people's instrument, of raced performance practices, of modernist antagonism); identities (the boy from the frozen north, land of mines and polkas); and affects (sobbing as a singer cannot). If at times Dylan's harmonica also seems to speak eloquently, it may not be to say anything definite. It gingerly approaches the condition of language only to retreat again, back into nonlinguistic sense. Let it drift, then, as the final Prague "Tambourine Man" solo plays. In the perforations between Dylan's brief phrases, meaning blooms for a moment and then fades. Perhaps the eloquence of this solo speaks to just that, to the delicacy of the transition between meaning and its absence, so like the transition between waking and sleep, or between breath bearing the word and breath free of it.

Chapter 8 audio examples:
soundingbobdylan.com/ch8

CHAPTER EIGHT

Piano

Seeking and Finding

Consider five scenes, strewn across sixty-two years:

April 5, 1957: Bobby Zimmerman, fifteen, is banging at the piano in his high school auditorium. He is doing his best Little Richard impersonation as front man for his band the Shadow Blasters. In his gusto, he breaks one of the instrument's pedals before the principal pulls the plug.

May 6, 1965: Backstage at Newcastle City Hall, the same pianist, now world famous and calling himself Bob Dylan, improvises at the piano in G♭, his fingers flat on the black keys. His producer Tom Wilson listens in. As Dylan puzzles through gospel-tinged changes, he stumbles onto a chord progression that will anchor one of his most famous songs, which he will record (with Wilson) in June.

August 12, 1970: In Columbia's Studio E, in New York, Dylan is at work on *New Morning*, seven of whose twelve songs will ride on his piano playing. Today he'll finally lay down the album version of "Time Passes Slowly," after many discarded takes. His galumphing piano sets the tone: an unsteady, bluesy waltz.

May 5, 1983: A few blocks away and thirteen years later, Dylan is again in the studio at the piano, feeling his way into a brooding chord progression in E♭ minor—more black keys. Mark Knopfler joins on twelve-string acoustic and an old tune made famous by Louis Armstrong, "St. James Infirmary Blues," morphs into "Blind Willie McTell," Dylan's most celebrated song of the decade.

July 3, 2019: Some thirty-six years on, the piano has become ever more prominent in Dylan's performing arsenal, handily edging out the guitar in the new millennium (fans wonder about arthritis). At the Roskilde Festival in Denmark, Dylan searches out novel chord voicings and pounces on odd snippets of melody at a grand piano, pedal-steel guitarist Donnie Herron shadowing his every move.

As these snapshots make clear, the piano has accompanied Dylan throughout his life, on stage, in the studio, and in casual moments of improvisation and compositional noodling. It was Dylan's first instrument, learned as a kid in Hibbing; in late life he once again came to play it more than any other. In the intervening years its prominence waxed and waned, but there is no period in his musical career in which it is entirely absent. The keyboard, in short, is as central to Dylan's musical life as are the guitar and harmonica.

As central, but not the same. For the piano is a radically different instrument musically, physically, and socioculturally. The guitar and harmonica were quintessential instruments of the folk revival—portable, affordable, and accessible. The piano was none of these. Moreover, it essentially straddled the space marked out by the folk revival's nascent counterculture. It was on the one hand an instrument of the bourgeois living room, a piece of furniture and an object of social distinction. Think of countless middle-class kids dutifully taking weekly piano lessons, as Bobby Zimmerman and his brother David did.[1] On the other hand, it had become a vehicle of racial fantasy and sexual transgression in the hands of Little Richard and Jerry Lee Lewis. The quintessential instrument of middle-class respectability had turned against itself. Crucially, neither of these registers—bourgeois domesticity or rebellious rock 'n' roll—coincided with the romanticized proletarian space that folk revivalists sought to cultivate with their humble guitars and harmonicas. "This machine kills fascists," said a sticker on Woody Guthrie's guitar. One can hardly imagine the same sticker adorning a Steinway grand.

The piano thus afforded Dylan not only a range of musical sounds unavailable on the guitar or harp, but also an array of distinct raced and classed identities, all of them more or less remote from Guthrie and the folk revivalists. Some of these pianistic identities aligned with Black expressive culture, others with white middle America. This racial duality fits almost too tidily with the colors of the keyboard—the piano in Black and white, if you will. Most important for our story, the instrument allowed Dylan to both escape from, and return to, his childhood roots. Think of it as a kind musical express train, taking him to points distant as well as back home. Let's trace that journey, which begins in an implausibly grand auditorium.

APRIL 5, 1957 (HIBBING)

The massive Hibbing High was built with iron ore money in the early 1920s, during Hibbing's flush days as "the richest village in the world."[2] By the time young Robert Zimmerman stepped onto the auditorium stage, the city had begun its decline into postwar depression, but the high school remained—and still remains—a reminder of the boom years.[3] The opulent 1,800-seat auditorium was, Dylan himself said, "no small music box theater but a professional concert hall like Carnegie Hall built with East Coast mining money, with curtains and props, trapdoors and orchestra pit."[4] There were also four massive chandeliers, faux-Greek urns, and a painting of the muses. In short, the room was decked out with emblems of the Old World, aspirational European high culture everywhere you looked. One imagines the locals—working-class stock descended largely from Finns, Slovenes, and Italians—swelling with pride on entering the room.[5]

And being horrified when they heard Abe Zimmerman's kid and his friends making such an unholy racket in the place. On

April 5, 1957, the Shadow Blasters played two Little Richard songs ("Jenny, Jenny" and "True Fine Mama"), as part of a variety show arranged by the student council.[6] Bobby would play in the auditorium again on February 6, 1958, his new band the Golden Chords offering up "Rock and Roll Is Here to Stay."[7] In 1957 the Shadow Blasters wore matching pink shirts and sunglasses, their hair swept back in bouffants. Bobby wanted it loud, so he added extra microphones. There was no Pete Seeger there to cut the cord with an axe, as the (apocryphal) story goes about Dylan's electric turn in Newport eight years later.[8] But a certain Principal Pederson did cut the power. Bobby, for his part, broke the piano's pedal. One recognizes the primal scene of Bob Dylan lore immediately: the confrontational musician on stage, opposed by the squares. But on this day in 1957 Robert Zimmerman had not yet become Bob Dylan. He was not even a Woody Guthrie disciple yet. Instead, at this point his goal in life was to "join Little Richard," as he put it under his yearbook picture.[9] The search for an identity was on. And the piano provided a vehicle. On stage at the Hibbing High auditorium, he played it as though he could pound his way to a new self, through sheer physical force.

The reaction, per Shadow Blasters guitarist Larry Fabbro, "went from shock to laughter to . . . booing."[10] Bobby was usually staid and bookish. To see him adopting Richard's mannerisms was too much for the students, administrators, "school system officials," and "Iron Range dignitaries" in attendance.[11] His friends, for their part, were embarrassed. Here is Echo Helstrom, Dylan's girlfriend at the time:

> He was playing the piano like Little Richard. He was standing up. And stomping on those little foot pedals and screaming and you know the way that he was singing, "I gotta girl and her name is Echo" and I was so nervous because I was always afraid something would go wrong because the people would boo and everything, you know, all the time and it embarrassed me. It didn't even bother him—he was just happy.[12]

Close friend John Bucklen offers a similar account:

> He got up there . . . in this talent program at school . . . came out on stage with some bass player and drummer, I can't remember who they were, and he started singing in his Little Richard style, screaming, pounding the piano, and my first impression was that of embarrassment, because the little community of Hibbing, Minnesota, way up there, was unaccustomed to such a performance.[13]

What were they accustomed to? The rest of the 1957 program gives an idea. The Shadow Blasters were just one of fifteen acts, which also included "tap dancing, magicians, an accordion player, and dramatic readings."[14] Amid this wholesome North Country fare—complete with accordion, presumably playing a polka—it's no surprise that Zimmerman's Little Richard routine provoked jeers and guffaws.

The school paper had paved the way. In announcing the 1957 variety show, the editors referred to the Shadow Blasters as a "jazz quintet," before alluding to them playing "a sensational novelty number which at the moment is top secret."[15] Both labels—jazz and novelty—were wide of the mark. Little Richard was neither.[16] But the editors may not have had a category for the music of a queer, Black rock and roller, or were not willing to name it explicitly if they did. "Novelty" was thus a handy euphemism for sexually licentious Black sound. It was surely a wink to the buttoned-up mainstream kids shuffling through Hibbing High's hallways, many of whom would soon be lustily booing in the auditorium.[17]

But what were they booing? The volume, perhaps. The dissonance between Bobby's quiet classroom persona and his wildness on stage, very likely. But these don't account for the level of hostility, which must have resulted at least in part from racial politics. Savor the euphemistic understatement of John Bucklen's account: "the little community of Hibbing, Minnesota, way up there, was unaccustomed to such a performance." It doesn't take a critical race theorist to catch the subtext of phrases like "little community" and "way up there" as code for rural, white, and insular. Those folks were unaccustomed to such noise and reckless energy, yes, but also unaccustomed to such a noisy encounter with Black expressive culture, especially coming from an awkward, middle-class Jewish kid.

And what was he *doing* to the auditorium's 1922 Steinway grand?[18] The room's quasi-European decor brought out the instrument's middle-class and Old World associations. But Bobby's playing insisted on its flipside, its affiliation with rock rebellion, setting the respectable white piano into dissonance with its Black other. Perhaps *this* dissonance offended most of all. For many of the students in the room had surely been dutiful piano pupils, studying their Hanon exercises and Clementi sonatinas, fingers arched and backs straight. What they saw and heard on stage dissonated with that white, middle-class regime of bodily discipline. One needed to look no further than the two Zimmerman brothers to sense the gulf between these poles. Bobby's younger brother David was evidently a model piano student, "who quickly learned his scales" and "loved his lessons." The school music teacher, Val Peterson, drew the contrast explicitly: "When Bobby played the piano he would stand and really pound it. But when David played, he sat and played very nicely."[19]

So, what did Bobby's standing and pounding sound like? Unfortunately, no recordings circulate of the two Hibbing High gigs. We do, however, have a recording of Bobby and John Bucklen goofing off in the latter's home in 1958, an excerpt of which we already heard in audio example 2.1. The song in that example, "Hey, Little Richard," features the two of them singing in call and response, with Bobby playing a heavy-footed, crude piano vamp on an F chord, transcribed in **figure 8.1. Audio example 8.1** presents a snippet of the recording.

We hear none of Little Richard's virtuosity—no manic triplet chords in the upper register, for example. Instead, we get hallmarks of Dylan's piano style, which will persist throughout his career: workaday mid-register chords in the right hand, supported by bass octaves in the left. We can in fact hear a similar texture eight years and a continent away, as Dylan plays piano for his producer Tom Wilson backstage.

FIGURE 8.1. Dylan's piano accompaniment to "Hey, Little Richard," recorded with John Bucklen in 1958.

MAY 6, 1965 (NEWCASTLE)

Dylan is seven dates into a tour of the UK, his every move being documented by filmmaker D. A. Pennebaker for his cinema verité classic *Dont Look Back*. Pennebaker catches Dylan on a few occasions playing upright pianos backstage. **Video example 8.1** shows an outtake from the film. To Dylan's right, partially obscured behind the piano, is Dylan's producer Tom Wilson.

In each of these moments of backstage piano noodling, Dylan plays in the same key, G♭ major. This puts the pianist's fingers almost exclusively on the instrument's black keys, a technique and sound Dylan had come to favor at the instrument. Many years later, he said to Paul Zollo,

> On the piano my favorite keys are the black keys . . . the songs that go into these keys right from the piano, they sound different. They sound deeper. Yeah. They sound deeper. Everything sounds deeper in those black keys.[20]

Given Dylan's indebtedness to Black keyboard traditions, from his earliest Little Richard imitations, it is hard not to hear racial resonances in his remark about the "deeper" sounds of the black keys. After all, one of the oldest stereotypes about Black music is that it is soulful, deep. Did Tom Wilson, an African American from Texas, hear any Black sounds in his artist's black-key playing, with its hints of gospel? To judge by his facial reactions, he may have. The camera focuses intently on Wilson, who listens enthusiastically, nodding his head, lips curled into a smile, at one point mumbling approval. Yet the thread between Wilson and Dylan is tenuous. Wilson is focused intently on Dylan and his playing, but the latter does not reciprocate, playing as though no one is there. If Dylan is searching for inspiration from Black music here—groping for the right chord, the right gospel groove—he searches alone, seemingly oblivious to the Black man right next to him. It's uncomfortable to watch.

It was probably uncomfortable for them, too. The relationship between Dylan and Wilson had become strained of late, and Wilson had flown in to join the tour in hopes of shoring things up and of potentially recording Bob in the studio in London if the mood struck.[21] Here in Newcastle, was Wilson perhaps listening for Dylan's next step, eager to keep pace? If so, he would have heard a snippet of it in the pianist's G♭ riffing. In **video example 8.2**, taken directly from *Dont Look Back*, Dylan begins with an unmistakable bit of music: it's the ascending chord progression from the verse of "Like a Rolling Stone."[22] As he plays, think of those opening lines ("Once upon a time you dressed so fine / Threw the bums a dime in your prime / Didn't you?") and you will hear the similarity immediately. To be sure, the key—that "deep" G♭ major—is very remote from the eventual C major of the studio version, which is all white keys, but Dylan is famous for changing keys. Indeed, "Like a Rolling Stone" didn't find its way into C until the day the final version was recorded. The day before, it was in D♭ major, which also uses all five black keys.

In Newcastle the song is taking shape under Dylan's fingers. Three nights later he will play it again, backstage at the Royal Albert Hall, as shown in **video example 8.3**.[23] In both cases the "Rolling Stone" progression dissolves into music that *won't* find its way into the famous song, making clear that this is just a riff so far, a chord progression that Dylan is toying with. It's not the backbone of a song yet.[24] But these clips reveal something important about Dylan's way with the piano, his approach to it as a tool for composition. In all the clips we see him experimenting intently, groping his way toward chords and grooves, trying out changes and melodies on the fly. His attitude at the instrument in these moments is a kind of musical rummaging. Whether he's feeling his way into a new song, trying to find an old one, or piecing together a melodic riff in live performance, his attitude is often one of mildly perplexed searching, as if hunting for mysterious sounds deep in the instrument's boxy interior. Think of someone at a large trunk of clothing, pulling out various pieces, turning them over and examining them, before dropping them and plunging arms back in to search some more. Dylan the pianist is, in this sense, a *curious* musician, in the full sense of that word: unusual, odd, but also inquisitive, seeking.

What does his rummaging turn up on this occasion? The "Rolling Stone" riff, yes, but also some other music that sounds little like that song. As already noted, it has a gospel vibe, and it may well be an actual gospel tune, barely held in memory. Wilson's surprise on hearing it suggests that it is new to his ears, though he would surely catch the idiom. The strongest gospel signal is a lick Dylan plays in octaves in his left hand, transcribed in **figure 8.2**. This is a pentatonic upbeat figure characteristic of gospel and often played at the "turn around," when the chord progression returns to its initiating tonic. It is especially idiomatic in G♭ major, as it can be played entirely on the black keys.

How striking, then, to hear a snippet of "Rolling Stone" flow into this music from the Black tradition. The main musical source usually cited for "Like a Rolling Stone," "La Bamba," is from a different nonwhite tradition.[25] But the music corresponding to that song is the chorus ("How does it *feel*?"). It features a simple loop of the I, IV, and V chords, familiar from countless other songs. The verse progression, by contrast, has an ascending stepwise progression uncommon

FIGURE 8.2. A left-hand gospel figure from Dylan's piano playing backstage in Newcastle, May 6, 1965.

in guitar rock, but one that Dylan would turn to more and more in these years, especially in piano-driven songs like "Queen Jane Approximately" and "Ballad of a Thin Man."

The footage from Newcastle suggests that this ascending phrase was cut from gospel cloth. Wilson would hear it again in June as he presided over the two days of studio sessions that would produce "Like a Rolling Stone." As it happens, it would be Wilson's last time working with Dylan. In one of the most rehearsed anecdotes in Dylan lore, when Al Kooper switched from guitar to organ Wilson objected, to Dylan's frustration. And just like that, Wilson was out, eventually replaced by another Columbia producer, Bob Johnston, who would man the board for the next several Dylan albums, including his most piano-heavy LP, 1970's *New Morning*.

AUGUST 12, 1970 (NEW YORK CITY)

Dylan has been out of the public eye since his motorcycle accident in 1966, mostly in retreat at his family home in the Byrdcliffe colony of Woodstock, New York.[26] A 1968 photo by Elliott Landy shows him short-haired and smartly dressed, playing a grand piano in his living room, his children Jesse and Maria on the rug in front of him. The instrument's lid is closed, its top cluttered with books, papers, and two pillows. The piano is a stunning Wm. Knabe & Co. grand, with ornately carved legs and deep, undulating figures in the woodgrain of the case.[27]

A decade earlier in the Hibbing High auditorium, Bobby Zimmerman's allegiances to the piano as an object of rock 'n' roll rebellion had been unambiguous, Little Richard all the way. The express train had left the station, at high velocity, heading to parts unknown. By 1965 it had taken him far from Hibbing, both geographically and musically. Backstage in Newcastle we hear him searching again, rummaging in the piano for sounds that might ground his next big song, gospel idioms in his fingertips. But now in 1970 it's time for a return trip, as Dylan the family man embraces the instrument's bourgeois, domestic flip side. To be sure, he is not playing a modest upright like those that graced most middle-class living rooms in Hibbing; fame and wealth have their benefits.[28] But the domestic setting in Landy's photo is unmistakable. One can imagine the sound, Dylan's idle plunking mixing with children's babbling and scurrying about on the rug. Dylan's mom Beattie, who came to visit in the same year the photo was taken, after her husband Abe's death, described the scene: "The kids are always around, climbing all over Bob's shoulders, and bouncing to the music . . . they love the music, sleep right through the piano."[29]

If all of this weren't proof enough that the instrument was once again a domestic fixture in Dylan's life, it would also find a prominent place on his most domestic album: 1970's *New Morning*, on which his piano playing drives seven of the twelve songs.[30] In one of them, the luminous "Sign on the Window," he sings over solo piano (**audio ex. 8.2**):

> Build me a cabin in Utah
> Marry me a wife, catch rainbow trout
> Have a bunch of kids who call me "Pa"
> That must be what it's all about

Dylan's piano playing under the verse is generous and warm, the simple chord progression decorated by arpeggios and turning figures—the sound of relaxed contentment. The key, as in Newcastle, is once again G♭ major, Dylan's pianistic happy place. But the song is not all blissed-out ease. The bridge (**audio ex. 8.3**) includes an arresting modulation to D major just before the line "Looks like nothing but rain." It is a remote key in the present context, containing only two black keys, in contrast to the five of G♭ major. But no sooner has Dylan established D major than he quickly departs it, drifting to yet another tonal station, B major, which arrives on the word "rain." This chord moves us back nearer the orbit of G♭ major, eventually acting as a pivot that returns us to that key. This is the tonic key, whose metaphorical status as "home" is by now familiar. Dodging the squall of rain, we return to our musical home, safe in the living room, domestic equilibrium restored. Warm and dry inside, the lyric persona can observe the rain through the window with slightly melancholic detachment, idly musing, "Sure gonna be wet tonight on main street / Hope that it don't sleet." Banal, domestic weather talk.

There are two things to notice about the bridge's harmonic convulsion. First, it is quintessentially pianistic. Such quicksilver leaps between remote keys do not happen in Dylan's guitar songs. The piano opens up different avenues of harmonic exploration.[31] Second, the convulsion coincides with a meteorological event, a cloudburst that interrupts the blue sky of domestic calm. In the previous song on side 2, "New Morning," Dylan had been "So happy just to see you smile / Underneath this sky of blue." But in "Sign on the Window" a cloud passes, the sunny idyll momentarily disturbed. Such moments of disequilibrium pop up elsewhere on the album, as we'll hear. For now, we should note that weather and nature are central to *New Morning*, an album that weds the domestic to the pastoral.[32] Roosters crowing, rabbits running, trout streams, bridges, cabins—the songs are stuffed with images of rural retreat, which set the scene for conjugal harmony. On the skater's waltz of "Winterlude," for example, the frozen winter landscape provides just the right contrast for a cozy evening by the fire.

Nowhere is the pastoral more overt than on "Time Passes Slowly":

> Time passes slowly up here in the mountains
> We sat beside bridges and walked beside fountains
> Catch the wild fishes that float through the stream
> Time passes slowly when you're lost in a dream

The music for this celebration of rural indolence did not come easy. Over multiple recording dates spread across months, Dylan and his producer Bob Johnston tried several arrangements, some of them elaborate.[33] The take Dylan eventually settled on, the final attempt on August 12, 1970, is stripped-down, raw, and piano-forward.[34] Like "Winterlude," it is a waltz, but a wobblier one. And the wobble is in the piano. **Audio example 8.4** presents the song's opening. The triple meter lurches forward, Dylan's blocky chords nudged by anticipations and grace notes, as shown in **figure 8.3**. The opening harmony is quizzical. Music theorists would call it a diminished triad in first inversion. The D♭ atop it makes it sound a bit like a bluesy tonic, but the B♭ in the bass also gives it a hint of dominant function. You need not understand all those music-theoretical details to sense the effect, though; it is an unsettled chord. The harmony looks at us askance, the musical equivalent of a side-eye. It is only when the band enters and Dylan begins to sing that we ease momentarily into a stable groove, simple triads sitting up straight on their chordal roots.

But stability doesn't last long. In two piano breaks between verses, Dylan comes perilously close to losing the groove. In the first (**audio ex. 8.5**), following verse 1, he embarks on a jazzy dialogue between right and left hands, shown in **figure 8.4**. The dialogue has a slapstick

FIGURE 8.3. "Time Passes Slowly," *New Morning* take, opening.

quality to it, a comic pratfall that lands too early on the octave E♭s, marked by a dagger (†). To confirm the meter, these low E♭s would need to arrive at the metric downbeat, the bar line. Instead, they come in the middle of the bar, an awkward one and a half beats early. But right on the heels of this ill-timed bass thud, Dylan recovers with his right hand, adding a tag on the downbeat that has the effect of a comic "ta-da!" Imagine a comedian executing a theatrical tumble when walking across the stage, only to end miraculously upright, arms triumphantly raised. Perhaps this is the kind of moment the guitarist on the session Ron Cornelius had in mind when he said, "You fall over laughing the first time you see [him play the piano], because his hands start at opposite ends of the keyboard, then just sorta collide in the middle. He does that all the time, but the way he plays just knocks me out."[35] Dylan's hands don't exactly start at opposite ends of the keyboard here, but the spirit of the quote fits.

Remember that the song is a waltz—that is, it has three beats to the bar. Musicians most often indicate such three-beat meters with the time signature 3/4. Any departure from the regular 1-2-3, 1-2-3 pattern of 3/4 will feel like a stumble, or a moment of imbalance. So, in these figures look for moments when a time signature *other* than 3/4 appears, for example, the 2/4 bar at the end of figure 8.4. This is a woozy moment of trying to regain metric equilibrium, attempting to dial the song's regular 1-2-3, 1-2-3 back in after the pratfall. Later stumbles have deeper metric repercussions. Consider the second

FIGURE 8.4. "Time Passes Slowly," *New Morning* take, first piano break.

FIGURE 8.5. "Time Passes Slowly," *New Morning* take, second piano break.

break, in **audio example 8.6**, which is transcribed in **figure 8.5**. Now there is no jazzy dialogue between hands, just bassline and chords. But this break wobbles metrically even more than the last one, as the two 2/4 bars indicate. Dylan has just sung, "Time passes slowly when you're searching for love." And search he does. At each of the 2/4 bars, Dylan is searching for 3/4 after losing it in a syncopated descent in the right hand. He tries twice to regain his metric footing at the piano, succeeding the second time and setting up the bridge that follows ("Ain't no reason to go in a wagon to town").

Pastoral relaxation does not always come easy for the city dweller, it turns out. Dylan's lyrics tell us as much: "Time passes slowly up here in the daylight / Stare straight ahead and try so hard to stay right." Staying right—present in the here and now, committed to this life in retreat, content with what is—this takes effort. One can *hear* the effort in **audio example 8.7**, as Dylan sings these lines in the climactic final verse. As **figure 8.6** shows, this is the melodic highpoint of the song, ascending twice to F4 in the two lines just quoted, and then surpassing that with high G4s on "blooms" and "Time" in the second system of the figure. There is a pinched tightness to the voice throughout the verse, an audible strain in the upper register, the opposite of chilled-out nature vibes. And the strain once again disrupts the meter, which stumbles into an awkwardly bulging 5/4 bar right after the line about staying right. Dylan does his best with the piano to steady the meter and hold onto the climax "up here in the daylight." As the bracket beneath the bottom system shows, his piano alternates between the V and IV chords in these bars. These repeated chords, built on scale degrees $\hat{4}$ and $\hat{5}$, create a plateau of harmonic energy as Dylan effortfully works to reground the music in 3/4.

But isn't this all simply a product of a shaky piano technique? And if so, am I reading too much into it? I may be. But it is useful to parse just what kind of artistic intention might be relevant here. It is indeed correct that I do not attribute conscious intention to Dylan in the moment of playing, as though he were deliberately stumbling at the piano in order to portray a faltering pastoral calm: "If I drop this beat here and add this beat there, it will create a sense of how hard it is to stay right." Such calculation is not his way. It is nevertheless telling that he chose *this* take for the record and not, say, the swashbuckling Joe Cocker–inspired rendition with full band.[36] That version never misses a step, surefooted and brash to the last. This is in large part due to the fiery arrangement for full band, which anchors the 3/4 groove. It never wavers. Perhaps Dylan sensed the dissonance between that confident arrangement and his unsteady lyric, preferring this ragged-but-right piano-led take instead.

Whatever its genesis, the uneasiness of the result speaks for itself. Christopher Ricks sensed it: "it assuredly isn't voiced as happily idle, a happy idyll. . . . [It] is rhythmically and vocally bumpy, jagged, pot-holed, unsettled and unsettling."[37] Blame the piano. While Dylan's singing is indeed "vocally bumpy," those bumps originate in the pot-holed surface below, the uneven keyboard accompaniment. With its lurching chords, its dropped and added beats, and its woozy solo licks, Dylan's piano searches for a settled rhythm—just as the lyric persona searches for love, for emotional steadiness, for peace of mind—and almost finds it. But the domestic pastoral remains elusive, ever fading away.

FIGURE 8.6. "Time Passes Slowly," *New Morning* take, final verse.

APRIL 11 AND MAY 5, 1983 (NEW YORK CITY)

By the time Dylan recorded "Blind Willie McTell" in 1983, the domestic pastoral was long gone. His marriage to Sara had ended in the late '70s, and he had marked the occasion in 1978 by circling the globe on his longest tour to date—114 shows (some snidely dubbed it the "alimony tour"). In other words, the opposite of retreat. And the opposite of the stripped-down musical intimacy he cultivated on *New Morning*. The 1978 band was his biggest yet, complete with backup singers, horns, and auxiliary percussion. This big-band approach would persist in some form through the gospel years that followed. Between 1978 and 1981 Dylan was backed by stellar keyboardists on stage and in the studio—Alan Pasqua, Terry Young, Willie Smith, Barry Beckett, Spooner Oldham—so he didn't play as much piano himself; the Stratocaster was his main prop. But he nevertheless did turn to the keyboard on some songs, most notably the live versions of "When He Returns" and "Pressing On."[38] Both show Dylan the pianist in full gospel mode, making explicit the generic affiliation that had only been implicit backstage in Newcastle some fifteen years earlier. Dylan also played piano in the studio on a small handful of songs that found their way onto album in the years after *New Morning*, including "Dirge" (*Planet Waves*, 1974), "Isis" (*Desire*, 1976), and "Lenny Bruce" (*Shot of Love*, 1981), as well as some that *didn't* make it onto albums, like "Let's Keep It Between Us" (1980), "Angelina" (1981), and the most famous non-album track of them all, "Blind Willie McTell" (1983). The song sees Dylan once again using the piano to venture far from his Hibbing roots, now into the deep south.

Most consider "Blind Willie McTell" his best song of the 1980s, and many place it among his best songs of all time. His decision to leave it off *Infidels*, rather than cutting weaker songs on the album (there are several candidates), has exasperated just about anyone with an interest in Dylan.[39] Was he unsatisfied with the song? He and producer Mark Knopfler tried several arrangements over three separate days of recording, including the first and last sessions for the album,

April 11 and May 5, 1983. Was there really no take in the bunch that Dylan liked? The song raises other questions too. For one, why does it sound so little like the music of the actual Blind Willie McTell? A twelve-string guitar virtuoso in the Piedmont blues tradition, McTell sang a wide repertory in a piercing tenor.[40] The high seriousness of Dylan's song bears no resemblance to the knowing wit of much of McTell's output, including his most famous number, "Statesboro Blues."

Though Dylan's lyrics take McTell's name for their refrain ("I know no one can sing the blues / like Blind Willie McTell"), the music comes from a different source: "St. James Infirmary," a standard sung by many, but most memorably by Louis Armstrong. His 1928 recording of the song struts proudly in a somber E minor, the gait—swung eighths and clear four-to-the-bar meter—familiar from countless march-based New Orleans numbers. Whether Dylan had Armstrong's version in his ears isn't clear, but there can be no question that his song is based on "St. James Infirmary" in some form—the resemblance in both melody and harmony is unmistakable. Dylan moreover nods to the borrowing in his final verse, in which he mentions the "St. James Hotel."[41] There are nevertheless two notable differences between Dylan's song and Armstrong's "St. James": key and rhythm. We will begin with key. One circulating studio take has Dylan trying a version in F minor, a semitone up from Armstrong.[42] But the best-known studio versions, which I will focus on here, are a semitone *down*, in flat-heavy E♭ minor.[43] This choice of key puts Dylan's fingers once again on the black keys, all five of which find a home in E♭ minor. This, then, is one likely reason Dylan chose to play the song on piano. Recall his comment about music played on the piano's black keys sounding "deeper." If any lyric of his needs deep resonance, it's this one, haunted by "the ghosts of slavery ships."

Figure 8.7 shows the chord progression that cycles throughout the song in both versions that we will study. The figure divides the progression into two beamed phrases, labeled *a* and *b*. Text underlays indicate the sung portions that correspond to each phrase. The *a* phrase is a simple oscillation between the tonic and dominant chords in E♭ minor.[44] Note the there-and-back motion of the bassline, indicated by the angled beam on the lower staff.[45] The *b* phrase also has a there-and-back bass motion, but now moving stepwise, first by descending semitones from E♭3 down to C♭3 before returning more quickly, via whole steps, back up to E♭3. Here, too, I have highlighted the motion with an angled beam. Dylan's right-hand chording acts as a counterpoint to these bass lines. In the *a* phrase, his three right-hand chords all have B♭4 as a shared upper pitch, indicated with an arrow in the figure. This note tolls funereally throughout, a veritable "undertaker's bell." Dylan re-sounds it twice at the beginning of the *b* phrase—it sits atop the same tonic and dominant chords—before the upper voice descends by step in the harmonic sequence that follows, ending on E♭4. But as the parenthesized chord shows, Dylan often substitutes the original voicing of the tonic triad here, reinstating the tolling B♭4.

There are three things to notice here. First is the particular resonance that Dylan draws from his preferred black keys, most obvious in the tolling B♭4. Dylan's right-hand pinky spends much of the song on this pitch, the rest of his hand often resting on the remaining two notes of the E♭-minor chord, lending the whole a hypnotic sense of stasis. The E♭-minor chord that sits so comfortably under Dylan's right hand—all black keys—is never far from our ears, the music always drifting back to it. It casts a sonic shadow over the whole song. The second detail to notice is the chromatic bass descent in the *b* phrase.[46] This kind of bass motion is much easier to achieve on

FIGURE 8.7. "Blind Willie McTell," piano chord progression.

the piano than the guitar, another likely reason for his choice of the instrument. Finally, note the cyclicity of the progression. The *a* and *b* phrases both have a circular trajectory, departing from tonic and returning to it. Moreover, the whole progression repeats cyclically, its opening chord returning at the end, like a snake eating its tail. There is thus a double cyclicity to the progression, loops within loops.

But the way Dylan animates this process rhythmically varies dramatically between these two takes. The April 11 version features a full band, including organist Alan Clark, bassist Robbie Shakespeare, drummer Sly Dunbar, and former Rolling Stone Mick Taylor on slide guitar.[47] But it starts with Dylan alone, voice and piano. **Audio example 8.8** provides the song's opening. He begins by improvising through the *a* phrase, decorating its chords in free time, no meter yet. The gospel feel is again unmistakable, like a pianist in church introducing the hymn in a kind of free fantasy, two arpeggiated chords to get the key in the congregation's ears. As Dylan begins to sing, the meter remains free, no clear beat yet. He is especially flexible with the chords of the *b* phrase, which he plays much more quickly than those of *a*, giving the chromatic descent a tumbling momentum. Then, a marvelous detail: in the second verse, right after Dylan sings "As they were taking down the tent," he begins to tap his foot audibly, prodding the band to enter (**audio ex. 8.9**). The groove is fully established two lines later when Dylan sings about the "charcoal gypsy maidens," who "can strut their feathers well." But this music struts differently than Armstrong's. Where his "St. James Infirmary" had swung eighths, in New Orleans fashion, Dylan's eighths, and his band's, are notably straight. It is an '80s groove, a reminder that this was, after all, the era of drum machines. But it also fits the high seriousness of the lyric, Dylan and band eschewing the playful unevenness of swing time in favor of a grimly even tread. This gives a sense of metric inevitability as the music cycles through the nested loops of the chord progression, a historical process with no escape, the dark cloud of E♭ minor ever looming.

Straight time was still in effect a few weeks later, on May 5, when Dylan and producer Mark Knopfler returned to the tune.[48] But now it was just a two-man track, Dylan's piano and Knopfler's twelve-string acoustic guitar, the latter the song's only sonic nod to the actual Blind Willie McTell. The music itself still sounds little like McTell's, though. It is spare and eerie, as one can hear in **audio example 8.10**. Unlike the April 11 take, this one starts out with the meter fully engaged, though we only recognize that from Knopfler's guitar, which quietly fills the space after Dylan's stark opening octave E♭s. As the track proceeds Dylan and Knopfler will trade off in keeping the meter going, Dylan generally filling the space in the first half of phrases, Knopfler the second half. The tread is now even more deliberate, but this does not decrease the sense of claustrophobic looping, stuck in the malevolent orbit of E♭ minor. Dylan's foot is once again audible at various points, marking time and keeping it straight. Indeed, he often taps on the offbeats, as though to ensure against a hint of jaunty swing. This is perhaps a final reason for Dylan's choice of piano: the instrument enables such time keeping (audible foot taps are awkward when standing with a guitar). This results in a metric feel that is the polar opposite of "Time Passes Slowly." There, crooked, stumbling time projected a sense of all-too-human fallibility, the difficulty of peacing out in nature. In "Blind Willie McTell," by contrast, the ticking straight time suggests a supra-human time scale, a historical process stepping inexorably forward, leaving suffering in its wake.

JULY 3, 2019 (ROSKILDE)

At the 2019 Roskilde Festival in Denmark, pedal-steel player Donnie Herron watches Dylan's fingers like a hawk. He's been watching this way for years, in fact, his lap steel positioned behind Dylan's piano bench, his eyes tracking and his hands following Dylan's every move at the keyboard.[49] Sometimes he creates a luminous halo by doubling Dylan's chords and melodic fragments. At others, he works to rationalize the sometimes puzzling keyboard riffs that Dylan hits on, knitting them into the rest of the band's musical fabric as best he can. Since the turn of the millennium, the keyboard has been Dylan's preferred instrument on stage, and for much of that time Donnie

Herron's pedal steel has been its double. As we will hear, Herron provides crucial connective tissue, helping tie Dylan's wayward playing into that of the band, as well as helping to lead him back home.

Video example 8.4 shows a piano-solo break in "Make You Feel My Love." Note how closely Herron watches Dylan's hands. Then watch his plucking hand as it mirrors Dylan's melody at one moment, before moving seamlessly into more independent chordal playing the next. **Figure 8.8** shows this process with italicized annotations, as Herron works to stitch Dylan's obstinate repeated phrase into the fabric of the tune. The top stave transcribes Dylan's right hand; his left hand (not shown) doubles it one octave lower. The bottom stave is a schematic representation of the song's harmonic progression, which the band realizes. NB: Dylan does *not* play these chords. This is crucial. His piano improvisation is largely impervious to the shifting harmony. He fixates on a five-note gesture, stepping up the D♭-major scale like a dutiful student, perhaps even like his brother David, that diligent practicer of scales.[50] These five notes traverse the D♭-major chord, and he repeats them throughout, even when the result clashes with the harmony. The most pronounced such clash is in measure 5. Here the band plays a G♭-minor chord; music theorists would call it a "minor iv." But Dylan's five-note lick remains doggedly *major* in this bar. This creates two notable clashes, indicated on the figure with a dagger (†) and an asterisk (*). The dagger marks the sourest note: an F, or major $\hat{3}$. An F♭ would have grated less against the underlying harmony. Somewhat less jarring is the asterisked A♭, which conflicts with the underlying G♭ chord but at least doesn't contradict its minor mode.[51]

Now note the italicized annotations between the staves, which indicate Donnie Herron's activity. He first doubles Dylan's ascending figure, giving it added pedal-steel shimmer with a hint of vibrato. Then, in bars 3 and 4, as the harmony drifts further from tonic, Herron moves into a more chordal style, his smooth transition blending Dylan's motive into the song's harmonic structure. Herron clearly anticipates the clash to come in bar 5, because he is ready with an elegant correction. He returns to single-note playing, following the rhythm of the motive, but he avoids the two bum notes in the figure

FIGURE 8.8. Interaction between Dylan (BD) and Donnie Herron (DH) in solo break from "Make You Feel My Love," Roskilde, Denmark, July 3, 2019.

that Dylan plays. Instead of stepping up from D♭, he simply iterates that pitch three times, before jumping up to G♭—*not* A♭—for the apex pitch. This G♭ reinforces the root of the underlying harmony rather than clashing with it.

Put simply, Herron makes the wrong notes right. But the moment's affective complexity relies on the tension between Dylan's dissonating part and the underlying harmony, a tension that Herron mediates but does not remove entirely. The clash falls at the most expressive chord in the verse, a brief minor-key chill in a song otherwise saturated with affirmational warmth. On one hearing, Dylan's major-key clash here is like the warm embrace that the lyric promises—a partnered security that persists even when things aren't going your way, when the rain of G♭ minor is falling. On another hearing, which I prefer, the effect is more unsettling, Dylan's part seeming oblivious to the harmonic shadow in bar 5. This complicates the song's simple message, giving us reason to doubt that the lyric persona really sees his beloved. He continues to spout bromides no matter the emotional weather. Herron's correction seems to confirm this hearing, in its anxious attempt to mediate the clash, to reestablish a secure bond between harmony and melody.

Herron maintains this mediating role elsewhere in the song. **Video example 8.5** shows a later moment in which Dylan reiterates high-register D♭ octaves as the chords shift underneath. Herron matches his rhythm exactly but integrates his repeated D♭s into the underlying chordal structure by playing full harmonies. Some moments are more lighthearted. For example, in **video example 8.6**, from the same song, Dylan plays a tremolo lick in octaves and then looks back at Herron, clearly pleased with what he's done. The same thing happens in "Like a Rolling Stone," shown in **video example 8.7**. Once again, Dylan plays his tremolo octave figure—which in this context sounds a bit like a poor man's Jerry Lee Lewis—and looks back at Herron, who responds with a wide grin. The moment attests to the proximity between the two musicians—physically, musically, and affectively—across the later years of the Never-Ending Tour.

Nowhere is that proximity more poignant than on the 2019 "Girl of the North Country." Dylan had unveiled this new arrangement in Stockholm on June 26, about a week before the Roskilde concert.[52] As we saw in chapter 6, this song was at first a quintessential guitar number, built on Martin Carthy's folk-baroque arrangement of "Scarborough Fair," with its complex suspended chords resulting from shifting fretted notes against fixed open strings. No such effects are available on the piano; there are no strings to fret or leave open, only keys to depress. But those keys make other things possible.

The new arrangement is metrically loose, dominated by Dylan's piano and Herron's pedal steel.[53] Strikingly, the rendition's emotional heart resides not in its sung verses but in an instrumental refrain. **Video example 8.8** shows the refrain as Dylan and Herron play it after the first verse. **Figure 8.9** transcribes the excerpt.[54] It is a simple tune in D♭ major, disarmingly direct, even sentimental. Herron follows Dylan closely, thickening the texture at one point to vibrato-sweetened chords, which create a shimmering halo around the tune.

FIGURE 8.9. "Girl from the North Country" melodic refrain, Roskilde, Denmark, July 3, 2019.

It's a melody so familiar, you could swear you've heard it before. That's because it harks back to some venerable models in America's musical past: parlor song and Protestant hymnody.

As for the former, the cut of the tune—its quarter-note tread, its foursquare phrasing, its deliberate $\hat{3}$–$\hat{2}$–$\hat{1}$ cadence, bracketed in the figure—distinctly recalls the music of Stephen Foster. Dylan released a stripped-down version of Foster's "Hard Times" on 1992's *Good as I Been to You* and decades later wrote feelingly about his song "Nelly Was a Lady" in 2022's *Philosophy of Modern Song*: "This is one sweeping song that is designed to make anybody who's ever lived a life just lie down and weep. A lot of sad songs have been written but none sadder than this."[55] Like "Girl from the North Country," "Nelly" is a song of loss and remembrance, but the loss is fresher: the lyric "I," working a logging boat, grieves his wife Nelly, who died the night before. Foster's melody does not match Dylan's piano refrain exactly, but there are striking similarities. Notably, the rhythm of the third bar of Dylan's tune echoes that in Foster's opening phrase ("Down on the Mississippi floating"), and the bracketed $\hat{3}$–$\hat{2}$–$\hat{1}$ cadence in the next bar matches Foster's cadence in both rhythm and scale-degree content. Strikingly, Dylan also refers to musical interludes when discussing his preferred version of "Nelly," by Alvin Youngblood, stating that "the guitar turnarounds are a slow cakewalk between heartbroken verses, loss shared on the front porch."[56] He could just as well be describing his own turnaround refrains in the 2019 "Girl from the North Country."

The deliberate $\hat{3}$–$\hat{2}$–$\hat{1}$ cadence pops up in other Foster songs, too, for example in "Jeanie with the Light Brown Hair," where it concludes each AABA verse (for example, at "Floating like a vapor on the soft summer air"). The lyrical resonance between "Jeanie" and "Girl from the North Country" is striking, and not only in Dylan's reference to his beloved's "hair hanging long." They are also both nostalgic songs of love lost, with abundant nature imagery. To be sure, the imagery in Foster's song is of spring and summer—Jeanie among the streams and daisies—while Dylan's girl inhabits the chilly, windswept north. But such seasonal and geographic differences cannot mask the similarity in sentiment between the two songs, which at times borders on uncanny:

> Oh! I long for Jeanie, and my heart bows low,
> Never more to find her where the bright waters flow.
>
> Now the nodding wildflowers may wither on the shore
> While her gentle fingers will cull them no more.[57]

There is also a subtle melodic link between the songs. As annotations above the staff in figure 8.10 indicate, the first arch of Dylan's melody tops out with a $\hat{5}$–$\hat{6}$–$\hat{5}$ figure. Foster's "Jeanie" starts with these very scale degrees, at "I dream . . ." ($\hat{6}$–$\hat{5}$).

We can hear even more explicit instance of the $\hat{5}$–$\hat{6}$–$\hat{5}$ figure in Protestant hymnody. For example, the tune "Nettleton," best known as the melody for the hymn "Come Thou Fount of Every Blessing" also features prominent $\hat{5}$–$\hat{6}$–$\hat{5}$ motions (first at "Come thou fount of every blessing / Tune my heart to sing thy grace").[58] Moreover, both the hymn tune and Dylan's refrain reach the high tonic pitch ($\hat{8}$) at their midpoints, and then descend stepwise from there. This occurs in Dylan's melody in bar 3 of figure 8.10, and in the hymn's B phrase, which first sets the text "Teach me some melodious sonnet." Once again, then, we hear echoes of the church in Dylan's piano playing. But where his earlier, gospel-infused playing indexed the Black church, in this refrain we hear *white* hymnody, the sound of flinty New England Protestantism.

Did Dylan have Stephen Foster or "Nettleton" specifically in mind when he crafted this refrain? Perhaps not. But the Stephen Foster connections are close enough, and his writing about "Nelly" heartfelt enough, to give me pause. He published *The Philosophy of Modern Song* only three years after the 2019 shows, but began working on it much earlier, in 2010. Perhaps he was writing entries on the tour bus or in hotel rooms during this very 2019 tour. But as with so much of Dylan's musicking, a one-to-one mapping is less important than the resonance, the piece of the American musical past sounding imperfectly in the present. As for imperfection, each time he plays the tune in figure 8.10, he blurs notes, hits extra keys, and otherwise smudges the tune, Donnie Herron always at his elbow to smooth out the rough edges. But Herron can only do so much, and that's a good thing. For Dylan's stray notes here are a source of pathos, the sound of rueful, stumbling regret.

* * *

What are we to make of Dylan's pronounced preference for the keyboard in recent decades, and of Herron's musical proximity to it? It is hard to answer without considering Dylan's age. Some fans blame arthritis, while others point to the weight of the electric guitar on his aging frame. Still others observe that Dylan typically has two other guitar players in his band, in *addition* to Herron on steel, so it would make sense for him to move out of that crowded guitar-playing field and sit behind the piano instead. (Of course, he could always hire fewer guitarists.) Or perhaps this is simply another left turn in his musical preferences, the aged performer returning to the instrument of his youth. Herron's shadowing also raises questions of age, for his pedal steel is like a musical prosthesis to Dylan's piano. As Dylan has aged, his playing on the instrument has become ever more idiosyncratic, strident and ornery one moment, lyrical and fumbling the next. Sometimes he repeats weird riffs ad infinitum. Flubbed notes, dissonant clusters, and harmonic mismatches abound. To draw on a concept first introduced in chapter 5, Herron's pedal steel takes these undercoded fragments and links them to the band's overcoded accompaniment.[59]

But Dylan's imperfect late piano is more than an emblem of his age. The piano is also for him a site of memory, and indeed of nostalgia, a faltering return to roots. Herron supports those faltering steps home, playing an instrument long associated with white Americana. Nowhere is this homecoming more evident than in the 2019 "Girl from the North Country." In this sentimental song about the frozen north, Dylan plays the first instrument he learned in frozen Hibbing, where "the wind hits heavy on the borderline." One can imagine young Bobby Zimmerman in the living room, rummaging for tunes in the recesses on the family piano, making his first musical sounds as the snow blew outside the window. He also overheard his brother practicing scales on the same Gulbranson spinet. In 2019, as he sings of the "north country fair," his pianistic memory machine drifts back to those childhood times and then bypasses them, receding further still, to an American nineteenth century dominated by Stephen Foster's songs and Protestant hymns. Both surely resounded in Frank Hibbing's young settlement in the 1890s, played on the first rickety uprights trundled to the remote outpost, drifting out of tune as they jostled on rutted roads. Listen closely and you can hear that past not only in Dylan's rough-hewn playing but in his words. "Remember me to one who lives there," he sings over simple piano chords, the reflexive verb sounding at one archaic and—could it be?—sincere.

PART III

Sounding "Hard Rain"

Chapter 9 audio examples:
soundingbobdylan.com/ch9

CHAPTER NINE

What Did You Hear, My Blue-Eyed Son?

The Musical Sources

Across eight chapters, we have filled our ears with Dylan's imperfect sounds, listening intently for their telling idiosyncrasies—and for what they tell. We are ready to return to "Hard Rain." When we left Dylan, he was noisily typing its words above the Gaslight, wondering how to set them to music. That he succeeded, we all know. But how? What wisps of music coalesced to form the song? And to what effect? Or, as I asked of the song in the introduction, "What do its sounds *do*? What do they make of the words that initially took shape on that typescript? Why is that hyphenated compound"—Words-Music—"so potent when it begins to vibrate in the air?" We are now ready to venture some answers.

This chapter explores the song's musical sources, those bits of the musical past conjured in the moment of composition. As we will hear, Dylan braids them into a structure that corrals the lyrics' wild energy and diverse literary registers into a sounding whole of eerie composure, at once poised and inexorable. It is tempting to call the result perfect, so snug is the fit between words and tune. But over the next five decades, that fortuitous alignment will prove to be the exception rather than the rule, an initial configuration whose inner bonds were more contingent than they seemed. The tightly joined song on *Freewheelin'* masks a fundamental looseness of conception. Here it is useful to remember Dylan's offhand comment in 1964 that "there was just no tune that really fit to it, so I just sort of play chords without a tune." The statement unnerves in part because it suggests a casualness in the relationship between words and sounds, even something arbitrary or haphazard in their linkage. This is hard to believe when we hear the song as it sounded in 1962. But Dylan's comment suggests the song's future mutability may have been baked into the creative process itself. And indeed, the more we listen across the decades, the dash between "Words" and "Music" atop the typescript comes to seem not a site of compositional fixity, nor a narrow channel to be hastily traversed, but a multidimensional space to inhabit again and again, a site of experiment, felicitous accident, and their abundant affordances. "Hard Rain," like all of Dylan's songs, becomes an occasion for change imperfection, for repetition with a difference. That will be the subject of chapters 11 and 12. In this chapter, we will attend instead to the song's genesis, and to the past musics that sound within it, now transformed. That, too, is repetition with a difference.

WHERE HAVE YOU GONE, LORD RANDAL, MY SON?

Before hearing the music Dylan eventually found for "Hard Rain," let's pause for a moment over a source he *didn't* choose. As already noted, the lyric begins with an explicit nod to the Child ballad "Lord Randal." When it came to finding a melody for the song, then, this would be the lowest-hanging fruit. Why not base "Hard Rain" on one of its many tunes? Dylan has, after all, never been shy about borrowing and repurposing melodies. He was doing a lot of it in 1962. In his 2004 interview with Robert Hilburn he provides the most familiar example:

> I wrote "Blowin' in the Wind" in 10 minutes, just put words to an old spiritual, probably something I learned from Carter Family records. That's the folk music tradition. You use what's been handed down.[1]

He more likely learned the spiritual in question, "No More Auction Block," from Odetta rather than the Carter Family, but no matter. The more general point stands. And indeed, *Freewheelin'* provides several textbook examples: "Girl from the North Country" is based on "Scarborough Fair"; "Masters of War" on "Nottamun Town"; "Bob Dylan's Dream" on "Lady Franklin's Lament"; and so on.

There can be little doubt that Dylan had heard "Lord Randal" both on recording and in live performance by 1962—it was a folk-revival staple. But "Hard Rain" in fact resembles no circulating version of "Lord Randal" that I have found, from commercial releases to field recordings. We know that Dylan consumed recordings voraciously, and he knew several of the musicians who recorded the ballad personally. I have also surveyed the many, many notated versions collected by Bertrand Bronson, who counts a staggering 102 variants of the tune.[2] These melodies are dizzyingly diverse, yet not a single one resembles the opening of "Hard Rain."[3] Of course, Dylan doesn't read music and wouldn't have consulted volumes like these. But it is at least plausible that he could have heard the tune sung in person in a version that doesn't circulate on recording. The Bronson collection shows that it is exceedingly unlikely such a tune would have resembled "Hard Rain."

To better hear the differences between "Hard Rain" and "Lord Randal," let's consider three versions of the ballad that would have circulated in folk-revival circles in the early '60s. Each represents a distinct style: Burl Ives's commercial folk, Ewan MacColl's Scottish balladry, and Jean Ritchie's laconic Appalachianism. **Figure 9.1** notates the first line of each of their versions, contrasting them with "Hard Rain" at the bottom of the figure. (I discuss the brackets in the latter below.) **Audio example 9.1** plays the excerpts back to back. First is Burl Ives, all plummy vowels and rounded tone. His rhythm is free, almost spoken; classical musicians would call it *parlando* (Italian for

FIGURE 9.1. The first line from three versions of "Lord Randal" compared with the first line of "A Hard Rain's a-Gonna Fall" (as sung on *The Freewheelin' Bob Dylan*).

"speaking"). Note the striking leap up at the end of the line, which mimics the inflection of a question. This is a good example with which to begin, as this tune was the template for many folk-revival versions of "Lord Randal," including those by Harry Belafonte, Josh White, Richard Dyer-Bennet, and Buffy Sainte-Marie. Next is Dylan antagonist Ewan MacColl, leaning into his thick brogue, which brings out the tune's Old World modal severity. Note especially the rising-then-falling contour, so different from Dylan's questions, which only descend. This is the ballad in its most self-consciously archaic, Scottish garb. Then comes Jean Ritchie's version, which also traces an arch-shaped contour, but rather than MacColl's modality her tune is pentatonic, a different kind of musical archaism. When the first line of "Hard Rain" hits our ears next, the contrasts are unmistakable. All three versions of the ballad differ from "Hard Rain" in ways subtle and not so subtle, from contour to mode to rhythm. In contrast to the up-and-down of the ballad lines, note the compact descent in Dylan's tune, which lends it an ear-catching concision.

VOICES OLD AND NEW

Before turning to the origins of Dylan's tune, let's consider his voice, so remote from Ives's rounded croon, MacColl's harsh brogue, and Ritchie's flat Kentucky drawl. Dylan's nasality and slight vocal roughness are by now familiar. This is his prematurely aged voice, first discussed in connection with "The Times They Are a-Changin'" in chapter 1. Sumanth Gopinath and Michael Cherlin hear the Southern twang crossed with Scottish pronunciation:

> Dylan pronounces *hard* with a very closed and emphatic /ar/ sound, suggesting a Scottish accent, if perhaps filtered through a southern (Appalachian?) accent. The personae of the song generally would seem to evoke the Scottish bard—with the well-known Lord Randal reference in mind here—the wavering voice of an old man, and the visionary and prophetic tone found in the middle parts of the verses. . . . The effect . . . is to convey the apocalyptic visions of the song through a subtly shifting persona in which the detached wisdom of the old seer then gives way to the emphatic Scottish bard (whose accent perhaps also signifies a working-class laborer, of an older time or remote geography) whose effort is used to depict the coming catastrophe.[4]

I would add that, for all its play of personae and accents, its timbral noise and grit, Dylan's voice is delicately balanced: his singing throughout the song is focused and concentrated, his enunciation careful and precise, even exaggerated. Listen, for example, to the emphatic /d/ plosives in the refrain ("And it's a har*da*, it's a har*da*").[5] This is an explicit Guthrie-ism, which had impressed the young Dylan:

> I was listening to [Guthrie's] diction, too. He had a perfected style of singing that it seemed like no one else had ever thought about. He would throw in the sound of the last letter of a word whenever he felt like it and it would come like a punch.[6]

As we will hear in a moment, this is not the only Guthrie imprint on the song.

For now, though, we should note that Dylan's delivery is not all high seriousness, the stoic bard foretelling doom. His rhythm is alert and sly throughout, his voice meeting the guitar's groove with the same folksy nonchalance we heard in "The Times They Are a-Changin'." Syllables cascade off the nearest beats, sometimes landing squarely, at other times slightly early. The resulting syncopation provides a further contrast with Ives, MacColl, and Ritchie, all of whom sing in pointedly *un*-syncopated rhythm. Brackets in figure 9.1(d) mark the syncopated moments in Dylan's opening line: quick pairs of syllables at "Where have," "you been," and "blue-eyed." These syncopations remind us of Dylan's devotion to a wide range of American vernacular and popular musics, from country and old-time to a range of Black musics, embracing rock 'n' roll and even some mainstream pop along the way. And yet the tight, two-syllable syncopations also gesture toward musics of the Old World, via the so-called Scotch snap, already discussed in chapter 2. Such snaps begin with a short, accented note on the beat followed by a longer, unaccented note off the beat. Dylan would have heard them in performances by the Clancy Brothers and Tommy Makem (for example, in "Brennan on the Moor") as well as from a range of ballad singers. In other words, Dylan's syncopations in "Hard Rain" do not derive exclusively from American vernacular traditions. And indeed, as Philip Tagg argues, Scotch snaps are ultimately indistinguishable from a wide range of syncopations in American working-class musics, white and Black.[7] What is notable is the pervasiveness of the syncopation in Dylan, which goes beyond the isolated snapped syllable to saturate the texture, creating a persistent vocal groove that nestles within the guitar's triple meter.

These overdetermined syncopations call to mind a critical commonplace: for many at the time, Dylan's music sounded at once old and new. Izzy Young, proprietor of the Folklore Center in Greenwich Village, stated that Dylan's early music sounded "like it was written today, but it sounded like it could've been written 200 years ago also. It sounded current and old at the same time."[8] To be sure, the sense of newness in "Hard Rain" arose in part from the lyrical content, the song's poetic daring and its vision of a modern world on the brink. Though it was not actually written in response to the Cuban missile crisis, it is shot through with Cold War anxiety. But this was not merely a question of new words and old sounds. Young clearly states that the music *sounded* new and old. It seemed to fold history, audibly mapping a musical past into the present. Sean Wilentz puts it eloquently: "Dylan's genius rests . . . on his ability to write and sing in more than one era at once," an ability that can "make the present and the past feel like each other."[9] The syncopations in "Hard Rain," a sounding gesture with roots in the Old World and a living tradition in the New, are one especially clear manifestation of this historical folding.

GUTHRIE, AGAIN

So where did Dylan's tune come from if not "Lord Randal"? **Audio example 9.2** offers a genealogy. It begins with the first line of Woody Guthrie's 1945 recording of "1913 Massacre"; followed by (1) Dylan's own performance of the same song at Carnegie Chapter Hall on November 4, 1961; (2) his studio recording of "Song to Woody," made about two weeks later in Studio A; and (3) the first line of the studio recording of "Hard Rain" from December 1962, about a year after that.[10] The keys vary across the performances, but the logic joining the links in the chain is immediately obvious to the ear. "Song to Woody" was explicitly based on "1913 Massacre," so that connection is no surprise.[11] But the similarity of those songs to the opening of "Hard Rain" *is* a surprise, hidden until one notices it, but after that, clear as a bell. The tunes all have the same contour, beginning on and holding scale degree $\hat{5}$ before descending to $\hat{1}$. The triple meter is also the same, as are the tempo, rhythmic profile, and harmony. This may sound vaguely persuasive in print, but the evidence is all in the hearing, right there in audio example 9.2.[12]

There is a tendency in Dylan studies to account for such borrowings via lyrical close reading—for example, by seeking a textual resonance between the words of "1913 Massacre" and those of "Hard Rain." But there is precious little resonance to be found. The Guthrie song soberly recounts the details of the Italian Hall disaster, a Christmas gathering of copper miners and their families in Michigan, at which mining bosses incited a panic that killed seventy-three. "Hard Rain" is, by contrast, a series of fantastical visions alluding to the end times, far removed from Guthrie's folksy realism. A lyrical connection between "Hard Rain" and "Song to Woody" is perhaps more plausible, especially its second verse:

> Hey, hey, Woody Guthrie, I wrote you a song
> 'Bout a funny ol' world that's a-comin' along
> Seems sick an' it's hungry, it's tired an' it's torn
> It looks like it's a-dyin' an' it's hardly been born

But even this is a stretch. The world of "Hard Rain" is indeed hungry ("I heard one person starve"), tired, torn, and dying, but it is hardly a "funny ol' world." Stylized Rimbaud is far from stylized Guthrie.

Rather than any such textual link, this was more likely simply the music that came when Dylan went to his guitar, searching for a tune. He had been singing Guthrie songs incessantly since 1960 and muscle memory alone would make a Guthrie melody a likely candidate. As Dylan moved to his instrument, armed with his new words, his body slipped into a familiar groove. We can practically hear the slippage right before our ears in audio example 9.2. It was made possible via a rather obvious formal similarity: the opening lines of "Lord Randal" and "Hard Rain" share the same prosody as "1913 Massacre" and "Song to Woody." As **figure 9.2** shows, all have four accented feet, all begin with a weak upbeat, and all end on a strong syllable.

Note the different stories told by audio examples 9.1 and 9.2 and their respective figures. While the former, with the three "Lord Randal" excerpts, exhibits textual continuity and musical discontinuity, the latter, beginning with "1913 Massacre," shows the reverse: the continuity is now musical, while the texts diverge. Words and music exhibit a degree of autonomy in figure 9.2. If their relationship is

		1		2		3		4
1913 Massacre:	Take a	trip	with	me	in	nine-	teen thir-	teen
Song to Woody:	I'm	out	here a	thou-	sand	miles	from my	home
Lord Randal:	Oh,	where	have you	been	Lord	Ran-	dal my	son?
Hard Rain:	Oh,	where	have you	been	my	blue-	eyed	son?

FIGURE 9.2. Prosodic similarity between "1913 Massacre," "Song to Woody," "Lord Randal," and "Hard Rain."

not arbitrary, it is at least somewhat fortuitous, a product of formal coincidence. They intersect in the tetrameter of the prosody, a shared property that acts as a sort of switching station, the site of the generic pivot in Dylan's recording. The words of "Hard Rain" may begin in the Scots-English border ballad tradition, but its music—pivoting on the four-foot prosody—begins in a different embodied practice, in Guthrie-esque sounding actions that Dylan had been performing nightly.

QUESTIONS-ANSWERS-REFRAIN

Those actions pervade the song. The opening, descending question resonates throughout the verse. Questions descend, answers descend, and the refrain's climactic line—"a hard rain's a-gonna fall"—descends yet again, the gesture now enacting the apocalyptic "fall" that the song foretells. Far from sounding static, however, the song moves with steady inevitability toward its climax, a result of Dylan joining these local descents into an overall *ascent*.

Before focusing on how that happens musically, it will be useful to review the words' three-stage arc. The "Lord Randal"–based questions establish antique balladry as the initial lyrical register. Yet note how Dylan collapses historical distance, replacing the archaic "Lord Randal, my son" with the affectionately detailed, "my blue-eyed son."[13]

In the ballad, these questions are followed by a single answer. But in "Hard Rain" we get a cascade of harrowing responses, those "chains of flashing images" with their literary ambitions. The result is a striking shift in textual register, from the balladic incantation of the questions to the literary "high style" of the answers, with their Symbolist and Beat resonances. Another arresting registral shift follows—this time a downshift, if you will—to a kind of folksy, hard-luck Americana in the "It's a hard" refrain. While the word "hard" will eventually link up with "rain," its initial iterations suggest intertextual affiliations with songs about hardship more generally. Among these are Guthrie's "Hard, Ain't It Hard" and "Hard Travellin'," as well as a Lomax field recording I will discuss in a moment. The song is thus a fusion of influences drawn from diverse literary and musical traditions, spanning centuries and continents, Old World and New, high and low.

A central challenge for Dylan the singer, then, was to stitch these textual registers together, to join them into a coherent sounding whole. He does this by draping the Guthrie-esque descending line over each of the song's three stages. **Figure 9.3** shows how. I've beamed together the descending figures in each section, marking their end points with open noteheads. Black noteheads show the pitches Dylan sings on the way down. The broken arrow above shows the large-scale ascent Dylan creates across these local descents. The questions depart from scale degree $\hat{5}$ (B in E major); the answers begin one step higher, on C♯ or $\hat{6}$; and the refrain reaches higher still, to the upper-octave tonic, E or $\hat{8}$. **Audio example 9.3** provides a sonic overview of the first verse, which one can listen to while following the figure.

Let's zoom in on some details. Note first the parenthesized annotations on the left side of the figure. "Closed" and "open" here refer to the relative conclusiveness of melody and harmony at the end of each of the parent's questions to the blue-eyed son.[14] The first question is closed, in that the melody descends to the tonic pitch, $\hat{1}$ (here, E), which is supported by the tonic chord on the guitar (an E-major chord). The second phrase, by contrast is melodically and harmonically open—it's left hanging. The melody descends only to $\hat{2}$ and the harmony is the dominant, or V. This creates a

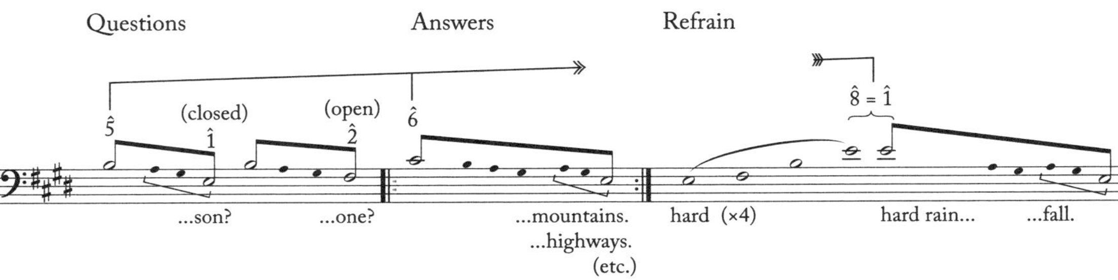

FIGURE 9.3. The melodic line of "Hard Rain," with (beamed) descending figures arranged into an overall ascent.

half cadence, which sounds open-ended. Music theorists often describe such cadences as musical "questions," awaiting the "answer" of an authentic (closed) cadence. The second question thus points forward musically as well as lyrically, awaiting the son's answers, musical and lyrical.

The closed cadence also points forward, but in a different way. Note the bracket at the end of the first question. This marks a three-note cadential gesture, A–G♯–E, or $\hat{4}$–$\hat{3}$–$\hat{1}$ in scale degrees. Dylan first sings this at the words "blue-eyed son," the affectionate detail I mentioned above. This cadential figure then resounds in the subsequent two sections, concluding each answer and marking the final cadence of the refrain, where it at once sets and enacts the word "fall." The bracketed gesture thus serves as a pre-echo of the song's climactic fall. **Audio example 9.4** gathers these together so you can hear this pre-echo. The three-note figure thus plays a crucial role in corralling the lyrics' wild energy and diverse literary registers. For one, it is present in each section of the verse—questions, answers, and refrain—thus providing a musical rhyme that ties together the lyrical registers of antique balladry, literary high style, and hard-luck Americana.

The musical rhyme is also potent more locally, within the answers themselves. Lyrically, the answers avoid end rhyme, each hanging like a loose thread. Dylan would have encountered such unrhymed strings of images in Ginsberg and Whitman[15]—they unspool over long stretches of "Howl" and "Song of Myself"—but no item in the folk-revival repertory attempted to integrate such a technique from free verse into a song. Question-and-answer ballads like "Lord Randal" and "Edward" are much more compact, each verse containing a single answer, sung once or twice. Dylan's iterated cadential gesture—the A–G♯–E figure that ends each question—offers a musical rhyme where the lyrics have none. Moreover, as Dylan put it to Studs Terkel in 1963, "Every line in ["Hard Rain"] really is another song. Could be used as a whole song, every single line. I wrote that when I didn't know how many other songs I could write."[16] This speaks to the weight of each image in the son's answers, and their relative independence. The melodic rhyme acts as a corrective to this too, a centripetal counter to the lyric's centrifugal energies.

ASIDE: THE ITERATIVE CORE

Before continuing with our survey of the song's overall melodic trajectory, as represented in figure 9.3, let's pause over the iterative structure of the answers in the song. Recall Tom Paxton's wonder at seeing the typed text, as well as Dylan's perplexity over how he might sing it. This was partly a problem of form. One sees the challenge immediately on glancing at the typescript: it does not *look* like a song. Yes, the visual organization clearly suggests a verse-refrain structure—each verse beginning with the balladic questions and ending with the "it's a hard" refrain (which Dylan marks visually on the typescript by indentation)—but in between, the son's answers create visual bulges, causing each verse to swell vertically as the surreal images pile up, one on top of another. And those piles grow: on the typescript, there are five answers in verse 1, six in verses 2 through 4, and twelve in verse 5.[17]

Dylan's solution—to devise a rotating melodic and harmonic figure that he could repeat as much as necessary in a given verse—was one of his novel formal strategies as a songwriter.[18] He may say he never invents his own melodies, but this technique, which I will call the "iterative core," is an exception, an invention borne of necessity. It was a musical response to lyrical pressure, specifically in those songs that fall into "chains of flashing images" or otherwise drop into lists that can expand and contract, accordion-style. "Hard Rain" was the first song in which he deployed the strategy, but it would not be the last. "The Lonesome Death of Hattie Carroll," "Only a Pawn in Their Game," "Who Killed Davey Moore?," and "Mr. Tambourine Man" all deploy the same technique.

Verses with an iterative core typically fall into three sections, which I will call the opening, the iterative core, and the cadence. In "Hard Rain," these correspond to the by-now-familiar sections of questions (opening), answers (iterative core), and refrain (cadence).

The opening often takes the form of a "shout and fall," a vocal gesture common in a wide range of vernacular music.[19] The "shout and fall" is just what it sounds like, an emphatic vocal utterance that begins in a relatively high register before falling away. "Who Killed Davey Moore?" provides an especially clear example, beginning with a chant in the upper register ("Who killed Davey Moore? / Why and what's the reason") before falling an octave for the concluding syllable ("for"). In "Hattie Carroll," the opening encompasses the first two lines, ("William Zanzinger killed poor Hattie Carroll / With a cane that he twirl'd round his diamond-ring finger"). The shout and fall here is terraced, a direct result of the pervasive strong-weak metrics of the prosody, which follow the stress pattern of the two characters' last names (-zínger, Cárroll).[20] Dylan sings these strong-weak patterns with descending minor thirds, tempering the outrage of the shout and fall with melancholy.

"Hattie Carroll" provides a useful example of the next two sections as well. The iterative core, which in verse 1 begins "At a Baltimore hotel society gatherin'," expands from four lines in verse 1 to nine in verse 4. In contrast to "Hard Rain," the iterations here project not a string of apocalyptic visions, but a mixture of detached reportage and a mimetic enactment of the of the numb repetition in Hattie Carroll's daily work. These come into dramatic conflict in the fourth verse: the dreary litany of tasks—underscored by the repetition of "table"—is suddenly interrupted by an account of Carroll's murder. Aptly, the iterated melody in the core circles tediously, ending with further descending minor thirds on a strong-weak stress pattern (e.g., "gátherin'," "fróm him," "státion," "múrder," "táble"). The resulting melody, like that in the opening, is pentatonic and austere, supported by an inertly looping chord progression. Music theorists would label the chords of this loop I–vi–iii. The two minor chords (vi and iii) are secondary harmonies that do not advance the music functionally, but circle in place, casting a minor-key shadow over the proceedings. But on the last statement of the iterative core, the lyrical subject rouses himself with a preparatory dominant chord, setting up the song's moral indictment ("You, who philosophize disgrace . . ."). This initiates the cadence section, which replaces the inert, melancholy pentatonicism of the first two sections with righteously diatonic moral certainty.[21]

The iterative core in "Mr. Tambourine Man" does its share of circling too, and aptly so, given the song's thematics of circling: the Rimbaudian "magic swirling ship" of verse 2, the ecstatic "laughing, spinning, swinging" of verse 3, and the Felliniesque singer "circled by the circus sands" in verse 4. The melodic figure of the iterative core circles around the pitches of the tonic triad, the dreamy iterations suggestive of spinning in place, going nowhere yet remaining ever in motion. The opening that precedes the core is once again a shout and fall. Now it takes the form of a vocative address, Dylan's "Hey, Mr. Tambourine Man!" updating the Homeric "Sing, O muse!" In the cadence, the melody circles once more on "jingle-jangle morning" before finally settling on the tonic, melodically and harmonically, at "following you."

ASCENDING—TO FALL

The overall trajectory in "Hard Rain" differs from these songs in telling ways. While "Hattie Carroll" is all about melancholic sinking followed by a bracing indictment, and "Mr. Tambourine Man" is about movement-in-stasis, blissed-out twirling, "Hard Rain" *builds*. Across the three stages of questions (opening)—answers (core)—refrain (cadence), the melody rises, as shown by the broken arrow in figure 9.3. The melody's overall rising trajectory invites comparison with an artist far from the hip enclaves of the folk revival, but one beloved by Dylan:

> I moved the dial up and down and Roy Orbison's voice came blasting out of the small speakers. His new song, "Running Scared," exploded into the room . . . With Roy, you didn't know if you were listening to mariachi or opera . . . He sounded like he was singing from an Olympian mountaintop and he meant business . . . Typically he'd start out in some low, barely audible range, stay there awhile and then astonishingly slip into histrionics.[22]

FIGURE 9.4. Vocal ascent in Roy Orbison's "Running Scared" (1961).

Figure 9.4 is an analytical image of "Running Scared" similar in structure to figure 9.3; **audio example 9.5** presents excerpts cued to the figure. Note the staged ascent, again marked with open noteheads and a broken arrow.[23] To be sure, "Running Scared" and "Hard Rain" are worlds apart stylistically, and I think it highly unlikely that Dylan had Orbison explicitly on his mind when working on the song. But the latter's operatic ascents clearly made an impression; "Hard Rain" matches them step for step. Greil Marcus agrees. Building on my linkage of the two songs at a 2019 talk I gave in Tulsa, he states:

> Dylan couldn't even imagine touching Orbison's three-octave range, but Orbison gave him ambition. "He sounded like he was singing from an Olympian mountaintop"—Orbison let Dylan see through those eyes.[24]

We will return to the mountaintop metaphor at chapter's end.

First, though, we survey the song's final musical borrowing, which is more direct. We can hear it in the "It's a hard, it's a hard" ascent, the only portion of the melody not enclosed in one of the descending beams in figure 9.3, and thus with no clear connection to the melodic shape that opens "1913 Massacre." As Todd Harvey and others have noted, there is good evidence that Dylan derived this from a specific source. **Figure 9.5** is a transcription of the song "It's Hard on We Po' Farmers," as published in John and Alan Lomax's 1941 collection *Our Singing Country*. **Audio example 9.6** is an excerpt from the field recording the Lomaxes made of Lemuel Jones singing the song in 1936 at the State Penitentiary in Richmond, Virginia. The first line shares

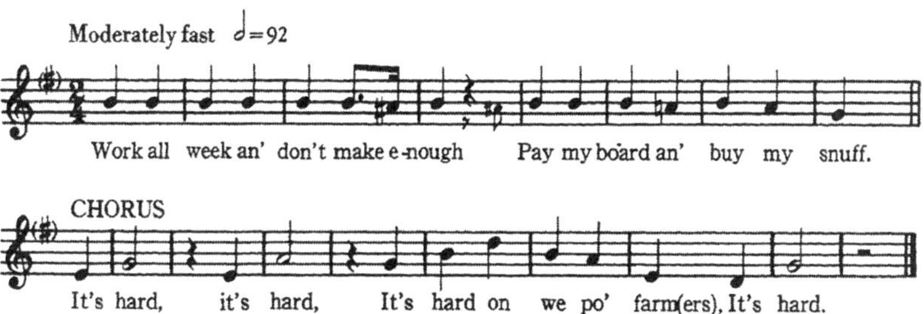

FIGURE 9.5. "It's Hard on We Po' Farmers," as sung by Lemuel Jones in 1936 and transcribed in John and Alan Lomax's *Our Singing Country* (1941).

no material with "Hard Rain," but the second, with its reiterations of "It's hard, it's hard" is a dead ringer. Note especially the ascending iterations and their even rhythmic spacing every two bars, both preserved in Dylan's song. We will discuss this metric issue further in subsequent chapters.

There is a French saying, *reculer pour mieux sauter*: stepping back to leap further. The "it's a hard" repetitions serve this role in "Hard Rain." They double back to survey the melodic ground covered so far, surpassing it in the leap to the prophetic enunciation that caps each verse. I often experience the melodic ascent here like the ascent on a roller coaster, specifically, those moments when the chain engages with a jerk ("it's a hard"—*jerk*—"it's a hard"—*jerk*—). We then pause at the summit—Dylan lingering over the nasalized diphthong of "rain," his guitar swinging from tonic to dominant—before the downward rush. If the theme-park metaphor feels too jarring, we can replace it with Alex Ross's aptly Old Testament one: "coming down the mountain of the song [Dylan] starts to sound like a prophet."[25]

A QUESTION ANSWERED

We are now in a position to answer a question posed near the beginning of this chapter: Why didn't Dylan base the music of "Hard Rain" on (some version of) "Lord Randal"? Quite simply, because no circulating tune for that ballad would lend itself to this kind of musical shaping. Dylan easily could have borrowed some version of the ballad for the song's first two lines, but how then to sing the tolling answers? They need to follow the questions with some sense of melodic consecution, at once answering them and pulling the listener forward toward the climax. One of the song's great achievements is that its momentum never flags, even as the answers pile up. Dylan's canny melodic invention carries the song ever forward, each verse a darkly compelling wave.

I hope it goes without saying that I am certain Dylan did not think of his melody in such analytical terms. And, again, I think there is a good chance he was even unaware of the melodic similarity to the opening of "1913 Massacre." If his 1964 quote is to be believed—that the song is just some chords "without a tune"—it seems possible that he didn't think consciously about the song's tune *at all.* But there is much in artistic creation that unfolds below the threshold of conscious awareness, particularly when the artist is as committed to Beat-like spontaneity as is Dylan.

Though he often doesn't possess technical language for it, Dylan has a remarkable musical instinct for formal proportion, pacing, and melodic design. This is true even in those songs in which Dylan explicitly borrows a tune. For example, "No More Auction Block" and "Blowin' in the Wind," on which it is based, differ melodically in crucial ways. The eminent singability—and memorability—of the latter is due almost entirely to Dylan's melodic interventions, his alterations of the original tune. The same can be said of "The Times They Are a-Changin'." Its melodic timing, overall contour, and energetic profile are unique, not to be found in "Deliverance Will Come," on which its opening gesture is loosely based. And so on. Dylan may disclaim a gift for melody, but his songs proclaim otherwise.

And there is more to "Hard Rain" than melody. Harmony, rhythm, and meter are also essential to the song's effect. They are most audible in Dylan's unassuming guitar part, to which we now turn.

Chapter 10 audio examples:
soundingbobdylan.com/ch10

CHAPTER TEN

Six Crooked Highways

Time and Harmony in the Guitar Part

The coalescing energy in the "it's a hard" ascent is not merely a melodic story. Harmony and meter are also crucial to the music's sweep. To get a sense of this, we will turn our attention to Dylan's guitar part in this brief chapter.[1] As we will hear, the meter is "crooked" in the questions and answers; it straightens out in the refrain, just as the harmony becomes more functionally purposeful. In short, when Dylan moves from answers and into refrain, the harmonic, metric, and melodic gears engage. The transition from answers to refrain is thus a pivotal moment in the song—a gathering together of energy and focus, the climax now within earshot.

STRUMMING

Let's dwell first on Dylan's right hand, so easy to overlook. It offers a classic example of the "bardic strumming" I discussed in chapter 6, with its simple alternation between up and downstrokes. But as so often in Dylan, his strumming projects a subtle balance between opposites, at once casual and exact. Given the song's dark shadows, its studied archaism and lofty citations, it is surprising that the guitar's bounce—the spring in its step—doesn't seem more incongruous. But rather than contradicting, as I noted in the book's introduction, it buoys, keeping the song afloat when it might otherwise sink under the weight of its ambition. The triple meter (1-2-3, 1-2-3) rotates gently, creating a loose coil or circuit that will cycle throughout the song. It is infectious, the rhythm *almost* swung, and yet the affect is strangely flat. Dylan's strumming is impersonal, unsentimental.

We know from chapter 6 that such adjectives do not apply to all of Dylan's guitar playing. We need only listen to other songs on *The Freewheelin' Bob Dylan* to get more sense of the particularity of his playing on "Hard Rain." There is of course the fingerpicking on "Girl from the North Country" and "Don't Think Twice, It's All Right," already discussed in chapter 6. Both are rueful songs of love past or failed, and, as we heard before, the close-miked fingerpicking projects a sense of intimacy, fleshy fingertips directly on strings, the various missed or muffled notes suggesting a fallible interiority. Moreover, a quick survey of the other flatpicked tunes on *Freewheelin'* reveals a range of styles and affects, from boisterous, open-tuned blues ("Down the Highway") to lively folk ("Oxford Town"). The guitar in "Hard Rain" stands out for its dryness and austerity. Anonymity is precisely one of its effects.

Dylan's archaic guitar would soon become a conventional signifier for the nascent counterculture, but in the mainstream auditory landscape of 1962 it was a striking dissonance. To re-experience that dissonance, we need not leave Studio A. Compare the guitar in "Hard Rain" with the lush arrangements backing some of Columbia's other marquee artists at the time, from Tony Bennett to Patti Page, Barbra Streisand to Johnny Mathis.[2] In sharp contrast with their glossy productions, strings and all, Dylan's guitar projects a sort of mythic simplicity, as though we are hearing an earlier stage of musical development.

THREE CHORDS AND THE TRUTH . . . OR IS IT FIVE?

This section discusses the song's harmonies and how Dylan plays them on the guitar. As in the analysis of "Girl from the North Country" in chapter 6, the music-theoretical incline gets a bit steeper here. The main takeaway point is that Dylan plays chord shapes that reinforce the sense of repetitive cycling in the answers before moving on to chord shapes that give more purposeful harmonic motion in the refrain. Readers who do not desire any more detail than that may wish to skip to the next section ("Meter, Crooked and True").

Like so many of Dylan's songs, "Hard Rain" uses only three harmonies, which music theorists would call the tonic, subdominant, and dominant—the three principal "harmonic functions" in tonal music. But on the studio recording Dylan actually plays the subdominant and dominant in two versions each. So, technically speaking, the guitar part consists of five chords but only three functional harmonies. This might at first seem like a very fine hair to split, but the difference in the guitar voicings of these chords plays a crucial role in the contrast between the iterative cycling of the answers and the coalescing momentum of the refrain.

Figure 10.1 shows the five chords that Dylan plays in the song. Figure 10.1(a) presents them on the fretboard, while 10.1(b) transcribes them in standard notation. Note that Dylan plays chord shapes that a guitarist would associate with the key of D, though the placement of the capo at the second fret for the studio recording makes them sound a whole-step higher, in E. As Dylan uses different capo locations for the song in the '60s—usually second or third fret—and as guitarists tend to think of these chords in terms of finger configurations rather than their absolute sounding pitch, the figure labels the chords in the key of D, irrespective of capo location. Figure 10.1(a) is arranged into rows and columns. The rows delineate two types of chords: open and half-barre. The open chords are familiar "first-position" chord shapes, which every guitar student learns in their earliest lessons. These fingerings differ only slightly due to the drop-D tuning, in which the sixth string is lowered from E to D. Dylan's fingering of the A chord, with the thumb wrapped around to stop the sixth string, is idiosyncratic. This allows him to strum freely, hitting the sixth string as desired, rather than carefully avoiding it.

(a)

Function:	Tonic	Subdominant	Dominant
Roman numeral:	I	IV	V

Tuning: Drop D (DADGBE)

	D	G	A
Open	capo → 0 0 0 1 3 2	x 1 0 0 3 (4)	T 0 1 2 3 (0)

		G*	A*
Half-barres		0 0 0 2 1 1	0 0 0 2 1 1

(b)

NB: Pitches in this figure are given without capo. With the capo on second fret, as on the studio recording, chords sound a whole step higher, i.e., in E. With the capo on the third fret, as in some 1960s live versions, the chords sound in F.

FIGURE 10.1. The five guitar chords in the studio version of "Hard Rain."

Nevertheless, it is an awkward fingering, as it is difficult to place all the fingers sufficiently near the second fret to produce a clean tone. One hears this on the recording—the chord is often muffled.

The half-barre chords reside higher on the neck and involve the use of the first finger laid flat across the first two strings. Beneath these half-barres, Dylan lets the lowest three open strings resound, creating a drone-like tonic pedal, above which the half-barres project G and A chords. To distinguish these chords symbolically from the open-position chords of the same letter name, I have adopted the labels G* and A*.[3] The arrow and open circles in the fretboard grid for A* indicate that Dylan slides up to this chord from G*, often quite audibly.

The columns group these chords into classes based on the three "functions" discussed above, adding roman numeral labels from the harmony classroom: tonic (I), subdominant (IV), and dominant (V). Dylan uses the two forms of IV and V to demarcate the form, playing the half-barres during the answers only. These chords float above the resounding low open springs, lending a quality of suspended animation to the answers, which differs considerably from the harmonic stage-setting of the questions or the purposeful cadential tread of the refrain.

METER, CROOKED AND TRUE

Figure 10.2 expands on this observation, showing how these five chords articulate the song's form and its large-scale rhythm. Labels along the left side of the figure indicate the three sections of each verse. Individual words or syllables provide cues for the vocal part (these are the accented syllables of the tetrameter, all of which fall on downbeats). Each beat is indicated with a slash, the first of which is sometimes replaced by a chord symbol, indicating the onset of a new chord. Numbers above these bars indicate what music theorists call "hypermeter": the grouping of measures into strong and weak patterns similar to those that inhere between the beats within a bar. This hypermeter is easy to hear in "Hard Rain," due to the unusual asymmetry in the questions and answers, in which Dylan employs a lopsided three-plus-four hypermeter. I have configured the example so that it is easy to follow while listening to the recording. While doing so, one can count along with the numbers atop the figure (aloud or silently) to better feel the three-plus-four hypermeter of the questions and answers. **Audio example 10.1** provides the first verse for this purpose.

It is no news that Dylan often adds and drops beats or bars. Metric irregularity has been a hallmark of his performance style throughout his career, to the frequent dismay of his backing musicians.[4] This metric flexibility has roots not only in his own idiosyncratic musical temperament—his elastic sense of musical time, his rhythmic indiscipline—but also in the American vernacular traditions he was so voraciously assimilating in the early '60s. Bluegrass musicians use the term "crooked tunes" to refer to songs or instrumental numbers in which dropped or added beats create moments of irregularity in a given metric layer.[5] The metrical irregularity of Dylan's playing is not merely accidental; he knew of this tradition. In his copy of Woody Guthrie's songbook *From California to the New York Island*, he highlighted a passage in Pete Seeger's introduction that advocates for just such a flexible approach to meter:

> To avoid a sing-song effect from repeating the same simple melody many times, Woody, like all American ballad singers, held out long notes in unexpected places, although his guitar strumming maintained an even tempo. Thus no two verses sounded alike. Extra beats were often added to measures.[6]

But unlike the unpredictable expansions and contractions in Guthrie's style—and much of Dylan's—on the studio recording of "Hard Rain" we hear a *regular* irregularity: the three-plus-four rhythm persists throughout the balladic questions and the cascading answers of the verse. Indeed, Dylan is remarkably consistent in this three-plus-four rhythm throughout the questions and answers of the studio performance; only once does he falter (testimony to his concentration during this take).[7] The result is a kind of uneasy, asymmetrical swaying, at once hypnotic and disconcerting.

The speed at which chords change within the questions and answers adds an additional layer of irregularity. In the answers, the G* chord sounds for two bars, A* for one, and then D for four. This enhances the sense of imbalance, of the half-barre chords ascending precariously, by unequal durations, before falling back down to the open-position D. That D is the tonic chord—the harmonic home base—and it provides an opportunity for the listener to absorb the image just described and regain metric balance before ascending once again for another vision. Through this all, the guitar's lowest three strings sound out the tonic drone, grounding the proceedings and acting as a counterbalance to the harmonic and metric instabilities elsewhere.

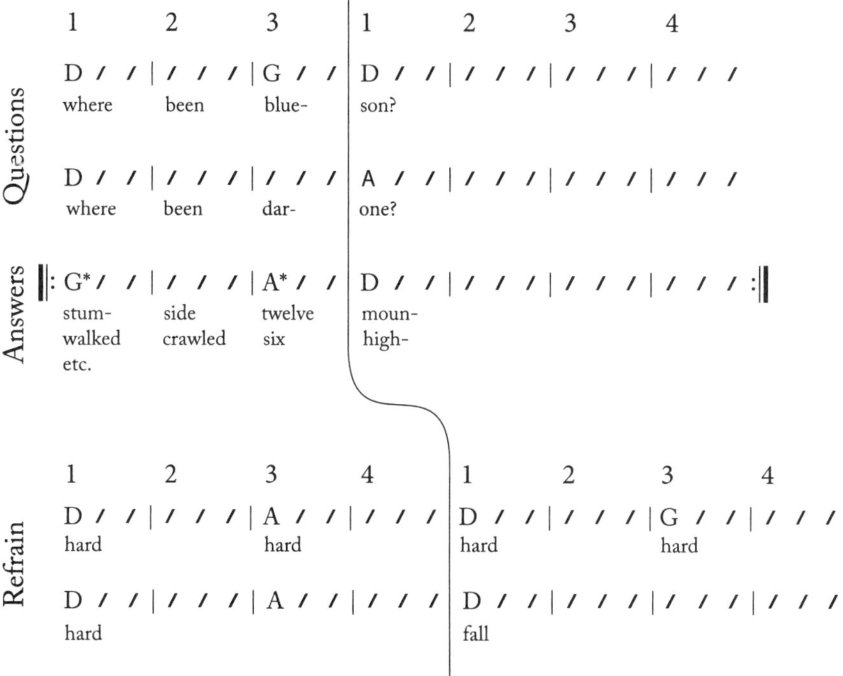

FIGURE 10.2. Chords and hypermeter in the studio version of "Hard Rain."

When Dylan swings into the refrain, the changes in hypermeter and harmonic rhythm are immediately striking. No longer the asymmetrical, three-plus-four swaying, we now move into a decisive (and stylistically normative) four-plus-four hypermeter. (Again, the reader is encouraged to count along while listening to sense this fully.) Moreover, the harmonic rhythm is now utterly regular, each chord lasting two bars, until the final D on "fall," which again lasts for four. This newfound regularity is also evident in Dylan's singing. Note how the spacing of syllables changes across the figure. In the questions and answers, the four accented syllables fall on successive downbeats, leaving a considerable vocal pause at the end of each line. The pauses correspond effectively to the rhythm of the conversation between parent and son: after each question a pause (awaiting an answer), after each answer a pause (as the image settles in). In the refrain, by contrast, the only accented word—"hard"—now falls every *two* bars in the first line (possibly under the influence of the Lemuel Jones performance in fig. 9.5 and audio ex. 9.6), stretching out across the entire eight-bar hypermetric structure. In the second line, this rhythm slows yet again: the only accented syllables now fall four bars apart, absorbing the previous momentum as the vocal line finally descends.

This metric-harmonic process—uneasy, crooked hypermeter in the questions and answers giving way to the sure tread of the refrain—is the energetic template for every live version of the song. But Dylan and his backing musicians navigate it differently each time, sometimes with surefooted confidence, at other moments stumbling on the refrain's steep ascent. But at their most effective—and affecting—even these flawed performances can achieve a kind of grace. Let's listen.

Chapter 11 audio and video examples:
soundingbobdylan.com/ch11

CHAPTER ELEVEN

I'll Know My Song Well

"Hard Rain" in Performance, 1962–1978

IMPERFECTING "HARD RAIN"

Chapters 9 and 10 tell the story of how Dylan made "Hard Rain" sound in the studio in 1962. We now turn, across two more chapters, to a survey of the ways he has made it sound since. The result is our most sustained discussion yet of Dylan's art of change imperfection. For, once composed, the song became not a fixed object but an occasion for difference in sounding, for unruly plenitude, for productive inconsistency.

This chapter begins with an overview of Dylan's performing career, before turning to the first sixteen years of the song's concert history, from the year of its composition through the massive world tour of 1978. This first phase begins with consolidation of the original arrangement in the 1960s followed by radical reinventions in the '70s, with each new "Hard Rain" pointing in a different direction. Chapter 12 picks up the thread when the song re-entered setlists late in Dylan's gospel period, tracing it through the '80s and its various iterations in the Never-Ending Tour. These versions follow a more continual evolution, a gradual process of change and development.

The wildly disparate genres of the song's '70s adolescence give way to a kind of wizened maturity and newfound lyricism, especially in the wake of a transformative performance in Japan in 1994.

On hearing "Hard Rain" morph before our ears across these chapters, we realize that it is less stable than we thought, and also more capacious. The song becomes more, not less, in its continual reinvention. Change proliferates meaning. "It used to be like that; now it goes like this," he taunted in 1966, only just then learning what doors that attitude could open, for any song. In this chapter and the next we walk through them, ears alert.

DYLAN ON STAGE: AN OVERVIEW

Figure 11.1 provides a bird's-eye view of Dylan's performing activity from 1962, when "Hard Rain" was written, up through 2023 (the most recent completed year of touring at time of writing). The gray bars plot the total number of concerts in a given year; black bars tally performances of "Hard Rain." **Table 11.1** presents the same information in numerical form.[1]

Solid brackets beneath the graph of figure 11.1 divide Dylan's performing career into four phases.[2] Dotted brackets beneath them mark three phases of "Hard Rain" performances, which I'll discuss below. We begin with an overview of the four career phases. The first, "early years," extends from 1961 to the motorcycle accident of July 1966. Dylan's concerts at the beginning of this period consisted mostly of coffeehouse gigs and shows at Greenwich Village folk-revival hot spots like Gerde's Folk City and the Gaslight Café. As his fame grew he began to perform more widely, traveling to London in December 1962, and embarking on his first tour of the United States in early 1964. Concert activity increased considerably in 1965 and 1966, building to a fever pitch in the "electric" world tour (with the Hawks) that extended from late August 1965 through May 1966. An eight-year hiatus from concert touring followed, beginning with the motorcycle accident in July 1966, during which time Dylan retreated to his home in Woodstock to recuperate with his family. He released

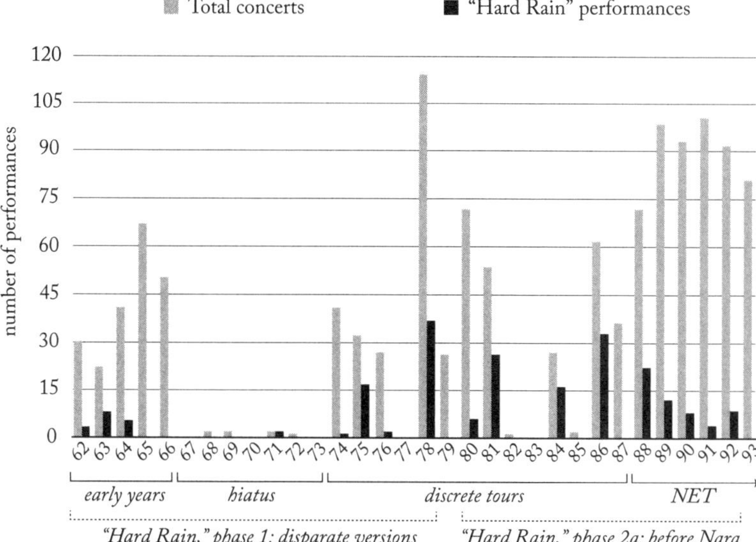

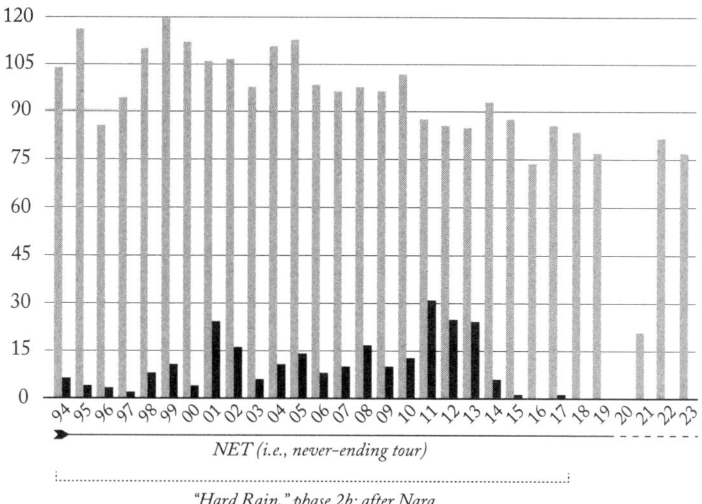

FIGURE 11.1. Dylan concerts (gray bars) and "Hard Rain" performances (black bars), 1962–2023.

TABLE 11.1. NUMBER OF DYLAN CONCERTS AND "HARD RAIN" PERFORMANCES, 1962–2023

Year	Total concerts	"Hard Rain" performances
1962	30*	3*
1963	22*	8*
1964	41*	5*
1965	67	
1966	48	
1967		
1968		
1969	2	
1970		
1971	2	2
1972	1	
1973		
1974	41	1
1975	32	17
1976	27	2
1977		
1978	114	37
1979	26	
1980	72	6
1981	54	26
1982		
1983		
1984	27	16
1985	2	
1986	62	33
1987	36	
1988	72	22
1989	99	12
1990	93	8
1991	101	4
1992	92	9
(continued)		
1993	81	
1994	104	6
1995	116	4
1996	86	3
1997	95	2
1998	110	8
1999	120	11
2000	112	4
2001	106	24
2002	107	16
2003	98	6
2004	111	11
2005	113	14
2006	99	8
2007	97	10
2008	98	17
2009	97	10
2010	102	13
2011	88	31
2012	86	25
2013	85	24
2014	93	6
2015	88	1
2016	74	
2017	86	1
2018	84	
2019	77	
2020		
2021	21	
2022	82	
2023	77	
Total	3961	461

**Conservative estimates based on extant set lists and recordings.*

several records in this period but made only seven concert appearances. He returned to concert life with a flourish in 1974, undertaking a massively successful US tour with the Band (the Hawks, renamed), and beginning an extended period of high-profile individual tours, including the celebrated Rolling Thunder Revue of 1975–76, an enormous international tour with large band in 1978, and the three "gospel tours" of his Christian phase in 1979–80. After a period of flagging inspiration on stage in the mid-1980s, Dylan recommitted himself to live performance in 1988, taking a cue from the Grateful Dead, with whom he had toured in 1987.[3] The phase of intense, almost uninterrupted touring that followed (and that continues at the time of this writing) has been dubbed the "Never-Ending Tour."[4] Dylan has performed with a revolving roster of musicians during this period, some for only a few months, others for many years (bassist Tony Garnier, for example, has been on the tour since 1989).[5] This phase has also seen Dylan's return to critical favor with 1997's *Time Out of Mind*, and his reconnection with what he has called "archaic" music—old-time folk, country, blues, and parlor song.[6]

Now let's attend to the dashed brackets marking the phases of "Hard Rain" in performance. These do not align with the career stages just discussed. This is often the case when one traces the performance history of individual songs. Arrangements and approaches to a given song regularly change in response to some local condition that does not coincide with other, more global changes in Dylan's performing career. In the case of "Hard Rain," the transition from the global tour of 1978 to the gospel phase that begins in the following year is a decisive inflection point for the song. And with good reason. The song's first phase, 1962–78, was a period of experimentation, the arrangement undergoing dramatic change from tour to tour. But after the mammoth 1978 tour, the song became more stable, its evolution more gradual. Dylan first revived it in late 1980, in the midst of his gospel phase, the song's spirit transformed by his close involvement with the music of the Black church. This version provided a template for the slowly evolving arrangement throughout the '80s and early '90s. The year 1994 then saw another inflection point in the song's history, with his orchestral performance of it in Nara, Japan. I have thus divided phase 2 into two halves, "before Nara" and "after Nara." More on this in the next chapter.

Let's now turn our attention to the black bars in figure 11.1. First, note how short they are. "Hard Rain" has never achieved the ubiquity of "All Along the Watchtower" or "Like a Rolling Stone" in Dylan's set lists. It is perhaps telling that the year with the most performances of it, 1978, saw it acting as an *instrumental* introduction, before Dylan even walked on stage.[7] Beyond that, it has remained a special item, a big song to perform selectively. Consider, say, 1994. Dylan performed 104 concerts that year but played "Hard Rain" only six times. The following year saw 116 concerts but only four renditions of "Hard Rain." And so on. The song's infrequent performances may be due in part to its demands on the singer. Dylan himself occasionally showed reluctance to sing it early on. On April 14, 1963, at the home of folk enthusiasts Eve and Mac McKenzie, Dylan demurred multiple times when Eve encouraged him to sing it, saying, "It's hard to sing it."[8] He eventually did perform the song, to everyone's astonishment. "Never [before] or since have I, or my folks, heard him pull out every line like that," writes the McKenzies' son Peter.[9] A couple weeks later, on Studs Terkel's radio program *Wax Museum*, Dylan once again demurred when Terkel asked him to play it, suggesting they could play the studio recording instead. Terkel pressed gently and Dylan eventually relented, performing the song in the studio.[10]

Why the demurrals? What makes "Hard Rain" so difficult to sing? It's not just difficult for Dylan. Patti Smith's poignant, stumbling performance of the song at the 2016 Nobel ceremony honoring Dylan makes clear that other seasoned musicians can struggle when attempting it. One obvious hurdle is length. There are five long verses, and the tolling answers are irregular: their number varies in each verse, and they lead to one another with no sense of logical connection or shared end rhyme. Anyone who knows the song well, including its author, soon gets used to which line follows which, but that kind of memory can become quite unreliable in the nervy context of performance (just ask Smith). Dylan has other long songs—"It's Alright,

Ma (I'm Only Bleeding)" and "Desolation Row" leap immediately to mind—which are also in the middle of the pack as regards number of performances. Like "Hard Rain," they are songs that require Dylan to marshal his forces. We can hear that in the studio chatter on January 15, 1965, when Dylan recorded "It's Alright, Ma" for *Bringing It All Back Home*. After an aborted take, and right before the sole complete take, Dylan says to producer Tom Wilson, "I really don't feel like doing this *song*, man. I have to do it, though. It's such a *long song*."[11]

But still, Dylan has performed "Hard Rain" less often (461 times) than even "Desolation Row" (594) or "It's Alright, Ma" (771).[12] This suggests that there is something beyond length that makes it difficult, or something about it that makes it more of a special item, often held in reserve. This likely involves the particular demands it makes as regards pacing, overall shape, and emotional tone—demands above and beyond those made by his other long numbers. But Dylan nevertheless *has* marshaled the resources to perform it hundreds of times. Let's listen to what that sounded like.

EARLY RENDITIONS (1962–1964)

Dylan's performances of the song in 1962–64 hew quite close to the studio recording. As Todd Harvey notes, "in terms of quantifiable elements (melody, tempo, meter, rhythm, text), the performances [in these years] are nearly identical. . . . The melody is remarkably stable, especially considering the constant variation in other songs."[13] These are all solo performances with acoustic guitar, which was of course Dylan's primary mode of performance in these years. The vocal tune is largely the same, though by 1964 he has begun curtailing the Guthrie-esque descents somewhat, often so that they end by hanging on scale degree $\hat{4}$. **Audio example 11.1** is a representative example, from the song's last circulating performance of this era, in San José, California on November 25, 1964. Note how Dylan clings to $\hat{4}$ at the ends of the answers, when singing "mountains," "highways," "forests," and so on. This is the first hint of melodic variation in a song he had been singing with notable discipline, focus, and consistency. Dylan's removal of the three-note musical rhyme (marked by the bracket in figure 9.3) gives the questions a sense of added urgency.

One other source of subtle variation in these performances is metric. Dylan generally hews quite closely to the three-plus-four hypermetrical structure that we explored in chapter 10. But he varies it more in live performance than on the studio recording. Most often he curtails the four-bar portion after each line, especially in the final verse, with the next line coming sooner than we would expect. This is evident in the earliest circulating recording of the song, from the home of Eve and Mac McKenzie.[14] In the final verse, excerpted in **audio example 11.2**, he compresses the hypermeter to two bars after "waters," "prison," and "forgotten," creating a sort of controlled acceleration. The effect is of gathering determination as the son tells where he is *going*, not just where he's been.

An additional detail that all these performances share with the studio recording: there is no harmonica. Indeed, this will become the norm for the song as Dylan performs it in the coming decades. It is, as a rule, not a harmonica song. Why? Why not perforate its flow of images—its ceaseless tolling of questions–answers–refrain—with some harmonica-led breathing room? I suspect that there are two reasons for this. First, there is not enough affective space in the song for the wordless emotional outpouring that Dylan's harmonica provides, discussed in chapter 7. It is a song overstuffed with images, shot through with a pervasive sense of doom mixed with luminous awe. The affective space is fully saturated; it neither welcomes nor needs the added emotion of Dylan's harp. Second, the song's momentum does not easily admit of a solo break. In the style of question-and-answer ballads, the next verse's questions typically follow hard on the heels of the previous verse's refrain, as though the parent were impatiently asking the next question of the blue-eyed son at the first opportunity, eager for *some* sort of legible information. To insert a solo—harp or otherwise—would interrupt this rhythm of continuous verbal exchange.

Dylan ceased performing "Hard Rain" for some time once he made his electric turn in early 1965.[15] This may have been because he now had another ambitious, visionary acoustic song, "Mr. Tambourine Man," which occupied the slot in set lists previously reserved for "Hard Rain." It could also be because the performative difficulties that "Hard Rain" presented had become too onerous, and "Mr. Tambourine Man" provided a welcome alternative. In any case, Dylan wouldn't sing the song on stage again for seven years. Once he did, it sounded utterly different.

AUGUST 1, 1971 (NEW YORK CITY)

Dylan played only one concert in 1971—or rather, two sets in George Harrison's back-to-back benefit concerts for Bangladesh, held on the afternoon and evening of August 1 in Madison Square Garden. Dylan was evidently very nervous about performing, almost backing out.[16] When he ultimately agreed to go on, "Hard Rain" was the first song of each set.

The Concert for Bangladesh finds Dylan on the opposite side of a watershed. In 1962 the ambitious young singer was hurtling toward international fame; in 1971 he was recovering from that fame in semi-seclusion. The counterculture was in a similar place in the bleary morning-after of 1971, in the wake of Altamont and Kent State, in the malaise of the Nixon years and incipient stagflation. In this context, Harrison's Concert for Bangladesh—the first such celebrity benefit concert, and the model for Live Aid fourteen years later—seemed to the editors of *Rolling Stone* "a brief incandescent revival of all that was best about the Sixties."[17] The cause was relief for victims of the Bangladesh Liberation War. Performers ranged from Ravi Shankar to Eric Clapton, with Leon Russell acting as musical director.

Dylan performed his set with light backing from Harrison (slide guitar), Russell (electric bass), and Ringo Starr (tambourine), but this was for all intents and purposes a solo acoustic performance. The backing is extremely sparse, all but inaudible except for the occasional murmur from Harrison's slide. In the film of the performance—**video example 11.1** shows an excerpt—the spotlight is (once again) trained on Dylan, with Russell and Harrison only partly visible,

Ringo nowhere to be seen. The simple fact of Dylan's presence with an acoustic guitar—dressed in a denim jacket—created a sensation, recalling the pre-electric Dylan. Jonathan Cott described the scene for *Rolling Stone*:

> He appeared on-stage in the dark: curly hair, Levi jacket, guitar and mouth harp. People cheered, but they didn't believe it, responding the way one does after having obtained something deeply hoped for with a kind of passionless disbelief.[18]

"Hard Rain," like so many Dylan songs, had by this time become an iconic piece of '60s lore. But as Dylan nervously played it for 20,000, it sounded the opposite of monumental. The performance is instead informal, laid-back, and unpretentious. The 1970s would find Dylan reinventing his songs in a host of ways; in 1971 the technique was countrified understatement.

As conveyed on the official release of the evening concert, the architecture of the song is more or less in place; the melody in particular follows the outline of the 1962 original. But differences abound in the details. For one, Dylan is no longer putting on the prematurely aged Guthrie voice. Nor does he employ the smooth country-crooner voice that he had used on 1969's *Nashville Skyline*, at the Isle of Wight concert in the same year, or on 1970's *Self Portrait*. His earlier timbral grit has returned, but the body of his voice is fuller, more resonant. In part this is due to the techniques Dylan must adopt in the cavernous arena—projecting into the large space, negotiating with the amplification, responding to what he can hear through the stage monitors, and so on. It is also likely a product of his new, more sedentary life in Woodstock, with its domestic ease and slow pace, his voice no longer pushed to the breaking point nightly.

But there is also a difference in vocal aesthetic. In place of the dry-as-dust prophetic voice of 1962, we now hear a host of little vocal ornaments, breaks, and inflections—relaxed country embellishments that would sound out of place on the severe *Freewheelin'* take. Jonathan Cott heard hints of Hank Williams and Roy Acuff in Dylan's delivery.[19] **Audio example 11.3** illustrates, juxtaposing passages from the questions, answers, and refrain in the 1962 and 1971 performances. **Figure 11.2** transcribes the first four phrases from 1971, using dashed boxes to indicate ornaments in each line. Dylan decorates both "son" and "one" with little melismas. He emphasizes "side" and "crawl'd" with country breaks in the voice (diamond noteheads indicate the vocal breaks). His voice breaks in the other answers too, as well as on the word "rain" itself.

What are we to make of these country inflections? Was this a provocation? An attempt at ironic defamiliarization? A generic stiff-arm? After all, country was a vernacular genre that the counterculture had been slow to absorb, due in no small part to its frequent association with white conservative politics. Those politics were sometimes overt: Merle Haggard's anti-hippie "Okie from Muskogee" had been

FIGURE 11.2. The first four vocal lines of "Hard Rain" as sung at the Concert for Bangladesh, August 1, 1971. Dashed boxes enclose country-inflected ornaments. Diamond noteheads indicate breaks in the voice.

released two years before the Concert for Bangladesh. Yet, by 1971 plenty of countercultural types had found ways to absorb country into their musical vocabularies, thanks in part to Dylan's own *Nashville Skyline*, as well as the work of a handful of Southern California groups centered around Gram Parsons. Moreover, Dylan's nerves and his eagerness to give a good performance—reported by Harrison—make provocation unlikely. More likely, this was Dylan's understated reaction to the adulation that had all but smothered him in the '60s. One way to evade that monumental myth was to cut "Hard Rain" down to size, to make it folksy and unassuming. After all, his explicit turn toward country in 1969 had come about in part as a strategy to back away from "Woodstock generation," as he called it. By 1971 country was something like a generic home base; it served his purposes well at Harrison's benefit.

Critical and fan reception of the performance was ecstatic. As the Cott quote above suggests, much of this had to do with Dylan's reappearance after years of relative isolation (with acoustic guitar and harmonica, no less), but there was also praise for his music making; it is difficult to find criticisms of its country aspects. Paul Williams calls both Bangladesh sets "stunning," praising them as "modest, confident, richly textured."[20] "Modest" is especially apt. Williams also hears affection in the performance, "Dylan feeling and communicating genuine love for the music he's playing."[21] Might he hear that affection in the very vocal ornaments we have been discussing? Country, with its conventional vocal signifiers of heightened emotion, conveys such affects with particular immediacy. What is striking is the stylistic mutability of the song. It accepts the generic resetting from folk to country like a skin graft.

There is also a *metric* mutability in the performance. If the studio recording resisted the kind of metric flexibility characteristic of bluegrass and other old-time musics, that flexibility returns emphatically here. Dylan now drops and adds bars throughout, replacing the regular three-plus-four of the answers with a constantly shifting hypermeter. **Figure 11.3** shows one representative verse, repurposing the notation from figure 10.2 for comparison. **Audio example 11.4** provides the verse in question.

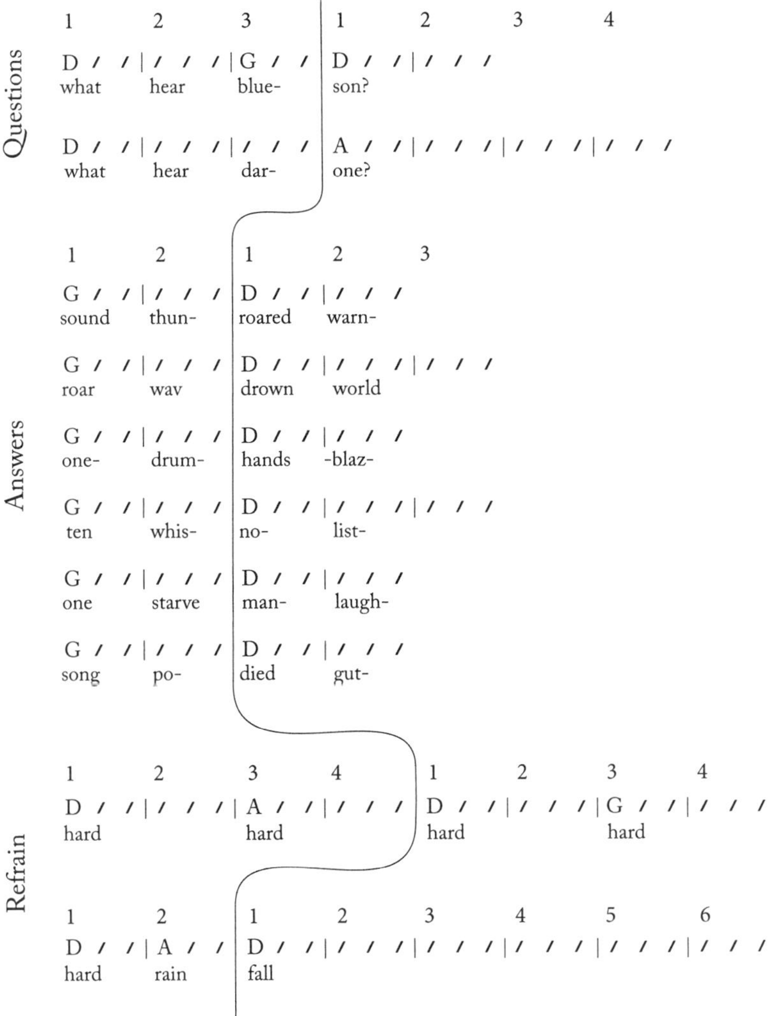

FIGURE 11.3. Irregular hypermeter in verse 3 of the Concert for Bangladesh version of "Hard Rain," August 1, 1971.

Again, I encourage the reader to listen along while following the figure. Under the pressures of the stage—with its nerves, adrenaline, and high stakes—the studio version's carefully weighted metric form is susceptible to buckling, denting, and bending. In addition to the metric variability, note the change in chording. The upper-position half-barres are gone; all chords are now open position. Moreover, the answers now lack a dominant harmony (A), instead cycling between subdominant G and tonic D. Crucially, the subdominant is usually considered a more "relaxed" harmony than the "tense" dominant, further evidence of an easing in tone. Note, too, that the harmony has slipped in relation to the vocal line. In the 1962 version, the tonic D chord arrived with the final word of each line, on the fourth accented syllable; now it arrives in the middle of the line, on the third vocal accent, casually early. The strumming is energetic but undetailed. Dylan's guitar slips away from the particularity of the studio recording to a kind of distilled outline, a rough sketch of the studio recording's harmonic moves. The metric inconsistency and harmonic relaxation further heighten the sense of an informal performance, far from the straight-backed discipline of the studio version. Note especially the abbreviation of the song's climax. In the studio, "rain" lasts ten beats (more than three bars); in 1971 it lasts just three (one bar). Dylan moves on quickly from the word, dialing back the climax's Mosaic intensity.

The overall effect is one of easy familiarity. That effect would be impossible without the precedent of the 1962 recording, its sounds presumably deeply etched into the memories of those present at the Garden in 1971. The result is a kind of aural double-focus: the memory of the studio recording organizes and inflects listeners' experience of the song as it sounds here and now. Again, this is a fact of all live music in the age of recordings; and again, the effect is heightened with Dylan. From the mid-1970s on, his performances open up an increasingly charged aesthetic space between sounds heard and sounds recalled.

FEBRUARY 4, 1974 (ST. LOUIS)

That space thrummed with energy when Dylan returned to touring in 1974, backed by the Band. This was most attendees' first chance to see him since the mid-'60s, and for thousands their first chance ever. Dylan nevertheless quickly soured on the tour. In the notes to 1985's *Biograph*, he stated that in 1974 he was

> just playing a role. . . . I was playing Bob Dylan and the Band was playing the Band. It was all sort of mindless. The people that came out to see us came mostly to see what they missed the first time around. It was just more of a "legendary" kind of thing. They've heard about it, they'd bought the records, whatever, but what they saw didn't give any clue to what was.[22]

Many collectors and critics nevertheless still praise the resulting performances, especially those documented on the live record *Before the Flood*, with rock critic Robert Christgau claiming the record contains "the craziest and strongest rock and roll ever recorded."[23]

The setlist was a veritable rundown of greatest hits, yet Dylan performed "Hard Rain" only once on the tour, his first performance of it since the Concert for Bangladesh. The song came during the acoustic set during the afternoon show in St. Louis, on February 4, in the slot typically reserved for "Gates of Eden." "Hard Rain" wasn't the only surprise of the evening. The concert also featured the only "Desolation Row" of the tour. Both songs receive focused, impassioned performances, Dylan's lyrical delivery impeccable (he does not flub a line in either song). This was evidently an afternoon for stretching out, for a revival of ambitious old songs.

And yet these are not performances of subtle nuance. "Hard Rain" is enthusiastic but lacks variation. **Audio example 11.5** presents the first verse. Dylan performs the song in G, which puts his voice in a higher register, with the vocal climax on G4 at the refrain's apex resounding through the cavernous arena.[24] This higher key suits the venue and the moment, allowing Dylan to harness his adrenaline of live performance for vocal projection into the big space. But the boomy acoustic and emphatic delivery—both characteristic of this tour—do not allow for the kind of intricate country detailing of the 1971 version. His country twang is also replaced here by a resonant chest voice, with exaggerated /ar/ sounds that recall Gopinath and Cherlin's comments about his Scottish bard voice. Metrically, the song is taut, the three-plus-four hypermeter in the answers now a more compact three-plus-two. It is a strong performance, but not a bold one. In the following year, fans would hear an astonishing new "Hard Rain" that was both.

DECEMBER 4, 1975 (MONTREAL)

The Rolling Thunder Revue—a star-cluttered tour that Dylan helmed in late 1975 and early 1976—was so many things at once that it defies easy description. It was a reunion of Village regulars; "an offbeat, underground, weird medicine show";[25] a revived commedia dell'arte; a protest tour aimed at raising awareness about the imprisoned boxer Rubin "Hurricane" Carter; promotion for Dylan's forthcoming album *Desire*; a traveling set for his film *Renaldo and Clara*, which would appear (to broad incomprehension and disdain) in 1978; a nightly citation of another film, Marcel Carné's 1945 epic *Les enfants du paradis* (Children of Paradise); and—most functionally—Dylan's attempt to recapture the spontaneity that he felt he had lost in 1974's corporate arena tour with the Band. Given the bewildering multiplicity that is Rolling Thunder, it is best to begin by taking in as much of this totality as possible. **Video example 11.2** shows a clip from *Renaldo and Clara* that includes the complete first verse of "Hard Rain" and the beginning of the second, as performed in the Montreal Forum on December 4, 1975.

We see Dylan in whiteface, the indelible image associated with the 1975 leg of the tour. The face paint and outfit—wide-brimmed felt hat with flower, tied scarf, vest—are an explicit reference to Jean-Louis Barrault's character Baptiste as he first appears in *Les enfants du paradis*.[26] Baptiste is a Parisian mime as well as a Pierrot figure, another link to the commedia dell'arte tradition. But Dylan's whiteface is also an enigmatic inversion of a more historically and geographically proximate mass-cultural phenomenon. Dylan would wrestle with blackface minstrelsy at various points in his career, up to and including his 2001 album *"Love and Theft,"* which takes its title from Eric Lott's book on minstrelsy. For David Yaffe the Dylan of the 1975 Rolling Thunder "turns minstrelsy inside out, reversing the poles of significance and showing the artificiality of the social constructs of race," his face "a painted vision of artificial whiteness."[27] Murray Leeder sees "an appearance between a ghost and a minstrel's photonegative."[28]

As if this weren't enough layered signification, Dylan the film editor adds yet another wrinkle. In *Renaldo and Clara* the complete Montreal performance of "Hard Rain" follows an extended scene of two white street preachers on New York's Wall Street addressing an increasingly hostile crowd. As **video example 11.3** shows, right before the cut to "Hard Rain," one of the preachers says, "I'll tell you this: whatever you say to a man of God, you say *direct* to God." Cue "Hard Rain" as fire-and-brimstone sermon.

But what we hear next is worlds removed from the church. For the song, this sacred text of the '60s, has become—shockingly—a raucous Chicago blues. Dylan's intensity at the mic matches the street preacher, but white religious fanaticism (in whiteface!) now meets an arrangement that draws explicitly on electrified urban blues. Most notable is a conventional blues tag, already mentioned in chapters 5 and 6. Boxed in **figure 11.4**, it is a variant of the IV–♭III–I stop-time figure familiar from Muddy Waters's "Hoochie Coochie Man" and "Mannish Boy," Bo Diddley's "I'm a Man," and countless blues that followed in their wake, from Elvis's "Trouble" (1958) to George Thorogood's "Bad to the Bone" (1982).[29] The tag was also in the air in 1975. Three years prior it had anchored David Bowie's glam anthem "The Jean Genie." This is not an incidental detail, for Bowie's guitarist from that session—Mick Ronson—was now, improbably, one of Dylan's guitarists for Rolling Thunder. Did Ronson suggest the lick? It's unclear from the sole circulating rehearsal of the song before the

FIGURE 11.4. "Hard Rain" groove, fall 1975; blues tag boxed.

tour, recorded on October 21, 1975. The rehearsal has Dylan's acoustic guitar out front and lacks the heavy blues shuffle of the eventual concert arrangement, which was fully in place at the first show of the tour in Plymouth, Massachusetts nine days later.[30] If the tag did come via Ronson, it would add yet another twist to the performance's tangled skein of racial signifiers, as a gesture from Black urban blues is filtered through British glam before reappearing stateside in Dylan's rollicking "Hard Rain."

It would be hard to overstate the audacity of the resulting arrangement. If the country-inflected version of 1971 was a mild generic affront, this version is a gleeful sacrilege, riding roughshod over the song in a galloping 12/8. But the irregularities of the song's metric surface make it an occasionally bumpy ride. As shown in **figure 11.5(a)**, the initiating questions have become asymmetrical, the first spanning two bars, the second three and a half. The added half bar in the latter—in which Dylan sings "darling young," indicated by a bracket in the figure—creates a metric hiccup of 6/8 that disturbs the regularity of the 12/8 groove. In contrast with this metric irregularity, the answers—which in 1962 had swayed asymmetrically, three-plus-four—are now as regular as can be: a repeating two-bar cycle shown in **figure 11.5(b)**. What had been a tenuous progression of half-barres high on the neck in the 1962 recording becomes a confident circular progression through the IV, V, and I chords (D–E–A), presented by the whole band in tight ensemble. The refrain, sketched in **11.5(c)**,

(a) Questions

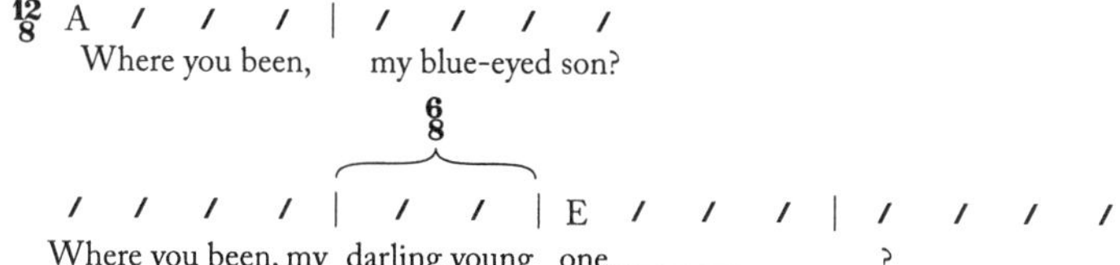

(b) Answers

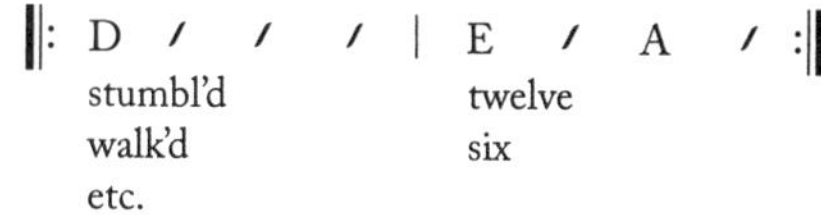

(c) Refrain

A / / / | E / / / | A / / / | D / / /
hard hard hard hard

A / E / | A / / / | / / / /
hard rain fall

FIGURE 11.5. Meter in the 1975 version of "Hard Rain." The 12/8 and 6/8 are represented by slashes that represent 12/8 as a four-beat bar, 6/8 as a two-beat bar. These beats are all subdivided into three parts, which gives the rhythm its shuffle feel.

essentially matches that of the 1971 version, compressing the climax on "rain" to a mere half bar.

This compression aside, the refrain is the only passage to retain a clear reference to the original melody, which is now a rowdy sing-along. Elsewhere the tune from 1962 is all but obliterated. In place of the descending figure from "1913 Massacre" and "Song to Woody," Dylan sings a series of short melodic bursts, freely contoured and rhythmically elastic. **Figure 11.6** transcribes the first few phrases as Dylan sang them in Montreal on December 4.[31] This is an early instance of Dylan's contour-inventive style, discussed in chapter 5, which would become a norm in the decades of touring that would follow Rolling Thunder.

FIGURE 11.6. The vocal line of "Hard Rain" at the outset of the December 4, 1975, performance in Montreal.

Dylan's vehement, inventive vocal delivery provides a sonic link to one of the performance's filmic paratexts, the Wall Street evangelist, reanimating the song's apocalyptic themes. But beyond this it is hard to synthesize the entire performance, with its riot of signifiers, the stray references to Carné, Pierrot, the commedia, blackface/whiteface, and the rest. While there is clearly a carnivalesque inversion at work—in the color of Dylan's face paint, in the band's blasphemous take on this hallowed song—the performance is so oversaturated with references that it resists a unified interpretation. If all of these are masks, to return to the familiar Dylan trope, the performance's semiotic opacity results from their simultaneous layering.[32] As a result, even the most culturally charged signifiers in this performance are hard to read clearly, occluded by mask upon mask. The urban blues becomes one sign system among many, a site of racial imagination and desire, yes, but also a sounding form that is ready to hand, a celebratory noise that remains audible above the signifying din.

MAY 23, 1976 (FORT COLLINS)

The second leg of Rolling Thunder was, by all accounts, a dour affair. Dylan's marriage was crumbling, he was struggling emotionally over the recent suicide of Phil Ochs, the musicians were dogged by illness, and the joyful carnival vibe of fall 1975 had curdled into malaise and anger.[33] The tour's dark apex came at an outdoor show in Hughes Stadium at Colorado State University in rainy, cold Fort Collins, on May 23, 1976, one day before Dylan turned thirty-five.[34] Some fans gamely held up a banner wishing him a happy birthday, but the concert was, on the whole, hardly celebratory, largely due to the weather. For the musicians—and (one presumes) a great many fans soaking in the stadium—it was an endurance test. The wet and cold penetrated so deep that multi-instrumentalist David Mansfield couldn't stop his leg from shaking as he tried to depress the pedals of his steel guitar.[35]

In all likelihood, it was with a touch of gallows humor that Dylan called for "Hard Rain" as the final encore for this rain-soaked concert. The song had made only one earlier appearance on the 1976 tour, on April 22 in a hotel ballroom in Clearwater, Florida. Notably, there were film crews on hand at both the Clearwater and Fort Collins shows. They were there to shoot a TV special. Dylan didn't like the Clearwater footage, so opted to reshoot a month later in Fort Collins. "Hard Rain" didn't make it into the circulating footage of the April 22 concert, but it is the first song on the Fort Collins film (despite the fact that it was the last song of the concert). The film and accompanying album were aptly called *Hard Rain*, though the song does not appear on the album. Video footage of the broadcast circulates widely, however. **Video example 11.4** shows the first verse.

Much has changed since the previous fall. Gone is Dylan's face paint. Instead, he sports a headscarf and hair falling in ringlets, looking almost Sephardic.[36] Gone, too is the barreling blues arrangement. In its place is a lopsided country waltz in G—lopsided because the slow tempo makes the song's metric irregularities that much more obvious. The questions and answers sit somewhat awkwardly across the slow hypermetric beats, and Dylan seems intent on contracting the space after each line, perhaps in an effort to keep the song from sagging. Drummer Howie Wyeth navigates the shifting hypermeter deftly, but this requires regular stutter steps on the snare, as the back-beat is disrupted. As on the studio recording, the meter straightens out at the "it's a hard" refrain, but even here there is a grinding of gears. On the 1962 studio recording the "it's a hard" iterations came every two bars (as illustrated in fig. 10.2). On stage in Fort Collins, the band members clearly expect Dylan to settle into this every-two-bars rhythm, coming in with the second "it's a hard," and its corresponding chord change two bars later. Dylan capitulates to his bandmates' rhythm in the first refrain, but in the second, as shown in **video example 11.5**, he turns and shakes his head, signaling them to slow down so that "it's a hard" occurs every *four* bars, not every two. Bobby Neuwirth, the de facto leader of the backing band (called Guam), can be seen in the background, nodding his head in encouragement when the musicians settle into the every-four rhythm. **Figure 11.7** shows the two competing timings, which I will refer to hereafter as the "every-two" and the "every-four" versions of the refrain. Dylan often opts for the every-four version in later decades, with fans regularly

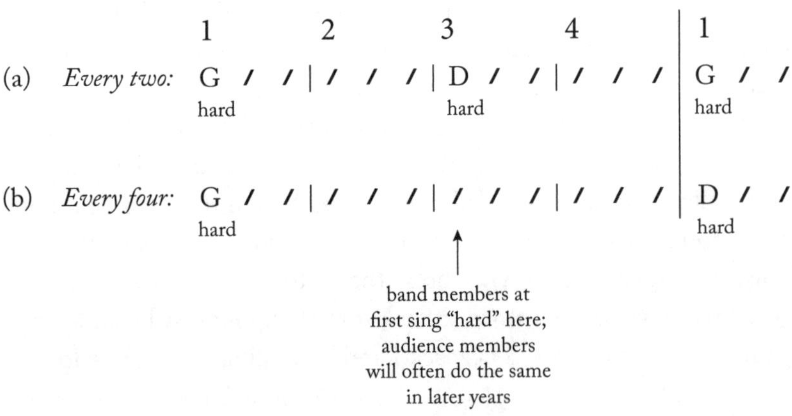

FIGURE 11.7. The "every-two" and "every-four" timings of the "Hard Rain" refrain, as heard in the May 23, 1976, Fort Collins performance.

wrong-footed as they sing the every-two version in the first refrain, just as Dylan's bandmates had in 1976.

The conflict between the every-two and every-four timing results in a moment of misalignment, a failure of coordination. When this happens in later concerts, it is a felicitous accident, opening a window onto fan participation that we might not otherwise hear. As fans sing the second "it's a hard" alone, we can hear just how fervently they join in on the chorus. The misalignment pries open a space between performer and audience, in which we hear fans' investment in Dylan and his song. We also hear their subsequent desire to be *back* in alignment with him as they adjust to the every-four timing. Dylan's band members did the same in 1976; now aligned with Dylan's every-four timing, they pull together once more. The resulting every-four timing makes the ascent effortful and ponderous, especially as it is weighed down by the heavy triple meter, so different from the joyful dash of the previous fall. The feeling is of slow chugging uphill, like the Little Engine that Could. When the engine finally reaches the melodic summit, it stalls. Rather than rushing through "it's a hard rain's a-gonna fall," as he had in 1975 and 1971, Dylan now pauses and the band ceases to play, the climactic line delivered in free meter and ragged harmony.

It is a performance of perseverance, of willing the song into sustaining its momentum, step by effortful step. It is also a performance of hard-won collectivity. The Rolling Thunder Revue was all about collectivity, after all, a motley band of musicians sharing the stage and making a racket together for hours each night. Dylan flattened the hierarchy as much as he could, letting various musicians take center stage and perform their own material over the course of the evening. By 1976 the collective bonhomie had waned. But on stage in Fort Collins, one senses the musicians' efforts to reconstitute that collectivity through "Hard Rain." Tellingly, Joan Baez harmonizes with Dylan throughout the song, standing behind him and to his right, offering vocal support on each phrase. Dylan's voice thus never sounds alone, as he sings his song about a lone son venturing into the apocalyptic wastes. After a grueling concert and a grueling tour, the effect by song's end is strangely hopeful, an exhausted victory.

FEBRUARY 28, 1978 (TOKYO)

This book began with the words of "Hard Rain" appearing on a typescript, the music as yet unrealized. We now turn to a performance in which the words are entirely absent, and all we hear is its music. "Hard Rain" is a strange song to hear without words, and not just because its lyrics are so famous. As we saw in chapters 9 and 10, the song's lyrics exert pressure on musical form, both in their meter and in the piling-up of answers, which creates the iterative core. Without those words sonically present, we hear only the musical bulges and asymmetries that they created.

For the enormous 1978 tour—114 concerts spread across the Far East, Europe, and North America—Dylan assembled the largest band he has played with to date: eight instrumentalists in addition to Dylan—including two percussionists, tenor saxophone, flute, fiddle, and mandolin—and three female backup singers. The production was garish, with the performers required to dress in stage outfits designed by Bill Whitten, who had also designed stage attire for Neil Diamond. Indeed, Diamond's live show was the model for Dylan's. He had attended a Neil Diamond concert in 1977, after which he secured the services of Diamond's manager, Jerry Weintraub, to oversee his own tour.[37] Dylan also based aspects of his show on Elvis's "comeback" concerts of the late '60s and early '70s, which Weintraub had also managed. Two of his musicians—saxophonist Steve Douglas and bassist Jerry Scheff (who joined the tour after its Far East leg)—had played with Elvis during that time.

If these associations seemed puzzling to Dylan's previous fans, the musical arrangements he employed—showbiz-y and stylistically eclectic—were, to many, positively perverse. Dylan stated in a 1978 interview with Ron Rosenbaum that he rearranged his songs because he "believe[d] in them."[38] But one can also hear his arrangements on this tour as antagonistic—an effort to further reclaim his catalog by aggressive defamiliarization. The arrangements have the effect of distancing self-quotation, as though Dylan were performing elaborate cover versions of someone else's songs. Howard Sounes aptly describes the resulting set list as a string of "show tunes in incongruous idioms."[39] These idioms ranged wildly, encompassing reggae (on "Don't Think Twice, It's All Right"), lounge ballad ("Tangled Up in Blue"), disco via Springsteen ("Shelter from the Storm"), Latin pop via the Doobie Brothers ("One More Cup of Coffee"), and something approaching heavy metal for "It's Alright, Ma."

The Japanese promoters had in fact sent a telegram that specifically indicated which songs Dylan was to play.[40] One imagines "Hard Rain" was on the list, though the promoters likely never expected it to be without words. The shows on the 1978 tour opened with an instrumental, in keeping with Vegas tradition. It's puzzling that Dylan chose "Hard Rain" for the first three dozen shows of the tour. The cycling melodic iterations of the son's answers make little sense without the words to justify their repetitions. As a result, it's nearly impossible to hear the instrumental version of the song without conjuring the words in the mind's ear. To make musical sense of the song in this live version, one needs to imagine the vocal part as a necessary, if silent, supplement.

Audio example 11.6 presents the first verse of the performance at Budokan on February 28, 1978. The arrangement is weirdly peppy, anchored by an up-tempo, straight-time pop groove that slips into a disco beat for the refrain, with Ian Wallace's open hi-hat prominent on the off beats.[41] Instead of voice, we hear a string of soloists stepping to the fore for each verse: capo-ed acoustic guitar (Steven Soles),[42] tenor sax (Steve Douglas), organ (Alan Pasqua), electric guitar (Billy Cross), and finally fiddle (David Mansfield). The mix of instruments and playing styles is itself jarring, a mélange of disparate genres, from Douglas's blaring rock sax to Mansfield's old-time fiddle, Pasqua's soulful organ to Cross's distorted shredding. Each soloist navigates the song's contours with gestures and licks idiomatic to their instrument and genre. Douglas and Cross in particular are generically remote from any "Hard Rain" we have yet heard. Strikingly, the band typically plays five iterations of the answer music in each verse. A more typical musical norm would be four; four-squareness is a default in most Western music, popular and classical. The five iterations here gesture toward the song's irregularity when sung. It always sounds like one iteration too many, giving us yet another opportunity to imagine the tolling answers in Dylan's voice, his lyrics silently bending the music into asymmetry.

The tour's reception in the United States was largely hostile, with critics dubbing it the "Vegas tour" (or the "alimony tour," as already noted in chapter 8). In the Far East and Europe the reception was more mixed, with some very enthusiastic reviews.[43] Fans in Japan had never seen him, and he hadn't played in Europe since 1966; many would see him for the first time on this tour. Derek Barker, editor of the British Dylan fanzine *Isis*, described the 1978 concert that he attended—his first Dylan show—as life changing.[44] "Hard Rain" was still opening the set then, but soon Dylan would replace it with "My Back Pages." It was an inspired choice. In addition to the ironies I mentioned in chapter 5—an instrumental song repudiating Dylan's old lyrics, before a concert stuffed with them—"My Back Pages" also has a more self-sufficient melody than "Hard Rain." One can hear it as complete in itself without the supplement of the imagined voice. "Hard Rain," by contrast, needs its words.

Perhaps sensing this, Dylan returned to the song in Nuremberg on July 1, giving a *vocal* performance, its sole sung version on the 1978 tour. Dylan sang it in the midst of the very long set, accompanying himself on acoustic guitar. **Audio example 11.7** presents verse 1. It is a focused return to the 1960s arrangement.[45] After the extravagant generic experiments of 1971, 1975, 1976, and earlier in 1978, the performance feels like gathering the song back together, recalling its original form. When he returned to "Hard Rain" two years later, he was once again ready to embark, piloting the song into yet new generic waters, change imperfection the wind in his sails.

Chapter 12 audio and video examples:
soundingbobdylan.com/ch12

CHAPTER TWELVE

I'll Tell It and Think It and Speak It and Breathe It

"Hard Rain" in Performance, 1980–2017

The story of "Hard Rain" across the next thirty-seven years divides into two halves: before Nara and after Nara. Recall the dashed brackets in figure 11.1. By "Nara" I mean the three stunning performances of the song that Dylan gave with an orchestra in Nara, Japan, on May 20–22, 1994. These transformative renditions are beloved by fans. They also act as a hinge in Dylan's approach to the song. Before the Nara concerts, he sang "Hard Rain" with a declamatory urgency, often deploying the bluesy, gospel delivery that he developed in the late '70s and early '80s. After Nara his singing became far more lyrical and tender, infused with a kind of gentle wisdom and wonder. The awestruck reverence of the song's early years returns. As for arrangements, in the before-Nara era, the song was typically part of the acoustic set, often solo, always performed in D, and relatively close to the 1960s arrangement as regards meter, groove, and form. After

Nara arrangements began to morph once again, taking on new keys, new instrumentation, new rhythmic feels. The Nara concert thus unfolded a new dimension of the song, teaching Dylan that it contained more potential than even *he* yet knew. In his performances of it from 1994 through 2017 he mines that potential, unearthing new expressive veins.

We begin, though, fourteen years before Nara, with a different transformative encounter between words and music, as the lyrics that Dylan typed in 1962 meet the gospel sounds he was making at the turn of the '80s.

GOSPEL RENDITIONS (1980–1981)

As the 1978 tour neared its conclusion in North America, Dylan experienced a spiritual awakening, becoming a born-again Christian. His ensuing gospel phase is one of the most controversial of his career, viewed by many longtime fans as a betrayal of his countercultural roots. It didn't help that, across three tours in 1979 and 1980, he played only Christian material, entirely eschewing his famous back catalog. Many fans nevertheless praise the concerts from these years, Dylan's newfound faith lending his performances a preacherly intensity. That intensity was supported and sustained by a backing band that included stellar gospel musicians, most notably a rotating cast of female background singers.

In the fall of 1980 Dylan began to reintroduce old songs into his setlists, aptly naming the fall tour "A Musical Retrospective." "Hard Rain" made six appearances across the tour's nineteen dates, typically as the final song of the encore, a privileged spot. At two shows late in the tour it took *another* privileged position, third in the set after Christian numbers "Gotta Serve Somebody" and "I Believe in You," in the slot usually filled by "Like a Rolling Stone." Thus, while "Hard Rain" appeared on fewer than a third of the tour's shows, it was clearly a highlight, prominent in the set.

On paper the arrangements are unremarkable. The triple meter of the original version is back, as is the asymmetrical swing of the questions and answers.[1] The full band plays, but the triple meter doesn't sag as it did in 1976. This band is much tighter than Rolling Thunder 2.0, and they navigate the song's hypermetric twists and turns admirably. The key is D, where the song will remain (with the notable exception of Nara) for the next twenty-two years. Again, unremarkable.

But such bean counting misses the essence of this rendition. The performative details are all. As Gayle Wald notes, "approaches that focus on the written text"—or in this case, the formal features of the arrangement—"overlook the performativity of gospel, in which a song's meaning is inseparable from singers' delivery of the lyrics and their ability to ignite the spirit in listeners."[2] So, how did Dylan and his background singers "ignite the spirit" in these gospel renditions of "Hard Rain"? We'll begin with Dylan's vocal delivery, before turning to his interaction with the background singers. Dylan typically begins the song with a loose gesture toward the original tune in the parent's initial questions. But after that he leaves the original melody behind, replacing it with impassioned, bluesy declamation that recalls his angriest gospel numbers, like "When You Gonna Wake Up," "Slow Train," and "Ain't No Man Righteous," or the more celebratory "Solid Rock." In fall 1980 Dylan delivers the "Hard Rain" answers in an emphatic minor-third toggle centering on D4 and F4. The latter pitch is a piercing blue third in D and Dylan delivers it with nasal intensity, causing it to dissonate fiercely against the D-major harmony. **Audio example 12.1** offers a representative sample from the performance in Portland, Oregon, on December 4. In the fall of 1981, when the song returned to the set, he began experimenting more with his vocal delivery. **Audio example 12.2** excerpts a portion of the final verse from October 27, 1981, at the Meadowlands in New Jersey. Now Dylan adds a third pitch to the toggle, making it a three-note descending gesture, G4–F4–D4, which he sings in frenzied loops during the son's answers.

The piercing bluesiness of Dylan's singing in both examples recalls the 1975 version, which also had a fire-and-brimstone quality. But the context is now radically different. Gone is the white street-corner crank from *Renaldo and Clara*, channeled by the white-face Dylan. In his place is a believer in the flesh, enveloped in the sounds of the Black church. Dylan the performer is no longer surrounded by a ragtag bunch of Village bohemians. Instead, he shares the stage with a mixed-race group heavy on gospel musicians. Each concert in the gospel era typically begins with a set by the gospel singers alone, thus establishing the tone and generic coordinates for all that follows. The sounds of the Black church permeate the space before Dylan even sets foot on stage. When he does, he recruits those sounds for his own ends, their aura infusing his singing. The ethics of the moment are complex. The ideology critique is easy to draw up, as the white star draws aesthetic and spiritual power—to say nothing of gospel legitimacy—from the Black musicians behind him.[3] But Dylan was also at this moment, by all accounts, a genuine believer. He shared the Christian faith with his fellow musicians and yielded the stage to them to express theirs directly, without him as an intermediary. Dylan does not merely recruit their sanctified sounds. In crucial moments—at the beginning of the concert and in solos during the show—he also gives their sounds the respect of his own silence.

This gets us to the second crucial aspect of these gospel versions of "Hard Rain": the interaction between Dylan and the background singers in the song's refrain. On the Musical Retrospective tour in fall 1980, the singers were Clydie King, Carolyn Dennis, and Regina McCrary.[4] All played significant roles in Dylan's personal and musical life; Dennis would become his second wife. As for King, Dylan said after her death in 2019, "She was my ultimate singing partner. . . . No one ever came close. We were two soulmates."[5] And McCrary was the only background singer to accompany Dylan on every concert of the gospel era. In a 2021 interview with Ray Padgett McCrary describes Dylan's gospel concerts as a "ministry," saying "Bob Dylan has always been called. God called him. . . . For me, it was as perfect as listening to him quote scripture and talk to the people and minister to the people as watching a baby being born. Very natural."[6] The interview makes clear McCrary's conviction that Dylan's faith was authentic. She speaks of Dylan and most of the band praying together before every concert.

The tight connection between front man and backing singers is audible in the refrain of "Hard Rain" as they sang it in late 1980. Here it will be useful to refer back to figure 11.7 and the surrounding discussion concerning the two ways Dylan has timed the "it's a hard" iterations in performance. He begins the Musical Retrospective tour singing them every two bars but ends singing them every four. **Audio example 12.3** includes a refrain from San Francisco on November 22, the first performance of the song that year, to demonstrate the every-two rhythm. Dylan makes the switch to the every-four timing in the middle of the song in Seattle on November 30, seemingly by accident. But it is a happy accident, for his background singers—King, Dennis, and McCrary—discover that it opens a space for them to answer him antiphonally, that is, in call-and-response fashion. They fill in the gaps of his every-four timing with their own "it's a hard" statements. The result is pure gospel call and response, the antiphonal singing of the Black church transplanted to Dylan's end-times epic. By the conclusion of the tour, in the Pacific Northwest, this antiphonal, every-four version was firmly in place, the background singers delivering their interjections with the passionate certainty of an amen choir, as one can hear on **audio example 12.4** from Portland, Oregon, on December 4, the final show of the tour.[7]

In a superb study of Dylan's gospel phase, Gayle Wald stresses the crucial role that female backing singers played for him during these years, specifically as musicians: "Dylan was attracted to the *creative authority* of the gospel chanteuse."[8] Drawing on the work of Horace Clarence Boyer and Anthony Heilbut, Wald emphasizes the "profound artistic discipline and personalized creativity" of these female gospel singers, speaking back to pernicious racist stereotypes that would portray gospel musicking—and Black musical expression more generally—as intuitive, spontaneous, and primitive, as opposed to white creativity, which is rational, disciplined, and intellectual.[9] By ceding the stage to these singers, Dylan demonstrated his respect for their profound artistry as well as their ability to sanctify through sound. None of this exonerates him, of course, from the fraught raced and gendered dynamics of the moment. As Wald notes, the gospel Dylan is hardly "innocent of the plunderous desire that characterizes the 'theft' side of the love-and-theft dialectic."[10] Even so, the 1980 "Hard Rain" sounds, for a moment, like a utopian suspension of such vexed issues, voices echoing one another in joyous exchange.

AN ACOUSTIC DECADE (1984–1993)

After the ecstatic heights of the gospel era, "Hard Rain" in the '80s and early-'90s settled into routine. The '80s were a famously fallow period for Dylan. Yes, there were triumphs in the studio—"Jokerman," "Blind Willie McTell," "Brownsville Girl"—and his concerts had their moments of inspiration. But on the whole he was in a deep trough, feeling

> whitewashed and wasted out professionally. Many times I'd come near the stage before a show and would catch myself thinking that I wasn't keeping my word with myself. What that word was, I couldn't exactly remember, but I knew it was back there somewhere. . . . I had no connection to any kind of inspiration. Whatever was there to begin with had all vanished and shrunk . . . My own songs had become strangers to me, I didn't have the skill to touch their raw nerves, couldn't penetrate the surfaces.[11]

"Hard Rain" was one of those impenetrable, unreachable songs. We can hear Dylan's efforts to connect with it throughout the decade, playing it solo and hewing pretty faithfully to the original arrangement, as though grasping after its old magic, trying to feel its nerves again. In these years the song was typically part of an acoustic set, keeping company with other chestnuts like "It's Alright, Ma," "It Ain't Me, Babe," and "Tangled Up in Blue." On the 1984 European tour, one of his least esteemed among fans, "Hard Rain" often opened the acoustic set. These performances are balanced, focused, and controlled, but on the whole rather perfunctory. Dylan rushes through the changes, often tightening the hypermeter in the answers from three-plus-four to three-plus-two and moving briskly through the refrain. He hews relatively closely to the melody in the opening verses, but gradually ascends until the answers are delivered on a chanted D4 reciting tone. This trajectory of overall ascent across the entire song—not just across one verse—will become increasingly important in coming years. As for 1984, the main attraction of these performances is in the audience interaction. Even when hearing an otherwise workmanlike "Hard Rain," fans often sing along to the refrain, a demonstration of the song's continued importance for them, some twenty-two years after its composition. **Audio example 12.5** provides a representative example from Barcelona on June 28, Dylan's unfussy every-two-bar timing allowing the audience to join their voices with his. I noted in chapter 1 that Dylan's capricious vocal variations and change imperfections often make it difficult for audiences to sing along. This has remained true of many of his songs throughout the decades.[12] But "Hard Rain" is a special case. The iterations of the chorus, whether delivered every two or every four bars, are less susceptible to temporal push and pull: Dylan sings them with considerable regularity, with the word "hard" typically arriving right on the downbeat, an easy target for fellow singers.

In 1986 Dylan went on tour with Tom Petty and the Heartbreakers. "Tom was at the top of his game," writes Dylan, "and I was at the bottom of mine."[13] All the same, these performances of "Hard Rain" show considerably more variety and invention than those in 1984. They are less hurried—the "it's a hard" iterations now come every four bars—and Dylan's phrasing is more supple. Occasionally he strikes out into genuine contour-inventive territory. **Audio example 12.6** presents one such example, from Sacramento on June 12. Dylan here hits on a new melodic idea for the answers, one unlike any we have yet heard before. It is a descending major third, F♯4–E4–D4, a striking departure from the bluesy minor-third toggle of 1981, whose blue F♮4 rubbed against the F♯ of the underlying D major. Dylan now exults in that major key, un-blue-ing its third and in the process giving the song a new kind of wide-eyed hopefulness. Cheers after nearly every phrase make clear the powerful effect on the audience.

Dylan did not play "Hard Rain" in 1987, but it reappeared in setlists when the so-called Never-Ending Tour (NET) commenced the following year. In the acoustic set in the early NET years, Dylan was accompanied by G. E. Smith, also on acoustic guitar. Smith gave these sets an extra kick, the driving propulsion of his strumming added to Dylan's already vigorous right hand. Smith's presence seems to have been both a support and a goad to Dylan, who rediscovers some the bluesy fire of the gospel version. Consider **audio example 12.7**, from New York's Beacon Theater on October 11, 1989. Dylan chants the answers on a strikingly blue $\flat\hat{7}$ (C♮), his enunciation occasionally becoming mannered and clipped ("with-uh blood that-uh kept-uh drippin'!"). As the NET continued, other band members gradually began to join the acoustic set, offering further prods to new invention. In Offenbach, Germany, on June 19, 1991, Dylan is evidently in good mood as he strums in the introductory D chord, a smile in his voice: "How is everybody? This is a song about a . . . a wet kind of time . . . a wet kind of song." Drummer Ian Wallace provides a nice lilt with his brushes on the snare, accenting beat 2 of every bar. This gives the song a metric lift, which Dylan explores in a melody that becomes progressively more exploratory. Strikingly, this exploration takes in his lower register in addition to his upper. As **audio example 12.8** shows, he dips down low in his register (the precise pitch is G2) for the beginning of several lines ("Saw a highway of diamonds . . ."; "Saw a black branch . . ."; etc.) and then ascends back to the tonic D3 by line's end. As with other performances from these years, though, his range expands upward over the course of the song, ending in his high register, chanting the answers on D4 by verse 5.

In these years we can hear Dylan's earnest attempts to recapture the song's magic, to "touch its raw nerves," with occasional success. But we also hear his blockage, his sense that he "couldn't penetrate the [song's] surfaces." The tactile metaphors are attractive, for in these years it is as though each time he attempts "Hard Rain" he is handling it like an object, picking it up, feeling its texture, turning it this way and that, looking for an opening. In 1994 he found one.

NARA, JAPAN: THE GREAT MUSIC EXPERIENCE (MAY 20-22, 1994)

A YouTube search for "hard rain best" typically brings up, as one of its first hits, a clip of Dylan performing the song with an orchestra in Nara, Japan, on May 22, 1994. This performance—the first and only time that Dylan has sung with an orchestra—was part of the Great Music Experience, three concerts (all basically identical) funded in part by UNESCO, organized by British impresario Tony Hollingsworth, and broadcast on international television.[14] A vast array of musicians were assembled for the event, ranging from taiko drummers and a traditional Japanese orchestra to a motley assortment of Western artists, including INXS, Joni Mitchell, Jon Bon Jovi, Ry Cooder, Wayne Shorter, the Chieftains, and Bob Dylan. UNESCO and Hollingsworth initially planned to present seven such events, in front of monuments across the world (including the pyramids and the Taj Mahal), with the purpose of drawing attention to those regions' traditional musics. In the end, only the Nara event took place, staged in front of the Great Buddha Hall of the Buddhist Tōdai-ji temple, at the time the largest wooden structure in the world.

The event would be easy enough to dismiss as a spectacle of 1990s globalist kitsch had Dylan's performance not become so beloved by fans. Much of the concert veers perilously close to the new-age world music of Yanni or Kitarō, but Dylan's performance with the Tokyo New Philharmonic Orchestra retains a singular strangeness and potency. Conductor Michael Kamen arranged three Dylan songs for orchestra—"I Shall Be Released" and "Ring Them Bells" in addition to "Hard Rain"—scoring them in the lush Hollywood style he had honed in his film work, as well as in his other orchestrations for rock musicians from Pink Floyd to Metallica. Asked in an interview if he had requested that Dylan sing a certain way, that he discipline his melodic invention and stick to a fixed tune, Kamen said "no":

> I think he's just responding to the reality of the musical situation. The orchestra's doing things in the music that he hasn't heard for a long time. I brought things out that I've always felt were in the music. His

> chords are beautifully simple; his words are deliciously complicated and heartrendingly pure. I was just sort of painting pictures with the arrangements, illustrating his words as if it were a Bach chorale—which, after all, doesn't have that many chords—and weaving lines inside and outside of each other to amplify the lines . . . illustrating the music in the vocal. And that inspired him to sing.[15]

Kamen clearly based his arrangement on the 1962 recording, matching its metric details exactly; the asymmetrical three-plus-four of the questions and answers returns, as does the climactic held pitch on "rain." Dylan, so used to dropping and adding beats at will, has to follow the orchestra closely. Unlike his bands, the orchestra cannot turn on a dime to follow his metric whims. As a result Dylan settles back into the pacing of the song as he had performed it for the microphone thirty-two years before. This also prods him back to some of the embodied actions from that studio rendition, including the full range of guitar chords in figure 10.1. Dylan had been playing the song in D for years, but on this night he used a capo at the first fret, raising the key to E♭ major. Though his guitar is hard to hear over the orchestra, his playing is clearly visible in **video example 12.1**, his performance of the song at the third concert, on May 22.

Dylan sings with melodic focus and restraint in the first verse, establishing a template that he will gradually depart from over the course of the song. He sings the initial questions to the exact tune of the *Freewheelin'* recording, and then establishes a new melodic shape for the answers. **Figure 12.1** sketches the contour of the answers and refrain in verse 1. In contrast to the Guthrie-esque descents of the original answers, Dylan now sings an up-then-down arch, marked by the angled beam in the figure, tracing an ascent from low tonic E♭ ($\hat{1}$), to the dominant pitch, B♭ ($\hat{5}$), before returning to E♭ ($\hat{1}$). Once he has established this gesture, Dylan is remarkably faithful to it throughout the verse, small rhythmic variants aside. The refrain is also very well behaved, though it differs in one crucial respect from the original: rather than reaching a climactic high E♭ ($\hat{8}$=$\hat{1}$), Dylan ascends entirely by step, topping out at B♭ ($\hat{5}$). Figure 12.1 uses an ascending broken

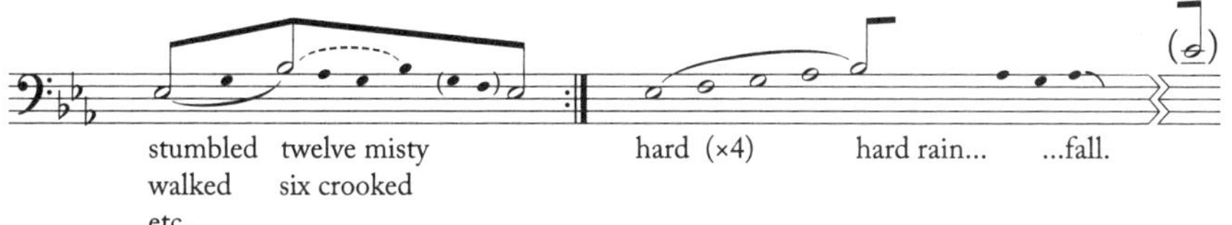

FIGURE 12.1. Melodic contour in verse 1 of "Hard Rain" on May 22, 1994, Nara, Japan.

beam from the B♭ apex, which connects to an implied high E♭ in parentheses on the right edge of the figure, indicating an implied melodic apex yet to come.[16]

This upper range—from B♭3 to the high E♭4—is notably silent in the first verse. This register thus becomes a charged space, a vocal range into which Dylan will gradually venture over the course of the song, eventually reaching the high E♭4, which becomes a climactic plateau in the final verse. Dylan first touches on the high E♭4 in the third verse, presented in **audio example 12.9**. Listen especially to "my darling" in the second question; the ascent to the same pitch at "ten thousand whisperin' and nobody listenin'";[17] and then its climactic sustain at "died in the gutter" and "cried in the alley." Dylan does not re-attain the E♭4 in the refrain, instead easing back down into the lower register with a series of new, artful melismas.

Audio example 12.10 presents the final verse. Now Dylan moves into the upper register with the fifth answer, eventually securing it as a kind of plateau. At this point he begins an oscillation between high E♭4 (bold) and B♭3 (italic):

5 Where the home in the valley **meets** *the* **damp** *dirty* **pri***son*
6 And the executioner's face is **alw***ays well* **hid***den*
7 Where the hunger is ugly, the **souls are** *for***got***ten*
8 Where black **is the color and none is** *the* **num***ber*
9 And I'll **tell it and think it and speak it and** *br***eathe** *it*
10 And **reflect from the mountain** *so* **all souls** *can* **see it**
11 And **I'll stand on** *the* **oc***ean un***til I start sinkin'**
12 And I'll **know my song well** *be***fore** *I start* **singin'**

Note the gradual increase in bold over the course of the answers, as the E♭4 plateau becomes more and more emphatic. Note, too, that the initial E♭4s fall on accented syllables only—reminiscent of the syllable-emphatic style—but beginning in answers 7, 8, and 9 he sustains the high pitch through intervening unaccented syllables as well. By answers 10, 11, and 12 the lines themselves end with a sustained E♭4, which hangs, tremulously, onto the final weak syllable of each line—the tremble despite the fact that E♭4 is not the top of his range in 1994. As evidence of this, in answer 11 Dylan even momentarily exceeds the E♭4, touching on F4 (at the first syllable of "sinkin'," underlined and bolded). The refrain then centers on the same charged interval between B♭3 and E♭4, oscillating tightly between the two pitches at the final climactic statement of "it's a hard rain":

> **Cause** it's a *hard*, it's a *hard*, it's a ha*rd*, it's *a* **ha***rd*,
> **It's** *a* **hard** *rain*———*'s* a-gonna fall

The epic sweep of the whole vocal performance matches the Hollywood crescendo of Kamen's orchestration. But Dylan's fragile voice remains a sound apart, inassimilable to the professionalized ranks of the orchestra. This separation is made visible by Dylan's position at the lip of the stage, physically far from orchestra and conductor and dwarfed by them. The result is a figure/ground relationship that thrums with tension and risk: at any moment Dylan's voice is entirely capable of violating the aesthetic contract of this occasion, this setting, this middlebrow musical arrangement. And even as it precariously follows the letter of that aesthetic contract, his voice in all its imperfection resists full assimilation to the musical code, the tightly regulated system of harmony, melody, and counterpoint fixed by Kamen's polished arrangement. Dylan's adherence to the script, his outward enactment of a mass-cultural epic narrative, paradoxically amplifies his difference-in-sounding. His tattered voice is an unsettling remainder, a literal dissonance, sounding apart (*dis-sonare*) from the festival's euphonious representations of global uplift.

Many find the result deeply moving, as a glance at the YouTube comments confirms. I suspect that this is in part due to the very dissonance mentioned above, the fragility of Dylan's voice in front of the professionalized orchestral mass. The result would hardly feel so heroic were it sung by a more conventional voice (imagine, if you dare, Michael Bolton singing it). Dylan himself knew that he had achieved something special in the performance, reportedly telling Hollingsworth that he hadn't sung so well in fifteen years.[18] He had moreover unlocked a new approach to the song, in two respects. First, he had discovered a new lyricism and tenderness in his delivery. Since the gospel shows fourteen years earlier, he had approached the song with fiery intensity, but now he sings it more gently, the parent's affection for the blue-eyed son infusing the whole. Second, he had now fully realized something that he had been working toward in previous years: a song-spanning vocal ascent. Recall the discussion of Roy Orbison's "Running Scared" in chapter 9, and my suggestion that its thrilling ascent influenced Dylan's singing of each verse. Orbison's ascent, however, spanned his entire song. Singing in front of Kamen's swelling orchestra, Dylan finds a way to draw out the ascent to song length as well, rising in stages across each verse until the final refrain sounds like a hard-earned triumph, an arrival at the summit. Both of these discoveries—renewed lyricism and song-spanning ascent—would reverberate in Dylan's performances of "Hard Rain" in the coming years and decades. He no longer puzzled at the song, turning it over in his hands and wondering how it had become such an inscrutable object. It was instead now open to new expressive possibility and, with it, chance and risk.

A NEW LYRICISM (1994–2002)

We can hear the transformative effect Nara had on Dylan's approach to "Hard Rain" in his very next performance of it. On August 17, 1994, he sang it in Hershey, Pennsylvania, as the final song of the encore. Dylan plays acoustic, accompanied by Tony Garnier on bass and John Jackson on a second guitar. The tone throughout is warm, generous, and tender. Dylan carefully sustains his sung pitches, gingerly traversing the D-major scale, with nary a hint of a blue note. **Audio example 12.11** provides a representative sample from verse 1. He sings the answers in the up-then-down contour of Nara, from tonic pitch to dominant and back again. By the time of the final verse, this gesture has transformed: now Dylan holds the upper, dominant pitch, A3, sustaining it in crescendo, as can be heard in **audio example 12.12**. In the chorus that follows, he exults with a sustained D4 until the final moments of the word "fall," when he tumbles gently downward back to A3. The performance thus traces the same song-spanning ascent as at Nara, which is remarkable, given its overall tone of unruffled lyricism. Nor was this a one-off. In Manchester, the following April 5, Dylan delivers another performance cut from the same cloth, differing only in small details of phrasing and in a more gradual overall ascent.

This proved a remarkably fecund approach to the song. As Dylan performed it over the coming years he did not depart from the post-Nara lyrical premise. **Audio example 12.13** juxtaposes four performances of the song's opening:

Portland, Maine (April 10, 1997);
Ljubljana, Slovenia (April 28, 1999);
Cincinnati, Ohio (July 11, 2000); and
Seattle, Washington (October 6, 2001).

One is struck immediately by both the consistency of the performances as regards key, tempo, and overall affect as well as by the countless subtle differences between them, as Dylan finds ever-new nooks and crannies for variation in vocal timing, articulation, and ornament.

The final performance excerpted in audio example 12.13 is from less than a month after the September 11 attacks. This was Dylan's second concert since that date, and the first to feature "Hard Rain." It is a performance as remarkable for what it doesn't do as what it does. There are no histrionics. Dylan does not overplay the song's apocalyptic imagery or exaggerate the song-spanning build of tension, now standard from night to night. Instead, he offers a performance of restraint, comfort, and determination. At least, that is how it strikes my ears. Listen to **audio example 12.14**, which presents verse 5 and see if you agree. First note the fine work of Dylan's guitarists, Larry Campbell and Charlie Sexton, who come up with a simple descending figure, which they play first in unison, and then in parallel sixths. This bit of musical bridging material spans the space between Dylan's lines, holding the listener secure in moments when the singing voice can't. As for the sung lines, each one is different, and each saturated with telling details. Note, for example, the breath-catching pause that separates the initiating "*s*" from the rest of the word "speak" in "I'll tell it and think it and speak it and breathe it." The effect is like a musical stutter, stuck on the plosive, a blockage in speech at the very moment when the singer promises to "speak it." One way to project determination is to project its obstacles. One can also hear determination in "I'll stand on the ocean until I start sinkin'," which moves to a higher pitch: B3, an arresting $\hat{6}$ in D major. Tellingly, Dylan does *not* descend from this pitch on the word "sinkin'," though musical convention would warrant a resolution to the more stable dominant pitch A3 ($\hat{5}$) at line's end. Dylan's voice refuses to sink. Then there is the refrain. Here, as often in this performance of the song, "It's a hard" sounds to me like "Yes, I *know* it's hard." We're all struggling. Indeed, his third iteration in the final refrain seems to suggest as much: "I seen, it's a *hard!*" The final iteration then includes a repetition rare in the refrain in any era—"It's a hard rain . . . *hard rain* gonna fall"—the italicized words clinging to a ragged D4 apex.

It's difficult to write objectively about such emotionally charged musical details, so I will not pretend to do so. I find this performance deeply moving. To these ears that broken D4 is laced with grief, fear, resolve, and solidarity. Its affective multiplicity reminds me of a comment Dylan made to Studs Terkel thirty-eight years before this performance, in 1963. Terkel assumed "Hard Rain" referred to "atomic rain," but Dylan quickly responded, "It's not atomic rain, it's just a hard rain. . . . I just mean some sort of end that's just gotta happen."[19]

The young Dylan resists a univocal interpretation of his song, an overliteral limit on its meaning. The Seattle "Hard Rain" delivers on the song's signifying multiplicity, its ability to sound not only comfort, or outrage, or determination, or fear, but all of them at once.

LATE "RAIN" (2003–2017)

The final phase of "Hard Rain" in performance sees a synthesis of the bluesy intensity of the gospel-era performances with the large-scale architectural sweep of Nara. The tenderness and lyricism of the latter are largely gone, however, replaced by Dylan's guttural late vocal style, replete with sharp barks, abrasive blue notes, and upsinging. The first performance of this new era comes on April 25, 2003, in New Orleans. After decades in D, the song is now in B♭. There are likely two reasons for this. First, while "Hard Rain" had always been a guitar song for Dylan up until this point, he now plays keyboard on it; B♭ feels great on the keys, but not on a guitar. Second, B♭ puts the whole song a major third lower, suiting Dylan's deepening voice as well as his penchant for upsinging. Indeed, the New Orleans performance comes from near the highwater mark of Dylan's upsinging, and many phrases follow the upsung template of the parent's first question: a guttural burst, followed by a leap to an upsung B♭3, with clean phonation. **Audio example 12.15** presents the opening questions and initial answers of the performance.

But Dylan doesn't get stuck in an upsinging rut. He and his musicians still maintain the sense of song-spanning build from the Nara performance. By verse 5, excerpted in **audio example 12.16**, they follow Dylan, who locks into a new rhythm of obstinate quarter notes, each syllable anchored to a single beat. The whole ensemble eventually picks up the rhythm, each quarter-note impulse seemingly heavier than the last. When the accumulated tension from these repeated impacts releases with the arrival of the refrain, there is a hearty cheer, the audience acknowledging the achievement of the song-spanning climax.

Some performances from this era show the mannerisms of Dylan's late style. In Byron Bay, Australia, on April 25, 2011, excerpted in **audio example 12.17**, he hits on a peculiar ascending major scale for each line. This is an inversion of the Guthrie-inspired descents of the original, and weirdly incongruous with the song's words. Other vocal inventions are more successful, such as the lovely descending figure he sings on one of the parent's questions two months later in Tel Aviv, presented in **audio example 12.18**. Throughout this era, Dylan is restlessly inventive in his phrasing, approaching the song with freedom characteristic of all of the post-Nara performances, but the affect is more ornery than tender. Indeed, at times one might hear a return of the street-corner crank from *Renaldo and Clara*, bellowing insistently, to the incomprehension of the onlookers.

As nice as it would be to tie up this story with a bow, it has no tidy conclusion. By 2017 this arrangement had run its course. Dylan performed his final "Hard Rain" (at time of writing) in Dover, Delaware, on June 17, 2017. It resembles its predecessors since 2003 in its key (still B♭) and its groove (a heavy-footed three to the bar), but differs, as always, in its idiosyncratic specifics.[20] As ever in the post-Nara era, the song builds to a climactic plateau in verse 5, with a new vocal figure in the upper register that Dylan repeats incessantly; **audio example 12.19** presents the fifth verse in its entirety. It is a ragged end to the tale, but that's perhaps as it should be. We know by now not to expect perfected closure when it comes to Dylan's sounds. Our tale that began with a noisy typewriter now ends with a different kind of racket, Dylan sending the song out to vibrate in the air one last time—imperfectly.

POSTSCRIPT

There the song hung when I finished this manuscript. But just as the book was entering copyediting, Dylan unexpectedly revived "Hard Rain" on the Outlaw Tour in late summer 2024. Isn't that just his contrary way? Across a dozen performances, he led it from the piano, fusing a gentle, post-Nara lyricism with the understated informality of the 1971 Concert for Bangladesh. Fans lauded the Outlaw Tour for its freewheeling unpredictability, and one can hear that in these "Hard Rain" renditions. He performs the song in no fewer than four different keys (B♭, B, C, and E) and tries out a variety of grooves and time feels, from swaying waltz to free-tempo declamation. Melodic and harmonic surprises abound. If, in 2017, the song's tale had seemingly come to a ragged end, now, seven years later, we hear Dylan once again tugging at its dangling thread. In the process, he imperfects this *book's* ending. Because of course he does.

Afterword

On Perfection

In a 2020 interview, Douglas Brinkley asked Bob Dylan, "What role does improvisation play in your music?" Dylan's answer:

> None at all. There's no way you can change the nature of a song once you've invented it. You can set different guitar or piano patterns upon the structural lines and go from there, but that's not improvisation. Improvisation leaves you open to good or bad performances and the idea is to stay consistent. You basically play the same thing time after time in the most perfect way you can.[1]

Nothing like a rebuttal of your main argument from the artist himself. Of course, Dylan is a famously cantankerous interview subject, so there's always the possibility that he's merely having Brinkley on. Given all that we have heard in this book—flux and flaw in glorious abundance—it may be tempting to dismiss this as yet another instance of Dylanesque misdirection. But I suspect there's something more to it than that. I'd like to take Dylan's answer seriously, in the hopes that it will open the door to a broader consideration of what artistic perfection might be, and how his generative imperfections might relate to it.

First, a note on context. The quote comes after a brief discussion of jazz. When Brinkley asks if any jazz musicians have influenced him, Dylan offers a few desultory thoughts about the definition of the word before name checking a handful of artists as inspirations, including Ella Fitzgerald, Thelonious Monk, and King Pleasure (Dylan regularly reaches for at least one obscure name in such moments). But in the next question about improvisation, Brinkley may have pressed the case too hard. I suspect that Dylan is quick to distance himself from improvisation in part because the word has such a close relationship to jazz. He knows that, whatever his approach to musical invention on stage, it is worlds removed from *that*. As a singer and instrumentalist he does not have the fleet technique or harmonic sophistication of a jazz musician in the post-bebop era, not even close. As we have heard time and again, his singing and playing are instead closer to a kind of strategic primitivism, untutored and raw. Dylan invents incessantly on stage, yes, but he does not improvise like Charlie Parker. It is for this reason that I've used the word "improvisation" only sparingly in the preceding chapters.[2]

What interests me more in the quote is Dylan's provocation as regards this book's thesis, his claim that "there's no way you can change the nature of a song once you've invented it." That sentence fascinates, considering how radically—and obviously—Dylan has changed his songs across decades of live performance. If we are to take him seriously, we have to interpret "the nature of a song" carefully. Clearly he means something more than the song's local musical details, which are always up for revision, as we've heard time and again. Considering the sentence that follows, in which he speaks of "structural lines," he seems to mean something more like the broader formal scaffolding of a song, its particular configuration of verses, refrains, bridges, and so on, as well as the prosody of its words. He may also consider a song's nature to include certain harmonic and melodic patterns, their points of departure and arrival, and the waves of waxing and waning energy to which all this give rise. But given the variation and mutability we've witnessed in all these musical parameters, it's tough to say if Dylan considers them fundamental to the song's nature.

The "nature of a song" may instead mean something like the *spirit* of a song, its governing ethos—say, the dreaminess of "Mr. Tambourine Man," the visionary comedy of "Desolation Row,"[3] or the awestruck foreboding of "Hard Rain." To be sure, we have often heard how Dylan's changeable performances inflect a song's emotional tenor. Think, for example, of the fire-and-brimstone "Hard Rain" from Rolling Thunder in 1975, as compared with the reverential Nara version, or the consoling one in Seattle in 2001. But for Dylan, perhaps all of these are merely inflections of a song's persisting character—the nature of the song, broadly construed. At the least, Dylan's comment to Brinkley suggests that *he* experiences his songs as having something fixed about them, perhaps a kind of stubbornness, a hard kernel that inhibits complete musical freedom. As much as he may revel in changing a given song, that song has its own obdurate "thingness," which holds musical fantasy in check. Any new sound must be answerable to the song, in tune with its fundamental "nature."

At the end of his response to Brinkley in the block quote above, I hear both an anxiety and a sort of mission statement regarding Dylan's late style. The anxiety is pretty clear. The language about "staying consistent" sounds like a check on a contrary impulse, like an addict proclaiming his sobriety. Despite this apparent praise for sameness, for decades Dylan has shown an unmistakable tendency toward generative inconsistency—it's been one of the throughlines of this entire book. But inconsistency is risky. Some bold experiments flop. Hence the anxiety, the protesting too much. As for the mission statement, by the time of the interview with Brinkley Dylan had settled into the most static period of his performing career. Beginning in 2013 setlists varied minimally from show to show and only gradually from year to year.[4] In an irony so delectable it must have been intentional, Dylan began nearly every show from 2013 to 2019 with the song "Things Have Changed." With the first notes of that song, astute fans knew that, no, things had *not* changed, and the setlist to follow would likely be all but indistinguishable from the show before and the show before that. So, when Dylan tells Brinkley in 2020, "You basically play the same thing time after time in the most perfect way you can," he is not speaking metaphorically or vaguely. He's describing an approach he took with his band across nearly 600 shows, from 2013 to 2019.[5] In this late era, difference and repetition were no longer in careful balance. The scales had tilted decidedly toward an embrace of rote repetition, at least at the level of the setlist.

One can sense a similar impulse toward minimizing difference in Dylan's Sinatra-inspired records from around this time. On *Shadows in the Night* (2015), *Fallen Angels* (2016), and *Triplicate* (2017), he and his band offer not new arrangements of these Tin Pan Alley standards, but note-for-note copies of specific recordings. Most are from Sinatra records, though not all. The arrangement of "That Old Black Magic" on *Fallen Angels*, for instance, is based on the 1958 hit version by Louis Prima and Keely Smith. As with all the songs on these albums, Dylan and his band copy every detail of this particular "Black Magic" arrangement, from its key to its groove to its novelty details, including a comical baritone-sax trill at the opening, which is played on guitar (likely by Charlie Sexton). Dylan on these records comes close to the kind of note-perfect duplication that he heard in his fellow folk revivalists as they copied every detail of old-time records. He may have sniffed at such fastidiousness back then, but now he applies the same approach to a repertory most revivalists abhorred: the Great American Songbook.

This is not to say that difference completely disappears in the face of such note-perfect repetition. On Dylan's Sinatra-inspired records, difference registers in timbre, most obviously in Dylan's tattered voice, so unlike Sinatra's. The timbral difference of the instruments is also striking. Gone are the smooth studio orchestras favored by Nelson Riddle, Gordon Jenkins, Axel Stordahl, and other arrangers. In their place is Dylan's "cowboy band," with lines once played by violins now taken by, say, pedal steel. The effect, as critic Stephen Thomas Erlewine aptly puts it, "is to slyly tie together various strands of American music, bringing Tin Pan Alley to the barrooms and taking the backwoods uptown."[6]

As for difference in concert, the consistency of arrangements and setlists since 2013 has allowed Dylan to become ever looser in his delivery. With (one assumes) fewer worries about memory slips with lyrics to distract him, he can turn his attention to varying micro-details of phrasing, articulation, and melodic contour, the latter especially after his Sinatra-ward turn.[7] He has also leaned into his piano playing, especially in the *Rough and Rowdy Ways* era. In short, the aging Dylan husbands his performing resources carefully, reducing the variables from night to night in the interest of honing finer and finer performative nuances.[8]

But for some longtime fans, such micro variation has felt like thin gruel. Many have missed the novelty, spontaneity, surprise, variety, and—yes—felicitous accident of the earlier Dylan, that careening risk-taker. The risk-taker made something of a return on the Outlaw Tour in 2024, as discussed in the postscript to chapter 12. But, for long stretches since 2013, Dylan's effort to "play the same thing time after time in the most perfect way [he] can" has come at a cost. What it sacrifices is the unruly plenitude that Dylanesque imperfection unleashes. If that imperfection is truly additive rather than subtractive, as I suggested in the introduction, then listening to the concerts since 2013 allows us to feel acutely just *what* imperfection added. With change and flaw imperfection drastically attenuated in these years, we become newly aware of their virtues. All of this suggests a reframing. In the search for note perfection—the effort to "play the same thing time after time in the most perfect way you can"—perhaps Dylan and his bandmates sacrificed a *different* kind of perfection. In other words, perhaps Dylan's earlier strategic imperfection aimed at a kind of supervening perfection all along.

I suspect many readers have been thinking something like this from the beginning of the book. "Well, yes, these musical imperfections are there, but don't they add up—in the best moments—to a kind of flawed perfection?" Indeed, the phrase "ragged but right," which I discussed in the introduction, says as much, with folksy directness. I largely agree with this sentiment, but I want to proceed carefully. Most importantly, I wish to avoid the tidy conclusion that Dylan traffics in "perfect imperfections," or something similarly trite. For the perfection we are now considering is elusive, hard to put into words. I propose that it is ultimately an ineffable quality, one that we can subjectively experience but that evades quantification or precise definition. I'll nevertheless do my best to wrap some words around it in these concluding paragraphs.

Let's start with the equivocal status of note perfection among musicians. Even in the world of Western classical performance, where instrumentalists practice for hours on end to play flawlessly, there is plenty of talk about the limitations of perfect technique. It is not uncommon to hear statements like, "His technique is perfect but his playing has no soul" or "She hit all the notes but missed the music." To be sure, there is usually more than a hint of sour grapes in such comments—envy of a technique better than one's own—but there is also insight into a whole set of musical values. Note how these statements gesture toward something ineffable: the *soul*, the *music*, the latter understood here as a kind of expressive surplus that transcends the mere notes. We will return to this idea of ineffability. For now, we can stick with the commonplace that music is clearly about far more than hitting the right notes at the right times. For nonmusicians this is glaringly obvious, but it's easy to forget when one lives in a music practice room. In any case, people rarely listen to music to experience mere note-perfection. They do so for a host of reasons—to dance, to work, to be transported, to be distracted, to be together, to be alone. And perhaps above all, to *feel*: emotion taken in through the ears.[9]

In this connection, consider a quote from Dylan's then-girlfriend Ellen Bernstein, regarding the *Blood on the Tracks* recording sessions. Speaking of an early take of "Tangled Up in Blue," she says: "you can hear the sound of his fingernails on the guitar—that didn't matter to him. What was important was the overall emotional weight of the song."[10] The imperfection of nails scratching the guitar is easy enough to pinpoint and, per Bernstein, didn't matter much to Dylan (though some fans treasure these sounds).[11] What mattered was the music's "overall emotional weight." And it is clear from the outtakes for the album—collected on the deluxe version of *The Bootleg Series*, vol. 14: *More Blood, More Tracks*—that Dylan was driven by something like perfectionism as he tried, take after take, to get that emotional weight just right.

Bernstein's wording ("emotional weight") is attractive, as it suggests heft, something one senses in holding an object. To return to a metaphor I used in chapter 12, think about hefting an object in your hand, judging its weight. There is indeed a kind of in-the-moment testing in such aesthetic judgments, a weighing up. Dylan, listening to playbacks in the studio, is engaged in the process, as are we when we listen at home. I suspect that one thing we are weighing up in these moments is a kind of emotional truth-effect, in the sense I explored it near the end of chapter 3. Do I recognize the emotion in the song? Does it touch me? Or—to recall a wording in chapter 3—does it "ring true"? One's answer will ultimately be first-personal and ineffable. One feels the emotion or one doesn't. But if one feels it with sufficient intensity—if the conviction has enough heft—one may well judge an artwork to have attained an ideal of emotional truthfulness. Or at least to have approached very near to it.

Is emotional truth a kind of perfection? Is this what we mean when we say that Dylan's imperfect sounds are in service of some higher-order perfection? Perhaps. Perhaps, in ringing true—when they do, for someone—Dylan's sounds approach a second-order perfection in their fidelity to imperfect life. Wallace Stevens offers support for that idea in his 1942 poem, "The Poems of Our Climate," the final four lines of which comprise this book's epigraph. The poem begins by meditating on the cold perfection of "Clear water in a brilliant bowl / Pink and white carnations. The light / In the room more like a snowy air, / Reflecting snow." In the second stanza, Stevens becomes dissatisfied with the image, saying that, even if contemplating it were to momentarily take us away from our cares, "Still one would want more, one would need more, / More than a world of white and snowy scents." Why? Because

> The imperfect is our paradise.
> Note that, in this bitterness, delight,
> Since the imperfect is so hot in us,
> Lies in flawed words and stubborn sounds.

That is, we delight in aesthetic imperfection because, in it, we recognize our imperfect selves. We feel alienated from cold, formal perfection because "the imperfect is so hot in us." The themes of temperature and interiors/exteriors—the cool bowl viewed externally, the flawed heat inside us—are striking, and link up with some relevant song lyrics by Leonard Cohen and Nick Drake. Both Cohen and Drake address imperfection as it relates to broken objects and people, focusing on the light that penetrates the fissure. The Cohen excerpt, from his 1992 song "Anthem," is the more famous of the two:

> Ring the bells that still can ring
> Forget your perfect offering
> There's a crack in everything
> That's how the light gets in

Drake, in "Things Behind the Sun," from 1971, offers a similar sentiment:

> So, open up your broken cup
> Let goodly sin and sunshine in
> Yes, that's day

Through the cracks and breaks come light, sunshine, day, and warmth, with their optimistic connotations of clarity, insight, growth, and health. There is much one could say about the contrast between the Stevens, Cohen, and Drake, and how they figure the relationship between the subject and imperfection. In Stevens the imperfection is hot in us, pressing from inside out; in Cohen and Drake imperfection lets light and warmth penetrate us, the heat coming from outside in. Drake also adds something more—at once malign and yet still joyful—in the paradoxical "goodly sin." This points to a kind of moral imperfection, but one that has its own subversive virtues, over and against cold moral perfection, grim adherence to a moral code with no room for human fallibility or caprice. These differences aside, across all three epigraphs, one senses a contrast between hot, fissured, imperfect life, and cold, static, closed perfection.

Whatever the perfections of Dylan's art, they are not cold, static, or closed. His music sounds a fidelity to flawed life—both personal and social—in constant flux. It is an art of songs permanently cracked open, like Cohen's and Drake's perforated vessels, open to revision, to accident, to the future. If there is perfection in this, perhaps it is an aspirational perfection, reaching for ideals that remain always just out of reach. That should sound familiar. After all, isn't it the subject of a famous lyric? "The answer, my friend, is blowin' in the wind"—just out of reach but seemingly so close. So many Dylan lyrics in fact work in this way, turning on questions that open toward uncertainty or that gesture toward an ineffable limit just beyond utterance.

Many of these lyrics are explicitly political, which reminds us that Dylan's sounding imperfections are not just about subjective, personal foibles and the flux of a life lived in the first person. They are also about a deeply flawed nation founded on the yet-unrealized promise of a "more perfect Union." Dylan's music has long sounded the roiling imperfections of the United States, the dissonance between its present and its stated ideals. Throughout these pages we have heard Dylan's sounds registering the country's social antagonisms—around race, class, gender, power, and more—like a seismograph. Or, to tweak the metaphor, we have heard his broken sounds like clefts through which we can glimpse social tectonic plates in poor alignment, ever shifting. Cracks that let the light in, but also let the dark out.

And yet the futurity of Dylan's art—its openness to change, the new, the possible, the answer just out of reach—saves it even in these moments from pure, diagnostic negativity. For there is always utopian potential in a music that refuses to sit still, that insists on the absolute novelty of the moment yet to come, in all its possibility and risk. Dylan's music keeps faith with that moment, its change energy surging ever on, bending flaws toward perfection.

ACKNOWLEDGMENTS

My first thanks—and my deepest—are to my partner Jennifer Iverson. She has been my keenest reader, my most incisive critic, and my emotional rudder during the long process of bringing this book into port. Our relationship began when I was a few years into its research. I may not have been stalled, but I wasn't exactly bounding ahead with confidence. Our conversations galvanized my thinking. I still remember an early one when the book's structure clicked into place, the argument suddenly clear. She has read every page since, her brilliant editorial interventions saving me from myself time and again while simultaneously lifting my spirits—not easy! Thank you, love. This book is dedicated to you.

I would also like to thank our children Elliott, Theo, Ian, and Della, who bring me profound joy every day. They never asked for this much Bob Dylan in their lives—lyrics quoted at the dinner table, obscure bootlegs on the car stereo. Sometimes it has baffled them. True story: One day when Elliott was eleven and Theo seven, I was driving them to school as "Rainy Day Women #12 & 35" played. They were quiet as we drove; we pulled into the parking lot just as the song ended. After a beat of silence, Theo asked, "Why are they stoning him, again?" Elliott, before I could answer: "That's the great thing about music: it doesn't have to make any sense." And scene. Sorry for the bafflement, guys. I love you all more than I can say. I also thank my mother Linda, who has offered decades of enthusiastic support for all of my musical and scholarly endeavors; my brother Mike, for sharing so generously of his philosopher's mind and encyclopedic music knowledge; my late father Dale, who I wish was here to hold this book in his hands; and my stepmom Penny and stepsisters Kim and Kristina for their love, support, and connection, especially during the weeks and months since his passing.

Elizabeth Branch Dyson, my editor at the University of Chicago Press, has been a wonder. She read every word and offered equal measures of praise for what was good and straight talk for what wasn't. Thank you, Elizabeth. I am also grateful to Mollie McFee for her expert assistance in guiding me through the nuts and bolts of getting the manuscript into shape and to Tamara Ghattas for overseeing the whole editing process. Some non–UChicago Press folks also helped with crucial publishing logistics, most notably Mark Nye and Amy McCarter, who lent their vision and design expertise to the website. Amy also deserves huge thanks for her marvelous cover design. Thanks to Therese Boyd for her eagle-eyed copyediting. A hearty thanks to Lizzy Lewis, who compiled the index with care and ingenuity, and John Lawrence, who caught countless slips—some subtle, some glaring—in his superb proofreading. Finally, Marta Tonegutti expressed interest in this book from an early stage, convincing me that Chicago was the place for it. I couldn't be happier to have the book appear from the press at the institution where I've taught for the last twenty years.

That institution, the University of Chicago, has supported this project in ways large and small for over a decade. I would first like to thank the three deans in the Humanities Division whose tenure overlapped with the book's writing, Martha Roth, Anne Robertson, and Deborah Nelson, all of whom have provided crucial support, especially in the form of research funds and research leaves. I would also like to thank the Franke Institute for the Humanities, where I was lucky enough to be a residential fellow twice during the book's writing, once in the very early stages, and once again just as I was finishing it. I warmly thank Jim Chandler and Richard Neer, who headed the Institute respectively during my two stints, and the rest of the staff: Verletta Bonny, Margot Browning, Bertie Kibreah,

Harriette Moody, and Mai Vukcevich. The Franke Institute also offered a generous grant to support the development of my website, for which I'm deeply grateful. Finally, I offer my thanks to the National Endowment for the Humanities, which supported the completion of the book with a Public Scholars grant. The ideas in these pages are mine, and do not necessarily reflect the views of the NEH.

I've taught portions of this book—or material related to it—in several courses over the years. I thank my students in those classes, who challenged me on points large and small and helped me sharpen and clarify my thinking. I'm especially grateful to the participants in two grad seminars who read and responded to big chunks of my writing: Liz Alvarado, Bethany Battafarano, Will Buckingham, Nadia Chana, Christina Colanduoni, Caroline Collins, Alejandro Cueto, Dana DeVlieger, Nina Goodman, Ted Gordon, Julianne Grasso, Chaz Lee, Anabel Maler, Samuel Marvin, Ameera Nimjee, and Braxton Shelley. My faculty colleagues at the University of Chicago Music Department have also heard me talk plenty about Bob Dylan over the years and have waited patiently for this book to appear. I would especially like to thank Martha Feldman, David Levin, and Seth Brodsky, with all of whom I thought much about voice in the early stages of this project. I also thank my music theory colleagues Thomas Christensen, Jennifer Iverson, and Larry Zbikowski, whose enthusiasm for the book carried me through early periods of doubt that it might not reward music-theoretical attention (a worry that now seems almost comically misplaced).

Many other scholars, fans, and musicians have shaped my thinking on Dylan over the years. I have learned a ton from Dylan fans online and am grateful to Karl Erik Anderson (of expectingrain.com) and Bill Pagel (of boblinks.com) for hosting sites on which Dylan obsessives can share, analyze, and interpret. The archive they have created is as valuable as any scholarly book on Dylan, and a trove for later researchers. On a more personal note, I would like to thank Johnny Borgan and Jonathan Hodgers, two international Dylan acquaintances whose friendship I cherish. Thanks as well to Greil Marcus, whose encouragement buoyed me in the home stretch. Sumanth

Gopinath and Ray Padgett both read the entire manuscript and offered invaluable perspective, criticism, and encouragement. I admire you both and am deeply grateful for your generous reading and suggestions. Jim Chandler, Timothy Hampton, Jonathan Lear, and Jacob Reed also read sizable chunks of the manuscript and offered sage feedback. Michael Jones has listened to me discuss this book every week for over six years. Thank you, Michael, for talking me off multiple ledges and convincing me I was not Rev. Casaubon after all. Harmonica virtuoso Joe Filisko was an invaluable resource for chapter 7. Our conversation about the instrument and Dylan's ramshackle playing of it amounted to one of the most rewarding and entertaining afternoons in my years of work on this book. Thanks, Joe.

My thinking is immeasurably richer for my interactions with all these individuals. The good ideas in these pages owe much to them. As for the bad ideas, that's all me.

ABBREVIATIONS USED IN THE NOTES

CV1 Bob Dylan, *Chronicles, Volume One*. Simon and Schuster, 2004.

DL1 Clinton Heylin, *The Double Life of Bob Dylan*, vol. 1: *A Restless, Hungry Feeling (1941–1966)*. Back Bay, 2021.

DL2 Clinton Heylin, *The Double Life of Bob Dylan*, vol. 2: *Far Away from Myself (1966–2021)*. Bodley Head, 2023.

EI Jonathan Cott, ed., *Bob Dylan: The Essential Interviews*. Wenner, 2006. NB: I have used the first edition throughout. Pagination is slightly different in the 2017 second edition.

EMPW Artur Jarosinski, ed., *Every Mind Polluting Word*, 2nd ed. Don't Ya Tell Henry, 2006.

MUtM Mark Davidson and Parker Fishel, *Bob Dylan: Mixing Up the Medicine*. Callaway, 2023.

NDH Martin Scorsese, dir., *No Direction Home: Bob Dylan*. 208 minutes. Paramount Pictures, 2005.

A NOTE ON URLS

Most URLs in the notes are in shortened "bitly" form.* I've given them intuitive back halves whenever possible. For example, the first web page cited in the book, a snippet from an interview in which folk singer Tom Paxton discusses Dylan, has the bitly address bit.ly/PaxtonOnDylan. To access this site, one would simply type this directly into a browser's URL bar. There is no need to add "http://," "https://," or "www." at the beginning. Note well: bitly addresses are case-sensitive, so one would need to capitalize the P, O, and D in this example.

* Created at bitly.com. The few URLs that are not in bitly format were already short and typable or could not be shortened due to proprietary restrictions.

NOTES

INTRODUCTION

1. Tom Paxton, interview with Ken Paulson as part of the "Speaking Freely" series, "Tom Paxton Remembers Bob Dylan," YouTube, November 29, 2000, bit.ly/PaxtonOnDylan.
2. Hugh Romney—whom B. B. King would later dub "Wavy Gravy"—has corroborated the story (see "About," Wavygravy.net, bit.ly/WavyGravyBio), and Paxton has told it more than once. In 1986 it went like this: "Once Dylan was banging out this long poem on Wavy Gravy's typewriter. He showed me the poem and I asked, 'Is this a song?' He said, 'No, it's a poem.' I said, 'All this work and you're not going to add a melody?' He did. It was 'A Hard Rain's Gonna Fall.'" Woliver, *Bringing It All Back Home*, 120. As to the date, no precise records exist, but the encounter most likely occurred sometime during August or September of 1962, as the earliest circulating recording of the song is from September 20, 1962, at the home of Eve and Mac McKenzie (Dylan performed it again two nights later at Carnegie Hall). NB: This puts the song's composition at least a month *before* the Cuban missile crisis, with which it has been associated since Nat Hentoff's liner notes for *The Freewheelin' Bob Dylan*. See Heylin, *Revolution in the Air*, 93–94.
3. See "Lot 71, Bob Dylan," Sotheby's, bit.ly/SothebysHardRain. The page includes color facsimiles of the typescript. While it is not certain that this is the exact typescript Paxton saw, Sotheby's hedges that "it is undoubtedly connected to the Gaslight text seen by Paxton." A manuscript copy of the lyrics in Dylan's hand sold at auction for $400,000 in 2014.
4. "Last Thoughts" is the notable metrical exception, with its loose tetrameter. On Dylan's early poems, see Heylin, *Behind the Shades*, 132–36. Heylin lists two talking blues items from 1962 that "seem to have been his earliest attempts at the freestanding word": "Talkin' Folklore Center" and "Go 'Way Bomb" (133). Written for the page or not, these texts tellingly emerge from an oral/aural tradition: talking blues. Dylan regularly performed talking blues—his own and Woody Guthrie's—during these years.

5. As documented on *The Bootleg Series*, vol. 9: *The Witmark Demos*.
6. "Lord Randal" is one of the so-called Child ballads, named for their inclusion in Harvard folklorist Francis James Child's collection *The English and Scottish Popular Ballads*. In "Lord Randal"—number 12 in Child's ordering—a mother questions her son about his whereabouts, what he has eaten, and so on, only to learn that he has been poisoned by his lover (usually by eating poisoned eels). Variants abound in English, Scottish, Irish, and Appalachian sources; relatives of the ballad have also been found throughout mainland Europe, including Italy, Germany, Hungary, Poland, the Low Countries, Scandinavia, and Catalonia. The name "Lord Randal" (sometimes spelled "Randall") is only one among several given to the son. For a penetrating study of the relationship between "Hard Rain" and "Lord Randal," see Portelli, *Hard Rain*.
7. On these literary influences, see Portelli, *Hard Rain*, 79–82. Portelli cites Alessandro Carrera, who claims (in *La voce di Bob Dylan*, 313) that Rimbaud's most celebrated poem, "Le bateau ivre" (The Drunken Boat), is the song's principal intertext. See also Thomas, *Why Bob Dylan Matters*, 155. On Dylan's early encounter with Ginsberg's poetry while still in Minneapolis, see Jarosinski, *Every Mind Polluting Word* (hereafter cited as *EMPW*), 877, and Wilentz, *Bob Dylan in America*, 66. *Every Mind-Polluting Word*, a self-published PDF assembled by the late Artur Jarosinski, is an invaluable resource for Dylan scholars and fans, cited often. It is meticulously thorough, well edited, and searchable. I have posted a PDF on soundingbobdylan.com.
8. Dylan himself coined the locution "chains of flashing images" in a 1966 interview with Ralph J. Gleason (*EMPW*, 302). Allen Ginsberg secured the phrase's place in Dylan lore in his 1973 poem "On Reading Dylan's Writings" (Hedin, *Studio A*, 93).
9. The typography gives no indication that "Words-Music B. Dylan" was added later: it is in-line with the title, by all appearances typed immediately following it. It is also in-line with the year to its right. The top of the second page includes a shortened header "W/M DYLAN," similarly sandwiched (in-line) between title and year. Paxton's story may still hold if this is a later typescript than the one he saw. Clinton Heylin suggests that "Hard Rain" may at first have hovered "somewhere between a song and a poem," but by the time Dylan typed this document, he clearly conceived it as a song. Heylin, *The Double Life of Bob Dylan*, vol. 1 (hereafter cited as *DL1*), 144–45.
10. *EMPW*, 80. Four years later, in conversation with musician and photographer John Cohen, Dylan revisited the topic. Cohen recalled Dylan showing him the song's lyrics "at Gerde's or upstairs from the Gaslight." Dylan's response: "I believe at the time you were wondering how it fit into music. How I was going to sing it." Cott, ed. *Essential Interviews* (hereafter cited as *EI*), 113; *EMPW*, 405.
11. As Todd Harvey notes, "The melody [in the 1960s versions] is remarkably stable, especially considering the constant variation in other songs." Harvey, *Formative Dylan*, 3.
12. Patti Smith sang the song, with touching fallibility, at the Nobel ceremony on December 10, 2016, an experience she recounted in *The New Yorker*: Patti Smith, "How Does It Feel," *New Yorker*, December 14, 2016, bit.ly/SmithHardRain.
13. For the record, the most-cited line is "Yes, I am a thief of thoughts," from the outset of the eighth epitaph. It is telling that this is the *first* line of one of the poems, visually

prominent on the insert page. My personal favorite bit comes several lines later, where Dylan writes of "weapons of words / wrapped in tunes," a lovely poetic take on the "words-music" alloy. Davidson and Fishel, *Mixing Up the Medicine* (hereafter cited as *MUtM*), 108, reproduces the typescript of this section of the poem. For a discussion of Kerouac and the Beats' influence on the epitaphs, see Stubbs, "11 Outlined Epitaphs: 'unspeakable visions of the individual.'"

14. For his part, Dylan took the tune for "Masters of War" from Jean Ritchie's version of the traditional song "Nottamun Town." This particular borrowing got him in legal trouble.
15. Bernstein, "Dances with Things," 69.
16. This is to say nothing of countless covers, from Bryan Ferry's arch Euro-pop version (on *These Foolish Things*, 1973) to Nana Mouskouri's anthemic French-language sing-along (*Au théâtre des Champs-Élysées*, 1974).
17. At the time of writing, Dylan has performed "All Along the Watchtower," "Highway 61 Revisited," and "Like a Rolling Stone" over 2,000 times each. "Hard Rain" sits solidly in the lower-middle of the pack, with 463 performances.
18. Most notable among these are the seventeen (and counting) volumes of Sony's *Bootleg Series*, which consist largely of previously unreleased material, much of it highly prized by Dylan enthusiasts.
19. The Grateful Dead performed 2,318 concerts before Jerry Garcia's death in August 1995. The vast majority of Dylan's ca. 4,000 performances circulate on recording. For example, for the period from Dylan's return to touring in 1974 through 2018, Olof Björner counts only 171 noncirculating concerts out of 3,661 total ("Uncirculated and Incomplete Shows, 1974–2018," bobserve, bit.ly/BjornerUncirculated). To be sure, the number of Dead bootlegs tops Dylan's if one counts multiple versions of the same concert (audience, soundboard, etc.), as well as bootlegs of post-Garcia iterations of the band, solo concerts, and spinoff groups.
20. This extends to sound quality and file type. The "Lossless Bob" project tracks Dylan recordings by audio fidelity, encouraging users to trade them in lossless formats such as FLAC, rather than in compressed formats like MP3. Every lossless recording is provided with a Lossless Bob (LB) catalog number and (often) a plea in a text file that accompanies downloads not to reseed the recording in a "lossy" format (see "Lossless Bob," losslessbob.wonderingwhattochoose.com). The movement—with its cobbled-together ethics and its discourses of loss and fidelity (sonic and otherwise)—merits a study in its own right. Jonathan Sterne's theory of "audile techniques" would provide a useful conceptual starting point. See Sterne, *MP3: The Meaning of a Format* and *The Audible Past*. Clinton Heylin and Michelle Engert consider the effects of digital technology on Dylan reception during the so-called Never-Ending Tour in "The Evolution of Fan Culture."
21. Reynolds, *Retromania*, 99.
22. Marcus's best-known writing on Dylan is his book on *The Basement Tapes* and Harry Smith's *Anthology of American Folk Music*; see Marcus, *The Old, Weird America*. See also his *Like a Rolling Stone: Bob Dylan at the Crossroads*, the collection *Bob Dylan by Greil Marcus*, and *Folk Music*. See also Padgett's fantastic blog, *Flagging Down the Double E's*, a rich trove of further interviews with Dylan's collaborators: www.flaggingdown.com.

23. Wilfrid Mellers's 1983 book, *A Darker Shade of Pale*, is a problematic case. It is at best half a monograph on Dylan's music, which Mellers does not begin discussing until page 111. Even then, the volume is thin on musical detail and thick with dubious racial generalizations.
24. These include Murphy, *Times a-Changin'*; Gray, *Song and Dance Man III*; Kim-Cohen, *In the Blink of an Ear*; Negus, *Bob Dylan*; Ross, *Listen to This*; and Koozin, *Embodied Expression in Popular Music*. Hampton, *Bob Dylan* is a special case: Hampton is a literature scholar, but he knows his music, as his frequent—and illuminating—discussions of the songs' chords and melodies attest.
25. These include Bickford, "Music of Poetry"; Cherlin and Gopinath, "Somewhere Down in the United States"; Daley, "One Who Sings"; Grier, "Ego and Alter Ego"; Ford, *Dig*, 147–50; Griffiths, "Talking about 'License to Kill'"; Koozin, "Guitar Voicing"; Murphy, "The Times Are A-Changin'"; and Zak "Bob Dylan and Jimi Hendrix."
26. Marshall, "Bob Dylan and the Academy," 108 and 109. See also Marshall, *Never Ending Star*, 25.
27. A video of the full panel, titled "The Inventions of Bob Dylan," November 19, 2009, is available at Philoctetes.org, bit.ly/RicksWilentz.
28. "Tombstone Blues," 1965.
29. Gracyk, "Valuing and Evaluating Popular Music," 211. For a similar argument, see Negus, *Bob Dylan*, 130–31.
30. On discourses of authenticity in Dylan reception see Cossu, *It Ain't Me, Babe* and Marshall, *Never Ending Star*. On constructions of authenticity in the folk revival more generally, see Cantwell, *When We Were Good*; Filene, *Romancing the Folk*; Marqusee, *Wicked Messenger*, 40–42; and Turino, *Music as Social Life*, 159–63.
31. Kinney, *The Dylanologists*, 1.
32. Gracyk, "When I Paint My Masterpiece," 177. He borrows the wording from Ted Gioia's article, "Jazz: The Aesthetics of Imperfection." See also Gioia, *The Imperfect Art*. For Gioia, jazz's imperfection—which he celebrates—is inseparable from its status as an improvised art, ever changing and running risks. These ideas are central to the broad understanding of imperfection I develop below.
33. See Rockwell, "Time on the Crooked Road."
34. "Ragged but Right" is the title of a traditional song from the early twentieth century, popularized by George Jones. The Jerry Garcia Band used it as the title for a live album.
35. See "Bob Dylan 2001.10.09 in Medford," bit.ly/MedfordReviews.
36. Ricks, *Dylan's Visions of Sin*, 17.
37. "She knows there's no success like failure / And failure's no success at all" ("Love Minus Zero / No Limit," 1965).
38. See "Bob Dylan 960416 at The Synphony [*sic*] Hall, Springfield, Mass.," April 17, 1996, bit.ly/SpringfieldReviews. Seth Rogovy (on the same web page) disagrees with Gart: "I guess I side with 'ragged but right.' I also thought he was doing some great melodic improvisational things, too."
39. Michael Cherlin deploys the term "imperfection" similarly in his monograph *Schoenberg's Musical Imagination*.
40. See Cohen, "The Imperfect Seeks Its Perfection," 146–47. Philosopher Jonathan Lear (in personal communication) has argued that there might still be an Aristotelian

perfection at work in Dylan's practice, that Dylan is a "teacher of human perfection" in his very embrace of finitude and fallibility. I return to this in the afterword.

41. Christopher Ricks disagrees, at least with respect to "The Lonesome Death of Hattie Carroll," which he calls a "perfect song," which receives its definitive performance in the studio version on *The Times They Are a-Changin'*. Ricks, *Dylan's Visions of Sin*, 15. I side with Alex Ross, who argues that the song's many performative variations can, at their best, activate meanings only latent in the original version. See Ross, *Listen to This*, 293.
42. The same is true of the very locution "sing-song." It repeats, with a difference. The author of "Lay Lady Lay" was well aware of the sonorous and playful potential of such minimal alterations in spelling, such near-repetitions.
43. Deleuze, *Difference and Repetition*.
44. Ambitious readers who want to wade into Deleuze's thought will find resonances with the present discussion, but also much that exceeds it. For useful primers on Deleuze's concepts of difference and repetition as they relate to music, see Gallope, "The Sound of Repeating Life," and Hulse, "Thinking Musical Difference." Political theorist Jane Bennett offers a lively introduction to Deleuze's theories of repetition in *The Enchantment of Modern Life*, 38–40.
45. Gray, *Song and Dance Man III*, 435.
46. This formulation, again, gestures lightly toward Deleuze. See Gallope, "The Sound of Repeating Life," and Hulse, "Thinking Musical Difference." For a penetrating and wide-ranging study on the cognitive bases of musical repetition, see Margulis, *On Repeat*.
47. According to David Evans, the revival of these years was actually the fourth "stage" of the folk revival, the first having begun early in the century, with a rise in academic interest and concert performance of folk music. The second stage began in the '30s, in explicit alliance with communist activists and the Popular Front. The third centered around recording reissues, most notably Harry Smith's 1952 *Anthology of American Folk Music*, which Dylan (and every other Village folkie) knew by heart. The fourth was led by young performers like Joan Baez, Dave Van Ronk, and Dylan himself. When I refer to the folk revival (without qualification) in this book, I mean Evans's fourth-stage revival. See Evans, "Folk Revival Music," cited in Hamilton, *Just Around Midnight*, 60 and 287. See also Marqusee, *Wicked Messenger*, 16–51; Wilentz, *Bob Dylan in America*, 17–46; Cantwell, *When We Were Good*; Rosenberg, *Transforming Tradition*; Filene, *Romancing the Folk*; and Cohen, *Rainbow Quest*.
48. Dylan, *Chronicles, Volume One* (hereafter cited as *CV1*), 70–72.
49. *EMPW*, 818; *EI*, 309–10. Some years earlier, he had wryly compared himself to two guitarist virtuosos, one classical, one flamenco: "I mean, I'm not Segovia or Montoya. I don't practice 12 hours a day." *EMPW*, 549; *EI*, 227. See also the liner notes to *Biograph*, 8 (LP), 11 (CD), and *EMPW*, 854: "Part of it was a technical problem which I never had the time nor the inclination for, if you want to call it a problem. But it didn't go down well with the tight-thinking people." Or, as he put it in "Goodbye Jimmy Reed," on 2020's *Rough and Rowdy Ways*: "You won't amount to much, the people all said / 'Cause I didn't play guitar behind my head."
50. *CV1*, 72.

51. For an additional Bourdieuian perspective on Dylan in the Village scene, see Hampton, *Bob Dylan*, 26–32 and 240n3.
52. See the essays collected in Bourdieu, *The Field of Cultural Production*, especially the first, "The Field of Cultural Production; or, The Economic World Reversed."
53. Crowe, liner notes to *Biograph*, 10 (in the LP booklet), 13 (in the CD booklet). Also in *EMPW*, 855.
54. Crowe, liner notes to *Biograph*, 10–11, photo on 20 (CD booklet); 7–8, photo on 10 (LP booklet). The photo comes from a March 2, 1962, recording session at Cue Studios in New York, at which Dylan played harmonica on recordings by Spivey and Big Joe Williams. See Heylin, *Bob Dylan: A Life in Stolen Moments*, 27–28.
55. Sounes, *Down the Highway*, 318.
56. Dylan titled his 2001 studio album *"Love and Theft,"* after Eric Lott's 1993 book *Love and Theft: Blackface Minstrelsy and the American Working Class*. Dylan's cheeky quotation marks are a postmodern nod to his own theft of the title. Blackface, Lott's subject, preoccupied Dylan in these years, figuring prominently in his 2003 film *Masked and Anonymous*.
57. The most thorough and engrossing account that I have read of Dylan's Jewish roots is Engel, *Just like Bob Zimmerman's Blues*. For further discussion of Dylan and Judaism, see Karp, "A Foreign Song I Learned in Utah"; Salkin, "Bob Dylan's New Book Is a Jewish Masterpiece"; and Chiat, "Jewish Homes on the Range." For a recent discussion of Jewishness and whiteness—a topic that re-entered mainstream discourse following Donald Trump's election in 2016—see Green, "Are Jews White?"
58. Wagner, *Judaism in Music*. I am grateful to Sumanth Gopinath for stressing this connection.
59. For the Beats' influence on Dylan, see Wilentz, *Bob Dylan in America*, 47–84.
60. For a brilliant study of hipness in the postwar era, see Ford, *Dig*. Ford places sound at the center of his concept of hipness. See especially his chapter 5 and his illuminating discussion of "Ballad of a Thin Man" (147–50).
61. From a 2001 interview with Robert Hilburn for the *Los Angeles Times*. *EMPW*, 1313. In the late 2010s Dylan used an excerpt from the *Rite of Spring* as his intro music in concerts.
62. Marcus, *The Old, Weird America*, xix. Dylan's modernism is a red thread that runs through Timothy Hampton's book *Bob Dylan: How the Songs Work*, with a particular emphasis on Rimbaud's dictum that "one must be absolutely modern."
63. Small, *Musicking*. For a virtuosic evolutionary study that deploys and develops Small's concept, see Tomlinson, *A Million Years of Music*.
64. Padgett, *Pledging My Time*.
65. Ray Padgett has also written a highly engaging book on covers, *Cover Me*. It is not about Dylan per se, but it does include a chapter on "Make You Feel My Love." See also his podcast on Dylan covers, *The Bob Dylan Covers Podcast*. My brother, Michael Rings, has also written important studies of cover songs from an analytical philosophical perspective. See, for example, his "Doing It Their Way."
66. Marcus, *Bob Dylan by Greil Marcus*, 366. See also Marcus, *Folk Music*, 5–6.

CHAPTER ONE

1. Barry Feinstein was the photographer for the album cover. Among photojournalist Dorothea Lange's iconic images of the Depression, "Migrant Mother"—which pictures Florence Owens Thompson and her children—is the most famous.
2. Hedin, *Studio A*, 259. Compare David Bowie's "a voice like sand and glue" in his 1971 "Song for Bob Dylan."
3. Indeed, Dylan's range on the album extends almost an octave below the lowest pitch in this song, down to the A♭2 that concludes each verse of "Boots of Spanish Leather." On his first album, recorded in late November 1961, he reaches all the way down to E2, brushing the pitch several times in "House of the Rising Sun" (his voice ranges across more than two octaves in that remarkable performance, which I discuss in chapter 3).
4. As Todd Harvey notes, the tune is related to that for the traditional hymn "Deliverance Will Come," which Dylan also used as the basis for "Paths of Victory" and "One Too Many Mornings." See Harvey, *The Formative Dylan*, 77–78, 84–85, and 111–13. "Times" nevertheless differs in crucial respects from those songs. Most notably, phrases 5 and 6 in figure 1.1—the highpoint of the verse—are entirely absent from the other three tunes, whose verses have only four phrases. And "Times" does not even track those tunes precisely in its first four phrases; resemblance is limited to the ascending gesture in lines 1 and 3. As with so many tunes, Dylan modifies his borrowed melody for "Times," giving it a new shape tailored to the prosody and affective trajectory of his words.
5. Heylin, *Trouble in Mind*, 51. Bennett heard Dylan sing in 1963 at a Columbia sales conference in San Juan, Puerto Rico; see Rotolo, *A Freewheelin' Time*, 221–22. Fifty-three years later Dylan would perform "Once upon a Time" at Bennett's ninetieth birthday celebration at Radio City Music Hall.
6. Compare Ecclesiastes 9:11 ("the race is not to the swift") and Matthew 19:30 ("But many that are first shall be last; and the last shall be first"), both quotes from the King James Version. See also Matthew 20:16, Mark 10:31, and Luke 13:30. Michael Gilmour's *Tangled Up in the Bible* is an invaluable resource for biblical allusions in Dylan. On this line from "The Times They Are a-Changin'," see the entry in Glimour's appendix.
7. There is also a harmonic component to this sense of suspended anticipation. The harmony at the end of phrase 4 is poised on the V chord (the dominant, D major), which points harmonically toward the I chord (the tonic, G major). But the resolving tonic chord does not sound until the beginning of phrase 6, which confirms it with a cadence in its fourth bar.
8. That image was made famous by Dr. Martin Luther King Jr., who first used it in a speech at the end of the Montgomery bus boycott in 1956. (He derived it from an 1853 sermon by abolitionist preacher Theodore Parker.) Dylan had shared the dais with King at the March on Washington on August 28, 1963, about two months before the recording session for "Times."
9. Their manager, Albert Grossman—also Dylan's manager—cultivated this image with great care. See, for example, the comments from Bruce Langhorne and John Cohen in *No Direction Home: Bob Dylan,* dir. Martin Scorcese (hereafter cited as *NDH*), 1:29:00–1:30:21.

10. Cherlin and Gopinath, "Somewhere Down in the United States," 225. See also Denning, "Bob Dylan and Rolling Thunder," 29; Titon, "Reconstructing the Blues," 221; and Wald, *Dylan Goes Electric*, 61–67.
11. Cherlin and Gopinath suggest that Dylan sought a third way between these two stylistic tendencies, especially in his pursuit of mainstream success, but his allegiances as a singer are clearly with Van Ronk and co.
12. Dylan was in close contact with Van Ronk in the months after his arrival in New York. Van Ronk's wife, Terri Thal, was Dylan's first manager and he crashed on their couch briefly.
13. Van Ronk with Wald, *Mayor of MacDougal Street*, 47.
14. Dylan was not unique in this. As Jack Hamilton notes, such a view of "authenticity" was endorsed by no less a figure than Pete Seeger, who "serv[ed] as a living example that musical expression and personal politics could intertwine even when the folksinger hadn't emerged from a dust bowl homestead or sharecropper's shack. Seeger's rhetoric was marked by self-making and rebirth, and the suggestion that the authenticity inherent to folksinging was a volunteerist proposition rather than a strictly socioeconomic one held tremendous appeal to young revivalists. In Seeger's telling, self-invention (or self-reinvention) could become its own authenticity, illustrating one's commitment to an identity that one has chosen, rather than what one has simply been born into." Hamilton, *Just Around Midnight*, 63. See also 288–89n76, which includes Seeger's comments on Ramblin' Jack Elliott along these lines.
15. For a study of Dylan's Minnesota roots, including some vestigial Minnesota-isms in his speech and lyrics, see Pichaske, *Song of the North Country*, chapter 2.
16. They may well have heard an advance pressing of the studio recording, via shared manager Albert Grossman. This demo version was released on *The Bootleg Series*, vol. 9: *The Witmark Demos*.
17. *NDH*, 2:19:15–20.
18. *NDH*, 1:40:30–35.
19. In addition to Baez, Dylan has sung with only a handful of other women, including Emmylou Harris (on 1976's *Desire*), Patti Smith (in a few live concerts in 1995), and background singers from his gospel years. These additional examples call out for a more extended study, which might explore (among other things) Smith's subversion of conventional feminine beauty ideals (not only in her appearance, but also in her singing), and the fraught racial dynamics of Black women singing behind a white man, lending him a kind of gospel credibility. On the latter, see Wald, "Gospel Music," especially 94–97. I discuss issues of gender and race in Dylan's gospel era in chapter 12.
20. The stylized spelling, with no apostrophe in *Dont*, was intentional, Pennebaker's attempt to "simplify the language." Sounes, *Down the Highway*, 175.
21. Hampton, *Bob Dylan*, 66.
22. Obama himself was especially fond of King's line about the arc of the moral universe (discussed in note 9 from this chapter) and repeated it often in speeches. Indeed, he paraphrased it that very night, in his victory speech at Chicago's Grant Park (perhaps at the very moment Dylan was performing "Times"?). Some have reported that Dylan himself said at the concert, "It looks like things are gonna change now," but that is

not audible on the audience recording that I have heard. See Latham, *The World of Bob Dylan*, 18.

23. For relevant discussion, see Lubet, "Listening to Bob Dylan."
24. The following discussion—in its successive focus on differences in vocal quality, pitch, and rhythm/articulation—takes its inspiration from Victoria Malawey's work on analyzing the popular singing voice. In *A Blaze of Light in Every Word*, Malawey identifies quality, pitch, and prosody (which includes rhythm and articulation) as the three principal domains in a conceptual map of vocal production.
25. The 1998 performance is from January 14, before Dylan's May 24 birthday.
26. Kane uses Greek terms throughout his discussion: *phoné* for voice, *echos* for sound, *logos* for word or meaning, and *topos* for site of bodily emission. My plain-English substitutions sound, word, and body for *echos, logos*, and *topos* are not perfect translations of his Greek, but they're close enough, and easier to remember. See Kane, "The Voice: A Diagnosis," and his more concise presentation in "The Model Voice." Kane's model departs from the work of Lacanian philosopher Mladen Dolar, specifically Dolar's book *A Voice and Nothing More*. For a thorough engagement with Dolar see Kane, *Sound Unseen*, 206–22.
27. Kane uses the Derridean term "spacing" to characterize the relationship between these three terms. Indeed, his entire project seeks to move beyond a philosophical impasse that Derrida creates for thinkers about voice. Readers interested in this philosophical debate are encouraged to consult Kane's "The Voice: A Diagnosis" and chapter 7 of his book *Sound Unseen*.
28. Kane calls these edges "crossings."
29. "Subterranean Homesick Blues," 1965.
30. Robin Witting makes a similar point about the musicality of Dylan's language in the book *Tarantula*. See Witting, *"Tarantula": The Falcon's Mouthbook*, 8–10; and Witting, *Help Those that Cannot Understand*, 2–3.
31. This is an anachronistic coincidence: there is no evidence that Dylan had D. A. Pennebaker in mind when he penned and recorded "Subterranean Homesick Blues." He recorded the song in January 1965 but wouldn't begin working with Pennebaker until late April of that year.
32. Kane, "The Voice: A Diagnosis," 94. Nina Sun Eidsheim begins her monograph on vocal timbre with the assertion that "the foundational question asked in the act of listening to a human voice is *Who is this? Who is speaking?*" Eidsheim, *The Race of Sound*, 1, emphasis original.
33. For a detailed scientific discussion of the ways listeners associate vocal timbre with various attributes of identity, see Kreiman and Sidtis, *Foundations of Voice Studies*, especially chapters 4, 5, and 9. For a more theoretical treatment, see Eidsheim, *The Race of Sound*.
34. For a brilliant study of such vocal personae, see Cherlin and Gopinath, "Somewhere Down in the United States." See also the suggestive discussions in Starr, *Listening to Bob Dylan*, 11–32, and Hughes, *Invisible Now*, 25–33.
35. Kane, "The Voice: A Diagnosis," 98.
36. Kane, "The Voice: A Diagnosis," 104.

37. Of course, there is a very small, closed circle of family, friends, and musicians that have had heard Dylan unamplified. ("The harmonica around my neck / I blew it for ya free," he sings in 1974's "Up to Me.") One thinks, perhaps, of Donovan and company listening stunned to "It's All Over Now, Baby Blue" in that tense 1965 hotel room in *Dont Look Back*. But even these encounters involve *technê* in Kane's sense of technique, discussed below. And—for us—Pennebaker's film thickly mediates that charged, intimate encounter through both audio-recording technology and the cinema verité visual aesthetic: gritty, handheld, black-and-white.
38. As a fellow Minnesotan who has performed at Northrup, I can attest to its unwieldy acoustics, with lengthy reverberation and a late slapback echo off the back wall.
39. Kane's book *Sound Unseen* is a detailed philosophical mediation on such "acousmatic" sounds, which are visually severed from their sources.
40. John Bauldie, for example, writes: "Each of the records had been brought with bated breath, and carried home in triumph, with the rest of the day set aside for lyric transcription." Bauldie, notes to *The Bootleg Series*, vols. 1–3: *Rare and Unreleased*, 1. Compare Betsy Bowden: "Listeners to each newly released Dylan album would first try to figure out exact words, especially if mumbled or garbled." Bowden, *Performed Literature*, 29.

CHAPTER TWO

1. As heard on *The Bootleg Series*, vol. 6: *Bob Dylan Live 1964*. The line comes at the end of track 6, after the second-ever live performance of "Gates of Eden."
2. For a theoretically ambitious study of Dylan's changeability—with a special focus on masks and Dylan's "trickster" persona—see Scobie, *Alias Bob Dylan: Revisited*.
3. Dylan, *Highway 61 Revisited*, back cover, ellipses and dashes as in the original. For a reading of this passage that has points of contact with mine, see Day, *Jokerman*, 8–9.
4. For more on Rimbaud's influence on Dylan in these years, see Hampton, *Bob Dylan*, chapter 3.
5. I am thinking here of theories about decentered subjectivity; the self as constituted through language; Derridean notions of writing, speech, and *différance*; and so on. On these Derridean concepts, see especially Derrida, *Of Grammatology*. For two early examples of poststructuralist Dylan interpretation, see Day, *Jokerman*, and Scobie, *Alias Bob Dylan: Revisited*. Yaffe, *Bob Dylan: Like a Complete Unknown*, offers a more recent exploration of Dylan's shifting identities, with light touches of theory.
6. That line comes from the celebrated, inscrutable "I'm Not There (1956)," recorded during the basement summer of 1967 (and officially released on *The Bootleg Series*, vol. 11). Todd Haynes's 2007 film *I'm Not There* takes mutable identity as its central conceit, famously casting six different actors in the role of Bob Dylan (including a woman, Cate Blanchett, and a young African American male, Marcus Carl Franklin, whose character—compounding the identity confusion—calls himself "Woody Guthrie").
7. Cavarero, *For More than One Voice*, 4. Quoted in Verma, "Screamlines," 98. Brian Kane critiques Cavarero's focus on the voice as a unique bearer of identity—don't we also (and even primarily) use vision for this purpose?—in *Sound Unseen*, 152–56. Cavarero's argument that the voice offers access to an interior part of the body, inaccessible to

sight, still retains some force, but Kane is right to question her assumption that this somehow discloses identity *more* than vision. Vocal identity need not be primary—or the ear the privileged organ of recognition—for the arguments in my main text to stand.

8. Verma, "Screamlines," 98.
9. *NDH*, 25:08–25:28. This complete Dylan performance has not been released officially, but it circulates on the so-called Minnesota Party Tape, which was recorded by Cleve Pettersen in Minneapolis's Dinkytown neighborhood, near the University of Minnesota.
10. Such rhythms are usually called "Scotch snaps," though they are present in musics throughout the British isles, not just in Scotland. For an excellent discussion, see Philip Tagg's "Scotch Snaps: The Big Picture": bit.ly/TaggScotchSnapsText.
11. Much of this debate took place in the short-lived fanzine *Fourth Time Around*, produced by Chris Hockenhull. Heylin alludes to it in *Behind the Shades*, 40. See also Heylin, *Recording Sessions*, 3.
12. Jeff Rosen, Dylan's manager, and the staff at the Dylan office evidently provided the audio of the Wallace Tape for the Scorsese documentary, as it is far cleaner than all unofficial circulating versions.
13. Heylin, *Behind the Shades*, 40 (for both the Koerner and Wallace quotes).
14. This voice is also amply in evidence on two *Bootleg Series* releases documenting these years: *Another Self Portrait* (vol. 10) and *Travelin' Thru* (vol. 15). Allen Ginsberg heard Bing Crosby in the voice. *MUtM*, 217.
15. On Dylan's contempt for "Woodstock Nation" and hippie culture during these years, see his 1984 *Rolling Stone* interview with Kurt Loder (*EMPW*, 764; *EI*, 301) and *CV1*, 116–24.
16. This recording circulates widely, though unofficially (it was first made available through a 1993 BBC-TV documentary). An even earlier recording—made in the Terlinde Music Store in St. Paul on Christmas Eve, 1956, when Dylan was fifteen—does not yet circulate. The recording, made with Hibbing friends Howard Rutman and Larry Kegan, features doo-wop tunes like "In the Still of the Night" and "Earth Angel" alongside Little Richard and Carl Perkins numbers. See Lee Ranaldo's discussion of it in *MUtM*, 39–41, as well as "1961 Concerts and Recording Sessions," bobserve, bit.ly/Bjorner1956.
17. On the chronology, see Heylin, *Bob Dylan: A Life in Stolen Moments*, 10. For Dylan's own account of his Guthrie obsession—including the colossal impression made on him by both Guthrie's voice and *Bound for Glory*—see *CV1*, 243ff.
18. The opening of "Blue Suede Shoes"—a Perkins song later popularized by Presley—is the most familiar example. Similar stop-time rhythm parts are in evidence in Perkins's "Honey Don't," "Everybody's Trying to Be My Baby," and "Boppin' the Blues," the latter of which Dylan performed with Rutman and Kegan on the noncirculating 1956 music-store recording discussed in n. 16 above. See "1961 Concerts and Recording Sessions," bit.ly/Bjorner1956.
19. This is also the underlying rhythm of Guthrie's models for "This Land Is Your Land": "When the World's on Fire" and "Pal of Mine," both Carter Family songs.

20. The blue third here and in the following measure is indicated with a quarter-tone-sharp symbol, indicating that it falls in the crack between F♮ and F♯, the minor and major third scale degrees (respectively) in D, an instance of the so-called neutral third in blues.
21. Middleton, *Studying Popular Music*, 18–21.
22. Whose songs Dylan had early heard sung by Hank Snow. See Gray, *Dylan Encyclopedia*, 159, 621.
23. We know that this was Dylan's method decades later when working on *Christmas in the Heart*, as backup singer Randy Crenshaw revealed in a 2023 interview with Ray Padgett: "He said *[Bob voice]*, 'Let's listen to some songs, we'll get some ideas.' He has a boombox and he puts on recordings of various classic Christmas songs." See Ray Padgett, "Inside the 'Christmas in the Heart' Sessions," December 20, 2022, bit.ly/PadgettCrenshaw.
24. See Rings, "Analyzing the Popular Singing Voice: Sense and Surplus," 665.
25. Bloom's output was vast, and the secondary literature on his theory of influence (pro and con) vaster still. The seminal texts nevertheless remain his early presentation of the theory in the books *The Anxiety of Influence* (1973) and its follow-up, *A Map of Misreading* (1975).
26. In his cranky preface to the 1997 edition of *The Anxiety of Influence*, Bloom claims that he "never meant by 'the anxiety of influence' a Freudian Oedipal rivalry, despite a rhetorical flourish or two in this book" (xxii). The frequency of reference to Freud, Oedipus, and the family romance in the main text nevertheless give one pause, seeming more than mere "rhetorical flourish." It seems more accurate to say, as Bloom does on p. 8, that his theory offers a revision of Freud's.
27. Taruskin, "Revising Revision," 115.
28. As told to Ken Paulson on November 29, 2000: "Tom Paxton Remembers Bob Dylan," YouTube, November 29, 2000, bit.ly/PaxtonOnDylan. While still in Minneapolis, Dylan had been brusquely informed by Jon Pankake, co-founder of the *Little Sandy Review* and a folk purist (Dylan calls him a member of the "folk police"), that Ramblin' Jack Elliott had beaten him to the Woody Guthrie–disciple game. Dylan's continued cultivation of a novel voice, set apart from both Guthrie's and Elliott's, could well have been a reaction formation to this news, stemming in part from his awareness that Elliott had gotten there first. On Dylan's encounter with Pankake and his initial hearing of Elliott, see *CV1*, 248–52, especially the final page, on which he writes explicitly of resisting Elliott's influence, proceeding as though he hadn't heard him. The Bloomian resonances are unmistakable.
29. The precise date of the Guthrie recording is unknown, though another recording of the song for Asch from 1944 is all but identical as regards key and vocal delivery. The present recording could well date from the same session. Both performances—plus a third with Cisco Houston—are available on vol. 1 of *Woody Guthrie: The Asch Recordings* (Smithsonian Folkways). The complete Dylan performance from Carnegie Chapter Hall is available on *The Bootleg Series*, vol. 7: *No Direction Home*.
30. The cover of the concert program is reproduced in *MUtM*, 104.

31. This, despite a line claiming the opposite in "Song to Woody," penned around this time: "The very last thing that I'd want to do / Is to say I've been hittin' some hard travelin' too."
32. On some lines Dylan anticipates even more, completing the entire phrase before the downbeat.
33. Bloom, *Anxiety of Influence*, 14.
34. As Tony Glover puts it in *NDH*, 25:07–25:08.

CHAPTER THREE

1. On the song's tangled history, including the many variants among the recorded versions, see Anthony, *Chasing the Rising Sun*. Though Dylan drops the *g* at the end of "Rising" in the title on the album jacket ("House of the Risin' Sun"), I've retained it throughout the chapter, in conformance with how the song is named on most other recordings.
2. Van Ronk with Wald, *Mayor of MacDougal Street*, 175–78; and *NDH*, 1:06:26–1:08:50.
3. Throughout this chapter I refer flexibly to the first-person "I" of a song as the "lyric subject," the "lyric persona," or the "protagonist." Though some theorists distinguish between such terms, I use them synonymously. For a relevant discussion of the many personae that can circulate in song, see Cone, *The Composer's Voice*, and Bicknell, *Philosophy of Song and Singing*.
4. The precise nature of that house—brothel? prison?—has long been in dispute, as Ted Anthony documents in *Chasing the Rising Sun*. Van Ronk, for his part, was convinced it was a women's prison (Van Ronk with Wald, *Mayor of MacDougal Street*, 178), while Dylan seems to have thought it a brothel, as he initially planned to have a performance of it precede a brothel scene in his 1978 film *Renaldo and Clara* (*DL2*, 267). Anthony also observes that the song's lyric persona was not always female. Clarence Ashley's early recording, for example, is sung from the perspective of a wayward boy, a "rounder." The protagonist is male again in the Animals' iconic version (musically based on Dylan's and Van Ronk's). But both Van Ronk and Dylan explicitly sing the song from a woman's point of view ("It's been the ruin of many a poor girl / And me, oh God, I'm a-one"), as did most folk revivalists. The ethnicity of the song's protagonist is also underdetermined, as Anthony notes, though the blues inflections in Dylan's and Van Ronk's performances clearly evoke Black expressive culture.
5. Bell, *Once Upon a Time*, 37.
6. Hughes, "Ulterior Significance," 23.
7. For a penetrating account of vocal personae in Dylan's early singing, with particular emphasis on comic code-switching, see Cherlin and Gopinath, "Somewhere Down in the United States."
8. Marcus, *Bob Dylan by Greil Marcus*, 366; cited in Hughes, "Ulterior Significance," 24n21. Dylan's vocal empathy is also the point of departure for Marcus's 2022 book *Folk Music: A Bob Dylan Biography in Seven Songs*.
9. In "The Lonesome Death of Hattie Carroll," "To Ramona," and "Seven Curses," respectively.

10. Or "North Country Blues" on *The Times They Are a-Changin'*, sung from the perspective of a woman in Minnesota's desolated Iron Range. The traditional song "Young but Daily Growin'" (a.k.a. "Long a-Growin'") is another example, in which the lyric "I" recalls her dead husband, who never outgrew his boyhood. Dylan versions circulate from 1961, 1965, and 1967.
11. Hughes, "Ulterior Significance," 23.
12. Christopher Ricks has spoken eloquently on the question of race and "tact" in these performances; Ricks, "All Because of the Color of His Skin," public lecture at the University of Chicago, May 12, 2017. His talk focused especially on "Black Cross" as Dylan performed it in October 1962 at the Gaslight Café, the same concert as the performance of "Handsome Molly" that Marcus praises.
13. See especially Cantwell, *When We Were Good*, and Filene, *Romancing the Folk*.
14. *CV1*, 256.
15. The term "gender shift" is Victoria Malawey's. In her article "An Analytic Model for Examining Cover Songs," Malawey refers to "cross-gender covers," but now prefers the term "gender-shifted," to "avoid the problematic binary implied with the modifier 'cross-'" (personal email, July 1, 2020). See also Malawey, *A Blaze of Light in Every Word*. Such gender shifts are also common in classical art songs (*Lieder*) and on the operatic stage, in so-called trouser roles (male parts sung by women). Suzanne Cusick discusses an example of the former—a performance by soprano Jessye Norman of Robert Schumann's controversial song cycle *Frauenliebe und Leben*—in her article "Gender and the Cultural Work of a Classical Music Performance." Kristina Muxfeldt offers a dissenting opinion in "*Frauenliebe und Leben* Now and Then," 30n9.
16. On gender politics in the folk revival—with a particular focus on Baez—see Cantwell, *When We Were Good*, 337ff.
17. Simone covered several additional Dylan songs, including "The Ballad or Hollis Brown," "Just like Tom Thumb's Blues," "I Shall Be Released," and "The Times They Are a-Changin'."
18. Roberta Flack similarly mixes third- and first-person pronouns ("she" and "I") in her cover version of the song from one year prior (1970). But unlike Simone, Flack introduces the first-person "I" right away, in the initial chorus.
19. Any short list of his songs that admit of a misogynistic reading would surely include 1978's "Is Your Love in Vain?" ("Can you cook and sew, make flowers grow / Do you understand my pain?") and 1983's "Sweetheart Like You" ("You know a woman like you should be at home / That's where you belong").
20. For relevant comments on the popular singing voice and its relationship to singers' carefully constructed personae, see Frith, *Performing Rites*, 183–202; and Turino, "Signs of Imagination," 239.
21. *CV1*, 256.
22. Precise date for Van Ronk's concert is unknown; released in 2013 on Dave Van Ronk, *Down in Washington Square* (Smithsonian Folkways). After Dylan recorded the song, an irate Van Ronk dropped it from his repertory. He did not make a studio recording of it until 1964, releasing it on that year's *Just Dave Van Ronk* (Mercury). The only other version that has seen official release is a live performance from 1993 (*Dave Van Ronk: On Air*, Tradition & Moderne, released 2007). Despite small differences

in key—his performances are in F♯ minor, F minor, and E minor, respectively, the capo descending by semitone for each subsequent rendition—the performances are remarkably similar as regards vocal delivery. I have chosen the Yale performance from 1961 as it documents how Van Ronk's performance sounded around the time Dylan learned it.

23. Van Ronk plays with a capo on the fourth fret, using D-minor chord shapes. His arrangement thus differs from Dylan not only in key but also in fingering and guitar chording.
24. Music theorists call this the "harmonic rhythm."
25. The Animals would take up Dylan's 6/8 lope in their 1964 version of the song. For a detailed study of such metric flexibility in singer-songwriter music, see Murphy, *Times a-Changin'*, which includes discussions of Dylan throughout.
26. On such stagings of vocal failure, see Martha Feldman's essay "Voice Gap Crack Break."
27. Dylan's verses track Van Ronk's relatively closely, though he repeats the first verse as the eighth, as discussed below (Van Ronk ends with verse 7). There are nevertheless some striking local differences in lyrics; for example, the gambler in verse 2 is the protagonist's father in Van Ronk's version, her "sweetheart" in Dylan's.
28. In this figure and in several subsequent ones in the book, I use musical notation flexibly, as music analysts are wont to do. Noteheads do not indicate durations. Here they capture details about vocal timbre, as the key at the bottom of the figure indicates. In other figures, different noteheads are used to indicate hierarchical distinctions, or to group notes into distinct lines, and so on. In all cases, I have striven to deploy them in a way that is intuitively readable at a glance.
29. Ricks, "Bob Dylan," 34.
30. That pitch is a painful, unresolved $\hat{7}$ in A minor, straining upward but never attaining the stable tonic ($\hat{1}$) of A4.
31. Cherlin and Gopinath, "Somewhere Down in the United States," 228–29.
32. "The 100 Greatest Singers of All Time," *Rolling Stone*, December 3, 2010, bit.ly/RS100Greatest. Bono is the author of the entry on Dylan, from which this quote comes. Though this line from Cooke is often cited, I have been unable to source it beyond Bono's mention here.
33. Remnick, "Bob Dylan, Extending the Line."
34. "I find the voice of Bob Dylan disturbing. Why do some people think that he is a good singer?" bit.ly/QuoraTruth.
35. In these years, as Bell relates, he was spinning yarns about "a life on the road, life with the carnival, life on the streets, of parents dead and gone." Bell, *Once Upon a Time*, 36–37.

CHAPTER FOUR

1. Mostly. There are of course those songs whose lyrics change in performance—several of them from *Blood on the Tracks*—and there are long songs in which Dylan regularly omits some verses. But these are exceptions that prove the rule. On a good night, with no memory slips, the lyrics to most songs remain largely as they are on the studio recording.
2. Barthes, "The Grain of the Voice," 181. Jacob Reed's dissertation-in-progress offers a brilliant analysis of this "fringe," offering many points of contact with my discussion in chapters 4 and 5.

3. There is a long ethnomusicological tradition of probing the porous boundary between speech and song. See, e.g., List, "The Boundaries of Speech and Song." For a more recent study that specifically discusses Dylan, see Bickford, "Music of Poetry."
4. Robert Shelton first published his review, "Bob Dylan: A Distinctive Folk-Song Stylist," in *The New York Times* on September 29, 1961. He reproduces it, with an introduction providing context, in *No Direction Home*, 86.
5. Sumanth Gopinath makes this point (about the incipient musicality of Dylan's speaking voice) in "Dylan's Speech: A Performative (and Musical) Poetics?" See also Pichaske, *Song of the North Country*, chapter 2, on the influence of Dylan's upper-midwestern speech patterns on his lyric writing and singing.
6. Rings, "Speech and/in Song."
7. Dolar, *A Voice and Nothing More*, 15.
8. They are also all white and associated with northern, urban traditions lionized by a critical elite: folk, punk, avant-garde. On the dynamics of race and class as regards speech in song, see Rings, "Speech and/in Song."
9. Released on *The Bootleg Series*, vol. 11: *The Basement Tapes Complete*.
10. Greil Marcus hears "a radio evangelist hawking his prayer rugs with a shit-eating grin on his face, a grin you can feel through the speakers." Marcus, *The Old, Weird America*, 81.
11. Marcus, *The Old, Weird America*, 81.
12. On sonic analogues, see Zbikowski, *Foundations of Musical Grammar*.
13. Many compared Dylan's stage manner in the early '60s to Charlie Chaplin. In a 1961 interview with Columbia Records publicist Billy James, he drew the comparison himself: "If I'm on stage, even my idol—my biggest idol on stage—the one that's running through my head all the time, is Charlie Chaplin . . . he's one of *the* men." *EMPW*, 17. See Joe Taysom's 2020 article on the Chaplin comparison in *Far Out*, which includes the quote: Taysom, "Bob Dylan Describes His Idol in His First Recorded Interview from 1961," *Far Out*, October 5, 2020, bit.ly/DylanChaplin.
14. *Bob Dylan's Theme Time Radio Hour*, episode 102, "Whiskey," part 2, 1:18:59–1:19:15. Transcript here: bit.ly/ttrh102.
15. The German word *Sprechstimme* translates literally as speech-voice, but it is usually rendered in English as speech-song. Two other German terms for the technique—*Sprechgesang* and *Sprechmelodie*—make its connection to song more explicit. Earlier composer Engelbert Humperdinck pioneered the technique, calling it *Sprechgesang* and using it for a musical genre known as melodrama, which involves dramatic recitation over musical accompaniment.
16. Schoenberg, *Verklärte Nacht and Pierrot Lunaire*, 54.
17. There is much debate among Schoenbergians as to whether the reciter in *Pierrot lunaire* should touch on precise pitches that coincide with the music's notated score. In practice, very few do.
18. The name is an homage to the late Adam Krims, who identified two styles of rap delivery as the "speech-effusive style" and the "percussion-effusive style." See his *Rap Music and the Poetics of Identity*, 50ff.
19. Syllabic emphasis is also central to Dylan's everyday speaking. Think of his delivery in interviews, especially in the mid-'60s: he swings from sentence to sentence like a

gibbon, emphasized syllables as his handholds. Alex Ross wryly observes that this effect is contagious among his fans at concerts: "In Dylan's vicinity, I noticed, everyone italicizes." Ross, *Listen to This*, 283.

20. Sondheim has often expressed his dissatisfaction with this very aspect of the song. See, for example, this PBS interview, starting at around 11:00: "Stephen Sondheim," *American Masters*, February 26, 1998, www.pbs.org/wnet/americanmasters/archive/interview/stephen-sondheim-2/.
21. The latter was released on *The Bootleg Series*, vol. 4.
22. The pentatonic scale is a five-note scale extremely common in musics of the world. To hear what it sounds like, play only the black keys on a piano. The particular transposition of the pentatonic scale in this song is nevertheless mostly white keys: D, E, F♯, A, B.
23. On this storied concert and its contexts, see Lee, *Like the Night (Revisited)*, and Heylin, *Judas!*
24. Lee, *Like the Night (Revisited)*, 151. On the same page, Lee states that "all the people who were there that night have agreed that it was the loudest thing they'd ever heard up to that date." See also the array of comments along these lines on 138.
25. "I felt like I was being forced back into my seat, you know? Like being in a jet when it takes off." Lee, *Like the Night (Revisited)*, 138.
26. The 1966 live performance is in the key of E major, a step up from the D major of the studio recording. Thus, Dylan's climactic pitch here is F♯4, a step above the earlier E4 climax.
27. In my article "Speech and/in Song" I refer to this phenomenon—moving the melody into an instrumental part while the singer speaks instead of singing—as melodic "ghosting."
28. Lee, *Like the Night (Revisited)*, 25.
29. See Lee, *Like the Night (Revisited)*, 25–43, and Jones, *Bob Dylan and the British Sixties*, 12–20. The "tenth-rate drivel" line is from Ewan MacColl, in MacColl, et al., "Topical Songs and Folksinging, 1965: A Symposium," 157. MacColl also calls Dylan a "mediocre talent," deriding the "cultivated illiteracy of his topical songs" and his "fourth-grade schoolboy attempts at free verse."
30. When Robert Hilburn asked about the song in a November 2003 interview, Dylan responded: "It's from Chuck Berry, a bit of 'Too Much Monkey Business' and some of the scat singers of the '40s." *EMPW*, 1343; *EI*, 438. Another intertext is Ricky Nelson's "Waitin' in School," also largely chant based, as noted in *DL1*, 315. Dylan admired Nelson, writing that he "sang his songs calm and steady like he was in the middle of a storm, men hurling past him." *CV1*, 14.
31. A blue third is a special inflection of scale degree $\hat{3}$ that typically hovers between minor and major. Berry and Dylan sing theirs closer to the minor third than the major, so I have notated their chants using that pitch.
32. I borrow this term from the analysis of Western liturgical chant (e.g., Gregorian chant).
33. I have written some of the lyrics in figures 4.7 and 4.8 on two lines. This is merely to conserve horizontal space; it does not indicate any change in pitch.

34. Another term borrowed from Western music theory, where it labels a basic technique of voice leading.
35. Though the actual pitch of the reciting and escape tones differ between "It's Alright, Ma" and "Like a Rolling Stone," they represent the same scale degrees: the reciting tone is $\hat{1}$, the escape tone $\hat{3}$. For more detailed analysis of "It's Alright, Ma" and its chant/escape delivery, see Rings, "A Foreign Sound."
36. It has appeared as recently as "I Contain Multitudes," the first track on 2020's *Rough and Rowdy Ways*.
37. Their discussions of the topic on expectingrain.com (see, e.g., "Upsinging Defined?" Expecting Rain Discussions, July 13, 2011, bit.ly/ERupsinging) represent a fascinating instance of vernacular music theory, in which posters identify various subvariants, such as "uprasping," "upbarking," and "upgrowling." One poster on the thread attributes the original term to a post from Doug Evans on the defunct discussion board dylanpool.
38. O'Connell, "Speech, Song, and the Minor Third," 443. O'Connell cites many previous writers who have also discussed the phenomenon, though none match his empirical thoroughness. See also Negus, *Bob Dylan*, 139–42 (a section that carries the subtitle "The magic of chant and the minor third").
39. Dale and Fairhall, "A Hipster Sneer: Dylan's Re-Coding of the Blue Third."

CHAPTER FIVE

1. I consider each verse to encompass these two phrases only. The music that follows—- e.g., beginning at "Freedom, just around the corner for you" in verse 1—I consider the prechorus.
2. This figure, like figures 3.2, 3.3, and several figures to come, uses musical notation flexibly, especially as regards notehead type. In figure 5.1, open noteheads indicate hierarchically prominent pitches, while solid ones indicate more ornamental notes.
3. Note that this chant/escape involves the same scale degrees as those in "It's Alright, Ma" and "Like a Rolling Stone": $\hat{1}$ and $\hat{3}$.
4. Subphrase C is a cadential—that is, ending—phrase. The word cadence comes from the Latin *cadere*, which means "to fall." It is an apt idea for Dylan's vocal cadences in "Jokerman," all of which end with a vocal fall of some kind (note the curved lines ending each C subphrase in figure 5.1; in figure 5.2 the fall is mostly stepwise to B♭).
5. Gray, *Song and Dance Man III*, 453.
6. On the centrality of instrumental riffs in much of Dylan's music, see Negus, *Bob Dylan*, 133–34.
7. A tetrachord is a four-note musical collection. I call this one a "blues" tetrachord because its B♭ is a blue third, rubbing against the B♮ present or implied in much of the accompaniment.
8. This is actually only the fourth verse of the performance, as Dylan skips verse 3 ("Now the moon is almost hidden"), his normal practice in these years.
9. For a powerful recent theorization of the circulation and appropriation of Black musical practices in popular culture, see Morrison, *Blacksound*. Morrison's book also includes a chapter on the Blackface legacy of M. Witmark & Sons, one of the first publishers of Dylan's songs.

10. Middleton, *Studying Popular Music*, 172–74. Middleton borrows the terms "undercoded" and "overcoded" from Umberto Eco.
11. From Selzer's review of a concert in Des Moines on August 22, 2012: "Reviews: Des Moines, Iowa," August 22, 2012, bit.ly/DesMoines2012reviews. See also Selzer, *Bobcat Nation*.
12. See the review from "RD" here: "Reviews: Chicago, Illinois," October 6, 2023, bit.ly/Chicago10-6-23reviews.
13. Or five albums, depending on how you count: 2017's *Triplicate* was a triple album, each of its three discs thematically unified.
14. The structure is not unlike the compound melodies of Bach's solo string music, in which a single line suggests multiple melodic strata at once.
15. The overall descent is from scale degree $\hat{5}$, thus $\hat{5}$–$\hat{4}$–$\hat{3}$–$\hat{2}$–$\hat{1}$. Music-theoretically savvy readers will recognize this as an archetypal descent from Schenkerian theory. I am making no Schenkerian claims here, nor do I recommend that style of analysis for Dylan's melodies more broadly, for both musical and ideological reasons. Dylan's tunes often do very un-Schenkerian things. Readers innocent of Schenkerian theory and all of the brouhaha surrounding it in recent years can disregard this note entirely.
16. Per the covers website SecondHandSongs (secondhandsongs.com). For the Dylan stats, see bit.ly/SecondHandDylan. Thank you to Ray Padgett for directing me to this site.
17. According to SecondHandSongs, "Long and Wasted Years" has exactly one cover, as compared to 232 for "Make You Feel My Love."
18. For an account of these definitional challenges, see Trippett, "Melody," which includes a historically thorough literature review.
19. When my wife and I searched for an instrumental version of the song on a streaming service, the first one (of many) that we found was indeed for piano and cello, with the latter taking the melody. It was delightfully cheesy.
20. On the importance of Kerouac to the song, and the album as a whole, see Hampton, *Bob Dylan*, 130ff.
21. Though Behan objected to Dylan's borrowing of the tune, Behan had himself borrowed it from traditional melodic stock. See Harvey, *The Formative Dylan*, 122–23.
22. This is a subtle example, though, as the second syllable of "American," which would be stressed in speech, gets a *metric* accent, occurring as it does on a downbeat. A similar thing happens in Bernstein/Sondheim's "Somewhere." Without getting too much into the theoretical details, suffice it to say that there are several different kinds of musical accent, involving contour, meter, duration, volume, articulation, grouping, or some combination of these. In "With God on Our Side," contour stresses the first syllable of "American," while meter stresses the second.
23. *EI*, 437–38; *EMPW*, 1342–43.
24. *CV1*, 119–20.
25. The film was promoted as a live concert, but it was neither—not live and not a concert. Set in a stylized, smoky jazz club, it features Dylan backed by musicians different than those playing on the recording we hear, often even holding different instruments. The music is entirely dubbed.

26. As such, it recalls the 1964 song "To Ramona," one of his most compassionate early songs, and another ambitious original melody.
27. *EI*, 17–18; *EMPW*, 85.
28. See my discussion of this in Rings, "Thoughts on Dylan's Nobel," November 3, 2016: bit.ly/RingsThoughtsNobel.
29. In the *Stereogum* article by Ryan Leas, "80 Artists Pick Their Favorite Dylan Songs for His 80th Birthday": bit.ly/80Artists.
30. See, e.g., a 2012 live performance from Louisville here: "Bonnie 'Prince' Billy, Brownsville Girl, Motherlodge Finale," YouTube, November 11, 2012, bit.ly /BPBillyBrownsvilleGirl.
31. The two covers listed on the website SecondHandSongs, by Reggie Watts and Himalayan Bear, also involve singing throughout.

CHAPTER SIX

1. Those sitting close to the stage experienced especially poor sound, as the speaker arrangement meant that they heard the instruments on stage but very little of Dylan's voice, which was coming through PA speakers directed past them. *DL1*, 350. Bobby Neuwirth also reports that the sound system failed during the performance, making Dylan's voice all but inaudible. *MUtM*, 159. For additional accounts of the concert, including its sound problems, see Wald, *Dylan Goes Electric!*, 257–74; Dann, *Guitar King*, 193–98; and *MUtM*, 158–61.
2. *DL1*, 350.
3. There is also, of course, the slang usage of "axe" for guitar, which Peter Yarrow adopted on stage that night to calm the crowd as Dylan went to get an acoustic for the encore.
4. Waksman, *Instruments of Desire*, 1.
5. Ethnomusicologist Thomas Turino defines two species of musical behavior that he calls participatory and presentational. In participatory musicking, "there are no artist-audience distinctions, only participants and potential participants performing different roles." By contrast, in presentational scenarios, "one group of people, the artists, prepare and provide music for another group, the audience, who do not participate in making the music or dancing." Turino, *Music as Social Life*, 26.
6. Brackett, *Categorizing Sound*; Kronengold, *Living Genres in Late Modernity*; Lena, *Banding Together*; Drott, "The End(s) of Genre." For an influential, if controversial, early study of genre in popular music, see Fabbri, "A Theory of Musical Genres," discussed and partially defended in Brackett, *Categorizing Sound*, 6–8.
7. For a good sampling of this polemical literature, see Heylin, *Judas!*, 16–31. Paul Nelson was one of the critics enthusiastic about Dylan's new sound.
8. See, for example, his interview with Nora Ephron and Susan Edmiston, *EMPW*, 173; *EI*, 47–48.
9. Helm with Davis, *This Wheel's on Fire*, 130. Emphasis original.
10. Hoskyns, *Across the Great Divide*, 96.
11. Heylin, *Behind the Shades*, 274.

12. Bending on the guitar involves pushing or pulling the string out of true with the left-hand fingers, causing it to rise in pitch. It is a hallmark of blues playing, and indeed of all rock playing that derives from the blues.
13. Wald, *Dylan Goes Electric!*, 216.
14. For example, folksinger Judy Collins says, "I loved his songs because they had that rock and roll energy." Hajdu, *Positively 4th Street*, 245. Or consider Pete Stampfel's quote on first hearing Dylan: "I saw him at Folk City, singing an old-time song called 'Sally Gal,' and it blew my mind. . . . His singing style and phrasing were stone rhythm and blues! He fitted the two styles together perfectly." Wald, *Dylan Goes Electric!*, 70. Recall, too, the Dylan quote to this effect from the latter part of the Introduction: "I played all the folk songs with a rock and roll attitude. This is what made me different and allowed me to cut through all the mess and be heard." Crowe, liner notes to *Biograph*, 10 (in the LP booklet), 13 (in the CD booklet). Also in *EMPW*, 855.
15. Some writers also cite Curtis Jones's "Highway 51 Blues" as Dylan's source, but that song bears no resemblance to Dylan's, musically or lyrically.
16. Robert Shelton (writing as Stacey Williams) points out the riff's similarity to the Everlys' in his notes on the back cover of Dylan's debut. Dylan's lifelong fondness for the Everlys is well documented. The unreleased 1966 film *Eat the Document* contains a scene in which he sings the Everlys' "When Will I Be Loved?" in a Glasgow hotel room; he would later cover two of their songs on his 1970 record *Self Portrait*. He even wrote a song for the duo in 1969—"The Fugitive," later called "Wanted Man"—which was performed by Johnny Cash at San Quentin (though never, as far as is known, by its original dedicatees). See Gray, *Dylan Encyclopedia*, 213–14. In 2006–9 Dylan featured six songs by the Everlys in his radio show *The Theme Time Radio Hour*. And in 2020 he name-checked "Wake Up, Little Susie" in his seventeen-minute epic on the Kennedy assassination and music in times of crisis, "Murder Most Foul." The Everlys' song was written by Boudleaux and Felice Bryant.
17. Everett, *The Foundations of Rock*, 151.
18. Later generations of guitarists would call these "power chords," that is, two- or three-note chords on the low strings, containing only the root and fifth.
19. The clash is specifically between G♯ (in the open tuning) and G♮ (the root of the ♭III chord).
20. As I noted in chapter 5, Dylan repurposed this very riff as the groove bed for his 2012 song "Early Roman Kings."
21. On "It's Alright Ma," as well as the other examples discussed in this paragraph, see Rings, "A Foreign Sound to Your Ear," ¶¶[18]–[20].
22. The song was banned in Boston, ostensibly for the lyrical content and its suggestion of teen sex. One wonders, though, how much the music's *sound*—and specifically its use of Black musical tropes, given new propulsion by increased tempo and syncopation—also played into this (mini) moral panic.
23. Jefferson, "Ripping Off Black Music," cited in Hamilton, *Just Around Midnight*, 1 2. See also Mahon, *Black Diamond Queens*.
24. Epstein, *The Ballad of Bob Dylan*, 5.

25. Several other live versions of the song from this era circulate. All are very close to the guitar style on the studio version.
26. Graves, *The English Ballad*, 9.
27. For a detailed study of the relatively free meter in such songs, see Murphy, *Times a-Changin'*.
28. Clinton Heylin has long argued that the fingerpicking on this track is not Dylan but Bruce Langhorne (*Behind the Shades*, 104; *DL1*, 180). He is wrong. The most obvious bit of evidence is Dylan's recording of the song for a Witmark demo in 1962 (released on *The Bootleg Series*, vol. 9), on which he also fingerpicks. This is undoubtedly the same guitarist, the playing marked by the same idiosyncrasies and blemishes. Langhorne was not at those Witmark sessions, nor would he have muffed notes the way Dylan does on both recordings. Moreover, as Eyolf Østrem has persuasively shown, subtle variations in the timing of harmonica, voice, and guitar in the *Freewheelin'* version make clear that the same person is doing all three. See "It Wasn't Bruce (A Musical Whodunnit)," Dylanchords, August 29, 2020, bit.ly/OstremDTT. Heylin's new argument in *DL1* that the guitar part is overdubbed does not hold water either, based on the timing issues that Østrem discusses, as well as the fact that, *were* it overdubbed, Dylan could clearly have played the overdub himself. Finally, there are many circulating recordings (official and unofficial) of Dylan's fingerpicking on other songs around this time, with which we can compare this one. One of them is right there on side 1 of *The Freewheelin' Bob Dylan*: "Girl from the North Country" (discussed below), which uses a nearly identical Travis picking pattern. In short, Dylan is indeed the fingerpicker on the studio "Don't Think Twice"—his guitaristic fingerprint is unmistakable.
29. Barthes, "The Grain of the Voice," 189.
30. Barthes develops the concept of grain specifically for the voice. His essay is much cited in popular music studies as well as voice studies more generally. It is nevertheless a difficult and sometimes vexing bit of writing, often misinterpreted. In the interest of accessibility, I only touched on the concept of grain gently in chapters 4 and 5, borrowing Barthes's concept of the "fringe of contact" between music and language.
31. Epstein, *The Ballad of Bob Dylan*, 205.
32. Dylan's sources for the song extend beyond country, ranging from British balladry to doo-wop. For more on this, see my 2015 lecture "'Don't Think Twice,' A Genealogy," available on soundingbobdylan.com.
33. The principal purpose of the trip was for Dylan to participate in the BBC drama *Madhouse on Castle Street*.
34. Dylan himself admitted the debt in a 1984 *Rolling Stone* interview with Kurt Loder: "Martin Carthy's incredible. I learned a lot of stuff from Martin. 'Girl From the North Country' is based on a song I heard him sing—that 'Scarborough Fair' song." *EMPW*, 769; *EI*, 296. The transcription in figure 6.4(a) is taken from the studio recording on Carthy's debut album, which was not released until 1965. We thus cannot be certain that it is identical to the way he performed the song in 1962 but, given Dylan's comment above and the explicit (and unusual) similarity in fingerboard voicing between the two songs, it seems likely that Carthy's arrangement did not change appreciably over these years. Simon and Garfunkel's version also begins with Carthy's chord.

35. A traditionally inclined analyst would likely read the A♯ and F♯ as non-chord tones—neighbors to the chordal B and G♯ of a tonic minor-seventh chord. But the fact that these pitches all ring and resound together weakens this interpretation. I am tempted instead to consider the whole chord a ringing, Dorian-tonic wash.
36. Timothy Koozin offers a detailed analysis of the song's harmony and guitar technique that accords well with my account here. See Koozin, *Embodied Expression in Popular Music*, 138–43.
37. Hurt's best-known recording of the song, which he made in 1928, was included on Harry Smith's *Anthology of American Folk Music* (1952), a treasure trove of early recordings beloved by the folk revivalists.
38. Dylan and Hurt crossed paths during the folk revival. For example, they were both featured performers at the 1963 Newport Folk Festival. *MUtM*, 100. In 2004 Dylan claimed he stayed in touch with Hurt until the latter's death in 1966. *EMPW*, 1346.
39. See Koozin, *Embodied Expression in Popular Music*, 147–60, for a suggestive analysis of Dylan's guitar playing on *Blood on the Tracks*, including the two songs I discuss here.
40. See his discussion of the album at "Blood on the Tracks (1975)," Dylanchords, 2001, bit.ly/EyolfBlood.
41. *CV1*, 282.
42. Per Sid Griffin, the scene was filmed in Fenway, Maine. Griffin, *Shelter from the Storm*, 130.
43. "To the magnificent Woodie [*sic*] Guthrie and / Robert Johnson / who sparked it off." Dylan, *Writings and Drawings*, unpaginated front matter.
44. There is a clear resemblance between Bloomfield's riff and certain riffs in Chicago urban blues, but I've not been able to source a specific antecedent. David Dann says the riff is based on the Paul Butterfield Blues Band's version of "Shake Your Money Maker," but I hear little resemblance. The rhythm guitar part in that song is a conventional double-stopped boogie pattern, rather than single-note lick high on the neck, as here. See Dann, *Guitar King*, 192. Three years after Newport '65, Jimmy Page of Led Zeppelin would use a very similar riff to Bloomfield's (in figure 6.10) to anchor the song "How Many More Times" on the band's debut album (Page's rhythm differs, though).
45. Electric guitars often have two or more magnetic "pickups" that capture the vibration of the strings and transform it into amplified sound. The bridge pickup is the brightest of these, located right next to the bridge, where the strings are affixed to the body, and thus at their tensest.
46. Musicians would call this a pentatonic collection, very common in blues soloing.
47. Waksman, *Instruments of Desire*, 4.
48. Certain traditional musicians whom they lionized were a different matter, however. Bascom Lamar Lunsford, for example, was a "racist, anti-Semitic white supremacist," who refused to come to Newport because of Pete Seeger's communist sympathies. Van Ronk with Wald, *Mayor of MacDougal Street*, 30.
49. Quoted in Marcus, *The Old, Weird America*, 14. See also Hoskyns, *Across the Great Divide*, 91, and Wald, *Dylan Goes Electric!*, 217: "[Bloomfield] had no patience with people who considered electricity an adulteration of the tradition, and was outraged that [John Lee] Hooker and [Muddy] Waters had been encouraged to play acoustic guitars at their Newport workshop sets."

50. See Wald, *Dylan Goes Electric!*, 205–7 and 224–25.
51. Wald, *Dylan Goes Electric!*, 219–23.
52. To be clear, I am not suggesting that fans thought Dylan was playing Bloomfield's leads: there were too many guitar players in the audience to be fooled by that. Anyone sitting close enough to see Dylan's open-position D chord would know that his was not the guitar emitting those wailing bends.
53. See "Bob Dylan's Controversial Electric Guitar Sold for Almost $1m," *The Guardian*, December 6, 2013, bit.ly/GuardianStrat.

CHAPTER SEVEN

1. This was, incidentally, the first time Dylan had performed this 1967 song live. That newness may well have contributed to the bad harmonica choice. He flubs quite a few of the lyrics, too. A terminological note: musicians refer to the harmonica by various alternate names, among them "mouth organ," "mouth harp," "French harp" (though it's of German origin), or simply "harp." Dylan plays a standard ten-hole diatonic harmonica, which players often call a "blues harp." I use the terms *harmonica* and *harp* interchangeably throughout this chapter.
2. It's an understandable mistake: second-position cross harp calls for a harmonica tuned a perfect fifth below the governing key; Dylan has chosen one a perfect fifth *above*.
3. This is the very question Greil Marcus encourages us to ask in *The Old, Weird America*, 53.
4. For a recent, insightful example, see Starr, *Listening to Bob Dylan*, 33–46.
5. A free-reed aerophone produces sound as air passes over a reed that vibrates freely. By contrast, a fixed reed vibrates against a hard surface, like a saxophone mouthpiece. For more on free and fixed reeds, as well as a discussion of the harmonica's ancestors, see Field, *Harmonicas, Harps, and Heavy Breathers*, 19–25, my source for this section. For more on the European reception of the *sheng* specifically, see Raz, "How the *Sheng* Became a Harp." For additional information on the harmonica's history and antecedents, see Pat Missin's online articles at www.patmissin.com. Thank you to Joe Filisko for pointing me to this resource.
6. A similar free-reed instrument also emerged around this time: the diatonic accordion. It produces the same notes as a diatonic harmonica, the pitch changing depending on whether one is pushing or pulling the bellows. Thank you to Joe Filisko for stressing this connection.
7. Field, *Harmonicas, Harps, and Heavy Breathers*, 13 and 14.
8. Licht, "Harmonica Magic," 211.
9. Depending on which holes you draw, this may also be a dominant ninth or a half-diminished seventh. No matter: these chords are all more or less equivalent in tonal harmony.
10. As Jonathan De Souza puts it, "the harmonica musicalizes respiration." De Souza, *Music at Hand*, 54.
11. Licht, "Harmonica Magic," 211.
12. Field, *Harmonicas, Harps, and Heavy Breathers*.

13. Alas, the gendering is all too accurate. As Field notes, "the professional harmonica realm is unrelentingly male." *Harmonicas, Harps, and Heavy Breathers*, 66.
14. Dylan saw Fuller play in Denver in 1958; most scholars speculate that this was his first encounter with a harmonica rack. (The rack was only one contraption among several in Fuller's remarkable one-man band, which also included a pedal-operated upright bass that he called a "fotdella.") Dylan claims he found his first real harmonica rack in a music-store basement in Minneapolis, having previously used a bent coat hanger (*CV1*, 256–57).
15. De Souza, *Music at Hand*, 54.
16. This is the same show we discussed in chapter 4, in connection with "I Don't Believe You" and the infamous "Judas!" shout, available on *The Bootleg Series*, vol. 4.
17. For an account of Dylan's modernism in this era, with a particular focus on Rimbaud, see Hampton, *Bob Dylan*, 83–117.
18. In this style, as Michael Licht notes, "a 'chugging' alternation of draw and blow chords, changing so rapidly as to produce percussive reed effects, is used to represent a locomotive, often accelerating and decelerating." Licht, "Harmonica Magic," 217. Licht observes that the train style is one of two common mimetic techniques on the instrument. The other is the fox chase, which is less relevant to Dylan's playing.
19. Dylan encountered that headlong rush in the first pages of Woody Guthrie's *Bound for Glory*, a vividly onomatopoetic account of hobo train travel.
20. Starr, *Listening to Bob Dylan*, 39. Starr goes on to mention "Midnight Special" as a classic instance of a train song. What he does not mention is that Dylan's first recording gig in New York was as harmonica player on Harry Belafonte's recording of that very song. Though Belafonte's loping shuffle rules out vigorous chugging, Dylan finds various ingenious ways to work in train-like rhythmic tattoos and bent pitches, as evidenced by the fascinating outtakes from the session, which circulate unofficially and are discussed below.
21. Christopher Ricks offers a reading of "Mr. Tambourine Man" that is finely attuned to its thematics of motion and stasis. See his *Dylan's Visions of Sin*, 136–44. See also Aidan Day's *Jokerman*, 19–28, a sensitive account of the centrality of artistic inspiration in the song.
22. The story goes that the original "Tambourine Man" was studio musician Bruce Langhorne, whose large tambourine inspired Dylan's central image for the song. See *MUtM*, 138–41, which includes photos of the tambourine and Langhorne playing it. Langhorne does play on the studio recording of "Mr. Tambourine Man," but not tambourine; he plays a gently undulating electric guitar instead. There *is* a tambourine in the Byrds' famous recording, which complements the jingle-jangle already created by Roger McGuinn's chiming twelve-string electric.
23. It is much easier to bend while drawing than blowing, and it is easier to bend on the lower holes than the higher ones.
24. It is admittedly an unusual blues formally: fifteen-and-a-half bar verses rather than the usual twelve, with an unusual descending chord progression in its second half. But the blues groove is unmistakable.
25. One can even hear Dylan say, "When we get done, I'm gonna dub in the harmonica," on *The Bootleg Series*, vol. 12: *The Cutting Edge 1965–1966*, Collector's Edition: CD 1, track 26.

26. The distortion increases over the course of the track, suggesting Johnston may have controlled it at the mixing board.
27. This description comes from Joe Filisko, in personal communication.
28. Marcus, *The Old, Weird America*, xviii.
29. This recalls the discussion of co-presence and melodic invention in chapter 5.
30. Powers, "Gender and Sexuality," 269.
31. Mackinnon, *The Jupiter Collisions*, 26–27.
32. For a suggestive discussion of the influence of Dylan's childhood soundscape on his music, see Negus, *Bob Dylan*, 12–18. See also the passages from *Chronicles, Volume One* that Negus cites: *CV1*, 31, 230, 273–74.
33. Johnson, "Bob Dylan Master Harpist part 2," from the blog *Untold Dylan*, April 17, 2019, bit.ly/MasterHarpist2.
34. Meyer, *Emotion and Meaning in Music*.
35. "Anyone else get kinda choked up at the end of Girl from the North Country?," bit.ly/GftNCharp. The original poster is u/chowder138, and the response is from kevinciviced7.
36. Starr, *Listening to Bob Dylan*, 38, 41.
37. Williams, *Bob Dylan, Performing Artist: The Middle Years*, 218.
38. Williams, *Bob Dylan, Performing Artist: The Early Years*, 24.
39. The Shakespeare reference is to Hamlet's comment to Horatio in act 5, scene 2 that "there is special providence in the fall of a sparrow." See also Matthew 10:29–30.
40. *The Bootleg Series*, vols. 1–3: *Rare and Unreleased*. He also performed a fine version at the Gaslight on October 15, 1962.
41. For guitarists, the shift is from an A-minor chord (with the capo at the fourth fret, creating C♯ minor) to a C/G chord. Dylan merely moves his third finger from the third string, second fret (above the capo) to the sixth string, third fret.
42. Analysts of vernacular and popular music sometimes refer to this situation as a "melodic–harmonic divorce." See Temperley, "The Melodic–Harmonic 'Divorce' in Rock," and Nobile, "Counterpoint in Rock Music: Unpacking the 'Melodic–Harmonic Divorce.'" Alternatively, one can hear G♯ and B as *part* of the A chord, turning it into a tender major 9th.
43. On melodic paraphrase in Dylan's harmonica playing, see Starr, *Listening to Bob Dylan*, 33–46.
44. The transcriptions in figure 7.3 are simplified, removing blurred adjacent pitches on neighboring holes, of which there are quite a few. I have not repeated the harmonic tablature for repeated notes, to lessen clutter.
45. The overall gesture is an instance of the shout-and-fall schema, which I discuss in chapter 5.

CHAPTER EIGHT

1. Bobby initially quit after one lesson with his cousin Harriet Rutstein, but then, after hearing Little Richard, resumed with a different teacher, Clarabelle Hamilton. Heylin, *Behind the Shades*, 15. David was the better student, as I will discuss below.

2. Engel, *Just like Bob Zimmerman's Blues*, 85; Marcus, "Hibbing High School," 5. As Marcus notes, the town's good fortune in the early twentieth century was due in large part to aggressive taxation of US Steel. When that tax burden eased under a new mayor, the town's fortunes predictably reversed course. The decrease in ore demand after the war played a role, too.
3. Harry Truman even knew of it: "I know Hibbing. . . . That's where the high school has gold doorknobs." Marcus, "Hibbing High School," 5; Engel, *Just like Bob Zimmerman's Blues*, 95.
4. *CV1*, 124–25. The auditorium was in fact modeled on New York's Capitol Theatre. As Stephen Scobie put it in 2003, "Every stage that Bob Dylan has played on over the forty-plus years since has been, after the Hibbing High School auditorium, an anticlimax." Scobie, *Alias Bob Dylan Revisited*, 18.
5. Chiat, "Jewish Homes on the Range," 17; Engel, *Just like Bob Zimmerman's Blues*, 15.
6. Larry Fabbro, guitarist in the group, confirmed the setlist in a March 4, 2003, article in the *Brainerd Dispatch*: "Guitar Donation Highlights a Bit of Bob Dylan History." See bit.ly/BrainerdDispatchDylan57. The article gives the group's name as the Cashmeres, but most sources have it as the Shadow Blasters. Either way, Fabbro indicates that Dylan made up the band's name on the spot at the request of the show's organizers.
7. Recollections about the two concerts vary, and memories of them seem to have gotten jumbled, the same event (like Bobby breaking the piano pedal) sometimes attributed to 1957, at other times to 1958, depending on whom one asks. See Wald, *Dylan Goes Electric!*, 41.
8. Wald, *Dylan Goes Electric!*, 280–82. *DL1*, 351.
9. See the photo and caption in *MUtM*, 37.
10. "Guitar Donation."
11. Thompson, *Positively Main Street*, 49. While the "school-system officials" and "Iron Range dignitaries" might be Thompson's fanciful embellishment, the *Brainerd Dispatch* article does say that the 1957 variety show was repeated for community members in the evening.
12. Scaduto and Trudeau, *Dylan Tapes*, 14. I've adjusted one word in the quote, substituting "stomping" for "something" in the first sentence; the latter is seemingly a mis-transcription from the interview audio. It is not obvious from the interview whether Helstrom is speaking of the 1957 or 1958 performance. She and Bobby dated in both years, attending the junior prom a few months after the 1958 gig. Gray, *Dylan Encyclopedia*, 305.
13. Heylin, *Behind the Shades*, 16.
14. "Guitar Donation."
15. Heylin, *Behind the Shades*, 16. See also *DL1*, 163.
16. Novelty songs were a relatively well-defined genre in the late '50s, including hits like "Transfusion" and "Ape Call" by Nervous Norvus, and "Charlie Brown" and "Yakety Yak" by the Coasters. Note also the mislabeling of the group as a quintet; the Shadow Blasters had only three members.
17. Toby Thompson, who visited the high school a decade later, refers to the "steady flow of starched chinos, monogrammed sweaters, and looseleaf notebooks" that "whisked

by [him] in restless satisfaction. Things couldn't have changed much." Thompson, *Positively Main Street*, 45.

18. *MUtM*, 35; Bell, *Once Upon a Time*, 103. Toby Thompson, who visited the school, says it was a Baldwin. Thompson, *Positively Main Street*, 49.
19. Heylin, *Behind the Shades*, 15. See also Engel, *Just like Bob Zimmerman's Blues*, 81.
20. *EI*, 375; *EMPW*, 1114. The Zollo interview was published in 1991.
21. *DL1*, 330.
22. Clinton Heylin states that Dylan played bits of "Phantom Engineer" (a.k.a. "It Takes a Lot to Laugh") for Wilson at this time. *DL1*, 330. There is no hint of that song in these clips.
23. Pennebaker shot at least one other clip of Dylan at the keyboard backstage, which made its way onto the extras on the Criterion release of *Dont Look Back*. This clip is again in G♭ major, but it differs from the others in its compound meter, loosely resembling a piano song of his from the previous year, "I'll Keep It with Mine." That song's first two lines were originally my subtitle for this section.
24. Dylan evidently finalized the song's chord progression back in the States at the home of Peter Yarrow (of Peter, Paul and Mary fame) the following month, June 1965. *MUtM*, 162. Yarrow would emcee Dylan's fateful electric concert at Newport a few weeks later.
25. Popularized by Ritchie Valens, "La Bamba" was in fact first a Mexican folk song.
26. On this (possibly apocryphal) accident, see Epstein, *The Ballad of Bob Dylan*, 180–81; Heylin, *Behind the Shades*, 277–68; *DL2*, 7–10 and 19; and *MUtM*, 195.
27. The instrument sold at auction for $217,600 in 2022. See "Bob Dylan: Played and Owned Personal Woodstock Piano (with Book)," Julien's, bit.ly/DylanPianoAuction.
28. His family's was a Gulbranson spinet (a short upright), which his father bought wholesale. Engel, *Just like Bob Zimmerman's Blues*, 81.
29. Thompson, *Positively Main Street*, 161.
30. These are "Time Passes Slowly," "Went to See the Gypsy," "Winterlude," "Sign on the Window," "The Man in Me," and "Father of Night." The instrument is also prominent on the Beat send-up "If Dogs Run Free," though Al Kooper, not Dylan, is playing.
31. This is evident in other piano-led songs from the preceding years. "Ballad of a Thin Man," for example, uses a chromatically descending bass progression that passes through a harmonic rarity in Dylan: an augmented triad (first heard at "with your pencil in your hand"). "Dear Landlord," from *John Wesley Harding*, is another example, its meandering chord progression departing from white-key C major in both the sharp and flat directions: an E7 chord on the sharp side (at "please don't put a price on my soul"), and a B♭-major triad on the flat side (underlying the line "I'm gonna give you all I've got to give").
32. For a study of the pastoral across Dylan's career, see Pichaske, *Songs of the North Country*, 105–43. Pichaske comments especially on Dylan's sensitivity to weather and landscape in many songs, an attentiveness he relates to the musician's Minnesota youth.
33. These include one with swirling organ from Al Kooper, released on *The Bootleg Series*, vol. 10, which all but quotes Joe Cocker's version of "With a Little Help from My

Friends." It was in fact labeled the "Mad Dogs & Englishmen" version on the studio log, after Cocker's tour from earlier that year. *DL2*, 137.

34. There's some confusion about the recording date, likely because the original session tapes are no longer extant (*DL2*, 131n). Heylin does not list this August 12, 1970, session in *Recording Sessions*, 84–85, instead putting the song's final take on June 2, 1970. Dundas (*Tangled Up in Tapes*, 51) and Björner ("1961 Concerts and Recording Sessions," bobserve, bit.ly/Olof1970) both say it was on August 12. Heylin seems to agree with them in *DL2*, 137n. But there he states that the "Mad Dogs & Englishmen" version *also* comes from this session, while *The Bootleg Series*, vol. 10, places that version on June 2. As I said, confusion. Still, a preponderance of evidence points to the album version being the eighth and final take on August 12, Dylan's last attempt at the song.
35. *DL2*, 132.
36. Released on *The Bootleg Series*, vol. 10: *Another Self Portrait* as "Time Passes Slowly #2 (Alternate Version)."
37. Ricks, *Dylan's Visions of Sin*, 125.
38. Dylan also plays piano on the studio version of "Pressing On," from 1980's *Saved*, but he is not the pianist on the studio release of "When He Returns" on the previous year's *Slow Train Coming*. The pianist on that track is Barry Beckett. A comparison of Beckett's florid gospel style with Dylan's deeply felt but simpler playing of the same song live is instructive, throwing Dylan's rough pianism into relief.
39. On the context for Dylan's decision to leave this track off *Infidels*, see *DL2*, 444–47.
40. For an excellent study of McTell's life, music, and Georgia environs, see Gray, *Hand Me My Travelin' Shoes*.
41. Also the name of a hotel in Red Wing, MN.
42. This outtake was released on a seven-inch 45-rpm record by Third Man Records, in coordination with *The Bootleg Series*, vol. 16: *Springtime in New York, 1980–1985*.
43. The first to circulate officially was the piano-and-guitar version that Dylan and Knopfler recorded on May 5, which was released on *The Bootleg Series*, vols. 1–3. A version with full band from April 11 is included on *The Bootleg Series*, vol. 16.
44. Dylan sometimes inserts an A♭4 after the dominant harmony, making it a momentary seventh chord.
45. Dylan varies the bass note underneath the B♭ chord in both legs of the progression, sometimes playing a D♮3, sometimes B♭3. The figure shows B♭3 in the *a* leg, which he most often plays when singing, and D♮3 in *b*, which clearly shows the chromatic descent.
46. The descent is chromatic in that it proceeds entirely by semitones, rather than the diatonic scale's combination of whole and half steps.
47. This version is available on *The Bootleg Series*, vol. 16.
48. This version of the song was released on *The Bootleg Series*, vols. 1–3. May 5 was the last *Infidels* session but one. On May 17 they returned to the studio to touch up "Neighborhood Bully."
49. Herron joined Dylan's band in 2005 and remained for nineteen years, until the summer of 2024. I have chosen the Roskilde concert because there is excellent fan-shot video showing Herron over Dylan's shoulder. The footage is actually of the large screen at the outdoor festival, on which Dylan and Herron were projected. But the

physical and musical proximity between them, Herron seated immediately behind Dylan's bench, was not unique to this concert.

50. Recall the discussion of the two Zimmerman boys in the first section of this chapter. Recall, too, that the melody of "Make You Feel My Love," which I analyzed in figure 5.7, traces a large-scale *descent* from A♭ to D♭. Dylan's solo figure here inverts that melodic progression.
51. On such conflicts between melody and harmony in popular music, see Temperley, "The Melodic–Harmonic 'Divorce' in Rock," and Nobile, "Counterpoint in Rock Music: Unpacking the 'Melodic–Harmonic Divorce.'"
52. My sincere thanks to Johnny Borgan, who sent me a clip of this version of the song just days after the Stockholm concert.
53. Drummer George Receli sits out, while bassist Tony Garnier discreetly bows his upright; Charlie Sexton's electric guitar is so tastefully restrained as to be all but inaudible.
54. I have included only the piano melody in figure 8.10. Dylan occasionally doubles it an octave below and/or adds some harmonic filler.
55. Dylan, *Philosophy of Modern Song*, 115.
56. Dylan, *Philosophy of Modern Song*, 115.
57. Jürgen Kloss writes persuasively on connections between "Girl from the North Country" and other Stephen Foster tunes on his website Just Another Tune: Songs and Their History (justanothertune.com): bit.ly/KlossGftNC.
58. Though the text for "Come Thou Fount" was penned in 1758 by English dissenter Robert Robinson, the American tune "Nettleton" did not appear in print until 1813, in *Wyeth's Repository of Sacred Music, Part Second.*
59. See the discussion of Richard Middleton and Umberto Eco in the vicinity of figure 5.6 in chapter 5.

CHAPTER NINE

1. *EMPW*, 1343; *EI*, 438.
2. Bronson, *Traditional Tunes of the Child Ballads*, 1:191–225. Bronson's collection also folds in the eleven examples found in Sharp, *Cecil Sharp's Collection of English Folk Songs*, 17–26.
3. Todd Harvey makes a similar observation. Harvey, *The Formative Dylan*, 4.
4. Cherlin and Gopinath, "Somewhere Down in the United States," 227–28.
5. Cherlin and Gopinath, "Somewhere Down in the United States," 227.
6. *CV1*, 244.
7. Philip Tagg, "Scotch Snaps: The Big Picture," bit.ly/TaggScotchSnapsText.
8. *NDH*, 1:17:01–07.
9. Wilentz, *Bob Dylan in America*, 12.
10. We could extend this chain back further to include Aunt Molly Jackson's version of "One Morning in May," which some authors claim is the basis for Guthrie's "1913 Massacre." See *DL1*, 39, and Arnold Rypens's discussion on his website The Originals: "Nightingale, The," bit.ly/RypensNightingale. "One Morning in May" dates back, in some form, to the seventeenth century, as discussed in Roud, *Folk Song in England*,

561–62 (see also Gammon, *Desire, Drink, and Death*, 52–53). Such a link would thus open a portal to a shadowy deep past of Dylan's tune. Nevertheless, the melodic similarity of Jackson's tune to Guthrie's—and thus to Dylan's—is shaky. On the 1935 field recording made by John Lomax (hearable at bit.ly/LomaxJackson), Jackson's melody begins by oscillating between $\hat{5}$ and $\hat{3}$, rather than simply holding $\hat{5}$ and descending; it also has a very different rhythm. Guthrie did admittedly have a personal connection to Aunt Molly Jackson in the years before the 1945 recording of "1913 Massacre" (see Klein, *Woody Guthrie*, 171), so there is perhaps *some* plausibility to the claim. But given the weak resemblance to Guthrie's resulting tune, any link from Aunt Molly Jackson to "Hard Rain" via Guthrie is tenuous at best.

11. Dylan also based his earlier "Song to Bonny" on Guthrie's "1913 Massacre," though no audio recording survives. See Heylin, *Revolution in the Air*, 33–34.
12. When I presented this material at the Bob Dylan conference in Tulsa in 2019, I played this clip during an A/V check as I was setting up. One early arrival heard it and said, "I'm convinced. Guess I don't have to stay for the talk."
13. On the racial implications of this detail of eye color, see Portelli, *Hard Rain*, 42–45.
14. On open/closed structures in a range of popular song forms, see Middleton, *Studying Popular Music*, 203–5.
15. Ian Bell speculates that he may also have encountered similar structures in the poems of Jacques Prévert, whose "J'en ai vu plusieurs," as translated by Lawrence Ferlinghetti, bears a strong resemblance to portions of "Hard Rain." See Bell, *Once Upon a Time*, 212–15.
16. *EI*, 6; *EMPW*, 52 offers a slightly different transcription of the interview.
17. The typescript differs from the final song in several respects, including the number of answers in each verse. On the *Freewheelin' Bob Dylan*, the successive verses embed five, seven, seven, six, and twelve answers.
18. Todd Harvey calls the technique "a hallmark of his original melodies." Harvey, *The Formative Dylan*, 64. To be sure, certain children's songs also have an iterative or accumulative structure, as do familiar carols like "The Twelve Days of Christmas." These nevertheless generally differ from Dylan's iterative songs in the regularity of their accumulation; Dylan's process is more variable (five lines in this verse, seven in that, and so on). Sumanth Gopinath discusses the importance of iterative structures in Dylan's expressly political songs in the mid-'60s in his unpublished MS "Dylan's Subroutines."
19. See Middleton, *Studying Popular Music*, 207–11.
20. Christopher Ricks has written virtuosically about this. See his *Dylan's Visions of Sin*, 221–22.
21. By "quasi-modality" I am thinking of the song's avoidance of the tonally purposeful IV and V chords in the opening and iterative core in favor of the more neutral circling progression I–vi–iii, which creates a sense of Old World modal stasis. The melody in this section is also pentatonic, reinforcing the musical archaism. When the chorus rolls around, with its withering indictment in the second person ("You who philosophize disgrace"), we enter the land of purposeful tonality. The progression is full of IVs and Vs, and the melodic descends through every step of the major scale before cadencing on $\hat{1}$ for the first time at "now ain't the time for your tears."
22. *CV1*, 33.

23. The figure includes only one lyric snippet for each stage, though there is some doubling back and repeating in Orbison's ascent.
24. Marcus, *Folk Music*, 131.
25. Ross, *Listen to This*, 289.

CHAPTER TEN

1. For an additional analytical perspective on this guitar part, which has overlap with mine, see Koozin, *Embodied Expression in Popular Music*, 144–47.
2. See Bell, *Once Upon a Time*, 219. Scorsese's *No Direction Home* makes the point nicely by juxtaposing Dylan's raucous "Sally Gal" with a Columbia promotional clip of Mathis singing "A Lovely Way to Spend an Evening," Mitch Miller conducting (*NDH*, 59:18–1:00:14).
3. Guitarists also often label such chords with slashes, for example, G/D and A/D, both of which indicate that D continues to sound in the bass. I have adopted the asterisk notation for its compactness.
4. For an in-depth exploration of Dylan's metric flexibility, see the many discussions of his music in Murphy, *Times a-Changin'*.
5. Rockwell, "Time on the Crooked Road."
6. Quoted in Heylin, *Behind the Shades*, 82, which also notes Dylan's highlighting of the passage. Tellingly, the three-plus-four hypermeter from "Hard Rain" also undergirds much of "Song to Woody," further evidence that "Hard Rain" emerged at least in part from the sounding actions of the earlier song. Nevertheless, Dylan is more flexible with the meter in "Song to Woody," drawing out certain syllables in exactly the manner that Seeger discusses, bending the hypermeter to follow his voice. Listen, for example, to the final line of the first verse (0:26–0:32): "Your pauperrrrrrrrs and peasants and princes and kings." Such flexible extensions abound in Guthrie's 1945 performance of "1913 Massacre"; Guthrie's guitar playing nevertheless shows no signs of Dylan's idiosyncratic three-plus-four hypermeter.
7. The misstep is at the beginning of verse 4 (3:44–3:56 on the *Freewheelin'* release). Perhaps as a result of stumbling over the words of the first question (Dylan sings "what did you meet" rather than "who did you meet"), he contracts the opening harmonic rhythm to three-plus-three as he seeks to regain his footing. When singing the second question he laughs slightly, signaling his awareness of the verbal slip. Remarkably, after the second question, Dylan *adds* a bar to the hypermeter, effectively compensating for the missed bar after the previous line. This was very likely a felicitous accident, but classical musicians will nevertheless recognize in it a surprisingly exact example of the technique of *rubato*—stealing time from one musical moment and paying it back in another.

CHAPTER ELEVEN

1. The principal sources for information on Dylan's performances are Olof Björner's "Still on the Road" web page (bobserve.com/olof/); Krogsgaard, *Positively Bob Dylan*; and Dundas, *Tangled Up in Tapes*. Björner is the acknowledged authority. Heylin's

Bob Dylan: A Life in Stolen Moments also provides valuable information about Dylan's day-to-day activities until 1995, including much corroborating information regarding concerts. Dylan's own website (bobdylan.com) purports to provide set lists and counts of song performances, but its information is incomplete and often unreliable. In surveying performances of "Hard Rain" I have relied primarily on Björner, supplementing and cross-checking with the other sources as necessary. As Björner focuses on performances that have circulating recordings or preserved set lists, there are some gaps in his accounting, especially for the early years. The entries for 1962–64, both total concerts and "Hard Rain" performances, are thus surely undercounts.

2. This is merely one heuristic periodization of Dylan's career, based on his performance activity. For a different periodization, see Scobie, *Alias Bob Dylan Revisited*, 20–26.
3. The onset of the NET also coincides roughly with Dylan's discovery of a mysterious "new vocal technique," which he discusses in *CV1*, 145–62. See also Eyolf Østrem's illuminating discussion of this passage at "What I learned from Lonnie," Dylanchords, bit.ly/OstremMath.
4. Fans debate whether or not the tour continues, with some arguing that the Never-Ending Tour in fact ended in 2020 as a result of the COVID-19 pandemic. I have reflected the ambivalence with a dashed line in figure 11.1.
5. For a compelling and entertaining personal account of Dylan's music making and stage manner in the Never-Ending Tour (through 2011), see Muir, *One More Night*.
6. *CV1*, 219. See also Sloman, notes to *The Bootleg Series*, vol. 8, 18–26. Dylan's renewed fascination with a wide range of early- to mid-twentieth-century vernacular musics was amply in evidence on his radio show, *The Theme Time Radio Hour*, which ran on Sirius XM from 2006 to 2009.
7. Dylan sang the song only once on that tour, as we will hear.
8. McKenzie, *Bob Dylan: On a Couch*, 78–80 (quote on 78).
9. McKenzie, *Bob Dylan: On a Couch*, 85.
10. Terkel's program was likely taped on April 26, 1963, and aired on May 1. See *EMPW*, 51, on questions of dating. For the exchange on "Hard Rain," see *EMPW*, 52. Cott edits out this exchange in *EI*, 6. One can hear it on the recording of the show, which circulates widely.
11. The reader can hear this exchange on *The Bootleg Series*, vol. 12: *The Cutting Edge*, deluxe edition, disc 2, track 17.
12. These numbers derive from the same sources and method discussed in n. 1 of the chapter.
13. Harvey, *The Formative Dylan*, 3.
14. This was about seven months before the performance at the McKenzie's discussed above, which occurred in April 1963. This earlier, September 20, 1962, rendition in their home was not necessarily Dylan's very first performance of the song. He may well have premiered it at the Gaslight earlier that month, as Paxton's anecdote at the beginning of the introduction suggests. Heylin has stated that he played it as part of an (uncirculating) three-song set at the club that September. See Heylin, *Bob Dylan: A Life in Stolen Moments*, 32.
15. Some sources list a single, uncirculating performance on March 17, 1965, at the Syria Mosque in Pittsburgh, a double bill with Joan Baez.

16. Greene, *Here Comes the Sun*, 191.
17. RS Editors, "The George Harrison Bangladesh Benefit," *Rolling Stone*, September 2, 1971, bit.ly/RSBangladesh.
18. Cott, "I Dreamed I Saw Bob Dylan," *Rolling Stone*, September 2, 1971, bit.ly/CottBangladesh.
19. Cott, "I Dreamed I Saw Bob Dylan," bit.ly/CottBangladesh.
20. Williams, *Bob Dylan, Performing Artist: The Early Years*, 263. Present-day fans continue to rave about the recording. Two posts from expectingrain.com: "He's in fine voice. What an astonishing performance. . . . he sings like an angel. True and pure." Posted by Richard—W on June 8, 2015. bit.ly/2yCtjPS. "At the Concert For Bangladesh Dylan's voice was 'cracking' like a real country singer, and I love every second of it. One of my favorite of his vocal incarnations." Posted by plainsgrizzly on December 5, 2006. bit.ly/2wh1BXc.
21. Williams, *Bob Dylan, Performing Artist: The Early Years*, 263.
22. Crowe, liner notes to *Biograph*, 24 (CD booklet), 22 (LP booklet); *EMPW*, 862.
23. "Bob Dylan/The Band," Robert Christgau, bit.ly/ChristgauOnBeforeTheFlood.
24. This is his first departure from D-major chord shapes for the song. He strums simple open-position G, C, and D chords, among the first chords that any guitarist learns.
25. Joan Baez to *Rolling Stone*, December 8, 1975: Chet Flippo, Ben Fong-Torres, Iris Brown, Bob Wallace, and Larry Stoman, "Bob Dylan Tour Snowballs: 'It's Not a Nightclub Show,'" December 8, 1975, bit.ly/RSRollingThunder.
26. On the many relationships between Carné's film, *Renaldo and Clara*, and the Rolling Thunder Revue, see Wilentz, *Bob Dylan in America*, 131–71, and Griffin, *Shelter from the Storm*, 101–4. In Martin Scorsese's semifictional 2019 film *Rolling Thunder Revue: A Bob Dylan Story*, Dylan claims that the face paint was an inspiration from the band Kiss.
27. Yaffe, *Bob Dylan: Like a Complete Unknown*, 78.
28. Leeder, "Haunting and Minstrelsy," 185. For additional accounts of Dylan's relationship to race, minstrelsy, and appropriation, see Nielsen, "Crow Jane Approximately" and Reginio, "'Nettie Moore'."
29. Willie Dixon wrote "Hoochie Coochie Man," the first song to use the stop-time lick, in 1953; Muddy Waters recorded it in January 1954. "I'm a Man" and "Mannish Boy" followed in the next year; Elvis's songwriters Lieber and Stoller adopted the tag for "Trouble" in 1958. In Dylan's version of the lick, shown in figure 11.4, there is a bluesy clash between C♯ in the guitar part and C♮ in Rob Stoner's bass. The two pitches sounding at once combine for a spiky, composite blue $\hat{3}$. (This clash disappears when Stoner occasionally plays an alternate figure here, which ascends from low E.)
30. The rehearsal is also in a different key, G. The concert version is in A. The rehearsal may be heard on the box set *The Rolling Thunder Revue: The 1975 Live Recordings*, disc 2, track 2.
31. This version is available on *The Bootleg Series*, vol. 5: *Live 1975: The Rolling Thunder Revue*.
32. Indeed, Dylan sometimes began his first Rolling Thunder set wearing a clear Nixon mask over his whiteface—a literal overlaying of two masks—singing "While I Paint My Masterpiece" alongside Bob Neuwirth.
33. *DL2*, 270–79; Griffin, *Shelter from the Storm*, 185–205.

34. This was the penultimate show of the tour, and the entire year. Two nights later the Revue performed its final concert in Salt Lake City. No recording circulates.
35. Griffin, *Shelter from the Storm*, 207.
36. Sid Griffin sees "a rather concerned, almost sinister, and somewhat underfed, Old Testament prophet." Griffin, *Shelter from the Storm*, 211.
37. Heylin, *Behind the Shades*, 473; Spitz, *Dylan: A Biography*, 521–22; Sounes, *Down the Highway*, 315.
38. *EMPW*, 549; *EI*, 225.
39. Sounes, *Down the Highway*, 316.
40. *DL2*, 303; Sounes, *Down the Highway*, 316. Sounes adds the stunning anecdote that, on receiving the telegram, Dylan "sent guitar technician Joel Bernstein to a bookstore to buy a copy of *Writings and Drawings* [the first publication of Dylan's lyrics, published in 1973]. 'He started flipping through it [and] playing things out of it that he hadn't played in years.'"
41. This version is available on *The Complete Budokan 1978* and the shorter *Another Budokan 1978*.
42. I had long been certain this was David Mansfield playing the mandolin, but Ray Padgett learned in an interview with Mansfield that it was in fact Soles. Thank you to Padgett for sharing this detail with me.
43. The lavish booklet for *The Complete Budokan 1978*, released in 2023, further attests to the warmth that Japanese fans still feel toward Dylan as a result of his visit there. The original 1978 *Live at Budokan* was one of Dylan's most derided releases at the time, though its critical fortunes have improved somewhat in the decades since.
44. Barker, *20 Years of Isis*, 218.
45. With one change: he adopts the slower, every-four-bars rhythm of the "it's a hard" iterations, as in 1976. The German fans soon catch on, adding their voices to his in each refrain.

CHAPTER TWELVE

1. Three-plus-two nevertheless predominates, rather than the three-plus-four of the 1962 studio rendition.
2. Wald, "Gospel Music," 88. For a compelling study of the musical means gospel artists use to ignite the spirit, see Shelley, *Healing for the Soul*.
3. For a similar point, see Wald, "Gospel Music," 94.
4. When "Hard Rain" returned to setlists in fall 1981, Carolyn Dennis was replaced in the lineup by her mother, Madelyn Quebec.
5. Booklet for *Bootleg Series*, vol. 13, 43. For an example of Dylan and King's tight harmonizing, listen especially to their extraordinary duet on "Abraham, Martin, and John" on the same *Bootleg Series* release. A video of another performance is on the *Trouble No More* DVD, which accompanies the deluxe version of the set.
6. Ray Padgett, "Regina McCrary Talks about Singing Gospel with Bob Dylan," Flagging Down the Double E's, November 1, 2021, bit.ly/McCraryPadgett.
7. Inexplicably—and disappointingly—when the song returned to setlists in fall 1981, the every-four rhythm remained but the antiphonal alternation did not. The vocalists now

sing with and behind each of Dylan's "it's a hard" iterations, rather than in alternation with him. It's a loss, both of the electrifying effect of the antiphonal exchange in 1980, and of the singers' relative autonomy in the song, their voices now covered by his.

8. Wald, "Gospel Music," 93.
9. On this stereotype, see Monson, *Freedom Sounds*, 284–87.
10. Wald, "Gospel Music," 96.
11. *CV1*, 147–48.
12. The chorus of "Just Like a Woman" is an especially vivid example: the audience often sings the tune from the *Blonde on Blonde* version, but Dylan typically waits until they're done, delivering the title phrase in a late burst.
13. *CV1*, 148.
14. For additional information on the concerts and all the planning that went into them, see Ray Padgett's interview with Hollingsworth: Ray Padgett, "30 Years Ago Today, Bob Dylan Sang with a 64-Piece Japanese Orchestra," Flagging Down the Double E's, May 20, 2024, bit.ly/PadgettNara.
15. Interview with Michael Kamen during the televised broadcast ("The Great Music Experience: Japan 1994," YouTube, March 21, 2013, bit.ly/Nara1994; interview begins at 59:47).
16. My thinking and notation here are indebted to Leonard Meyer's theory of melodic expectation. See especially his *Explaining Music*.
17. This moment coincides with an artful bit of reharmonization in Kamen's arrangement: the bass instruments, rather than resolving from B♭ to the tonic E♭, ascend to a deceptive C, which supports a minor harmony. Dylan seems sensitive to this reharmonization: he often ascends to the high E♭ when it sounds.
18. As reported on Tony Hollingsworth's website (Peter Elman, "The Great Music Experience," bit.ly/HollingsworthNara).
19. *EMPW*, 54; *EI*, 7.
20. It bears noting that two performances from this era are in a different key. On the fall 2013 European tour, Dylan played "Hard Rain" twice: in Milan on November 4, and Padua on November 8. Both times it is in G major. This experiment—perhaps an attempt to descend yet lower to accommodate Dylan's voice—did not stick. By the following year the song is back to B♭.

AFTERWORD

1. Douglas Brinkley, "Bob Dylan Has a Lot on His Mind," *New York Times*, June 12, 2020: nyti.ms/48JHS3P.
2. It is worth noting, though, that many of the backing musicians whom Ray Padgett interviews in *Pledging My Time* refer to the jazz-like aspects of playing with Dylan. I suspect these musicians are referring primarily to the spontaneity of the performance environment, not to the specifics of the musical style. Percussion Gary Burke, who played on Rolling Thunder 2.0 in 1976, says as much: "The most common question I get is, 'What's it like to play with Dylan?' I say, 'Oh, it was the greatest jazz gig I ever played.' People look at me like I'm crazy. I don't mean stylistically it was like a jazz gig,

but in terms of the mindset. It was very spontaneous. You never knew where he's going to go. You weren't given directions ahead of time." Padgett, *Pledging My Time*, 176–77.

3. On the humor in "Desolation Row," especially evident to its first audiences, see Hewitt, "How Long Can We Falsify," *Dylan Review* 5, no. 1 (Spring/Summer 2023): bit.ly/HewittDylanHumor.
4. See Ray Padgett's excellent blog post on variety in Dylan's setlists across his career: "A Deep Dive Into Bob Dylan Setlist Data," Flagging Down the Double E's, December 17, 2023, bit.ly/PadgettSetlists.
5. In his return to touring after the pandemic, for the *Rough and Rowdy Ways* tour, setlists were once again pretty static, though they show a slightly higher statistical variation, particularly due to varied covers in 2023. See "A Deep Dive Into Bob Dylan Setlist Data," bit.ly/PadgettSetlists. With the Outlaw Tour of summer 2024, Dylan returned to much more variable setlists.
6. Bob Dylan, *Fallen Angels*, bit.ly/ErlewineFallenAngels.
7. On this subject, see Ray Padgett's fascinating exploration of variation in arrangement and delivery across the *Rough and Rowdy Ways* tour, with its largely static setlist: "Rough and Rowdy Ways Tour Finale II: The Arrangements," Flagging Down the Double E's, April 9, 2024, bit.ly/PadgettRRW.
8. There is much to say about the relationship of these observations to the question of "late style" in Dylan, building on Adorno and Said. Thankfully, Franz Nicolay has already explored this issue better than I could. See his fine essay "Love, Death & Knock-Knock Jokes," *Spectrum Culture*, July 22, 2009, bit.ly/NicolayLateStyle.
9. For more on the everyday uses Westerners make of music, see DeNora, *Music in Everyday Life*.
10. *DL2*, 227. I have removed Heylin's editorial additions to the quote.
11. Most often one hears fans rhapsodize about the buttons on Dylan's vest clacking on the back of the guitar in these sessions. For a compelling study of listeners' emotional attachment to such sounds in the world of recorded classical music, see Beaudoin, *Sounds as They Are*.

REFERENCES

Anthony, Ted. *Chasing the Rising Sun: The Journey of an American Song*. Simon and Schuster, 2007.

Barker, Derek, ed. *20 Years of Isis: Anthology Volume 2*. Chrome Dreams, 2005.

Barthes, Roland. "The Grain of the Voice." In Barthes, *Image–Music–Text*, 179–89. Hill and Wang, 1977.

Beaudoin, Richard. *Sounds as They Are: The Unwritten Music in Classical Recordings*. Oxford University Press, 2024.

Bell, Ian. *Once Upon a Time: The Lives of Bob Dylan*. Pegasus, 2012.

Bennett, Jane. *The Enchantment of Modern Life: Attachments, Crossings, and Ethics*. Princeton University Press, 2001.

Bernstein, Robin. "Dances with Things: Material Culture and the Performance of Race." *Social Text 101* 27, no. 4 (2009): 67–94.

Bickford, Tyler. "Music of Poetry and Poetry of Song: Expressivity and Grammar in Vocal Performance." *Ethnomusicology* 51 (2007): 439–76.

Bicknell, Jeanette. *Philosophy of Song and Singing*. Routledge, 2015.

Bloom, Harold. *The Anxiety of Influence: A Theory of Poetry*. 2nd ed. Oxford University Press, 1997. First edition published by Oxford in 1973.

Bloom, Harold. *A Map of Misreading*. Oxford University Press, 1975.

Bourdieu, Pierre. *The Field of Cultural Production*. Columbia University Press, 1993.

Bowden, Betsy. *Performed Literature: Words and Music by Bob Dylan*. 2nd ed. University Press of America, 2001.

Brackett, David. *Categorizing Sound: Genre and Twentieth-Century Popular Music*. University of California Press, 2016.

Bronson, Bertrand. *Traditional Tunes of the Child Ballads*. Vol. 1. Princeton University Press, 1959.

Cantwell, Robert. *When We Were Good: The Folk Revival*. Harvard University Press, 1996.

Carrera, Alessandro. *La voce di Bob Dylan: Una spiegazione dell'America*. Feltrinelli, 2017.

Cavarero, Adriana. *For More than One Voice: Toward a Philosophy of Vocal Expression*. Translated by Paul A. Kottman. Stanford University Press, 2005.

Cherlin, Michael. *Schoenberg's Musical Imagination*. Cambridge University Press, 2007.

Cherlin, Michael, and Sumanth Gopinath. "'Somewhere Down in the United States': The Art of Bob Dylan's Ventriloquism." In *Highway 61 Revisited: Bob Dylan's Road from Minnesota to the World*, edited by Colleen J. Sheehy and Thomas Swiss, 225–36. University of Minnesota Press, 2009.

Chiat, Marilyn J. "Jewish Homes on the Range, 1890–1960." In *Highway 61 Revisited: Bob Dylan's Road from Minnesota to the World*, edited by Colleen J. Sheehy and Thomas Swiss, 15–24. University of Minnesota Press, 2009.

Child, Francis James. *The English and Scottish Popular Ballads*. 5 vols. Dover, 2003. Originally published from 1882 to 1898.

Cohen, David E. "'The Imperfect Seeks Its Perfection': Harmonic Progression, Directed Motion, and Aristotelian Physics." *Music Theory Spectrum* 23 (2001): 139–69.

Cohen, Ronald D. *Rainbow Quest: The Folk Music Revival and American Society, 1940–1970*. University of Massachusetts Press, 2002.

Cone, Edward T. *The Composer's Voice*. University of California Press, 1974.

Cossu, Andrea. *It Ain't Me, Babe: Bob Dylan and the Performance of Authenticity*. Paradigm, 2012.

Cott, Jonathan, ed. *Bob Dylan: The Essential Interviews*. Wenner, 2006. NB: I have used the first edition throughout. Pagination is slightly different in the 2017 second edition.

Crowe, Cameron. Liner notes to *Biograph*. Columbia C5X 38830 (LP) or C3K 65298 (CD), 1985. I have provided page numbers for both the LP and CD booklets, as the pagination varies.

Cusick, Suzanne G. "Gender and the Cultural Work of a Classical Music Performance." *repercussions* 3 (1994): 77–110.

Dale, Pete, and Adam Fairhall. "A Hipster Sneer: Dylan's Re-Coding of the Blue Third." Paper presented at *The World of Bob Dylan Symposium*, Tulsa, OK, June 2, 2019.

Daley, Michael. "'One Who Sings with His Tongue on Fire': Change, Continuity and Meaning in Bob Dylan's Vocal Style, 1960–66." Masters thesis, York University, 1997.

Dann, David. *Guitar King: Michael Bloomfield's Life in the Blues*. University of Texas Press, 2019.

Davidson, Mark, and Parker Fishel. *Bob Dylan: Mixing up the Medicine*. Callaway, 2023.

Day, Aidan. *Jokerman: Reading the Lyrics of Bob Dylan*. Basil Blackwell, 1988.

De Souza, Jonathan. *Music at Hand: Instruments, Bodies, and Cognition*. Oxford University Press, 2017.

Deleuze, Gilles. *Difference and Repetition*. Translated by Paul Patton. Columbia University Press, 1995.

Denning, Michael. "Bob Dylan and Rolling Thunder." In *The Cambridge Companion to Bob Dylan*, edited by Kevin J. H. Dettmar, 28–41. Cambridge University Press, 2009.

DeNora, Tia. *Music in Everyday Life*. Cambridge University Press, 2000.

Derrida, Jacques. *Of Grammatology*. Translated by Gayatri Chakravorty Spivak. Johns Hopkins University Press, 1998. First published (in French) in 1967.

Dolar, Mladen. *A Voice and Nothing More*. MIT Press, 2006.

Drott, Eric. "The End(s) of Genre." *Journal of Music Theory* 57 (2013): 1–45.

Dundas, Glen. *Tangled up in Tapes: A Recording History of Bob Dylan*. 4th ed. SMA Services, 1999.

Dylan, Bob. *Writings and Drawings*. Knopf, 1973.

Dylan, Bob. *Chronicles, Volume One*. Simon and Schuster, 2004.

Dylan, Bob. *Philosophy of Modern Song*. Simon and Schuster, 2022.

Eidsheim, Nina Sun. *The Race of Sound: Listening, Timbre, and Vocality in African American Music*. Duke University Press, 2019.

Engel, Dave. *Just like Bob Zimmerman's Blues: Dylan in Minnesota*. River City Memoirs-Mesabi, 1997.

Epstein, Daniel Mark. *The Ballad of Bob Dylan: A Portrait*. HarperCollins, 2011.

Evans, David. "Folk Revival Music." *Journal of American Folklore* 92, no. 363 (1979): 108–15.

Everett, Walter. *The Foundations of Rock: From Blue Suede Shoes to Suite: Judy Blue Eyes*. Oxford University Press, 2008.

Fabbri, Franco. "A Theory of Musical Genres: Two Applications." In *Popular Music Perspectives*, edited by David Horn and Philip Tagg, 52–81. IASPM, 1982.

Feldman, Martha. "Voice Gap Crack Break." In *The Voice as Something More*, edited by Martha Feldman and Judith T. Zeitlin, 188–208. University of Chicago Press, 2019.

Field, Kim. *Harmonicas, Harps and Heavy Breathers: The Evolution of the People's Instrument.* Cooper Square, 2000.

Filene, Benjamin. *Romancing the Folk: Public Memory and American Roots Music*. University of North Carolina Press, 2000.

Ford, Phil. *Dig: Sound and Music in Hip Culture*. Oxford University Press, 2013.

Frith, Simon. *Performing Rites: On the Value of Popular Music*. Harvard University Press, 1996.

Gallope, Michael. "The Sound of Repeating Life: Ethics and Metaphysics in Deleuze's Philosophy of Music." In *Sounding the Virtual: Gilles Deleuze and the Theory and Philosophy of Music*, edited by Nick Nesbitt and Brian Hulse, 77–102. Routledge, 2010.

Gammon, Vic. *Desire, Drink and Death in English Folk and Vernacular Song, 1600–1900*. Ashgate, 2008.

Gilmour, Michael J. *Tangled Up in the Bible: Bob Dylan and Scripture*. Continuum, 2004.

Gioia, Ted. *The Imperfect Art: Reflections on Jazz and Modern Culture*. Oxford University Press, 1988.

Gioia, Ted. "Jazz: The Aesthetics of Imperfection." *Hudson Review* 39 (1987): 585–600.

Gopinath, Sumanth. "Dylan's Speech: A Performative (and Musical) Poetics?" Paper presented at the annual meeting of the Society for Music Theory, Indianapolis, IN, November 5, 2010.

Gracyk, Ted. "Valuing and Evaluating Popular Music." *The Journal of Aesthetics and Art Criticism* 57 (1999): 205–20.

Gracyk, Ted. "'When I Paint My Masterpiece': What Sort of Artist Is Bob Dylan?" In *Bob Dylan and Philosophy: It's Alright, Ma (I'm Only Thinking)*, edited by Peter Vernezze and Carl J. Porter, 169–81. Open Court, 2006.

Graves, Robert. *The English Ballad: A Short Critical Survey*. Ernest Benn, 1927.

Gray, Michael. *The Bob Dylan Encyclopedia*. Continuum, 2006.

Gray, Michael. *Hand Me My Travelin' Shoes: In Search of Blind Willie McTell.* Bloomsbury, 2009.

Gray, Michael. *Song and Dance Man III: The Art of Bob Dylan*. Continuum, 2000.

Green, Emma. "Are Jews White?" *The Atlantic*, December 5, 2016.

Greene, Joshua M. *Here Comes the Sun: The Spiritual and Musical Journey of George Harrison*. Wiley, 2006.

Grier, James. "Ego and Alter Ego: Artistic Interaction between Bob Dylan and Roger McGuinn." In *Sounding Out Pop: Analytical Essays in Popular Music*, edited by Mark Spicer and John Covach, 42–62. University of Michigan Press, 2010.

Griffin, Sid. *Shelter from the Storm: Bob Dylan's Rolling Thunder Years*. Jawbone, 2010.

Griffiths, Dai. "Talking about 'License to Kill.'" In *The Dylan Companion*, edited by Elizabeth Thomson and David Gutman, 260–66. Macmillan, 1990.

Hajdu, David. *Positively 4th Street: The Lives and Times of Joan Baez, Bob Dylan, Mimi Baez-Fariña, and Richard Fariña*. Picador, 2001.

Hamilton, Jack. *Just Around Midnight: Rock and Roll and the Racial Imagination*. Harvard University Press, 2016.

Hampton, Timothy. *Bob Dylan: How the Songs Work*. Zone, 2019.

Harvey, Todd. *The Formative Dylan: Transmission and Stylistic Influences, 1961–1963*. Scarecrow, 2001.

Hedin, Benjamin, ed. *Studio A: The Bob Dylan Reader*. Norton, 2004.

Helm, Levon, with Stephen Davis. *This Wheel's on Fire: Levon Helm and the Story of The Band*. A Cappella, 2000.

Hewitt, Harrison. "How Long Can We Falsify and Deny What Is Real: Bob Dylan Is the Funniest Person Alive, and Why We Need to Talk about It." *Dylan Review* 5, no. 1 (2023), bit.ly/HewittDylanHumor.

Heylin, Clinton. *Behind the Shades: The 20th Anniversary Edition*. Faber and Faber, 2011.

Heylin, Clinton. *Bob Dylan: A Life in Stolen Moments. Day by Day: 1941–1995*. Schirmer, 1996.

Heylin, Clinton. *Bob Dylan: The Recording Sessions, 1960–1994*. St. Martin's, 1995.

Heylin, Clinton. *The Double Life of Bob Dylan*. Vol. 1, *A Restless, Hungry Feeling (1941–1966)*. Back Bay, 2021.

Heylin, Clinton. *The Double Life of Bob Dylan*. Vol. 2, *Far Away from Myself (1966–2021)*. Bodley Head, 2023.

Heylin, Clinton. *Judas!: From Forest Hills to the Free Trade Hall, A Historical View of the Big Boo*. Lesser Gods, 2016.

Heylin, Clinton. *Revolution in the Air: The Songs of Bob Dylan, 1957–1973*. Chicago Review Press, 2009.

Heylin, Clinton. *Trouble in Mind: Bob Dylan's Gospel Years—What Really Happened*. Route, 2017.

Heylin, Clinton, and Michelle Engert. "The Evolution of Fan Culture and the Impact of Technology on the Never Ending Tour." In *Refractions of Bob Dylan: Cultural Appropriations of an American Icon*, edited by Eugen Banauch, 207–21. Manchester University Press, 2015.

Hoskyns, Barney. *Across the Great Divide: The Band and America*. Hal Leonard, 2006.

Hughes, Glen. "Ulterior Significance in the Art of Bob Dylan." *Journal of Macrodynamic Analysis* 6 (2011): 18–40.

Hughes, John. *Invisible Now: Bob Dylan in the 1960s*. Ashgate, 2013.

Hulse, Brian. "Thinking Musical Difference." In *Sounding the Virtual: Gilles Deleuze and the Theory and Philosophy of Music*, edited by Nick Nesbitt and Brian Hulse, 23–50. Routledge, 2010.

Jarosinski, Artur, ed. *Every Mind Polluting Word*. 2nd ed. Don't Ya Tell Henry, 2006.

Jefferson, Margo. "Ripping Off Black Music." *Harper's*, January 1973.

Jones, Tudor. *Bob Dylan and the British Sixties: A Cultural History*. Routledge, 2019.

Kane, Brian. *Sound Unseen: Acousmatic Sound in Theory and Practice*. Oxford University Press, 2014.

Kane, Brian. "The Model Voice." *Journal of the American Musicological Society* 68 (2015): 671–77.

Kane, Brian. "The Voice: A Diagnosis." *Polygraph* 25 (2015): 91–112.

Karp, Jonathan. "A Foreign Song I Learned in Utah." *Jewish Review of Books* (Winter 2017). bit.ly/KarpOnDylan.

Kim-Cohen, Seth. *In the Blink of an Ear: Toward a Non-Cochlear Sonic Art*. Continuum, 2009.

Kinney, David. *The Dylanologists: Adventures in the Land of Bob*. Simon and Schuster, 2014.

Klein, Joe. *Woody Guthrie: A Life*. Delta, 1999.

Koozin, Timothy. *Embodied Expression in Popular Music: A Theory of Musical Gesture and Agency*. Oxford University Press, 2024.

Koozin, Timothy. "Guitar Voicing in Pop-Rock Music: A Performance-Based Analytical Approach." *MTO* 17, no. 3 (2011). bit.ly/KoozinGuitar.

Kreiman, Jody, and Diana Sidtis. *Foundations of Voice Studies: An Interdisciplinary Approach to Voice Production and Perception*. Wiley-Blackwell, 2011.

Krims, Adam. *Rap Music and the Poetics of Identity*. Cambridge University Press, 2000.

Krogsgaard, Michael. *Positively Bob Dylan: A Thirty-Year Discography, Concert, and Recording Session Guide, 1960–1991*. Popular Culture, inc. 1991. Revised and updated version of Krogsgaard, *Master of the Tracks: The Bob Dylan Reference Book of Recording*. Pierian Press, 1988.

Kronengold, Charles. *Living Genres in Late Modernity: American Music of the Long 1970s*. University of California Press, 2022.

Latham, Sean, ed. *The World of Bob Dylan*. Cambridge University Press, 2021.

Lee, C. P. *Like The Night (Revisited): Bob Dylan and the Road to the Manchester Free Trade Hall*. Helter Skelter, 2004.

Leeder, Murray. "Haunting and Minstrelsy in Bob Dylan's *Masked and Anonymous*." *Journal of Popular Film and Television* 40 (2012): 181–91.

Lena, Jennifer C. *Banding Together: How Communities Create Genres in Popular Music*. Princeton University Press, 2012.

Lerner, Murray, dir. *Festival!* Eagle Rock, 1967.

Licht, Michael S. "Harmonica Magic: Virtuoso Display in American Folk Music." *Ethnomusicology* 24 (1980): 211–21.

List, George. "The Boundaries of Speech and Song." *Ethnomusicology* 7 (1963): 1–16.

Lott, Eric. *Love and Theft: Blackface Minstrelsy and the American Working Class*. 20th-anniversary edition. Oxford University Press, 2013.

Lubet, Alex. "Listening to Bob Dylan." *Cognitive Critique* 5 (2012): 37–58.

MacColl, Ewan, et al. "Topical Songs and Folksinging, 1965: A Symposium." In *The American Folk Scene: Dimensions of the Folksong Revival*, edited by David A. De Turk and A. Poulin Jr., 150–66. Dell, 1967. The symposium was originally published in the September 1965 issue of *Sing Out!*

Mackinnon, Lachlan. *The Jupiter Collisions.* Faber and Faber, 2003.

Mahon, Maureen. *Black Diamond Queens: African American Women and Rock and Roll.* Duke University Press, 2020.

Malawey, Victoria. "An Analytic Model for Examining Cover Songs and Their Sources." In *Pop-Culture Pedagogy in the Music Classroom: Teaching Tools from American Idol to YouTube*, edited by Nicole Biamonte, 203–32. Scarecrow, 2010.

Malawey, Victoria. *A Blaze of Light in Every Word: Analyzing the Popular Singing Voice.* Oxford University Press, 2020.

Marcus, Greil. *Bob Dylan by Greil Marcus: Writings 1968–2010.* PublicAffairs, 2010.

Marcus, Greil. *Folk Music: A Bob Dylan Biography in Seven Songs.* Yale University Press, 2022.

Marcus, Greil. "Hibbing High School and 'the Mystery of Democracy.'" In *Highway 61 Revisited: Bob Dylan's Road from Minnesota to the World*, edited by Colleen J. Sheehy and Thomas Swiss, 3–14. University of Minnesota Press, 2009.

Marcus, Greil. *Like a Rolling Stone: Bob Dylan at the Crossroads.* PublicAffairs, 2005.

Marcus, Greil. *The Old, Weird America: The World of Bob Dylan's Basement Tapes.* Picador, 2001. Originally published as *Invisible Republic: Bob Dylan's Basement Tapes.* Holt, 1997.

Margulis, Elizabeth Hellmuth. *On Repeat: How Music Plays the Mind.* Oxford University Press, 2013.

Marqusee, Mike. *Wicked Messenger: Bob Dylan and the 1960s.* Seven Stories, 2005. Revised and expanded edition of *Chimes of Freedom: The Politics of Bob Dylan's Art.* New Press, 2003.

Marshall, Lee. *Bob Dylan: The Never Ending Star.* Polity Press, 2007.

Marshall, Lee. "Bob Dylan and the Academy." In *The Cambridge Companion to Bob Dylan*, ed. Kevin J. H. Dettmar, 100–109. Cambridge University Press, 2009.

McKenzie, Peter K. *Bob Dylan: On a Couch and Fifty Cents a Day.* MKB, 2021.

Mellers, Wilfrid. *A Darker Shade of Pale: A Backdrop to Bob Dylan.* Faber and Faber, 1984.

Meyer, Leonard B. *Emotion and Meaning in Music.* University of Chicago Press, 1956.

Meyer, Leonard B. *Explaining Music: Essays and Explorations.* University of Chicago Press, 1973.

Middleton, Richard. *Studying Popular Music.* Open University Press, 1990.

Monson, Ingrid. *Freedom Sounds: Civil Rights Call Out to Jazz and Africa.* Oxford University Press, 2007.

Morrison, Matthew D. *Blacksound: Making Race and Popular Music in the United States.* University of California Press, 2024.

Muir, Andrew. *One More Night: Bob Dylan's Never Ending Tour.* CreateSpace, 2013.

Murphy, Nancy. "'The Times Are A-Changin'': Metric Flexibility and Text Expression in 1960s and 1970s Singer-Songwriter Music." *Music Theory Spectrum* 44 (2022): 17–40.

Murphy, Nancy. *Times a-Changin': Flexible Meter as Self-Expression in Singer-Songwriter Music.* Oxford University Press, 2023.

Muxfeldt, Kristina. "*Frauenliebe und Leben* Now and Then." *19th-Century Music* 25 (2001): 27–48.

Negus, Keith. *Bob Dylan.* Indiana University Press, 2008.

Nicolay, Franz. "Love, Death, and Knock-Knock Jokes: Adorno, Said, and Late

Style in Dylan." *Spectrum Culture*, July 22, 2009, bit.ly/NicolayLateStyle.

Nielsen, Aldon Lynn. "Crow Jane Approximately: Bob Dylan's Black Masque." In *Highway 61 Revisited: Bob Dylan's Road from Minnesota to the World*, edited by Colleen J. Sheehy and Thomas Swiss, 186–96. University of Minnesota Press, 2009.

Nobile, Drew. "Counterpoint in Rock Music: Unpacking the 'Melodic-Harmonic Divorce.'" *Music Theory Spectrum* 37 (2015): 189–203.

O'Connell, Jeremy Day. "Speech, Song, and the Minor Third: An Acoustic Study of the Stylized Interjection." *Music Perception* 30 (2013): 441–62.

Padgett, Ray. *Cover Me: The Stories Behind the Greatest Cover Songs of All Time*. Union Square, 2017.

Padgett, Ray. *Pledging My Time: Conversations with Bob Dylan Band Members*. EWP, 2023.

Pennebaker, D. A., dir. *Dont Look Back ('65 Tour Deluxe Edition)*. Docurama, 2007.

Pichaske, David. *Song of the North Country: A Midwest Framework to the Songs of Bob Dylan*. Continuum, 2010.

Portelli, Alessandro. *Hard Rain: Bob Dylan, Oral Cultures, and the Meaning of History*. Columbia University Press, 2022.

Powers, Ann. "Gender and Sexuality: Bob Dylan's Body." In *The World of Bob Dylan*, edited by Sean Latham, 264–77. Cambridge University Press, 2021.

Raz, Carmel. "How the *Sheng* Became a Harp." *Sound Studies* 6 (2020): 239–56.

Reginio, Robert. "'Nettie Moore': Minstrelsy and the Cultural Economy of Race in Bob Dylan's Late Albums." In *Highway 61 Revisited: Bob Dylan's Road from Minnesota to the World*, edited by Colleen J. Sheehy and Thomas Swiss, 213–24. University of Minnesota Press, 2009.

Remnick, David. "Bob Dylan, Extending the Line." *New Yorker*, February 9, 2015.

Reynolds, Simon. *Retromania: Pop Culture's Addiction to Its Own Past*. Faber and Faber, 2011.

Ricks, Christopher. "Bob Dylan." *Threepenny Review* 40 (1990): 33–35.

Ricks, Christopher. *Dylan's Visions of Sin*. Ecco, 2004.

Ricks, Christopher. "All Because of the Color of His Skin." Colloquium lecture at the University of Chicago, May 12, 2017.

Rings, Michael. "Doing It Their Way: Rock Covers, Genre, and Appreciation." *Journal of Aesthetics and Art Criticism* 71 (2013): 55–63.

Rings, Steven. "Analyzing the Popular Singing Voice: Sense and Surplus." *Journal of the American Musicological Society* 68 (2015): 663–71.

Rings, Steven. "A Foreign Sound to Your Ear: Bob Dylan Performs 'It's Alright, Ma (I'm Only Bleeding),' 1964–2009." *MTO* 19, no. 4 (2013): bit.ly/RingsDylanMTO.

Rings, Steven. "Speech and/in Song." In *The Voice as Something More*, edited by Martha Feldman and Judith T. Zeitlin, 37–53. University of Chicago Press, 2019.

Rings, Steven. "Thoughts on Dylan's Nobel." *OUP blog*, November 3, 2016: bit.ly/RingsThoughtsNobel.

Rockwell, Joti. "Time on the Crooked Road: Isochrony, Meter, and Disruption in Old-Time Country and Bluegrass Music." *Ethnomusicology* 55 (2011): 55–79.

Rosenberg, Neil V., ed. *Transforming Tradition: Folk Music Revivals Examined*. University of Illinois Press, 1993.

Ross, Alex. *Listen to This*. Picador, 2011.

Rotolo, Suze. *A Freewheelin' Time: A Memoir of Greenwich Village in the Sixties*. Aurum, 2009.

Roud, Stephen. *Folk Song in England*. Faber and Faber, 2017.

Salkin, Jeffrey. "Bob Dylan's New Book Is a Jewish Masterpiece." *Salt Lake Tribune*, December 7, 2022.

Scaduto, Anthony. *The Dylan Tapes: Friends, Players, and Lovers Talkin' Early Bob Dylan*. Edited by Stephanie Trudeau. University of Minnesota Press, 2022.

Schoenberg, Arnold. *Verklärte Nacht and Pierrot Lunaire*. Dover, 1994.

Scobie, Stephen. *Alias Bob Dylan: Revisited*. Red Deer, 2003.

Scorsese, Martin, dir. *No Direction Home: Bob Dylan*. Paramount, 2005.

Selzer, Adam. *Bobcat Nation: Life Among the Dylan Fans*. A Goon Attack Press, 2010.

Sharp, Cecil. *Cecil Sharp's Collection of English Folk Songs*. Oxford University Press, 1974.

Shelley, Braxton. *Healing for the Soul: Richard Smallwood, the Vamp, and the Gospel Imagination*. Oxford University Press, 2021.

Shelton, Robert. *No Direction Home: The Life and Music of Bob Dylan*. W. Morrow, 1986.

Small, Christopher. *Musicking: The Meanings of Performing and Listening*. Wesleyan University Press, 1998.

Sounes, Howard. *Down the Highway: The Life of Bob Dylan*. Updated ed. Grove Press, 2011.

Spitz, Bob. *Dylan: A Biography*. Norton, 1991.

Starr, Larry. *Listening to Bob Dylan*. University of Illinois Press, 2021.

Sterne, Jonathan. *The Audible Past: Cultural Origins of Sound Reproduction*. Duke University Press, 2003.

Sterne, Jonathan. *MP3: The Meaning of a Format*. Duke University Press, 2012.

Stubbs, Will. "11 Outlined Epitaphs: 'unspeakable visions of the individual.'" In *Bob Dylan's Words: A Critical Dictionary and Commentary*, edited by Richard David Wissolik and Scott McGrath, 9–14. Eadmer, 1994.

Taruskin, Richard. "Revising Revision." *Journal of the American Musicological Society* 46 (1993): 114–38.

Taysom, Joe. "Bob Dylan Describes His Idol in His First Recorded Interview from 1961." *Far Out* (October 5, 2020). bit.ly/DylanChaplin.

Temperley, David. "The Melodic-Harmonic 'Divorce' in Rock." *Popular Music* 26 (2007): 323–42.

Thomas, Richard F. *Why Bob Dylan Matters*. HarperCollins, 2017.

Thompson, Toby. *Positively Main Street: Bob Dylan's Minnesota*. University of Minnesota Press, 2008. First edition published by Coward-McCann and Geoghegan in 1971.

Titon, Jeff Todd. "Reconstructing the Blues: Reflections on the 1960s Blues Revival." In *Transforming Tradition: Folk Music Revivals Examined*, edited by Neil V. Rosenberg, 220–40. University of Illinois Press, 1993.

Tomlinson, Gary. *A Million Years of Music: The Emergence of Human Modernity*. Zone, 2015.

Trippett, David. "Melody." In *The Oxford Handbook of Critical Concepts in Music Theory*, edited by Alexander Rehding and Steven Rings, 397–436. Oxford University Press, 2019.

Turino, Thomas. "Signs of Imagination, Identity, and Experience: A Peircian Semiotic Theory for Music." *Ethnomusicology* 43 (1999): 221–55.

Turino, Thomas. *Music as Social Life: The Politics of Participation*. University of Chicago Press, 2008.

Van Ronk, Dave, with Elijah Wald. 2005. *The Mayor of MacDougal Street: A Memoir*. Da Capo, 2005.

Verma, Neil. "Screamlines: On the Anatomy and Geology of Radio." In *The Voice as Something More: Essays Toward Materiality*, edited by Martha Feldman and Judith T. Zeitlin, 91–112. University of Chicago Press, 2019.

Wagner, Richard. *Judaism in Music*. Translated by Edwin Evans. W. Reeves, 1910. Originally published in 1850.

Waksman, Steve. *Instruments of Desire: The Electric Guitar and the Shaping of Musical Experience*. Harvard University Press, 1999.

Wald, Elijah. *Dylan Goes Electric!: Newport, Seeger, Dylan, and the Night that Split the Sixties*. HarperCollins, 2015.

Wald, Gayle. "Gospel Music." In *The World of Bob Dylan*, edited by Sean Latham, 88–99. Cambridge University Press, 2021.

Wilentz, Sean. *Bob Dylan in America*. Random House, 2010.

Williams, Paul. *Bob Dylan, Performing Artist: The Early Years, 1960–1973*. Omnibus Press, 1991.

Williams, Paul. *Bob Dylan, Performing Artist: The Middle Years, 1974–1986*. Omnibus Press, 1992.

Williams, Paul. *Bob Dylan, Performing Artist: Mind Out of Time, 1986–1990 and Beyond*. Omnibus Press, 2005.

Witting, Robin. *"Tarantula": The Falcon's Mouthbook*. Exploding Rooster, 2005.

Witting, Robin. *Help Those That Cannot Understand Not to Understand: A Guide to Reading "Tarantula."* Isis, 2023.

Woliver, Robbie. *Bringing It All Back Home*. Pantheon, 1986.

Wyeth, John. *Wyeth's Repository of Sacred Music, Part Second*. 2nd ed. Da Capo, 1964. Originally published in 1820 (1st ed. in 1813).

Yaffe, David. *Bob Dylan: Like a Complete Unknown*. Yale University Press, 2011.

Zak, Albin J., III. "Bob Dylan and Jimi Hendrix: Juxtaposition and Transformation 'All Along the Watchtower.'" *Journal of the American Musicological Society* 57 (2005): 599–644.

Zbikowski, Lawrence M. *Foundations of Musical Grammar*. Oxford University Press, 2017.

INDEX